Travels in the Morea.

William Martin Leake

Travels in the Morea.
Leake, William Martin
British Library, Historical Print Editions
British Library
1830
3 vol. ; 8°.
1047.d.7-9.

The BiblioLife Network

This project was made possible in part by the BiblioLife Network (BLN), a project aimed at addressing some of the huge challenges facing book preservationists around the world. The BLN includes libraries, library networks, archives, subject matter experts, online communities and library service providers. We believe every book ever published should be available as a high-quality print reproduction; printed on- demand anywhere in the world. This insures the ongoing accessibility of the content and helps generate sustainable revenue for the libraries and organizations that work to preserve these important materials.

The following book is in the "public domain" and represents an authentic reproduction of the text as printed by the original publisher. While we have attempted to accurately maintain the integrity of the original work, there are sometimes problems with the original book or micro-film from which the books were digitized. This can result in minor errors in reproduction. Possible imperfections include missing and blurred pages, poor pictures, markings and other reproduction issues beyond our control. Because this work is culturally important, we have made it available as part of our commitment to protecting, preserving, and promoting the world's literature.

GUIDE TO FOLD-OUTS, MAPS and OVERSIZED IMAGES

In an online database, page images do not need to conform to the size restrictions found in a printed book. When converting these images back into a printed bound book, the page sizes are standardized in ways that maintain the detail of the original. For large images, such as fold-out maps, the original page image is split into two or more pages.

Guidelines used to determine the split of oversize pages:

- Some images are split vertically; large images require vertical and horizontal splits.
- For horizontal splits, the content is split left to right.
- For vertical splits, the content is split from top to bottom.
- For both vertical and horizontal splits, the image is processed from top left to bottom right.

1947. ok. 8

TRAVELS

IN

THE MOREA.

VOL. II.

G. WOODFALL, ANGEL COURT, SKINNER STREET, LONDON.

TRAVELS
IN
THE MOREA.

WITH

A MAP AND PLANS.

BY

WILLIAM MARTIN LEAKE,

F.R.S. ETC.

IN THREE VOLUMES.

VOL. II.

LONDON:
JOHN MURRAY, ALBEMARLE STREET.

MDCCCXXX.

CONTENTS

OF

VOL. II.

CHAPTER XII.

ARCADIA.

Temple of Apollo Epicurius at Bassæ. — From the temple to Andrítzena.—Karítena.—Sinánu.—Megalopolis.—To Londári and Tripolitzá 1

CHAPTER XIII.

ARCADIA.

From Tripolitzá to Alonístena.—To the Site of Methydrium, near Vitína.—To Dhimitzána.—Teuthis.—To Fanári.—Alipheræ.—To Platianá.—Typaneæ.—To Ai Ianni.—Heræa 51

CHAPTER XIV.

ARCADIA.—ACHAIA.

From Ai Ianni to Vyzítza.—Thelpusa.—Strézova.—Karnési.—Kalávryta.—Nezerá.—Patra.—Patræ.—Castle of the Moréa.—Rhium.—Antirrhium 94

CHAPTER XV.

ACHAIA.—ELEIA.

From Patra to Karavostási.—Olenus.—Dyme.—Teichus.—To Lekhená, Kastro Tornese, and Gastúni.—Myrtuntium.—Cyllene.—Hyrmine 151

CHAPTER XVI.

ELEIA.

Geography of the ELEIA Proper, in the time of the Trojan War.—BUPRASIUM, PETRA OLENIA, Mount SCOLLIS, ALEISIUM.—Geography of the PISATIS.—LETRINI, PHEIA, Promontory ICHTHYS, HERACLEIA, SALMONE, DYSPONTIUM, CYCESIUM, MARGANEÆ, AMPHIDOLI, Mount PHOLOE, EPITALIUM, LASIO, ACROREIA, THALAMÆ.—Geography of TRIPHYLIA.—EPEIUM, BOLAX, PHRIXA, PISA, SCILLUS 179

CHAPTER XVII.

ELEIA.—ARCADIA.

From Gastúni to Tripótamo.—ELIS.—PYLUS of ELEIA. River LADON of ELEIA.—Tripótamo.—PSOPHIS.—Siege of Psophis by Philip, in the Social War.—Routes of Pausanias to and from PSOPHIS.—To Sopotó.—River and Mountain ERYMANTHUS.—To Karnési.—CLEITOR, town and river.—To Tara.—Rivers AROANIUS, LADON, TRAGUS.—To Levídhi and Tripolitzá.—ORCHOMENIA, MANTINICE 219

CHAPTER XVIII.

ARCADIA.

On the description by Pausanias of the eight roads which centered in MEGALOPOLIS, namely :—1. From HERÆA to MEGALOPOLIS.—2. From MEGALOPOLIS to MESSENE.—3. To CARNASIUM.—4. To SPARTA.—5. To METHYDRIUM.—6. To MÆNALUS.—7. To PHIGALEIA.—8. To PALLANTIUM and TEGEA................ 286

CHAPTER XIX.

ARGEIA.

From Tripolitzá to Argos.—Mount Parthenium.—Akhladhókambo.—Ancient Roads from Tegea to Argos and Thyrea.—Tribes of Tegea.—Hysiæ.—Trochus.—Source of the Erasinus.—Ancient Road from Argos to Hysiæ.—To Anápli.—Tiryns.—Nauplia 326

CHAPTER XX.

ARGEIA.

Mycenæ.—Heræum.—Argos.—Ancient routes from Argos.—Œnoe.—Lyrceia.—Orneæ 364

CHAPTER XXI.

Ancient Geography of the Argolic peninsula.—Mideia.—Lessa.—Hierum of Epidauria.—Epidaurus.—Ægina.—Temple of Jupiter Panhellenius.—Trœzen.—Calaureia.—Methana.—Hermione.—Halice.—Mases.—Asine.—Islands of the Argolic and Hermionian Gulfs 416

CHAPTER XXII.

ARGEIA.—LACONIA.

From Argos to the Mills of Anápli.—Lerna.—Mount Pontinus.—Fountain Amymone.—Temenium.—To Kivéri.—Genesium.—Abobathmi.—To Astró and Luku.—Anigræa.—The Deine.—Astrum.—Thyrea.—Anthene.—Neris.—To Prastiótika Kalývia.—Prasiæ.—Cyphanta.—To Kastánitza.—

Tzakonía.—Tzakonic dialect.—Eva.—To Tzítzina.— River Tanus.—Mount Parnon.—To the Monastery of the Forty Saints.—Ancient road from Argos to Sparta.—Scotita.—Sellasia.—Caryæ.—River Œnus.—To Sparta and Mistrá.......................... 469

TRAVELS

IN

THE MOREA.

FIRST JOURNEY.

CHAPTER XII.

ARCADIA.

Temple of Apollo Epicurius at Bassæ.—From the temple to Andrítzena.—Karítena.—Sinánu.—Megalopolis.—To Londári and Tripolitzá.

May 7.—At 1.5 I set out for the ruins of the temple of Apollo Epicurius, for which the natives have no other name than that of the *Columns*, στοὺς στύλους, as they are here more Hellenically called: our Greeks from Kalamáta used the Italian word κολόνναις. We soon begin to ascend Mount *Cotylium*, which is therefore correctly placed by Pausanias at a distance of forty stades from Phigaleia; for though the temple is at least a two hours' walk of a man or horse from the ruins of the city, we may be allowed to apply the forty stades to the nearest part of the mountain on which the temple stands. After ascending for half an hour through pasture land, in which there are some sheep-folds [a] belonging to Tragói, we enter the forest of oaks which covers the summit of all these ridges. The path winds among the trees for half an hour, when I am suddenly startled from the indolent reverie which such a pleasant but unexciting kind of road often produces, by the sight of one of the component cylinders of a Doric shaft of enormous size, lying half buried in earth and decayed leaves, on a level spot, by the road side, just wide enough to hold it. A detached fragment of this kind sometimes gives a greater impression of grandeur than an entire building, or the ruin of a large portion of one, because in these the dimensions of the parts are lost in the harmony of the whole; even the magnitude of a perfect building is not felt unless there is some vulgar object at hand to form a scale of comparison: as a St. Peter's or a St. Paul's would fail of producing their just effect without houses and churches in sight, or as the Pyramids of Memphis seldom impress the traveller with their immensity as long as he has nothing but hills to compare them with, and until he is near enough to judge of the size of

[a] μάνδραις.

the masses of stone of which they are formed, by the scale of his own height. I had no conception, until I had measured the fallen piece of column on the ascent to *Bassæ*, that its diameter was scarcely the half of that of the columns of the Parthenon. About 150 yards farther I came in sight of the ruined temple. The cylinder belonged undoubtedly to the column which stood at the south-western angle of the peristyle, one of the pieces of which rolled down the hill when the column fell.

The large proportions of these ruins, and the perfection of their workmanship, prove them to be the remains of the temple of Apollo Epicurius, though it is only from the few words which Pausanias bestows upon the temple that we obtain that certainty. Without those few words, the existence of such a magnificent building in such a wilderness, must ever have remained a subject of wonder, doubt, and discussion. As to a description of this fine ruin, the first in preservation of the temples of Greece, except the Theseium, it must be left to the painter and the architect; for the latter in particular there would be sufficient employment for some weeks. Indeed until some attempt be made to clear away the ruins of the cell, which form an immense confused mass within the peristyle, it will hardly be possible even for an architect to understand thoroughly all the particulars of the building.

In general terms the temple may be described as a peripteral hypæthral hexastyle, with fifteen columns on the sides, 126 feet in length, 48 broad, and facing nearly north and south. The columns are three feet eight inches in diameter at the base, and twenty feet high, including the capital. As usual in peripteral temples, there were two columns in the pronaos and as many in the posticum, so that the total number in the peristyle was forty-two, of which thirty-six are standing, and, with one exception only, covered with their architraves. There are twenty shallow flutings in the shafts, as usual in the Doric order. As they measure only three feet under the capital, and are five times the lower diameter in height, they are both more tapering and shorter in proportion to their height than the columns of the Parthenon. As a necessary consequence of their being more tapering, the echinus of the capital is longer than in the Athenian temple, and forms a more acute angle with the plinth, the order thus more resembling the examples of the Doric at Corinth, and in the ruins of Sicily and Pæstum. There were several projections on either side of the cell, terminating in fluted Ionic semi-columns: one of these is standing, and it is the only part, either of the cell, or pronaos, or posticum, that is in that condition, though all the lower part of the cell is still in situ. Of the outer columns of the peristyle, on the contrary, all are standing, except the two angular columns of the southern front; nor are these wanting, as all the component cylinders are lying on the ground, so that both the peristyle and the cell might be restored to their original state without much deficiency, if wealth and power, taste and science should ever be restored to Greece.

The stone of which the temple is constructed is a hard yellowish-brown lime-stone[a], susceptible of a high polish, which explains the obser-

[a] Baron Haller and Mr. Cockerell have since discovered the frize, which is now in the British Museum, representing battles of Centaurs and of Amazons with Greeks. For a delineation of these sculptures, and an able elucidation of them by Mr. Taylor Combe, see the Description of the Marbles of the British Museum, Part 3. By the excavation which followed the discovery of the frize, the complete plan of the temple was ascertained. It was found that the frize, the capitals of the Ionic semi-columns, and that of a single column which occupied a situation at the end of the cell, were of white marble. This last-mentioned column is a very curious specimen of art, being a variety of the Ionic order, with helices and leaves of acanthus, and consequently the earliest specimen of the order, which, having been first executed at Corinth, was called Corinthian. It is remarkable that Vitruvius, l. 4. c. 1., ascribes the invention of the order to Callimachus, who lived about the same time that the temple at Bassæ was built, having made the golden lamp and brazen palm-tree in the temple of Minerva Polias at Athens.

vation of Pausanias, that this temple was superior in harmony[a] to all the temples of the Peloponnesus, except that of Tegea, for it is evident, from other passages [b], that by ἁρμονία he meant the nice adaptation of the stones to each other, or, in other words, the fine execution of the masonry, and not the general harmony of the proportions of the temple. It may easily be conceived that such workmanship would be most finished in a temple of white marble, like that of Minerva Alea at Tegea, and least so in a building of soft conchite lime-stone, like that of the temple of Jupiter at Olympia; and this accords with the order of the three temples as to harmony in the idea of Pausanias, namely, first the Tegeatic, next the Phigaleian, and lastly the Olympian. In the temple of Apollo Epicurius, as in the Parthenon, the stones are wrought and adjusted to one another with such accuracy that the junctures in some places are not visible without the closest inspection; in others the superficial decomposition of the edges has formed a natural cement uniting the stones together.

Although the Phigalenses made a present of

---

[a] ἁρμονίας εἵνεκεν.
[b] Particularly in the following description of the walls of Tiryns:—λιθία ἐνήρμοσται πάλαι, ὡς μάλιστα αὐτῶν ἕκαστον ἁρμονίαν τοῖς μεγάλοις λίθοις εἶναι.

their colossal statue of Apollo Epicurius to the city of Megalopolis, only seventy years after his temple was built, this removal does not appear to have taken place in consequence of any disaster which had dilapidated the building. The remark of Pausanias on its roof shews that it remained uninjured until his time. The cause of its present state of ruin one cannot well imagine to have been any other than the repetition of those concussions of the earth to which Greece is so subject,—which at first sight seem sufficient to have prevented the Greeks from having ever made any great advances in architecture, but which may perhaps in reality, by obliging them to encounter difficulties and to study solidity, have been one of the causes of their excellence in the art: in fact, though earthquakes are very frequent in this country, they seldom occur with such violence that a single shock would cause irreparable damage in buildings so well constructed as those of the Greeks; as far therefore as their destruction has been the effect of these concussions, it has rather been caused by a repetition of shocks upon former injuries left unrepaired in consequence of that neglect of the public monuments, which increased as the power, and wealth, and spirit of the nation declined. At Athens two or three explosions of gunpowder destroyed in an instant what the successive earthquakes of twenty-two centuries had left uninjured. The mode adopted by Ictinus, the architect of the temple at Bassæ, to prevent the horizontal motion of the earth from separating the component cylinders of the columns was, to fill up a cavity left in the centre of two adjoining cylinders with a piece of lead. I could not find any of the lead, but the peasants informed me they had often taken pieces away. In the Parthenon the wood of the juniper, which is still called by its ancient name Κέδρος (cedar), was used for the same purpose, as well as lead, and I believe sometimes iron.

The preservation of all the parts of the temple shews that the ruins have never been plundered for the sake of building materials. Indeed there is little temptation to transport these immense masses over such mountains as surround them, nor even to break them into smaller stones, by which barbarous process many other Hellenic remains have been destroyed, for there is no inhabited place nearer than Sklirú, a small village, distant about one mile and a half from the temple, on a part of the mountain where the ground is a little more level than in most other parts, and where alone there seems any possibility of cultivating corn.

There is certainly nothing in Greece, beyond

the bounds of Attica, more worthy of notice than these remains. The temple of Ægina in some of its accidents or accompaniments may be more picturesque, and the surrounding prospect more agreeable; but undoubtedly there are many persons who will prefer the severe grandeur, the wildness, and the variety of this Arcadian scene, in which, amidst a continued contrast of rugged mountain, forest, and cultivated land, there is no want of objects interesting to the spectator by their historical recollection. That which forms, on reflection, the most striking circumstance of all, is the nature of the surrounding country, capable of producing little else than pasture for cattle, and offering no conveniences for the display of commercial industry either by sea or land. If it excites our astonishment that the inhabitants of such a district should have had the refinement to delight in works of this kind, it is still more wonderful that they should have had the means to execute them. This can only be accounted for by what Horace says of the early Romans:

> Privatus illis census erat brevis,
> Commune magnum [a].

This is the true secret of national power, which cannot be equally effective in an age of selfish luxury.

[a] Carm. l. 2. od. 15.

Mount *Cotylium* branches from the great *Lycæan* ridge, between the summits Dhiofórti and Fanarítiko, the former of which is in a line with Karítena, the latter more to the northward. The summit of *Cotylium* looks down to the westward on the hollow watered by the torrent which flows between Tragói and Puikádhes, and eastward into a more deep and narrow valley, which receives the waters from about Sklirú. The stream which is collected from the latter feeders is that which I crossed yesterday, at 3 P.M., just above its junction with the branch which flows from Tetrázi and from some fountains between that mountain and Ambelióna. Thus we have three streams contributing to form the river which passes near the ruins of Phigaleia. Pausanias in like manner speaks of three tributaries of the Neda, namely, the Lymax, which joined the Neda about twelve stades above Phigaleia, the Plataniston, which the traveller coming from Megalopolis by Despœna crossed at thirty stades short of Phigaleia, and the Neda Proper, which had its origin in Mount Cerausium. The two distances here given by Pausanias shew that the *Lymax* was the river of Tragói, and that the *Plataniston* was that which descends from the hollows about Sklirú, into the glen on the eastern side of Mount *Cotylium*: consequently, that the proper *Neda* was that which has its origin in

Mount Tetrázi. Hence also it appears that this mountain was the ancient Cerausium, of which word the modern name is perhaps a corruption. The observation of Pausanias as to the extremely winding course of the Neda, must be applied to it below Phigaleia, for its course is very direct upwards from thence towards the peak of Tetrázi, as is particularly apparent from the Acropolis of Phigaleia. Strabo remarks[a], that the Neda rises at a fountain in Mount Lycæum, which was fabled to have been caused to flow by Rhea, being in want of water when she brought forth Jupiter[b]; from Pausanias however it is evident that this was not the true Neda, but its branch, the Lymax, so called from the λύματα of Rhea upon that occasion.

In the prospect from the temple, the steep mountains on the eastern side of the glen of *Bassæ* are blended with the great summits of Mount *Lycæum,* called Karyátiko and Dhiofórti. To the right of this range, and in the direction of the course of the *Plataniston,* the majestic summit of Tetrázi presents itself, with a cultivated space at the foot of it, around the village of Kakalétri[c]. To the right of Tetrázi Mount *Ithome* appears above the part of the

---

[a] Strabo, p. 348. [b] Pausan. Arcad. c. 41. [c] Κακαλίτξι.

ridge of Tetrázi which I crossed coming from Skala; and to the right of *Ithome*, the *Messenian* gulf, Koróni, Mount Lykódhemo, and then the range of Kondovúni. A higher summit of the ridge on which the temple stands intercepts the view for a short distance to the right of Kondovúni: but beyond it, to the right again, is seen the lofty mountain behind Arkadhía, and that town with its castle, from which, consequently, I might have seen the temple, had I been aware of it, and the weather permitted;—then occurs a part of the sea-coast, and the country about Pávlitza. Another summit of Mount *Cotylium* now intercepts the view, but by mounting a few paces I obtain the bearing of the peaked summit above Fanári, and see the champaign country of the *Alpheius* between Fanári and Lalla, with the rock of Sandaméri rising above the table-heights of Lalla. Mount Málevo, of Tzakonía, is seen a little to the right of the Karyátiko.

It may be inferred, I think, from Pausanias, that Bassæ[a] and Cotylum were two subordinate villages, or castles, of the Phigalenses, and it appears that they were not far removed from one another, for he describes both Bassæ and the temple as being in the mountain which took its name from Cotylum. Bassæ therefore, I infer, was at the temple itself, and Coty-

[a] Βῆσσαι, saltes, *Dor.* Βᾶσσαι.

lum gave name to the mountain which rose above the temple to the westward, and the nearest part of which was forty stades from Phigaleia. Some remains of the temple of Venus may perhaps be concealed in the recesses of the forest, and these would determine the site of Cotylum.

I am informed by some of the peasants, that there are vestiges of Hellenic walls at Kakalétri, which prove that place to have been the position of a third dependent fortress, or fortified village of the Phigalenses. Its cultivated slopes, indeed, lead at once to the presumption, that if the Phigaleian district extended to the crest of the Lycæan range, as one can hardly doubt, Kakalétri must have been one of its subordinate places. This name, although of Hellenic origin, has not the semblance of being ancient. It is more likely that the fortress, or fortified κατοικία, which occupied the site of Kakalétri, bore the same appellation as the mountain under which it stood, namely, Cerausium; for we find in every part of Greece, that the most remarkable summits, with the exception perhaps of the highest and most inaccessible of all, have been fortified, or have had fortresses near them, bearing generally the same name as the mountains themselves. The insecurity which caused such situations to be resorted to never ceased, even in the most civilized ages of Greece, to be a characteristic of the country, multiplying works of defence in every part of it; so that, with the exception of Attica, the Eleia, and a few other districts, there were, in strictly Hellenic times, very few inhabitants who did not protect themselves from danger at night within the walls of a fortress. At present, when insecurity, though not exactly arising from the same causes, is greater than it ever was, there is a still larger proportion of the natives driven to the mountains, and we find, as in ancient times, that there generally exists near every remarkable summit a village, which either derives its name from, or gives its name to the mountain.

Some persons, perhaps, may be inclined to think that Kakalétri is the position of *Eira*, and that Tetrázi was that Mount *Eira* into which the Messenians retired when they were driven out of the country situated immediately on its southern side.

It would certainly be a natural refuge under such circumstances: I must also admit, not only that the lofty summit of Tetrázi, covered with snow half the year, agrees better with the " white mountain " of Rhianus[a], than any other near the *Neda* to the westward; but that the

---

[a] Οὔρεος ἀργεννοῖο περὶ πτύχας ἐστρατόωντο,
Χείματά τε ποίας τε δύο καὶ εἴκοσι πάσας.
　　　　　　　　Rhian. ap. Paus. Messen. c. 17.

position of Kakalétri, immediately overhanging the *Neda*, is very much in accordance with the circumstances related of the fortress of Eira. Even these reasons, however, seem to me insufficient to contravene those which I have already alleged, in favour of Eira having been on a part of the river *below* Phigaleia.

I had scarcely been long enough at the temple to take a few measurements, and to obtain a general idea of the building, when I found the day fast advancing to a close, and the rain beginning to fall. I was therefore obliged to hasten away, not at all to the regret of my janissary, who, being a native of the soft climate of Kalamáta, was greatly annoyed by the cold damp air of the mountain, and sat huddled up at the foot of a column, endeavouring to keep out the enemy, with a pipe.

Leaving the temple at 4.25, we descend the hill by the same route we came, but soon turning to the right along the western face of the mountain through the forest, we have a view to the left of a fine cultivated slope on the south-western side of Mount Fanarítiko, upon which are the villages of Vervítza and Linístena[a], the latter containing 150 houses. The waters of this slope, after uniting, enter the *Neda* below Pávlitza. Linístena is about four miles distant

[a] Βερβίτζα, Λινίστενα.

from our road in a direct line. At 5.15, in a little vale where the planes are just in leaf, and the oaks beginning to bud, we join the road from Tragóï to Andrítzena at the point where the ridge is lowest and most practicable: here a stream descends to the glen below Tragóï. It seems to be the main branch, or at least the most distant tributary of the *Lymax*, of which river, Pausanias says, that a spring, pointed out to him in Mount Cotylium as such, was certainly not the origin, and that he did not think of inquiring where the sources were situated [a]. We continue through a forest of planes and oaks mixed with shrubs, and approach the pointed summit of Fanarítiko, or the hill of Fanári, on which are the ruins of a castle; at length, leaving that height to the left, and passing between it and another summit, called Ai Eliá (St. Elias), which overhangs Andrítzena, I command a fine view of the vale of the *Alpheius* and adjacent country, on either side of the river from Andrítzena to the sea, with the islands of Kefalonía and Zákytho in the distance.

After a descent of half an hour, we arrive at 6.30 at Andrítzena, whither I had sent my baggage and servants in the morning from Tragóï. Andrítzena [b] is beautifully situated in an elevated hollow under the summit of Ai Eliá, at the

[a] Pausan. Arcad. c. 41.   [b] Ἀντρίτζενα.

head of a hilly, fertile, and well cultivated tract, which slopes gradually to the *Alpheius*. A little higher up the mountain, and on the western side of a small ravine, watered by a rivulet which descends to the same recipient, stands the separate quarter of Apanokhóra. There is another in the same direction, called Tjanália [a], and a third, Gufóplo [b], on a summit towards Fanári. The four together contain about 500 houses. Andrítzena itself is larger than the three other villages put together; and has a tolerable bazar. The staple article of external commerce is prinokókki, which is gathered from the kermes oak in the neighbouring mountains. The houses standing amidst trees on the side of a steep declivity rising above one another, give the town an imposing appearance at a distance.

Fanári is similarly situated under the peaked summit, called Fanarítiko, or Zakkúka; the latter name is that of the ruined castle upon its summit. Fanári is two miles in a straight line to the north-west of Andrítzena. It contains about 300 houses; the inhabitants, with the exception of a very few shop-keepers, servants, and cultivators of the soil, are entirely Turks; those of Andrítzena all Christians.

May 8.—At 1.5, P. M. I set out from Andrít-

[a] Τζανάλια. [b] Κουφόπουλον.

zena for Karítena, having procured horses from Fanári, which is the head of the Kázasi,—descend obliquely along the side of the mountain by a winding road, until, at 2.30, we enter a valley inclosed between the hill of Lavdha, half a mile on the left, and the mountain of Dhiofórti, two miles on the right. A river from the south traverses the valley and joins the *Alpheius* between Lavdha and Andrítzena. At 2.45, near the end of this valley, I quit the direct road, and, turning to the left, mount the steep and lofty hill of Lavdha, upon which are the remains of a small fortified Hellenic town, now known by the name of the castle of St. Helene[a]: the walls inclosed all the summit of the hill, at one end of which there was a citadel forming, like that of *Phigaleia*, an inclosure near one side of the outer walls, but entirely separated from them. This citadel is about 150 yards in diameter, more circular than that of Phigaleia, and without any tower or keep. In it stood a temple, of which the lower parts of seven Doric columns of one foot eight inches in diameter, are still standing in a line in their original places. Here is also a very large quadrangular stone, with an excavation of the same form in it. The walls are of the most irregular species of the second

[a] τῆς Ἁγίας Ἑλένης τὸ κάστρον.

order, and have suffered much from time and the exposed situation of the place. There is a round tower near one corner of the citadel, which a Lavdhiote peasant tells me was once a windmill, but it seems rather to have been a signal tower in the line of communication between the castle of Karítena and that of Zakkúka, on the summit of Mount Fanarítiko, for those two buildings appear to have been nearly of the same period of the middle or lower ages. The hill forms an even slope to the northward and westward, and is covered with a fine turf: towards the eastern end it is bounded by a precipice of no great height, from the foot of which there is a steep descent to the *Alpheius*, which runs in a dark ravine below, and is distant from the citadel about 800 yards in a straight line.

Midway stand two villages, both called Lavdha[a], containing, together, about forty houses. Mount Dhiofórti, a lofty round summit, which I believe to be the proper *Lycæum*, presents itself directly before us to the south-east. From the right bank of the *Alpheius*, in the opposite direction, rises the mountain which contains the towns Dhimitzána and Zátuna. The two great ridges approach each other at Karítena, and form, from thence to near Andrítzena, an αὐλὼν, or narrow opening, at the bottom of which flows

[a] Λάμβδα, or Λαύδα.

the Alpheius in its passage from the upper plain, or that of which *Megalopolis* was the chief place, to the lower, in which *Heræa* was the principal town. To the east is seen the mountain of Alonístena; a little to the westward of north that of Sandamério: Tzimbarú, a little to the left of Dhiofórti. The wind blows strong and keen through the aulon, and my Messenian janissary is once more almost deprived of the power of moving. There is, indeed, a great difference between the maritime climate of the Peloponnesus and that of the Arcadian mountains. " 'E un' aria troppo rigida," observed to me the Ragusan consul at Mothóni, speaking of the interior of the peninsula. The average climate of *Arcadia* is in fact cooler, by several degrees, than that of the consul's native town, though the latter is situated so much farther north. In summer, I believe the sea-coast of the Moréa to be more healthy than many of the close valleys of Arcadia; but the cool air of the hills, in particular situations, must in that season be a most agreeable and beneficial change from all the lower situations of the Peninsula.

At 4.25 I rejoin the Karítena road near the place we quitted it, and cross the hills at the foot of Mount Dhiofórti; these, like some of the slopes towards Andrítzena, are covered with dwarf oaks about two feet high. At 5.30 arrive on the bank of a rapid stream running from the south, shaded with planes, and turning some mills; steep hills rise from either bank. It joins the *Alpheius* a little below Karítena. After following it for a short distance, I find, to my surprise, that it issues from the side of the mountain in a single body; the road to Karítena passing round the head of it. The village of Tragománo[a] is one mile and a half to the right on the side of Dhiofórti. We now cross the lower part of that mountain, which terminates to the left in precipices, divided only by the Alpheius from a similar termination of the steep hill of Karítena. To avoid this impracticable gorge, the road makes such a circuit in reaching Karítena, that its hill remains behind us as we descend into the plain to the southward of the town. We leave, a little on the left, the ruins of a mosque and a small village called Xero-Karítena, and cross the *Alpheius* by a bridge, which appears to be of the same date as the castle of Karítena. They were both probably built by one of the Frank princes of the Moréa, in the thirteenth century. There is a small chapel of the Panaghía attached to one side of the bridge, intended as a sacred protection to it against the wintry floods. It takes near half an hour to ascend from the bridge to the town:

[a] Τραγομάνο, or Δραγομάνου.

we do not arrive till 7 p.m. though the direct distance from Andrítzena is not more than eight miles.

Karítena is one of the most important military points in the Moréa. The castle, which is now abandoned, occupies the summit of a high rock, extremely steep towards the Alpheius, and connected eastward with the mountain which lies between the adjacent part of the plain of the Alpheius, and the vale of Atzíkolo; on the north and south the hill slopes more gradually, and on these sides the town is situated. The hill stands at the southern extremity of the Στενὰ, or straits, of the Alpheius, which, as I have already observed, separate the upper from the lower great valley of that river.

The vilayéti of Karítena contains upwards of 100 villages, and extends to the northward as far as that of Kalávryta. Some of the villages are large, as Stemnítza, Zigovísti, Dhimitzána, Zátuna in the nearer hills northward of Karítena, and farther in the same direction, Alonístena, Vitína, Magulianá, Valtesiníko, Langádha, Vizítza, Vervítza: except the part of the *Alpheian* plain near Karítena, the whole district is mountainous, though in general fertile. It produces nearly equal quantities of wheat, barley, and maize; cheese, and butter are made in large quantities in the higher villages, and cotton, flax, and vines are grown in the lower valleys. Prinokókki is gathered in all the woody parts of the district. The pináki of wheat weighs about sixty okes, that of kalambókki fifty-five, of barley forty-five.

The town of Karítena is much depopulated of late; there now remain about 200 families, of which not more than twenty are Turkish: the emigrants have chiefly gone to the territory of Kara Osmán Oglu, in Asia Minor, where they are subject only to the land-tax and kharátj, and are chiefly employed in cultivating the rich lands of Pergamum and Magnesia. The master of the house I lodge in, has within a year paid 300 piastres as his share of the impositions laid upon the town.

The mukatá of Karítena belongs to the same sister of the Sultan who has the Emlátika Khoría. Mistrá and Argos, or the territories of the Atreidæ, are the appanage of another sister of the Barbarian king.

May 9. At eight this morning, following the side of the mountain above the right bank of the Alpheius, I arrive in half an hour at the point where the river of Dhimitzána, or of Atzíkolo[a], as it is here more commonly called, unites with the *Alpheius*, or river of Karítena. The Atzíkolo is a fine stream, wide, clear, and rapid. We proceed along the hill above its left bank,

[a] τὸ ποτάμι τοῦ Ἀτζικόλου.

and at 9 cross it by a bridge; then, ascending the opposite hill, leave the monastery of Kalámi at 9.20 on the right, situated on the brow of a precipice above the river. Half way down the same cliff I perceive the ruin of a more ancient monastery, and a church in a cavern in the cliff itself. On the side of the hill, which rises above the monastery, stands the village of Atzíkolo, which we leave on the left, and then, crossing a height, arrive at the ruins of a small Arcadian polis, which occupied a level summit, bordered by precipices, on the right bank of the river: the city, I think, was Gortys, the river the Gortynius, otherwise called

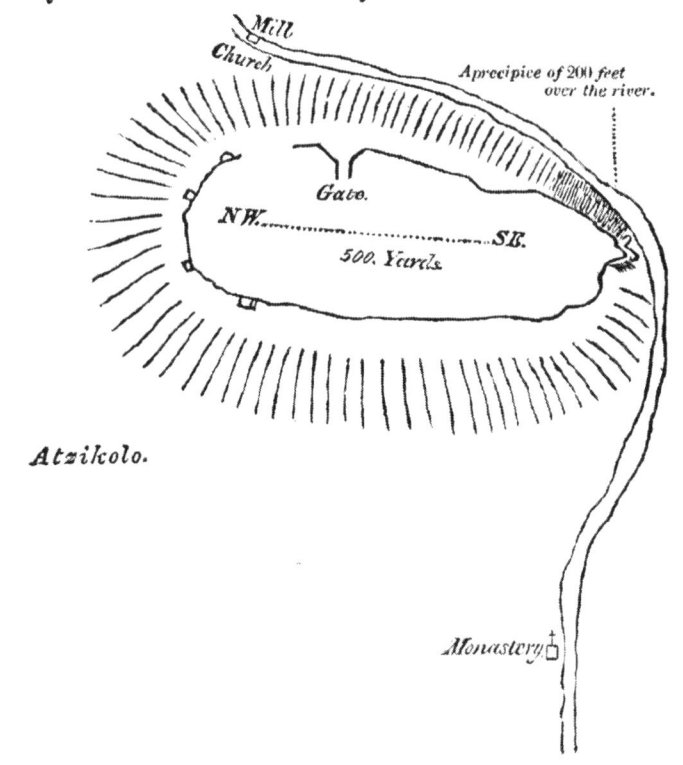

Lusius. The position is nearly in a direct line between Karítena and Dhimitzána, neither of which is visible. Stemnítza is seen on the face of a mountain to the north-east, and a little tower on one side of it, on a sharp peaked rock. On either side of the principal gate of Gortys the walls are a fine specimen of the polygonal or second order: the stones are accurately joined, and in good preservation. One of them is six feet eight inches long, three feet six inches high, and as much thick: in general, their contents are equal to cubes of two, three, and four feet. The entrance was strengthened by being placed in a re-entering angle, thus:—the gate itself being at the end of a passage between two parallel walls, or perhaps there was a gate at either end of the passage. The ancient town was nearly of the same size as that at Lavdha. On the south-western side of the town, I observe the remains of an artificial platform and some scattered fragments of white marble; it is probably the site of the temple of Æsculapius, described by Pausanias as having being built of Pentelic marble, and as containing statues, by Scopas, of Æsculapius and Hygieia[a]. It

[a] Pausan. Arcad. c. 28.

is mentioned by Cicero as being the sepulchre of one of the Æsculapii, of whom he reckoned three[a]. Scopas had represented the Æsculapius of Gortys without a beard, and armed with a thorax and spear, which were said to have been dedicated by Alexander the Great: of the spear only the point remained, in the time of Pausanias. It is evident, from these distinctions, but especially from the materials of the building, which must have been brought with great labour from Athens to these Arcadian mountains, that the temple was one of the most remarkable in the Peloponnesus. In another passage (in the Prior Eliacs) where Pausanias describes the river Gortynius as flowing from Gortys, he shews the importance which he attached to the temple, by adding the words, " where stands the temple of Æsculapius."[b] As usual, however, he supplies no means of judging of its dimensions or structure, nor could I find any remains serving to indicate even its order of architecture. It happens, unfortunately, that buildings of white marble have

[a] Tertius (Æsculapius) Arsippi et Arsinoæ, qui primus purgationem alvi, dentisque evulsionem, ut ferunt, invenit, cujus in Arcadiâ, non longè a Lusio flumine, sepulchrum et lucus ostenditur. Cicero de Nat. Deor. l. 3. c. 22.

[b] παρὰ δὲ Γόρτυνα, ἔνθα ἱερὸν Ἀσκληπιοῦ Γορτύνιος ῥέων. Paus. Eliac. Prior. c. 7.

less chance of preservation than those of ordinary stone, as the material is in request for the making of lime and stucco, a circumstance which may account for the total disappearance of the Asclepieium of Gortys.—I return at noon to Karítena.

Within the castle of Karítena I find the ruin of a long building, with a Gothic window and several large cisterns, the work probably of the Frank prince to whom the castle and its dependencies belonged. At 3.35 I leave Karítena for Sinánu: cross the bridge at 3.52 and proceed rapidly along the plain till 4.40, when I cross the river a second time, fording it to the right bank: it is here wide and shallow. Between the two passages I passed the village of Mavriá and then that of Kyparíssia. Above Mavriá, at the foot of the *Lycæan* range, there are said to be some remains of antiquity. Higher up are Karyés and Kuruniós, belonging to the vilayéti of Karítena, and Póvergo and Strábovo to that of Londári. Above Karyés rises the mountain called the Karyátiko: it is the highest point of the *Lycæum*, except Dhiofórti and Tetrázi; and seems to have been the summit of what Pausanias calls the Nomian mountains [a], which comprehended apparently all the ridge connecting Dhiofórti with Te-

[a] Pausan. Arcad. c. 38.

trázi. Farther to the south is the village 'Ysari[a], belonging to Fanári. At Kyparíssia there are some appearances of an ancient site, and a brook, which we cross near it, is called Vathýrema[b], a name which contains some vestiges of that of the place *Bathos*[c] mentioned by Pausanias[d].

Proceeding at a moderate pace, at 5.6 we leave Vromoséla half a mile on the right. One *tufek*, or musket-shot, above that village, according to the expression of my guide, the river of Daviá joins that of Barbítza: the former is clearly the *Helisson*, the latter the *Alpheius*. At 5.30 we turn off along the bank of the *Helisson*, and crossing it near the theatre of *Megalopolis*, arrive at Sinánu at 5.50.

May 10.—Sinánu, from Sinán, a common Turkish name, contains about twenty Greek families and the pyrgo of the spahí, who is a Turk of Londári. When I asked one of the cottagers why he did not sow more corn in such a fertile soil,—" Where are we to get seed?" was the answer. The Turk of the pyrgo unable, in consequence, to obtain his spahilík on the crops, torments the peasants with extraordinary extortions of every kind, and this fine plain, naturally one of the richest in Greece, remains, with the exception of a few spots round some

---

[a] Ὕσαρι.   [b] Βαθύ-ρευμα.   [d] Pausan. Arcad. c. 29.
[c] χωρίον Βάθος.

of the villages and Turkish tjiftliks, quite uncultivated.

The decline of the culture and population of Arcadia dates from a very distant period. Strabo[a] refers it, or at least the conversion of the corn lands into pasture, to the time of the foundation of Megalopolis, when many of the small towns were abandoned. It is probable, however, that the cultivation of this plain was improved by that event: while an opposite effect may have been produced in all the surrounding districts. So greatly had the agriculture of Arcadia declined in the time of Strabo, that it was then chiefly noted for its breed of horses and asses. It would seem, therefore, that although Megalopolis gave a momentary strength and importance to Arcadia, it assisted in the depopulation of the province, and itself flourished only for a short time. This "youngest of cities"[b] soon fell into decrepitude, Sparta being still too powerful a neighbour, except in some conjunctures, when Megalopolis was fortunate in its alliances. Cleomenes plundered and partly destroyed the place about 150 years after its foundation[c], and from this shock it probably never recovered, gradually declining, until, according to a comic poet

[a] Strabo, p. 388.   Arcad. c. 27.
[b] νεωτάτη πόλεων. Pausan.   [c] Plutarch. in Cleomen.

quoted by Strabo[a], the "great city was nothing more than a great desert."[b] Its vast dimensions, more extensive, according to its native historian, than those of Sparta itself[c], and always disproportioned to its inhabitants served only to render its desolation the more remarkable.

During the first two centuries of the Roman empire; when Greece and Asia enjoyed a degree of security to which they had long been strangers, and more happiness perhaps than they had known for several centuries, it cannot be doubted that Arcadia partook in the general improvement, and that Pausanias found this province in a condition far less wretched than that which Strabo has described. Megalopolis itself, however, was in a more ruinous state than any of the other great cities of Greece, as appears, not less from the description which Pausanias has given of the several buildings, than from his general reflections in the thirty-third chapter of the Arcadics.

Though the appearance of this noble basin might be rendered more agreeable by a certain degree of culture, desolation has not deprived it of its natural beauties, as seems to have happened in the other great *Arcadian* valley of

[a] Strabo, p. 388.
[b] Ἐρημία μεγάλη 'στιν ἡ Μεγάλη Πόλις.
[c] Polyb. l. 9. c. 21.

Tripolitzá, which, having lost its three cities, its cultivation, and its forest Pelagus, (the latter a fine contrast, probably, to the rocky steeps on either side,) is now an uninteresting monotonous level. The valley of Megalopolis, on the contrary, abounds in delightful scenery. The sides of the majestic mountains Karyátiko and Tetrázi, and the hills at the southern end of the plain beyond Londári, are covered with oaks, chestnuts, and other trees. The eastern range in its higher regions is more naked than the others, but the lower hills are clothed both with underwood and large trees, among which are forests of oaks, extending in some places into the plain, particularly a little to the southward of Megalopolis. The valley itself, varied with hillocks, undulated ground, and detached copses, refreshed with numerous rivulets, shaded by planes, and watered by a larger stream winding through the middle, may almost rival the plain of Sparta in picturesque beauty; to which it is inferior only in the grandeur of the mountains, and their magnificent contrasts with the other features of the Spartan valley. In the present sylvan and uncultivated state of the country around the site of Megalopolis, we have a scene more resembling an ideal Arcadia, than could have been presented, when there was a large city in the centre of the valley: and thus we have another example of a resemblance between the Greece of the earliest ages of its history and that of the present day. The country is now clothed in all the beautiful verdure and flowery luxuriance of a Grecian spring.

Though little remains of the Great City, except its mountain of a theatre, the position of the agora is sufficiently traceable, and the two together furnish some illustration of the description of the city by Pausanias[a]. "The Helisson", he says, "divides Megalopolis into two parts, like the canals[b] at Cnidus and Mitylene." "The agora was on the right bank, or northern side of the Helisson[c]: opposite to it stood the theatre on the southern side of the river[d]. In the agora there was an inclosure of stones, the space within which was sacred to Jupiter Lycæus, and had no entrance, all its contents being exposed to public view, namely, two altars of the gods, two tables, two eagles, and a statue in stone of Pan Synoeis. Behind this inclosure there was a figure of Polybius, son of Lycortas, in relief, on a pillar[e]: elegiac verses were inscribed on the pillar, stating that he had wan-

[a] Pausan. Arcad. c. 30, 31, 32.
[b] οἱ εὔριποι.
[c] ἐν μέρει τῷ πρὸς ἄρκτους, δεξιῷ δὲ κατὰ τὸ μετέωρον τοῦ ποταμοῦ. Pausan. Arcad. c. 30.
[d] ἡ δὲ ἐπέκεινα τοῦ ποταμοῦ μοῖρα ἡ κατὰ μεσημβρίαν παρείχετο θέατρον. Pausan. Arcad. c. 32.
[e] ἀνὴρ ἐπειργασμένος ἐπὶ στήλῃ, Πολύβιος.

dered over every sea and land, had fought for the Romans, and had appeased their wrath against the Greeks. The council-house [a] was to the left of this statue. In front of the temenus of Jupiter Lycæus, stood the brazen statue of Apollo Epicurius, twelve feet high, which had been brought from Bassæ by the Phigalenses to adorn Megalopolis. To the right of the Apollo there was a small statue of the Mother of the Gods; of her temple the columns only remained. Before it were some pedestals of statues, on one of which there was an elegy shewing that it once supported a statue of Diophanes, son of Diæus, who was the first to unite all Peloponnesus in the Achaian league [b]. The stoa called the Philippeium was so called in compliment to Philip, son of Amyntas; the temple of Mercury Acacesius, which adjoined to it, had been overthrown [c], and nothing of it was left but a lintel of stone [d]. A smaller stoa, contiguous to the Philippeium, contained the Archives [e]: these were six apartments [f], in one of which there was a statue of Diana Ephesia, and in another a brazen Pan, a cubit in height [g], surnamed Scoleitas, because the statue was brought from a hill of that name within the city, from which

[a] βουλευτήριον.
[b] Ἀχαϊκὸν σύλλογον.
[c] κατεϐέϐλητο.
[d] χελώνη λίθου.
[e] τὰ ἀρχεῖα.
[f] οἰκήματα.
[g] χαλκοῦς Πὰν πηχυαῖος.

issued a stream of water flowing to the Helisson. Behind the Archives stood a temple of Fortune, with a statue of stone five feet high. The agora contained also a stoa called Myropolis, built from the spoils of the Lacedæmonians under Acrotatus, when they were defeated by the Megalopolitæ under Aristodemus. Another stoa in the agora was called the Aristandreium, because it was built by Aristandrus, a native citizen. Near it, eastward, stood a peripteral temple [a] of Jupiter Soter, containing a statue of Jupiter seated on his throne, with Megalopolis standing on his right, and Diana Soteira on his left; they were of Pentelic stone, and made by the Athenians Cephisodotus and Xenophon. Adjoining to the Aristandreium, on the west, was the sacred inclosure [b] of the Great Goddesses, as Ceres and Proserpine were called; the latter was named Soteira by the Arcadians (instead of Core, as in most other parts of Greece). Before the entrance were represented in low relief [c], on one side Diana, on the other Æsculapius and Hygieia. The statues of the Great Goddesses were fifteen feet high, that of Ceres was entirely of stone, the drapery of the Soteira was of wood. Before them stood statues of two young women in long

[a] κεκόσμηται πέριξ κίοσι.
[b] ἱερὸς περίβολος.
[c] ἐπειργασμένοι ἐπὶ τύπων.

drapery [a], bearing flowers in baskets, a small Hercules, and a table adorned with figures of the Hours, of Pan, and of Apollo in relief, and which supported statues of the nymphs, Neda, Anthracia, Hagno, Archiroe, and Myrtoessa [b], bearing appropriate symbols. The peribolus of the Great Goddesses contained also a temple of Jupiter Philius, whom Polycleitus of Argos, had represented in the character of Bacchus, with a cup in one hand, and a thyrsus in the other, distinguishing him as Jupiter only by an eagle on the thyrsus. Behind this temple there was a small grove of trees surrounded with a fence [c], into which there was no admission [d]. Before it stood statues of Ceres and her daughter, three feet high. The other contents of the sacred peribolus were a temple of Venus,—a building containing the statues of four persons, who were supposed to have been the teachers of the mysteries to the Megalopolitæ,—a large temple in which the ceremony [e] of the Great Goddesses was performed; and to the right of the latter a sanctuary of Core (Proserpine), containing a statue of marble eight feet high; men were admitted into this sanctuary only once a year, but women at all times. Be-

[a] ἐν χιτῶσι ἐς σφυρά.
[b] The names of rivers or fountains in Arcadia.
[c] θρίγκῳ.
[d] ἔσοδος οὐκ ἔστιν ἀνθρώποις.
[e] τελετή.

fore the entrance of the above-mentioned temple of Venus were some ancient wooden statues of Juno, Apollo, and the Muses, brought from Trapezus. Within it were a wooden Mercury, and an acrolithic statue of Venus Mechanitis, the works of Damophon. In another part of the inclosure of the Great Goddesses, there were six statues of deities, of that square form which Pausanias elsewhere tells us that the Arcadians particularly affected.

"The Gymnasium adjoined the Agora to the west. Behind the Philippeium were two small heights, on one of which stood the ruins of the temple of Minerva Polias, on the other those of Juno Teleia; at the foot of the latter was the spring of water, named Bathyllus, which flowed to the Helisson.

"On the southern side of the river, stood the theatre, in which there was a never-failing source of water[a]. Near the theatre were foundations of the council chamber[b] of the Ten Thousand Arcadians, called, from the person who founded it, the Thersilium; and near the latter, a private house formerly built by the Megalopolitæ, for the King Alexander, son of Philip, before which stood a hermaic statue[c] of Ammon, with the horns of a ram. Of a temple sacred to Apollo,

[a] ἀένναος ὕδατος πηγὴ.
[b] βουλευτήριον.
[c] τοῖς τετραγώνοις Ἑρμαῖς εἰκασμένον.

Hermes, and the Muses, there remained only a few foundations, together with a hermaic figure of Apollo, and a statue of one of the Muses. There remained, also, the pronaos and some ruins of a temple of Venus, and three statues of Venus, one called Urania, another Pandemus; to the third, no epithet was given. Near this temple, there was an ancient altar of Mars. The Stadium, which contained a fountain [a] sacred to Bacchus, was contiguous to the theatre on one side, and on the other, to a few remains of a temple of Bacchus. Of a temple of Hercules and Hermes, which stood near the Stadium, only the altar remained. In this division of the city, on a hill towards the east, stood the temple of Diana Agrotera, dedicated by Aristodemus; to its right was the temenus of Agrotera, containing a temple of Æsculapius with statues of Æsculapius and Hygieia, and a little below it, hermaic statues of the five gods, called the Ergatæ, namely, Minerva Ergane, Apollo Agrieus, Hermes, Hercules, and Lucina. At the foot of the same hill, there was a temple of Æsculapius the Boy [b], with an upright statue of him, about a foot and a half high [c]. In this temple there was an Apollo, seated on a throne, six feet in height, and some bones of one of the giants; near it a source of water flowed to the Helisson.

"Just without the city, on the road towards

[a] κρήνη.   [b] Ἀσκληπιοῦ Παιδὸς ἱερὸν.   [c] πηχυαῖον μάλιστα.

Thocnia, stood the temple of Neptune Epoptas; of the statue the head only remained."[a]

On the site of the Agora, amidst numerous foundations and portions of columns, many of which are either standing in their original places or only fallen from their bases, I measured some Doric shafts of two feet eight inches in diameter. Farther north is what appears to have been a quadrangle of columns in a double row, within a wall. The inner row, or those towards the middle of the quadrangle, were Ionic, two feet four inches in diameter, with *filled* flutings; the others were pure Doric, two feet seven inches in diameter. This quadrangle I take to have been the Gymnasium, though it is situated rather northward, than westward as Pausanias indicates, of that which appears to have been the central part of the Agora. But the ancients were seldom very accurate as to the points of the compass. The distance of the ruins alluded to from the Helisson is not less than 300 yards, which shows the great extent of the public buildings in and around the Agora. Proceeding from the Agora, westward, along the current of the Helisson, I met with a rough mass of masonry on the bank, apparently the ruins of a bridge, and a little beyond it a small portion of a paved street, formed of a double row of long squared stones carefully wrought, and

[a] Pausan. Arcad. c. 30.

lying in a direction which forms an acute angle with that of the river. A little beyond this pavement there are two brooks, joining the Helisson, and between them a barrow. Of the theatre there remain only a few fragments of the seats, and a part of the exterior wall of the cavea; the rest is an immense mass of earth. Between the front of the theatre and the river, I observed two parallel walls, which seem to have been a prolongation of the two sides of the proscenium as far as the river, thus apparently connecting the theatre with the Agora, and forming of both one magnificent *piazza*, with the river running through it. Perhaps the foundations in front of the theatre may have belonged to the Thersilium, a building which, though it may have been subservient to the uses of the council of Ten Thousand[a], could hardly have been employed for its actual assemblage, as such a multitude could only have been seated for purposes of business, in a theatre-shaped edifice. I could not find any appearance of the source of water in the theatre, nor could I discover any vestiges of the Stadium. As to the dimensions of the theatre, which Pausanias has described as the greatest in Greece[b], and

[a] For the Μυρίοι Ἀρκαδες, or Arcadian Council of Ten Thousand, see Xenophon Hellen. l. 7. c. 1. and Diodorus, l. 15. c. 19.
[b] μέγιστον τῶν ἐν τῇ Ἑλλάδι.

to which such dimensions were, perhaps, given chiefly for the purpose of accommodating the multitudinous Arcadian council—although it is too much ruined to admit of any detailed or accurate measurements, it is sufficiently preserved to afford the means of forming some judgement of its original diameter, which I believe to have been about 480 feet, or from twenty-five to thirty feet greater than the diameter of the theatre of Sparta. It seems, moreover, to have been a greater effort of labour and expense than the theatres of Athens, Argos, Sparta, or any theatre in Greece, of which there exist any considerable remains, having had the advantage only of a slight rise in the ground, at the back of the structure, and having, with this exception, been raised, entirely by art, from the lowest level of the plain.

I could not ascertain the position of the hill of Agrotera, at the foot of which there was a source of water, but in fact, with the exception of the theatre, the difference of level in every part of the site of Megalopolis is very slight; the land abounds too in sources of water, and it may easily be conceived, that the process of ruin in the city, or natural causes, may have altered the situation of the issues of some of those springs from the ground. It is very possible that many remains may lie hid among the shrubs, which cover a great part of the site, and may thus have escaped my notice; and still more so, that the deep alluvial soil may conceal and preserve some of those works of art which Pausanias has described.

One is curious to understand the reasons which induced so experienced a soldier as Epaminondas to choose the middle of the plain for the site of the new capital of Arcadia, such a position being very different from that of the generality of Grecian cities. An unfailing supply of water, which could not be intercepted, was probably one recommendation, but those advantages of a level country, of which a modern engineer can avail himself, so as to make a fortress in a plain almost as strong as any that is favoured by natural difficulties of ground, seem scarcely applicable to the ancient art of war. Nevertheless, one can hardly doubt that some such principles were acknowledged at this meridian period of Greek strategy, since we find the Mantinenses at the same time choosing a level situation for their new city, in preference to its old position upon a hill.

In the village of Sinánu I found a marble inscribed with a few names, and a large ancient tile made of very fine earth, one foot ten inches square and two inches thick; both of them had been turned up by the plough. Coins are often procured here in the same manner; those which were brought to me were chiefly of Megalopolis or of Arcadia. At Kassími, two miles to the w.n.w. of Sinánu, I found the trunk of a draped female figure of the human size. I observed also some vestiges of the walls of Megalopolis, as well as of a ditch, among the pasture land and bushes not far from Sinánu, which place being very little more than half a mile from the theatre, will give a circumference of three miles and a half, at the utmost, to the ancient city, if we suppose, as seems probable, that the theatre and agora were about the centre. These are much below the dimensions which Polybius ascribes to Megalopolis.

At the end of forty minutes, the road from Sinánu to Londári crosses the main stream of the *Alpheius*, here called Kutufarína, from whence it gradually ascends for twenty minutes to Londári[a]. The Londári Kázasi contains sixty villages in the *Megalopolitis* and adjacent part of *Messenia*, and extends south-westward as far as the foot of Mount *Ithome*. The Turks of the town of Londári own the greater part of the land, which, though naturally not less fertile than the generality of the interior of the Moréa, is, in consequence of their poverty, idleness, and extortion, in a wretched state of cultivation.

[a] Λοντάρι, properly Λεοντάριον.

Many Greeks have lately removed from this district to Nisí. There are about 250 Turkish and forty Greek houses in the town, which stands on the side of a long acclivity rising to a summit clothed with oaks, which is connected southwards with Mount Xerovúni, the northern great summit of the *Taygetic* range. The branch which terminates at Londári is separated to the eastward by the valley of the main stream of the *Alpheius*, from the summits now called Tjimbarú [a] and Khelmós [b], and to the westward by another tributary of the same river from the mountains Makryplái and Elenítza. On the northern side of the town are the remains of a castle on a commanding height; it contains some ruined churches and a Turkish mosque, which was formerly a large Greek church; both the castle and the churches are constructions of the time of the lower empire. Londári probably attained to importance, and received its present name in the same ages which gave rise to Mistrá, Tripolitzá, and several other modern Peloponnesian towns, which owed their existence, or at least their augmentation, to the strength of their position in times of insecurity. I do not however find the name of Londári in the Byzantine history, until after the conquest of Constantinople, when it figures as one of the

---

[a] Τζιμπαροῦ.   [b] Χελμός.

chief places of the Moréa in the narratives of Chalcocondylas and Phranza. One cannot but suppose that such an advantageous position was the site of one of the numerous small πόλεις of ancient Arcadia, though Pausanias affords no support to this opinion, nor have I been able to find any Hellenic remains at Londári. The principal place in this vicinity in the middle ages of ancient Greece appears to have been at Samará, a village on the left bank of the Xeriló-potamó, or above-mentioned western branch of the *Alpheius*, not much more than a mile distant from Londári. Here are the remains of the walls of a Hellenic city, which appears from Xenophon and Pausanias to have been Cromnus, or Cromi[a].

May 11.—From Londári to Tripolitzá. I set out at 6.15, and in leaving the town, see the traces of chariot wheels in the rocks. After having crossed the Kutufarína, we enter a forest of oaks not very thickly planted; they extend to the right as far as Mount Khelmós, an insulated mountain of no great height, distant about five miles, standing about midway between Xerovúni and Tjimbarú. Having arrived at the end of the forest, at 7.40, we begin, at 8, to ascend Mount Tjimbarú, leaving Rapsomáti considerably on the left and Gardhíki on the

[a] Xenoph. l. 7. c. 4.—Pausan. Arcad. c. 34.

right. My route from Arkadhía to Tripolitzá on the 5th March, passed on the other side of Rapsomáti. Gardhíki, which Chalcocondylas writes Καρδικίη, was a place of some importance when it was taken by Mahomet the Second in the year 1460. At 8.30 pass the ruins of the village of Anemodhúri on the summit of the ridge of Tjimbarú, the highest point of which remains half a mile on the right, and is one of the most conspicuous objects in the centre of the Moréa. At 8.50, entering the plain of Frangóvrysi, Pápari is in the plain on the right, near Mount Tjimbarú, and 'Alika at the foot of the mountain on the left; this is perhaps the ancient Alycæa, one of the old Arcadian towns which contributed to people Megalopolis. At 9.5 we halt five minutes at the head of a causeway of stone which crosses the western end of a large marsh. In coming from Arkadhía I left this marsh entirely on the right; it occupies all the central part of the plain, and extends to the rock at the foot of Mount Tjimbarú. At the south-eastern end of the plain I observe a peaked hill with a ruined church on the summit, behind which there is said to be a valley, and a small stream flowing to the Vasilipótamo [a]. The marsh is chiefly formed by the stream which originates in the spring of Frangóvrysi and the others near it. The river Gdhani

[a] Eurotas.

flows out of the marsh and passes into the plain of *Megalopolis*, through the deep rocky gorge on the northern side of Mount Tjimbarú, which was on my right, on the 5th of March, as I ascended the heights from Rapsomáti.

After crossing the marsh we proceed along the banks of the rivulet of Frangóvrysi, which turns some mills, and at 9.40 join the road from Arkadhía to Tripolitzá at the foot of the height, upon which are the Hellenic remains already described[a], undoubtedly those of Asea. In the marshy plain, at the foot of the hill, I observe the foundations of a round tower, together with those of a piece of curved wall, within which the tower stood. The ruins are called Zurlómylo[b], a name first applied probably to the round tower. At 9.55 we arrive at the Khan of Frangóvrysi, and halt there five minutes. The neighbouring spring which gives name to the Khan is joined by the waters of another copious source, which issues near the foot of the opposite mountain one third of a mile distant, and afterwards by those of a third under the Paleókastro. The united stream turns the mills which I passed in approaching Frangóvrysi. The Khan stands at the foot of a rocky height, which is separated from that of the Paleókastro by a narrow valley, branching up near a mile towards the mountains: there is

---

[a] March 5th.   [b] ζουρλό-μυλος, crazy mill.

another similar valley after passing the Khan. Our road follows the latter, and at 10.30 begins to ascend the hills which separate the valley of *Asea* from that of *Pallantium*, leaving on the right the rocky summit now called Krávari, and anciently Boreium.

At 11.25 we enter the vale of Pallantium, leaving the inundation of the Taki at the foot of Mount Boreium on the right. It is as plentiful as when I saw it last, and fills up all the space between that mountain and the rocky ridge, on which stand the villages of Birbáti and Thána, and which is continued quite to Tripolitzá. The castle of Tripolitzá may be considered the extreme point of it. The Manthuric plain of Pausanias is evidently that part of the Tegeatic plain which surrounds the Taki. We leave on the right Birbáti, and then Thána, each about two miles distant, and Boléta on the left half a mile, gradually approaching the ridge as the plain narrows, until, at 12.5, having arrived at the end of the valley, we cross the ridge and enter Tripolitzá at 12.35.

May 12—19.—I find a white marble column hollowed out, and serving for a horse-trough at a well, one mile from the gate of Tripolitzá on the Anápli road. Its dimensions being precisely the same as those of the two columns in the mosques of the city, it is evident that they all belonged to the same colonnade at *Tegea*; I was told at Pialí that fifteen similar columns had been carried away from the same excavation at that place.

In the basement of one of the mosques of Tripolitzá I observe a marble, on which is inscribed the name of Lucius Mummius, the celebrated conqueror of Corinth: spelt Λεύκιος Μομμ — the remainder of the name wanting. The marble probably came from *Tegea*, as well as another which I found in the merchants' okkal; it is a child's sarcophagus, on which are the letters ΠΟΛΙΣ ΤΕ . . . . the remainder of the word Τεγέα, or Τεγεατῶν being broken off. The inscription of Mummius serves to shew the form of letters used about the year 145 B.C.

One afternoon I rode to Thána. Though the place seems to have had nothing to recommend it to the ancients for the site of a town, there are many fragments of buildings and of ancient pottery around the village, and I found two broken inscriptions, one in a church in the village, the other at a small distance from it in a church of St. Euphemius. The latter records the erection of a bath and stoa, and mentions the name of Hadrian with the epithet of Panellenius.

During my absence from Tripolitzá, the

Pashá has assembled all the vóivodas, agás, and hodjá-bashis, upon the subject of a firmáhn of the Porte, ordering a reinforcement of troops to the Moréa, in consequence of the alarm respecting the French. The firmáhn directed that they should be fed and paid by the Moréa: 600 men, chiefly Albanians, arrived from Rúmili, whose leaders required twelve piastres, about sixteen shillings, a month for each soldier. The Pashá would only consent to eight; at length it was agreed in council that they should be dismissed with fifteen purses, and that the Pashá should represent that the peninsula was unable to support them, on account of the failure of the last harvest,—he expecting in return that the assembly should unite in a representation to the Porte, laudatory of his conduct, and recommending the renewal of his Pashalík for another year. The Spahís who came from Rúmili were retained, because they are entitled to provisions only, but there can be little doubt that they will soon return home without waiting for permission. Such is the mode in which the Turks prepare for war. Another firmáhn directs that no Frenchman shall be allowed to land from a ship of war.

One of the chief landed proprietors of the Moréa is Arnaút Oglú of Tripolitzá, who owns 300 tjiftliks. Bekír Bey, brother of Nuri Bey of Corinth, has 500, the gross produce of which may be worth 1000 purses, or 30,000*l.* sterling a-year.

The gardens attached to the houses of Tripolitzá are chiefly planted with mulberry-trees, from which about 2000 okes of silk are made every year. There is not a single tree or garden outside the walls, and the vegetables brought to market are chiefly from Argos or Nisí, though the climate would suit admirably any of our potherbs and even potatoes.

An idea prevails here, which I have heard repeated in several parts of the Moréa, that the swallows come in the spring from Africa on the backs of the cranes[a]. A person of good credit has assured me, that he has seen a crane light upon a ship at sea with swallows on its back. The storks[b] arrive in the Moréa at the same time as the cranes, but are not swallow carriers, whether from want of charity, or want of strength, I cannot learn.

[a] γεράνοι. [b] λελάκοι.

CHAPTER XIII.

ARCADIA.

From Tripolitzá to Alonístena.—To the Site of METHY-DRIUM, near Vitína.—To Dhimitzána.—TEUTHIS.—To Fanári.—ALIPHERÆ.—To Platianá.—TYPANEÆ.—To Ai Ianni.—HERÆA.

MAY 20.—Quitting Tripolitzá, at 4.10 P.M., by the Karítena road, I enter the pass of Mount *Mœnalus*, or *Mœnalium*, at the back of the town:—at 4.25 see tracks of chariot wheels in the rocks. At 4.50, in the middle of the mountain, leave the Karítena road to the left; at the summit of the ridge look down upon the vale of Daviá, and the opposite range of mountains, which extend to the plain of *Megalopolis*. On the left are Sylímna, and the other places which I visited March 16. Sylímna, perhaps, stands on the site of *Sumatia*. Descending the hill, we turn to the right under Apanokhrépa, and at the bottom leave a pyrgo and zevgalatía at the head of a little bay at the foot of the steep. It is the same mentioned March 16. We then pass along the foot of Mount Mænalium, ascending the valley of Daviá, and leaving four or five miles on the left the Stená, through which the Helisson passes, between two steep fir-clad mountains, into the plain of Megalopolis. In some part of the valley towards those passes, the site of Lycoa might probably be recognized. At 5.50 we leave Daviá[a] a little on the right, on the rise of Mænalium, consisting of twelve poor huts.

The town of *Mænalus* stood probably higher up the mountain, at the foot of the highest summit, which is now called Aidín.

On the opposite side of the *Helisson*, a rocky projection of the hills which border that side of the valley reaches nearly to the river side: the summit is encircled by remains of Hellenic walls, of which I observe a handsome piece on the part of the hill overlooking the river. This is doubtless the position of Dipæa, which Pausanias describes as a small city of the Mænalia[b] on the banks of the Helisson[c]. It was famous for a battle fought here about the year 470 B.C., between the Lacedæmonians and all the Arcadians, except the Mantinenses[d]. In the latter ages of the Greek empire, Daviá was in the

---

[a] Νταβιὰς or Δαβιὰ.
[b] ἐν τῇ Μαιναλίᾳ πόλισμα Ἀρκάδων.—Pausan. Lacon. c. 11.
[c] Pausan. Arcad. c. 30.
[d] Pausan. Lacon. c. 11. Arcad. c. 8.

possession of the Albanians, of whom there were many settlements at that time in the peninsula. Those of Lalla and Bardhúnia are probably the remains of them, though I do not find either of the names in the Byzantine historians.

We continue to ride along the foot of the mountain, the nearest heights of which are covered with firs, and leave the Helisson flowing from a narrow gorge on the left, in which direction, on the side of the mountain rising opposite to the Mænalium to the west, there is a little cultivation around the village of Piána. At 6.10 cross a torrent flowing from Mænalium towards the Helisson. At 6.27 ascend the hills which terminate the vale of Dipæa, and connect Mænalium with the mountains which extend south-westward to Karítena. All the highest summits of the Mænalian ridge are covered with large firs. At 6.40 we enter upon an elevated valley, in which are corn-fields mixed with firs. At 7.20 cross a stream; at 7.30 another; at 7.35 arrive at Alonístena: the baggage at 8.15.

The first of the two streams just mentioned, rises in the mountain on the right, a bare white rock, on which are a few pines near the top, and farther down a forest of the same trees. The second stream issues from a copious fountain in the village of Alonístena. The source of the western branch is in the village of Piána. As the spring of Alonístena is the principal source of the river, the village should stand, according to Pausanias, on the site of the town Helisson[a], though I cannot find any remains of antiquity here, nor has it any of the usual attributes of an ancient site. The modern appellation is perhaps one of those corruptions in which the name has assumed a new meaning, while preserving a similarity in sound to the ancient word. Though Alonístena means the pass of the threshing-floor, it seems very possible that it may have been derived originally from Helisson, in the usual Romaic form of the accusative case. It is by no means unlikely also that the source at Alonístena is the emissory of the katavóthra of the *Ophis*, or river of *Mantineia*. The mountain behind the village is one of the highest summits of the *Mænalian* ridge, and is contiguous northward to Mount Aidín. Between it and another which runs northward, and then eastward, towards Tara[b], there is a pass leading from Alonístena to Levídhi.

Alonístena contains about seventy houses, and is in the district of Karítena, which town

[a] ὁ Ἐλισσῶν ἀρχόμενος ἐκ κώμης ὁμωνύμου. Pausan. Ar- cad. c. 30. [b] Τάρα.

is reckoned eight hours distant. It is prettily situated on either side of the ravine, at the bottom of which the river issues, and which is closed around by steep mountains covered with firs. The situation of the village being very lofty, the natives enjoy a fine air, and have none of those diseases which torment the inhabitants of the plains in the summer and autumn. In return, they often have three feet of snow upon the ground in the winter. The land produces a small quantity of wheat, which is very good; but sheep[a] and their produce are the principal riches of the place: no benefit is derived from the firs which surround it, except firewood. I am lodged in the house of the protógheros; the best, that of a Kyr Dhimítri being pre-occupied by certain Lalliote armatolí, hired by the vilayéti of Karítena to clear the country of robbers, and who are living at free cost upon the village.

May 21. At 5.50 A.M. we ascend the ravine behind the village, through a forest of firs between the rocky summit of the *Mænalian* range on the right, and a lower woody mountain on the left;—at 6.20 arrive on the crest of the ridge which connects the two mountains; it commands a view of the vale of Alonístena and the range of hills on each side of it, with Mount

[a] πρόβατα.

Málevo (of St. Peter's) in the distance. In the opposite direction is seen the vale of Vitína, and beyond it, to the north-westward, a high ridge, upon the face of which is the village of Magulianá, containing about seventy houses, distant four or five miles from us, in a straight line. At the crest of the pass the road to Vitína and Kalávryta separates from that leading to Dhimitzána, the former descending along the side of the mountain to the right, the latter along the range to the left. We pursue the latter, and in the descent perceive to the north the town of Vitína, at a direct distance of about three miles, and in the same direction, the plain and village of Tara, with a lofty mountain at the back of it, eight or ten miles distant.

Vitína is divided into two parts; the larger stands on a height, at the back of which a river runs through a deep rocky ravine, and takes its course towards the plain of Tara. This river is formed by four streams; the southernmost descends from Nimnítza, the second from Pyrgo, both of which are small villages on the mountain bordering the valley to the south-west; the third is from Magulianá, on the mountain which borders the valley to the north-west; and the fourth from the vicinity of a small village to the north of Magulianá.

Vitína is the largest town in this part of *Arcadia*, and has a schoolmaster, who teaches Hellenic.

After a halt of twenty minutes for the baggage under Nimnítza, we cross, at 7.20, the stream from that village, and at 7.30 arrive at the walls of an ancient city on a height, below Pyrgo, otherwise called Pyrgáko, which is prettily situated on the side of the mountain. At 7.35 arrive at another ancient wall built along the bank of the rivulet which descends from Pyrgo, and joins that from Nimnítza a little below the ruin. The walls were of the second order, but very little of them remains. If they belonged, as I have little doubt, to Methydrium, they probably extended considerably farther to the northward, as far perhaps as the junction of the rivulet of Magulianá with the united stream from Pyrgo and Nimnítza; for Methydrium was one of the most important towns in Arcadia. After a few minutes' delay, we proceed over the roots of the Nimnítza mountain along the brook which rises near Magulianá, and at 8 arrive at the foundations of an ancient building thirty feet long and fifteen broad. Two minutes farther I perceive other ancient wrought stones, brought probably from the same building, now mixed with many rude masses, and forming a modern fence. They seem to be the remains of a temple, perhaps that of Neptune Hippius; for though Pausanias says that this temple was in Methydrium[a], these words do not absolutely require, according to his mode of expressing himself, as exemplified on other occasions, that the temple was *within* the walls of the city: indeed, as he adds that the temple was on the Mylaon[b], it was more probably without the city walls. On this supposition the river of Magulianá was the *Mylaon*. It is doubtful which of the streams descending from Pyrgo and Nimnítza was the *Molottus*, and which the *Malœtas*; or, rather, there is reason to suppose that one of these names is an error in the text of Pausanias for the other, and that he only meant to speak of one river besides the Mylaon. If the Mylaon was the river of Magulianá, it will follow that the mountain above Pyrgo and Nimnítza was that which Pausanias describes as being above the Molottus, and as being called Thaumasium, though I cannot confirm it by any tidings of the cave of Rhea[c]. It must

[a] ἐν Μεθυδρίῳ.
[b] ἐπὶ τῷ Μυλάοντι.
[c] Ὠνομάσθη μὲν δὴ Μεθύδριον, ὅτι κολωνός ἐστιν ὑψηλὸς Μαλοιτᾶ [Μολοττοῦ?] τε ποταμοῦ καὶ Μυλάοντος μέσος, ἐφ᾽ ᾧ τὴν πόλιν ὁ Ὀρχομενὸς ᾤκιζε..... Ἔστι δὲ ἐν Μεθυδρίῳ Ποσειδῶνός τε Ἱππίου ναός· οὗτος μὲν ἐπὶ τῷ Μυλάοντί ἐστι· τὸ δὲ ὄρος τὸ Θαυμάσιον καλούμενον κεῖται ὑπὲρ τὸν ποταμὸν τὸν Μολοττόν. ..... ἔστι δὲ πρὸς τῇ κορυφῇ τοῦ ὄρους σπήλαιον τῆς Ῥέας.
Pausan. Arcad. c. 36.

be allowed that one part of the description of Methydrium by Pausanias, does not very well agree with the position of these ruins. He says that it was built by Orchomenus on a *lofty hill* between the two rivers; whereas it was rather surrounded with mountains than built upon one: the rivers, however, leave little doubt of the identity; and the elevation of the place above the level of the sea must be very considerable, as it is so near to some of the most distant sources of the *Alpheius;* in this sense, therefore, it was built upon a mountain.

Continuing to ascend the rivulet of Maguliana, we pass, at 8.15, over the traces of wheels in the rocks; at 8.16 leave the road to Maguliana, as well as the rivulet, to the right. Ascend till 8.22, when, arriving at the highest part of the pass between the mountains of Nimnítza and Maguliana, we leave on the left a small plain, at the foot of the fir-clad heights of the former range. This plain gives rise to a rivulet which runs towards Dhimitzána; the pass therefore separates the waters of the *Ladon* from those of the *Gortynius*. The rivulet enters a ravine, and we follow the steep and rocky side of the hill which rises from its right bank. At 9, in a small plain belonging to Dhimitzána, it is joined by another torrent from the mountain on the right: it is now much increased in size, and a canal is diverted from it to turn some mills. The plain is marshy, and the land prepared for kalambókki: at 9.30, at the end of the plain we are saluted by a heavy shower of rain and a strong cold wind directly in our faces: soon enter a pass through which the river, now nearly as large as at Atzíkolo, is precipitated over a rocky bed between two steep mountains. Descending along the side of that which overhangs its right bank, we arrive in half an hour in a narrow vale, from whence the town of Dhimitzána is visible on the opposite side of the river, standing on the summit of a high ridge, and surrounded on all sides by steep and lofty mountains. At 10.15 cross the bridge of Dhimitzána, and, immediately passing between two high perpendicular rocks, separated by an opening of only six or eight feet, we mount the hill, and arrive in the town at 10.45. When the Tartar inquires for the hodjá-bashi, "We are all hodjá-bashis", is the reply; soon alarmed, however, by the oaths of the Turk, or not apprehensive of any ill treatment from an Englishman, they find us a good konák, as well as lodging for the horses.

In the afternoon I visit the school of Dhimitzána, the most renowned in the Moréa, and which probably existed before the Turkish conquest. I find the dháskalo, or master[a], in his library, which contains some valuable editions of the classics, many of Aldus, and numerous theological works, but no manuscripts. At present the school has few disciples, and those who learn ancient Greek read little more than the Fathers of the Greek Church, and Lucian, which is generally the first book put into their hands by the master. I have remarked this practice at other places; it had its rise, perhaps, in the early ages of Christianity, for the sake of the ridicule which the author throws on the Pagan deities. The school of Dhimitzána, though still considered the best in the Moréa, has much declined of late. With the increasing misery and depopulation of the Peninsula, the pursuit of letters has diminished in proportion. The study of Hellenic, though so easy to those who have more than half learned it with their mother tongue, is discouraged because it leads to nothing: meantime smaller schools have been established at Mistrá, Argos, Vitína, and Kalávryta, in which is taught that mere smattering of the ancient language which is thought sufficient for boys intended for the Church. The poor didascalus complains piteously

---

[a] διδάσκαλος, vulgarly δάσκαλο.

of these changes from bad to worse, the effect of which is, that his means of existence fall off, and that he is at a loss to find any person who really esteems his occupation, or with whom he can entertain a conversation on the subjects which interest him. He seems a sensible, pleasant character, with a tolerable knowledge of the ancient authors, and a good memory; but, as usual among the modern Greeks, he is quite devoid of sound criticism, and scarcely attempts to form a judgement for himself of the authors whom he reads.

He persists in maintaining that Dhimitzána is the ancient Psophis, that the mountain of Stemnítza, or, as it is sometimes called, Klínitza, is Lampeia, and that the river is the Erymanthus. It is in vain that I turn to Pausanias, and endeavour to shew him that those places must have been some thirty miles distant from hence. He produces Meletius, though he acknowledges him to be full of errors, in support of the tradition which he received from his predecessor in the school, and which the people of Dhimitzána have been so long accustomed to, that they will probably adhere to it as long as Greece remains in its present state of darkness.

The dháskalo accompanies me to the bishop,

an ignorant monk from Cyprus, who lives in the eastern part of the town, on a ridge branching towards Zygovísti. He then conducts me to the other parts of the town, and we make the circuit of it as far as a rocky summit overhanging the river, which forms a semicircle around the precipitous peninsula. All round the crest of the ridge occupied by the town are the remains of a Hellenic wall, some parts of which are intermixed with the yards, and walls, and foundations of the private houses: in some places there are several courses of the masonry remaining, which is partly of the third order, but contains also some fine massy pieces of the polygonal kind. If Atzíkolo was *Gortys*, and there is any truth in Pausanias, these must be the ruins of Teuthis. There are some Hellenic foundations among the vineyards on the slope of the mountain, shewing this slope to have been a part of the ancient city. On the other hand, the portion of the modern town lying on the ridge to the eastward, seems to have been excluded from the ancient inclosure. The walls traceable round the modern town are probably those of the Acropolis only.

The situation of Dhimitzána is cool, healthy, and extremely beautiful. To the south it commands a view of the western part of the plain of *Megalopolis* and the mountains behind Londári. I am informed that the river which encircles the hill is a mere torrent[a], which fails in the summer, and that the permanent source of the *Gortynius* is a great kefalóvrysi, or spring, at the foot of the mountain of Stemnítza.

The situation of the place, the rocky streets, or rather narrow passages between the houses, and the ancient remains, forming a part of some of the modern walls, remind me of Khimára; but the people here have more concord among themselves, and are far less uncivilized. The Mukatá of Dhimitzána and its dependent villages, of which Zygovísti and Stemnítza are the chief, belongs to Osmán, one of the twelve hodja-kháns of Constantinople: he holds them on condition of paying three purses to a certain mosque in Constantinople, and four to the Porte for the kharátj. Osmán's agent receives twelve purses from Hassán Bey of Tripolitzá, brother of Alí Effendi: the hodjá-bashi and primates of Dhimitzána rent it of Hassán Bey for thirteen purses this year, and generally for more. The dhekatía on the cultivators is one in seven: the proprietors of the land are all Greeks. In the town there are 300 families all Greek.

[a] χείμαρρος.

May 22.—This morning, at 5.50, I begin to descend from Dhimitzána, and passing through the vineyards by a steep rugged zigzag path, arrive at 6.10 at the river, which we cross by a bridge just below a place where the water descends fifty feet in a distance of as many yards, tumbling over large masses of rock between lofty precipices hung with shrubs; the hill and town of Dhimitzána appear above this fine foreground in the most picturesque manner. We ascend the opposite hill, which is still more steep and lofty than that of Dhimitzána, and just under the brow arrive at the large village of Zátuna, situated in a climate which is so far behind that of the plain, that the figs and mulberries are only coming into leaf. There are about 150 houses, many of which are large and have gardens of mulberry and walnut mixed with cypress, and lefka, or white poplar. I observe several shops of artisans, and a manufacture for tanning and dyeing leather. We halt ten minutes at the highest part of the village, and then, proceeding under the brow of the mountain, leave to the left, at 7.10, the road to Karítena, which town is distant four hours. At 7.15, on the summit of the pass, we became involved in a thick fog. The western side of the mountain is barren, and little cultivated; at 8 the small village of Sérvoi is on the left; here the fog clears away and discovers a grand prospect of the opposite mountains of Fanári, and the fine slopes on either side of the lower vale of the *Alpheius*. Andrítzena and Fanári are both hid by the hills in front of them. On the slope of those below Andrítzena, across the hollow of the Alpheius, I see the village of Matésh[a], two miles to the north-westward of Lavdha. The river of Andrítzena, which is called Servatá, joins the Alpheius a little below Matésh.

At 8.15 we halt ten minutes; on the left I perceive, at a distance of two or three miles to the south-west, an ancient Greek ruin with walls of the third order: it occupies the summit of a woody hill overhanging the right bank of the Alpheius, opposite to and a little below Matésh. It is called the Castle of Leódhoro[b], or, more vulgarly, Lódhoro, and is said to have been built by a lord of that name who owned all the adjacent country, which from him was called Leódhora[c]. This may be a true account of a part of its history; and a castle of the middle ages may have been added to the Hellenic walls: but these belong, in all probability, to Melæneæ, which Pausanias[d] and the Peutinger Table place hereabouts, on the road from Heræa to Megalopolis. Pausanias says, that in

---

[a] Ματέσι.
[b] τὸ Κάστρον τοῦ Λεοδώρου.
[c] Λεόδωρα.
[d] Pausan. Arcad. c. 26.

his time Melæneæ was deserted and inundated with water; it would seem, therefore, that the town was on the river side, and that the remains which I see are those of the citadel only. They are about due north of the Castle of St. Helen at Lavdha, which is also in sight.

The sides of the hills on the right as far as Lalla, are rich, well wooded, and abound in corn. After halting ten minutes, we continue to descend, and at 8.45 cross a stream shaded with planes, and flowing from right to left towards the *Alpheius*. It is probably the *Buphagus*, at the sources of which was *Buphagium*[a]. I am told that it is dry in summer. We continue to descend through fields of corn in ear, intermixed with wild pear trees, and natural copses of a great variety of shrubs, and at 10.5 arrive at the *Alpheius* just where it emerges from the straits of Karítena and Lavdha into the lower valley or champaign country, of which the chief town was *Heræa*. Throughout this part of its course, and indeed as far as the sea, there is a narrow level on either bank, inundated in winter, and planted with maize in summer; the river is wide and shallow, and its banks produce a great number of large plane trees. After crossing it, we ascend the culti-

---

[a] Pausan. Arcad. c. 26.

vated slope of Fanári: at 11.20 pass along the side of a mountain overhanging a ravine to the right, which is formed on the opposite side by a hill, crowned by the walls of a Hellenic fortress, now called the Castle of Neróvitza.

From thence we descend into a little plain situated at the foot of the mountain of Fanári, and watered by the stream, which, after having half-encircled the hill of Neróvitza, descends from thence to the Alpheius. Having crossed this plain and stream, we ascend Mount Fanarítiko, and at 12.15 arrive at Fanári. This town, which is almost entirely inhabited by Turks, stands in an elevated situation between two high peaks, on the south-eastern of which, towards Andrítzena, are the remains of a castle of the Lower Empire, called Zakkúka. From the two peaks descend two streams, which are conducted in numerous artificial rills to the gardens, houses, mills, and public fountains of the town, which covers a large space of ground. The gardens of fruit trees surrounding the houses, and some fine plane trees in the open spaces near the mosques, as well as along the course of the two brooks, give the whole a beautiful appearance. The air is pure, and is said to be cool even in the midst of summer.

I am visited by the Greek Hodjá Bashi of Andrítzena, Papa Alexi Ikonómu, who assists the Turkish vóivoda of Fanári in transacting the business of the vilayéti, and has, in fact, the principal direction of it. There are five or six mosques in Fanári, and three or four hundred houses.

May 23. Pass the morning in taking geodæsical observations on the summit of Zakkúka, the highest or south-eastern peak of the Fanarítiko, or mountain of Fanári. Zakkúka, it seems, was the name of a castle which stood upon the peak. It is an hour's ride thither from Fanári, passing through the town from the lower part of it, and then up the hill by a zigzag path. The view may be said to comprehend all the Moréa except *Achaia*, the north-eastern part of *Arcadia*, and the extremities of *Argolis* and *Laconia*. To the north is seen the whole range of 'Olonos, and a little more westward, at the foot of that mountain, the *Eleian* hills, with the hill of Sandamério and Kefalonía rising above them. To the right of 'Olonos, the two other great mountains, Khelmós and Zýria close the view; within which are seen all the secondary *Arcadian* summits, from the range of *Erymanthus* to that of *Mænalus*, both included. Still nearer, are the mountains and hills which inclose the vale of the *Alpheius* on the north-east, forming a chain from the valley of the *Ladon* to Mount Tjimbarú, in face of

Londári. Still more distant than the *Mœnalian* summits are seen Turníki and Parthéni, Mount Málevo of St. Peter's (*Parnon*), and then two other remarkable peaks in the same great ridge which occupies all the eastern side of *Laconia*; over its southern extremity I can clearly recognize the pointed hill of Beziané, near the head of the *Laconic* Gulf.

Mount *Taygetum* forms a noble object in the south-east, overlooking the lower summits near Mistrá and in Mani. The plain and gulf of *Messene*, Koróni, Mounts Lykódhemo and Kondovúni, and the *paralia* between Navarín and Arkadhía, fill up the prospect to the right of *Taygetum*, in which direction the nearer objects are the *Lycæan* mountains, with their valleys and cultivated slopes. The latter range forms, together with the *Triphylian* mountains, one distinct body, bounded by the *paralia* of *Triphylia* on the west, by the pass of Kokhla and the plain of *Messene* on the south, by the plain of *Megalopolis* and the valleys of the lower *Alpheius* on the east and north. Of the summits of this division of the *Peloponnesian* mountains, Tetrázi has the appearance, perhaps from its pointed shape, of being the highest; that upon which I stand seems nearly equal in height with the others, namely, Karyátiko, Dhiofórti, and the mountains of 'Alvena and

Smerna, anciently called *Minthe* and *Lapithus*. The Fanarítiko forms the connecting link between *Lycæum* and those two summits, and *Lapithus* terminates the range at Khaiáffa, and towards the mouth of the *Alpheius*. To the right of the latter mountain are seen the plain of Pyrgo, Cape Katákolo, and all the sea shore of the *Eleia* between that cape and Kastro Tornése, with Zákytho in the distance. The most beautiful part of this extensive prospect is to the northward, where the fine champaign slope presents itself to view, which extends five or six miles on both sides of the *Alpheius*, and in the middle of which stands the town of Lalla, in the highest part of the elevated country to the north-east of *Olympia*. The large houses of the three brothers, Seid, Mustafá, and Hassán, and of the son-in-law of one of them, Ali Fermáki, are very conspicuous objects.

The castle of Zakkúka is probably of Frank construction: there are remains of a round tower on the summit of the peak, and of a few houses on the slope. Stunted oaks are scattered over the highest parts of the hill, and among them are some shepherds tending their flocks.

This afternoon I visit the Hellenic remains called the Castle of Nerόvitza[a], which lay on

[a] τὸ Κάστρον τῆς Νεροβίτζας.

our right yesterday as we approached Fanári. At two-thirds of the distance thither I observe the foundations of an ancient wall, but too distant from Nerovitza to have been a part of the city which stood there. The hill of Nerovitza is surrounded on the eastern and partly on the northern and southern sides by the torrent of Fanári. It has a tabular summit about 300 yards

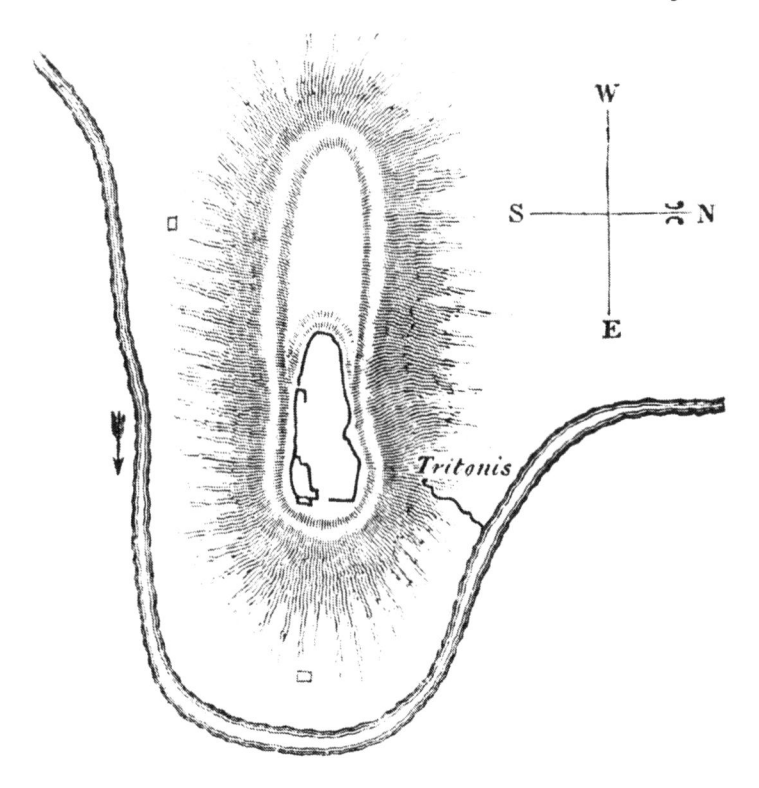

long in the direction of east and west, 100 yards broad, and surrounded by remains of Hellenic walls. At the south-eastern angle, a part rather higher than the rest formed a keep to this fortress; it was about seventy yards long, and half as much broad. The entrance appears to have been in the middle of the eastern wall, between two square towers, of which that to the left only now remains. Beyond this tower, in the same direction and just below the eastern wall of the keep, a lower terrace still retains some foundations of a temple, together with portions of the shafts of columns not fluted, two feet two inches in diameter. There are remains of another temple, with some fragments of columns of the same dimensions, towards the western extremity of the outer fortress near the brow of the height. The whole summit is carpeted with a fine close turf, as usual on the Arcadian hills, where the atmosphere is generally sufficiently moist, even in summer, to maintain the verdure and to furnish an excellent pasture for sheep. I descend from the hill on the northern side through some fields of wheat full grown, but quite green; in the midst of which I find some large flat stones accurately cut, which apparently formed part of a ceiling. A little farther on is a source of water. From thence, after winding round the eastern side of

the hill to regain the road to Fanári, I find the foundations of one of the gates of the lower city. This part of the fortification was flanked with towers, of which there are the remains of two or three, together with considerable pieces of the intermediate walls on the western side, where the ground is very rocky and overgrown with bushes. The masonry is in general of the second order, and has suffered much from time and the exposed situation.

Pausanias and Polybius accord in proving that these are the ruins of Aliphera. The place is so well described by Polybius, and the topography of the surrounding country so well illustrated by a comparison of the two authors, that I shall here subjoin extracts both from the description of the Greek traveller, and the narrative of the historian. "The river Tuthoa", says Pausanias[a], "flows into the Ladon at the boundary of the Thelpusii and Heræenses, which the Arcadians call Pedium[b]. The Ladon joins the Alpheius at the island of Crows[c]. The founder of the Heræenses was Heræeus, son of Lycaon. The city lies on the right bank of the Alpheius, the greater part on a gently-rising ground, the remainder on the bank of the river,

[a] Pausan. Arcad. c. 25, 26.
[b] κατὰ τὸν Θελπουσίων ὅρον πρὸς Ἡραιεῖς, καλούμενον δὲ ὑπὸ Ἀρκάδων Πεδίον.
[c] Κοράκων Νᾶσος.

where are baths and walks of myrtle and other cultivated trees. Here are two temples of Bacchus, one surnamed Polites, the other Axites: attached to them is a building in which the orgies of Bacchus are celebrated. In Heræa there is likewise a temple of Pan, who, to the Arcadians, is a native deity. Of the temple of Juno some columns and other ruins only are left. Proceeding into the Eleia from Heræa, at the end of about fifteen stades you will cross the Ladon, from whence to the Erymanthus there are twenty stades. According to the Arcadians, the Erymanthus is the boundary of Heræa towards the Eleia; but the Eleians say that their limits are at the tomb of Corœbus, upon which there is an epigram, attesting that he was the first who conquered at Olympia, and that he was buried on the confines of the Eleia.

" Aliphera is a small city; many of the inhabitants of which abandoned it when the Arcadians collected together in Megalopolis. In proceeding from Heræa to Aliphera, you will cross the Alpheius, pass over a plain ten stades in width, and then ascend thirty stades through a mountain. The city was named from Alipherus, son of Lycaon. Here are temples of Æsculapius and Minerva: the latter deity is particularly revered among the Alipherenses, because, as they say, she was born and nourished among them.

They have dedicated an altar to Jupiter Lecheatas, as having here brought forth Minerva, and they have given the name of Tritonis to a fountain, to which they apply that which is generally reported concerning the river Triton. The statue of Minerva is made of brass; it is the work of Hypatodorus, and is worthy of admiration both for its magnitude and its workmanship. The Alipherenses celebrate a public festival to one of their deities, I think to Minerva."

The narrative of Polybius is to the following effect[a]:—It was in the Social War, B. C. 219, that Philip, after having taken Psophis and plundered the Eleia, marched from Olympia to Thelpusa, and thence to Heræa, where he repaired the bridge over the Alpheius for the purpose of passing over into Triphylia. It happened at the same time that Philidas, who had been sent from Ætolia with 600 men to assist the Eleians, entered Triphylia at the head of those troops, reinforced by 1000 men of Elis and nearly as many mercenaries in the service of that state. Triphylia (remarks the historian) took its name from Triphylus, one of the sons of Arcas; it was situated in the maritime part of Peloponnesus, between Eleia and Messenia, and contained nine cities, namely, Samicum, Lepreum, Hypana, Typaneæ, Pyrgus, Æpium,

---

[a] Polyb. l. 4. c. 77.

Bolax, Styllangium, and Phrixa. These the Eleians had not long before gained possession of; they had also, by an exchange with Lydiades, a tyrant of Megalopolis, obtained Aliphera, which had before been attributed to Arcadia. Philidas having sent the Eleians to Lepreum and the mercenaries to Aliphera, waited at Typaneæ to observe the movements of Philip, who speedily crossed the bridge over the Alpheius at Heræa, and moved to Aliphera. "This city", adds Polybius, "stands upon a hill precipitous on every side[a], to which there is an ascent of more than ten stades. The citadel is on the summit of the hill, and contains a statue of Minerva remarkable for its beauty and magnitude. It is not known by whom or upon what occasion this statue was dedicated, but all agree that it was made by Hypatodorus and Sostratus, and that it is one of their choicest works." On the morning after his arrival, the weather being serene and clear, Philip ordered ladder bearers to proceed to various parts of the town walls, escorted by mercenaries, who were followed by parties of Macedonians; while he led in person a chosen body of men through some difficult and rocky places[b], to the citadel. The assault was made at sunrise. The Alipherenses, intent on resisting the attack of the Mace-

[a] κρημνώδους πανταχόθεν.   [b] διά τινων κρημνῶν.

donians on the town walls, left the citadel undefended, so that Philip easily gained the outer inclosure[a], and set fire to it. The Alipherenses, seeing the flames, and alarmed for the safety of the Acropolis, retired into it, and thus allowed the Macedonians to enter the town on all sides: soon afterwards they sent proposals of capitulation to Philip. Philidas having quitted Typaneæ and marched to Lepreum, the Typaneatæ surrendered their city to Philip, and their example was followed by Hypana and Phigaleia. The Lepreatæ, whose city was occupied by some Lacedæmonians and Cretans, as well as by the Eleians and Ætolians brought thither by Philidas, required these troops to leave the place; but it was not until Philip approached the town that their demand was complied with, when the Cretans marched towards Messenia on their way home, and Philidas, with the Spartans and Eleians, retired to Samicum. Lepreum then submitted to the king: as soon as he approached Samicum, the Ætolians and Eleians requested and obtained his permission to march unmolested homeward; Samicum was then also taken, all the other towns surrendered, and the whole of Triphylia was thus reduced in six days.

It appears from the remains of the outer walls

[a] τὸ τῆς ἄκρας προάστειον.

of Aliphera, on the western side of the hill of Neróvitza, that here stood the main body of the lower town. On this side, therefore, it should seem that the escalade took place while Philip made his way through the rocks and bushes on the eastern side, and under that cover surprised the προάστειον, or outer citadel, which probably occupied the lower and larger portion of the tabular summit. The small fortress at the north-eastern angle I take to have been that which Polybius called the Acra or Acropolis, and into which the garrison retired. The temple which stood on the terrace, under the eastern side of the upper citadel, I conceive to have been that which contained the celebrated colossal Minerva, the situation being such as is likely to have been dedicated to that deity as the protector of fortresses; it will follow that the temple in the lower level, or proasteium, was that of Æsculapius. The fountain which I have mentioned towards the north-eastern side of the city, seems to have been the Tritonis of Pausanias.

The summit of the hill of Neróvitza is higher, I think, than Fanári; it is more pervious to the breezes, and more conveniently situated, with respect to the valley of the Alpheius, than that place, but wants its fine streams and plentiful supply of water. I return after sunset to

Fanári by the same road I came, along the valley of the torrent which flows to Nerovitza: here the murmuring of the rivulet, the songs of the nightingales, and the aromatic perfume of the shrubs on the hills, brought by a gentle zephyr, contribute to form the perfection of a Grecian evening in May.

I purchase from a Turk of Fanári an intaglio on an onyx, about an inch in length, representing a Minerva armed with spear and shield, and clothed in a short tunic hanging in graceful folds over a χιτὼν ποδήρης, or loose robe reaching to the feet. The design is of the best times, but the preservation is not good. Around the figure is the word ΑΓΗΣΙΠΟΛΙΑΣ, which leaves no doubt on my mind that the figure represents the colossal and much admired statue of Minerva, by Hypatodorus, which stood in the temple of the goddess at Aliphera; for the Greeks often represented their most celebrated or revered statues upon gems and coins, or copied them in miniatures of brass or clay; and I have observed that it is not uncommon to find such representations of them near the places where they were worshipped.

May 24.—At 6.15 I set out for Platianá. After winding round the hill of Fanári to the westward, descend at 6.48 into a small plain crossed by a rivulet, which rises behind the western peak of the Fanarítiko. In its passage through the hills, below the plain, it makes a bend so as to approach Neróvitza; on issuing from the hills, it crosses the valley of the Alpheius, and joins that river nearly opposite to Aiánni[a]. These hills, of which Neróvitza is one of the most remarkable, are an advanced lower chain parallel to the Fanarítiko. At 6.56 we cross the small stream above mentioned, and at the end of the plain pass over a low ridge into another vale, which is separated from the lower *Alpheian* valley by a lofty summit ranging in a line with that of Neróvitza. The heights on both sides of the valley which we pass through are covered, but not very thickly, with trees: on the slope of that upon the right are two small villages. Several torrents rush down on either side from the hills, and unite in the vale, which is diversified with woods and cultivated ground. At 7.30 we cross a bridge at the junction of two of the streams flowing to the right; then proceed along the left bank of the united river, among planes and other trees, and occasionally over the foot of the hills which bound the valley to our left: at 7.45 cross another stream flowing from a steep shady ravine on the same side. At 8.30 again cross a rivulet of the same kind, descending directly from the moun-

[a] St. John.

tain of 'Alvéna. The name Vunúka, which is also given to this mountain, is derived from a castle which formerly stood on the summit, and which was probably of the same date as that of Zakkúka on the Fanarítiko.

The river formed from the several streams which we have passed, now takes its course to the right to the Alpheius, through an opening between the heights. We ascend the hill of Platianá, which rises from the left bank of the river, and arrive at a Paleókastro on the summit at 9.15. This is the ruin of a small Hellenic πόλις, similar to those of *Arcadia*. A narrow level on a long summit surrounded with precipices formed an Acropolis; a space on the face of the hill, a little shorter, and of about thrice the breadth was the inclosure of the town. All the walls are of the third order; some of the towers have the flanks considerably longer than the face, as in the ruins at Pávlitza. The citadel is narrower in proportion to its length than any other I have seen, being nearly 700 yards long, with a breadth in no part of more than twenty or thirty. There are cross walls dividing this long space into several inclosures, one of which is eighty-five yards in length, and on a higher level than the others; it is divided from the main lower citadel by a curved wall, and is separated on the opposite side by another wall,

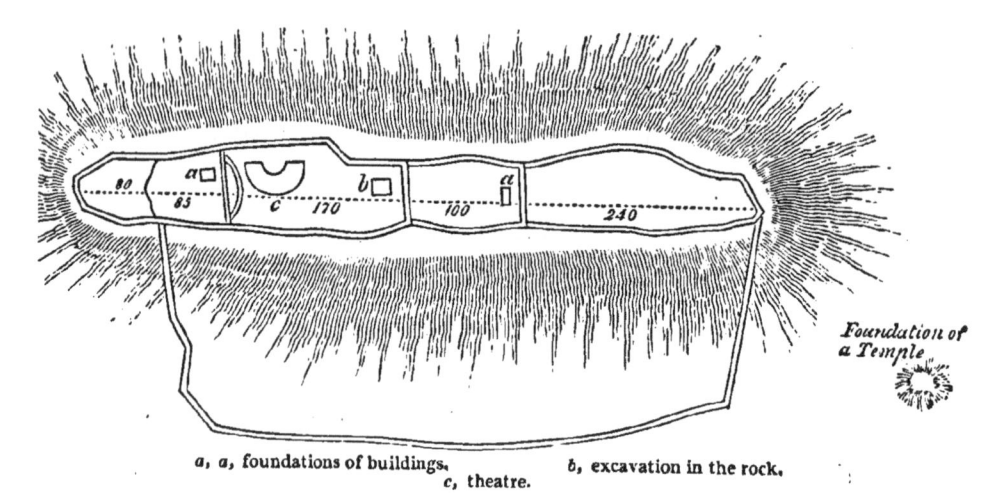

a, a, foundations of buildings. *b*, excavation in the rock.
c, theatre.

from a narrow rocky promontory, which forms the termination of the summit to the westward. In the lower citadel, just below the curved wall eastward, I find the *emplacement*, and a few of the seats of a small theatre, fifteen or twenty yards in diameter, so situated immediately behind one of the walls of the citadel, as not to command any prospect of the country. Though it is not to be supposed that the spectators in Greek theatres could always command a view of the external objects, as the scene must have prevented it, it may be suspected that they did in some instances, especially where the theatre was chiefly used for sacred or political assemblies; for it is observable that the theatres of Greece are generally placed in the most beautiful and commanding situations. In the present instance, the wall in front of the theatre is so near that it might itself have served for the scene. About one hundred yards beyond the theatre, in the lower inclosure eastward, is a quadrangular excavation in the rocks, probably a cistern, and then the foundations of another wall crossing the Acropolis; one hundred yards farther are the remains of some public edifice, and another wall of separation: from thence the hill descends towards the east-north-east, which is the general direction of the height; and terminates at about 240 yards beyond the last-mentioned transverse wall. I conceive, from the narrative of Polybius already cited, that these must be the ruins of Typaneæ; for the situation was perfectly adapted to the object of Philidas, after he had sent forward the greater part of his forces to Lepreum and Aliphera, namely, that of observing the motions of Philip at Heræa.

From the summit of the Paleókastro the sea-coast about the Khan of Ai Sídhoro is seen; —a vale which separates the mountain of Smerna, or *Lapithus*, from Vunúka, or *Minthe*, leaves the prospect open. The latter mountain rises directly opposite to the Paleókastro to the southward, and 'Alvena is seen immediately under the summit. This village may possibly stand on the position of *Hypana*, for this name seems to indicate a lofty situation; and as Aliphera, according to Pausanias, was the frontier town of Arcadia on this side, and was even included in Triphylia at the time of the Social War, we may conclude that Mount Vunúka was also a part of *Triphylia*, to which district it has been seen that Polybius ascribes Hypana. From Strabo, as well as Polybius [a], Hypana clearly appears to have been at no great distance from Typaneæ, and to have been in the hills above the maritime plain of Lepreum. A low transverse ridge in the vale above mentioned, which separates the two mountains, divides the course of the waters. Eastward flows the stream which I crossed at $8\frac{1}{2}$; in the opposite direction, through a deep ravine between the two mountains, runs that which crosses the maritime plain below Zákari, and falls into the sea a little southward of the Khan of Ai Sídhoro, where I crossed it February 28th. This river appears to be the Pamisus, or Mamaus, or Arcadicus, or Amathus of Strabo, and that which runs eastward is perhaps the Diagon of Pausanias [b].

Proceeding from the eastern termination of the Acropolis, I arrive, after a descent of 250 yards to the eastward, at a small height in a hollow between the hill of Platianá and another toward the *Alpheius*. Here, on a rising ground in a corn-field, are the foundations of a small

---

[a] Strabo. p. 344.—Polyb. ubi sup.   [b] Pausan. Eliac. post. c. 21.

temple or other public edifice. From thence I descend to the village of Platianá, which stands under the Paleókastro hill, on the northern side. The most agreeable lodging I can find here is under a fig tree, and the best dinner, some new cheese and milk from a mándhra on the hill, with a loaf of maize flour from one of the cottages. Platianá contains about thirty families divided into two hamlets, and is beautifully situated on the slope of the hill amidst gardens, woods, and fountains. Below it, to the northward, there is a great hollow space with a most uneven surface, surrounded by hills and intersected with torrents: its declivities are adorned with copses of firs mixed with a great variety of shrubs, and its ravines are shaded with planes. The ground, as at *Olympia* and in many parts of the circumjacent country, is broken into little abrupt precipices, where the white argillaceous soil forms a striking contrast with the verdure of the turf and forests. A ridge separates this irregular vale of Platianá from the lower valley of the *Alpheius*. The woody and diversified country which begins here extends westward as far as the maritime plains of the *Eleia*, and northward as far as the steep acclivities of Mount 'Olonos. It was in the midst of this sylvan region, so well adapted to a sportsman, that Scillus, the residence of Xenophon, was situated, at a distance of only two miles and a half from Olympia. Wild boars, one of the great objects of the ancient chace, are common in this woody district, though not generally found in the lower open country near the Alpheius, nor indeed in any other part of the Moréa, except in the higher and more woody mountains.

Sending orders to my Tartar and Agoyátes, whom I had left at Fanári, to meet me at Aiánni, I proceed with a Turkish guide to a ruin called the Paláti, or Palace[a], near the bank of the Alpheius. Leaving Platianá at 2 p. m., I cross the valley in an eastern direction, and then passing over the height which separates it from the vale of the Alpheius, and which is covered with large firs[b] and pines[c], descend on the other side by a rugged, steep, and winding road, and arrive, at 3.30, at the Paláti. The ruin stands not far above the river, in the midst of a fertile corn country near the side of a woody hill, at the foot of which are many fine planes and terebinths, with a shady fountain constructed in the Turkish style, which stands on the side of the road from Lalla to Fanári. I am not a little surprised to find that the palace is the ruin of a Gothic church or hall, of which one end is entire, terminating above in a high acute angle: the low side walls

[a] τὸ Παλάτι.   [b] ἐλάτια.   [c] πεύκοι.

which supported the high shelving roof still remain with a row of windows in them. The centre of the high end-wall is pierced with a great window of the annexed form.

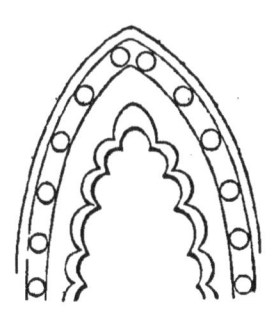

On one side of this building stands a square church of the same kind of architecture, with a Greek cross over one of the windows, thus;

on the opposite side there are some remains of other buildings belonging to the monastery, for such these ruins seem to have been. The whole has the appearance of a ruined abbey in England, and the scenery around is well adapted to increase the illusion. I have already remarked that there is a Gothic ruin at Karítena of a similar style: it cannot be doubted that they are works of the same age, that is to say, of the thirteenth or fourteenth century, when, after the conquest of Constantinople, there were several Frank principalities in the Moréa. In all the dry places about the Paláti I observe great numbers of the formica leo in its inverted conical habitation. These animals are here called ζουζούνια.

At 4 P.M. I descend obliquely towards the Alpheius: at 4.35 cross a bridge over the river, of which I passed several of the tributaries towards their sources in Mount Vunúka and the adjacent hills, and its westernmost branch just before ascending the hill of Platianá. As the junction of the *Erymanthus* and *Alpheius* is in sight at the bridge, about half a mile to the left, it seems evident that the river is the Diagon, which Pausanias describes as falling into the Alpheius nearly opposite to the mouth of the Erymanthus, and as forming the line of separation (southward of the Alpheius) between Pisæa and Arcadia[a]. The Diagon is probably the same as the Dalion of Strabo[b], whose Acheron may possibly be the next stream to the eastward, which I crossed towards the upper part of its course this morning at 6.56.

There is a narrow level on either side of the Alpheius shaded with planes, sown with kalam-

[a] Pausan. Eliac. post. c 21.   [b] Strabo, p. 344.

bókki, and subject to inundations. Our road passes over a height rising from this valley, through shrubs among which the Paliúri [a] predominates. The small village of Bizbárdhi [b] stands on the hill to our right:—at 5.5 arrive on a bank immediately overhanging the *Alpheius*, and opposite to the mouth of the *Ladon*, which at its junction forms a delta. This delta is the Coraconnasus, or Island of Crows, mentioned by Pausanias [c], whose observation, that there is no island in the Ladon as large as a ferry-boat [d], was assuredly not meant to be applied to the Coraconnasus, which is nearly a quarter of a mile in circumference, and contains a fine grove of planes. The *Ladon* enters the *Alpheius* with a narrow, but rapid, deep, and turbid stream: having passed opposite to the junction of the rivers, we soon enter upon the narrow level which borders the Alpheius.

A Lalliote soldier, in the Albanian dress, who meets us, asks my Turkish guide, the only person accompanying me: " Who is that infidel [e] you have got with you? Is he a physician?" [f] " No ", says my guide in the same contemptuous tone, " he is one of those *Mylords* [g] that

---

[a] παλιούρι, rhamnus Paliurus.
[b] Μπηζιμπάρδη.
[c] Κοράκων Νᾶσος. Pausan. Arcad. c. 25.
[d] νηὶ πορθμίδι.
[e] Ghiaour.
[f] Ἰατρὸς εἶναι;
[g] Μιλιόρδοι.

look for old castles, and has been to see the Palace." At 5.48 we cross the Alpheius, which is wide and reaches to the horse's belly, the water white and turbid; just below the ford there is a fall of several feet in a short space. Arrive at Aiánni at 6: find a servant arrived, but no Tartar, horses, or baggage. Aiánni and Anemodhúri are two small villages 500 yards asunder, standing on a height which overlooks the low level on the banks of the Alpheius, which is here called the river of Karítena. In each hamlet there is one stone house; the remaining habitations are thatched huts shaped like a great oval tent;—a large post in the middle supports the roof, which slopes to within three or four feet of the ground, where a wall of that height, made of pliant wicker branches interwoven with upright sticks, forms the rest of the structure. I procure a lodging in one of these huts.

In the fields between the village and the brow which looks down upon the level of the Alpheius, I find the remains of a small Roman building, near which are several squared blocks of stone. Many coins are found in ploughing or in digging the surrounding fields. These vestiges, inconsiderable as they are, are sufficient, I think, when combined with the descriptions of Polybius and Pausanias, to fix this spot for the site of Heræa. The fifteen stades of Pausanias from Heræa to the Ladon, his twenty stades from the Ladon to the Erymanthus, his ten stades across the level of the Alpheius, and his thirty stades of ascent to Aliphera[a], are all found to be perfectly accurate on the supposition of Aiánni and Neróvitza having been respectively the sites of Heræa and Aliphera.

Near the summit of the mountain to the eastward of Aiánni, some remains of a Hellenic fortress are described to me at the ruined village of Papadhá; here are the sources of a torrent, dry in summer, which flows to the Alpheius, and seems to be the same which I crossed in the descent from Zátuna to the Alpheius on the 22d. The position of Papadhá answers to that of Buphagium, for Pausanias says: "that Buphagium stands above Melæneæ at the sources of the river Buphagus, which descends to the Alpheius."[b]

Pliny, Theophrastus, and Ælian, concur in reporting that the wine of Heræa had the property of making men mad and women fruitful[c]. A sweetish red wine is still made here, and it has more flavour and body than almost any

[a] Pausan. Arcad. c. 26.
[b] Pausan. Ibid.
[c] Fecunditatem feminis, viris rabiem.—Plin. H. N. l. 14. c. 18.—Theophr. de Plant. l. 9. c. 20.—Ælian. Var. Hist. l. 13. c. 6.

wine I have met with in the Moréa. In sufficient quantities, therefore, it might produce for a time one of the effects anciently attributed to the wine of Heræa: as to the other, its reputation at least is gone: and certainly the poor women of modern Arcadia never drink of it for the sake of the virtues ascribed to it by the ancients. There were some fables of the same kind related of the wine of Trœzen and of Ceryneia in Achaia.

I find the unfortunate inhabitants in expectation of the arrival, to-morrow, of eighty Lalliotes, for whom they are preparing ten or twelve sheep, with wine and bread. These men are making a tour of the country under pretence of keeping it clear of robbers.

CHAPTER XIV.

ARCADIA. ACHAIA.

From Ai Ianni to Vyzítza.—THELPUSA.—Strézova.—Karnési.—Kalávryta.—Nezerá.—Patra.—PATRÆ.—Castle of the Moréa.—RHIUM.—ANTIRRHIUM.

MAY 25.—Having hired two horses from the village, and left orders for the Tartar and baggage to follow, I set out, at 5.45, on the road to Vyzítza and Kalávryta, passing through woods of oak beautifully intermixed with corn-fields, vineyards, and copses of shrubs. At 5.55, Loti, a small village, is on the right. At 6.25, ascending the hills in the direction of a new built pyrgo belonging to Arnaút Oglú, of Tripolitzá, I halt for 10 minutes at a ruined church to which the Aianniotes had directed my attention, but where I find nothing remarkable. Belesh[a] is situated on the right bank of the *Ladon*, half an hour from its mouth. Having passed the tower of Arnaút-Oglú, which stands on the summit of a ridge sloping towards the junction of the Alpheius and Ladon, we descend through a forest of oaks, and at 7.4 enter a pleasant

[a] Μπέλισι.

valley watered by the river of Langádha [a], the ancient Tuthoa, which receives its modern name from a town on a mountain six or seven miles to the right in the direction of Dhimitzána. Though now shallow, this river is rapid and large in winter, as its wide and stony bed indicates. A little above the place where I crossed it at 7.12, it is joined on the left side by a small torrent descending through a deep gorge from Zulátika, a village on the side of a hill three or four miles distant, where the Lalliotes burnt a house the other day under the pretence that it belonged to a thief.

The *Tuthoa* joins the *Ladon* one mile and a half to the left, opposite to the small village of Renési, which stands on a high bank. I find that the Ladon throughout this country is called Ruféa, Rufiá, or Rofiá; and that the Alpheius bears that name only below its junction with the Ladon; above which it is usually called the River of Karítena. Higher up however the Ladon is more commonly called the Foniátiko, or river of Foniá: here it flows, for the most part, between high, steep, woody banks, which inclose a narrow level on either side of the stream. We proceed along the summit of a ridge included between the Tuthoa and Ladon,

[a] ποτάμι τῆς Λαγκάδας.

and halt, at 8.15, for a quarter of an hour at a commanding eminence, from whence there is a gradual slope of two miles to the banks of the Ladon, where is a conical height like a great tumulus. On a projection of the opposite or right bank of the river, stand Tumbíki and a khan which is in the road from Tripolitzá to Lalla.

A little above Tumbíki, on the left bank, there are said to be some remains of a Hellenic city, at a ruined village called Vánena. Below us, to the right, at a small distance, is the village of Kokhla. Our direction is now towards the mountain of Vretembúga[a], upon reaching which we ascend the foot of it, and pass round it, with the summit on the left; at 9.20, leave the Tripolitzá road on the right and descend into a little vale, where, at 9.35, the village of Alvánitza remains close on the right; from thence, after passing up another small valley under the mountain of Vretembúga we arrive, at 10, at Vyzítza, a village with a large church and several good houses, some of which, however, are in ruins. Another village, called Vervítza, somewhat larger, is on the side of the same hill, half a mile distant. Both enjoy a fine air and a plentiful supply of good water. The people of Vyzítza stoutly assert that their water is the better

[a] Βρετεμποῦγα.

and lighter of the two, and the Vervitziotes probably say the same. The merchants of Tripolitzá come to these villages to buy butter and cheese. Of the former alone 1000 kantars [a] are yearly brought for sale from the neighbouring country. I lodge in the house of Kyr Niko, the tailor, shoemaker, and archon of the village. His dwelling is one long chamber, with a fireplace for a kitchen at one end; he and his sons' families all live together. My baggage, &c. arrive at 2.30: the computed distance for loaded horses from Fanári is eight hours and a half.

May 26.—This morning I visit the ruins at Vánena, setting out at 5.45, and arriving at the ruins at 7.15. From Vyzítza the road leads through the vale under Vervítza, and then through a narrow valley included between a hill which overhangs that village and the mountain of Vretembúga; it then descends upon Vánena along the side of the latter mountain, which is covered with wood, chiefly oaks and wild pears. Some tents on one of the heights near the *Ladon* now shelter all the remaining inhabitants of what once was the village of Vánena [b]. A brook from Vretembúga joins the Ladon, which is here called Rufiá. Another brook, which joins the former, comes from behind a height

---

[a] cwt.   [b] Βάνενα.

which has two conical summits. Here probably stood the Acropolis of the ancient city which occupied this position, and which seems clearly to have been Thelpusa. No remains of walls now exist on the height; but on its slope towards the Ladon I find some Hellenic foundations, and the lower parts of six columns, one foot nine inches in diameter, standing in their original places. Towards the rivulet are the remains of a Roman building about twelve yards long and six wide, with the ruins of an arched roof. One of the corners of the building has a stone with an ornament upon it, to which I find a corresponding fragment in a ruined church of St. John not far from the brook.

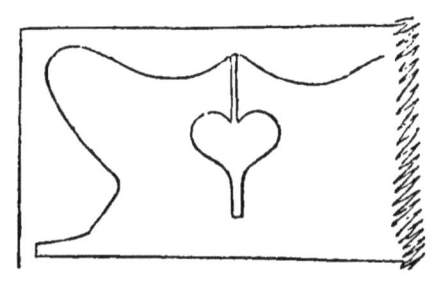

Here likewise are several other wrought stones; and among the shrubs around the ruined church are some Hellenic foundations, a small portal in its place, and many fragments of plain columns two feet in diameter. On the opposite bank, lying in the water, I find a small fluted Doric column with twenty shallow flutings, the diameter one foot, the length four feet five inches. The ruined church stands in a fine grove of oaks and kotríves [a], as the Moreites call the terebinth [b], which grows plentifully, and sometimes to a considerable size, in the moist and shady situations of Arcadia.

By the guidance of a man of Vánena I ford the Ladon, which is deep and rapid, and here embraces a large island bearing some plane-trees, and covered with fennel; by the side of which is a smaller one, so that I have three streams to pass. The water comes up to the horse's shoulder: my guide boasts of sometimes passing it in winter up to his neck. The only danger to the inexperienced, he says, is from giddiness [c], arising from the rapidity of the current. In the ruined church of St. Athanasius the Miraculous [d], on the right bank, I find a plain column one foot three inches in diameter, another with twenty Doric flutings, one foot nine inches in diameter, and a Doric capital of the same diameter, three feet square at the plinth. Two large plain columns, one foot three inches in diameter, form the door-posts of the church, and a great Roman tile serves for the holy table [e]. The saint, as his epithet imports, has the reputation of performing miracles.

[a] κοτρίβαις.
[b] pistacia terebinthus.
[c] σκότισμα.
[d] Ἅγιος Ἀθανάσιος ὁ θαυμαχτός.
[e] ἁγία τράπεζα.

Not long ago, according to my guide, he half strangled one night a Turk of Lalla, who had begun to plunder the saint's church to complete his pyrgo. The cultivated land about the church is called Zamba, perhaps from a village which once existed here. The hills beyond it are woody, steep, and very picturesque.

It is not surprising that the modern Peloponnesians should consider the Ladon the main stream of the Alpheius, or that they should have given it the name of Ruféa, which is a corruption of Alpheius, in preference to the Karítena branch [a], for it is the handsomest river in the Peninsula, by its depth, its rapid, even, unfailing course, and its beautiful banks; compared to it the others are rocky or sandy torrents. As high as Spáthari, a bridge and village three or four miles above Vánena, it produces the κέφαλος, or gray mullet, the λαμβράκι, or perch, and the χέλι, or eel; all which, observes my Thelpusian guide, are fish of the sea: in every other part of its course are found the πέστροβα,

---

[a] The process of change in this instance illustrates what I conceive to have taken place at Troy. Seven or eight centuries after the time of Homer, the name Scamander was applied not only to the united river, but to the branch also, which in the time of the poet was called Simoeis. The examples of such changes in the names of rivers are by no means rare. See Journal of a Tour in Asia Minor, c. 6.

or trout, the τριχιὸ, and the μουστάκι. I know not exactly to what fish he applies the last two names; but considering the etymology of the words μουστάκι and *barbel*, it may be conjectured that they are the same fish; τριχιὸ would seem to imply a fish with hair upon it, or perhaps of a form extremely slender. Half a mile below the church of St. Athanasius stands the village of Tumbíki, where a promontory projects into the bed of the river; on the summit of it there is a mound apparently artificial. Just above this position a torrent joins the Ladon.

Of Thelpusa, and the course of the Ladon below that city, as far as its junction with the Alpheius, Pausanias thus writes[a]: "Below the temple of Ceres Eleusinia, the Ladon passes the city Thelpusa, which is situated on its left bank, on (or at) a lofty hill, but the greater part is now deserted, so that the Agora, which was formerly in the middle of the city, is now at the end of it. In Thelpusa there is a temple of Æsculapius, and another of the Twelve Gods, the greater part of which is now levelled with the soil. Beyond Thelpusa the Ladon descends to the temple of Ceres in Onceium: the Thelpusii call the god-

---

[a] Θέλπουσαν τὴν πόλιν ὁ Λάδων παρέξεισιν ἐν ἀριστερᾷ, κειμένην ἐπὶ λόφου μεγάλου, τὰ πλείω δὲ ἐφ' ἡμῶν ἔρημον.

Pausan. Arcad. c. 25.

dess Erinnys[a]. According to report, Oncus was son of Apollo, and reigned over the place[b] named Onceium in the Thelpusia. The statues in the temple are of wood, except the faces, hands, and feet, which are of Parian marble. That of Erinnys bears the box called Ciste in the left hand, and a torch in the right, and is about nine feet high. The statue of Ceres Lusia is about six feet high. The Ladon, leaving the temple of Erinnys, passes that of Apollo Onciates on the left, and on the right that of the Boy Æsculapius, where is the sepulchre of Trygon, who is said to have been the nurse of Æsculapius. The river Tuthoa falls into the Ladon at the place called by the Arcadians 'Pedium', which is the boundary of the Thelpusii and Heræenses. At the junction of the Ladon with the Alpheius is the Island of Crows. Some think that Enispe, Stratie, and Rhipe, places mentioned by Homer, were inhabited islands in the Ladon; but those who hold this opinion must be mistaken, for the Ladon con-

---

[a] An allusion to the temple of Erinnys, near Thelpusa, occurs in Lycophron, v. 1038:—

Χέρσου πατρώας οὐ γὰρ ἂν φονῇ ποσὶ
Ψαῦσαι, μέγαν πλειῶνα μὴ πεφευγότα,
Δίκης ἰάσει τάρροθος Τελφουσία,
Λάδωνος ἀμφὶ ῥεῖθρα ναίουσα σκύλαξ.

[b] χωρίον.

tains not any islands equal even in magnitude to a ferry-boat, and though second to none of the rivers, either of the Barbarians or Greeks, in beauty, is not of such a magnitude that islands can exist in it like those of the Ister and Eridanus."

The mountain of Vretembúga answers to the λόφος μέγας, or great hill, of Pausanias; he seems therefore to have intended to say that the town was situated at or near, and not upon, a high hill. Above Vánena, on the same bank of the river, some vestiges of the temple of Ceres Eleusinia might perhaps be found; and if Tumbíki, the only remarkable site on the right bank between Thelpusa and the Tuthoa, be the site of the temple of Æsculapius, and the tumulus on that promontory the tomb of Trygon, as I suspect, the temple of Apollo Onciates was nearly opposite to it on the left bank, and between the latter and Thelpusa stood the temple of Erinnys at Onceium. I cannot, however, hear of any remains at those places to tempt me to explore farther. There is an island in the Ladon nearly opposite Tumbíki, which appears to me not less than three or four hundred yards in length, and that which I crossed is as much. They bear plane-trees and shrubs, and are inundated in winter. Either, therefore, Pausanias was deficient in his usual accuracy, when he said that the Ladon contained no island larger than a ferry-boat, or the islands must have been formed since his time. I return by the same road to Vyzítza.

Vyzítza and Vervítza contain together about 150 families. All persons above twelve years of age pay twenty-five piastres a year, and those above fifteen, fifty, to the $\chi\rho\acute{\epsilon}\eta$, or share of the contributions to government. A learned Vyzítziote tries to persuade me that the river at Vánena is the ancient Alpheius, and the ruins those of a city which he calls $Βοιήαν\ πόλις$, and of which name he supposes Vánena to be a corruption. Where he got this idea I cannot discover.

At 3 p.m. I proceed towards Kalávryta. At 3.20 on the descent, after crossing the heights behind Vyzítza, the castle of Galatá and a place with four houses so called, is half a mile on the right. The castle, which is a structure of the middle ages, has several high round towers, and stands on a precipitous hill; it is reckoned three and a half hours from Dhimitzána. Soon afterwards we pass a church situated in a grove of gigantic prinária, or holly-oaks, and at 3.35 pass through the little village of Katzuliá.

From thence we descend through a forest of

small but lofty oaks[a], and at 4.10 leave the village of Syriámu Kurtághi[b], otherwise called Syriamáki, half a mile on the right. There is another Siriámu on the opposite side of the Ladon, where a plain of no great extent branches out of that of the Ladon, which is here narrow and subject to inundations. Having descended into the vale of the river, we cross, at 4.35, a small tributary of the Ladon flowing from a gorge on the right, beyond which is Kerpení. We cross it just above its junction with the Ladon, and then pass a small level grown with kalambókki, beyond which the Ladon flows between steep cliffs, under which a little slope on the riverside is shaded with plane, oak, cornel[c], and arbutus[d], the river running rapidly through the grove; it is said to be ten feet deep in some parts, the breadth is from fifty to eighty yards: the waters are turbid, and there are little cataracts at intervals. The road continues to follow the left bank of the river through this woody pass till 5, when, at a small level opening, we cross the river by the Lady's Bridge[e], as it is called. A road to the right here leads to Kerpení and Valtesiníko, from whence the distance is nine hours to Karítena by Dhimitzána,

---

[a] δενδρά.
[b] Συριάμου Κουρτάγη.
[c] κρανιά.
[d] κουμαριά.
[e] τὸ Γεφύρι τῆς Κυρᾶς.

or Zygovísti, and the like to Tripolitzá by Magulianá.

After a halt of ten minutes at the bridge, we cross a little plain of kalambókki, and following up the river at a quick pace, arrive, at 5.30, in a plain, beyond which the river comes through a gorge to the north, in the direction of Mount Zýria. We here quit the Ladon, and passing up a plain which branches to the north-west, arrive, at the end of a mile, at the foot of the hills which border it to the north-eastward; here stands the village of Podhogorá.—Ascend these woody heights, and arrive at Strézova, a town of 100 or 150 houses in a lofty situation. The baggage was four hours and a half from Vyzítza. Strézova belongs to the vilayéti of Kalávryta. A Turkish agá possesses a pyrgo, and there is a Greek captain of Armatolí named Makri Vasíli, who resides here with twenty-five men, maintained by the district. This mode of keeping the roads safe from robbers seems to shew that the state of society in this country is something similar to what it was in England in the reign of Alfred, who is said to have thrown upon the villages the expense and responsibility of keeping the country clear of robbers.

May 27. At 5.50 descend from Strézova into a plain belonging to it, called Paleá Kátuna; the descent is over a woody hill; the plain is watered by a stream, of which the sources are said to be an hour distant; it enters the plain from a gorge on the left, and to the right joins the Ladon: we cross it at 6.21. Near the bank there is a wood of oaks and other trees, which is not a very common occurrence in the valleys of Greece. Ten minutes beyond the river we pass through another cultivated tract belonging to Strézova, called Kúvelo. Behind us I see the monastery and village of Khassiá on the side of the mountain, to the west of Strézova. The vale now runs nearly north: the greater part of it is uncultivated and covered with a fine long thick grass, interspersed with oak trees. At 7 the village of Tjarnalí[a] is half a mile to the left, at the foot of the mountain. At 7.12, at the end of the plain, we begin to cross a ridge which connects a high mountain on the left with a lower on the right, at the foot of which stands the little village of Mamalúka. At 7.30 halt ten minutes on the summit of the ridge, and then descend through a forest of oaks into a vale, watered by a rivulet running from left to right. Halt from 8 to 9 on the bank of this stream, then crossing it, ascend the hills on the opposite side, and arrive, in half an hour from our last halt, at Karnési. The plain below this place is about three miles long,

[a] Τζαξιαλί.

surrounded by high mountains, and watered by several small rivers. On a little insulated height, in the middle of the plain, stands a hamlet called the Kalývia of Mazi[a], which is a village on Mount Khelmós: beyond this the streams flow in one body southward instead of eastward, which was their former course, and at length join the Ladon. From the north-eastern side of the plain rises a great mountain which adjoins Khelmós on the south, and is named Turtována. The river we crossed is called the river of Klítoras, as flowing from a village of that name. *Clitor*, therefore, is probably at no great distance.

Leaving, however, the exploring of this site for the present, I prosecute the route to Kalávryta, and descend from Karnési through a forest of oaks: at 10.7 cross a torrent, then pass over another ridge covered with a similar forest, and at 10.20 descend into a plain, which at first is half a mile wide, lying in a north and south direction, but which afterwards branches up to the right, to the foot of Mount Khelmós, where stand two large villages, Sudhená and Pera Sudhená, situated under the mountain, upon the higher parts of which are seen extensive woods of firs, and large patches of snow. The ordinary road from Tripolitzá to Kalávryta passes through Sudhená, and from thence

[a] Μαζέϊκα, or Μαζείτικα, καλύβια.

crosses a root of Khelmós, and descends upon Kalávryta. Instead of falling into this road, we continue to the left of it, and pass three copious fountains, the sources of the stream which runs through the gorge of Karnési into the valley of *Clitor;* at the middle fountain of the three I observe some ancient foundations; at the third source, at 10.48, we leave to the right the branch of the plain towards Sudhená, and, mounting the hill which closes the plain, arrive at 11.20 on the summit of a high ridge which commands a view of the plain of Kalávryta, and of the village of Visoká, the latter near the summit of an opposite range of mountains, over which is seen Mount Voidhiá.

On the descent the large monastery of St. Laura[a] remains half a mile on the left, in which direction appears also the whole range of Mount 'Olonos. The road now descends obliquely to the right, as far as the town of Kalávryta, where we arrive at 12.20; a quarter of an hour short of the town are some copious fountains, the streams from which fall down the steep declivity, and water some cultivated grounds in their passage; a part also is diverted into the town by an aqueduct. If Kalávryta be *Cynætha,* this spring must be the *Alysson,* which was so called from its reputation of being a

[a] Ἁγία Λαῦρα.

cure for the bite of a mad dog[a]. It will follow also that the plain of Sudhená is the territory of *Lusi*, situated between *Clitor* and *Cynætha*, which was plundered by the Ætolians at the beginning of the Social War, and where, in the time of Pausanias, remained the temple of Diana Hemeresia[b]. The ancient remains at the fountains of the river of Karnési, indicate perhaps the site of that building.

Kalávryta[c] evidently takes its name from the "fine sources"[d] which I have mentioned. The town stands just above the edge of the plain, on either side of the bed of a wide torrent, descending directly from Mount Khelmós, the western summit of which, covered with snow, is seen over the back of the town. A mountain attached to it on the west is called Kiniú[e]. Kalávryta contains scarcely 100 Turkish families: the rest, to the number of 500, are Greek. Both Turks and Greeks possess farms[f], cultivated by Greek metayers on the usual terms, but the greater part of the 114 villages of the district are Kefalokhória, inhabited by Greeks cultivating their own lands, or by a still greater number who subsist by the produce of their

---

[a] κυνὸς λύσσῃ. — Pausan. Arcad. c. 19.
[b] Polyb. l. 4. c. 18.—l. 9. c. 34.—Pausan. Arcad. c. 18.
[c] τὰ Καλάβρυτα.
[d] καλαὶ βρύσεις, or καλὰ βρύτα.
[e] Probably Κυνηγοῦ, "the hunter's mountain."
[f] ζευγαλατίαις.

flocks, or by tending those belonging to Turkish or Greek proprietors; the export productions of the district being principally butter and cheese. The number of kharátjes is upwards of 6000; and as the vilayéti has maintained its population better than any other in the Moréa, except Máni, the capitation to each person is not heavy.

Two hours from hence under a precipice overhanging the right bank of the river, on the road to Vostítza, stands the convent of Megaspílio[a], the largest in Greece, and so called from its being formed out of a great cavern. It possesses many Metókhia, some of which are entire villages. The valley of Kalávryta lies in the direction of east and west; a deep stream, which issues from the lower heights of 'Olonos, flows through it, and then follows the gorges of Megaspílio to the sea, which it joins at Dhiakófto to the east of Vostítza. The valley is marshy, particularly opposite to the town, and the mountains being too high and too near to allow a good ventilation, the situation is one of the most unhealthy in the Moréa. In the two afternoons which I passed at Kalávryta I found the air more close and disagreeable than I have yet experienced since the warm weather began, though the elevation

[a] Μεγασπήλιον.

above the sea must be considerable, and though the sky was covered as it generally has been, after mid-day, since I entered Arcadia. Polybius describes the climate and situation of Cynætha as the most disagreeable in Arcadia[b]. The plain is said to have become more productive as well as less pernicious to health, since the practice of draining the land has prevailed, though it is still done very imperfectly.

The only remains of antiquity I can discover are on the edge of the valley, immediately opposite to the town. Here are two catacombs excavated in the rock, containing each a single chamber with ledges in the sides for coffins. One of the catacombs has been converted into the sanctuary of a church, of which there are still some traces of constructed walls on the outside of the cavern, together with two pieces of a small plain column with a Doric capital.

May 28.—There is a high rocky hill with a flat summit a mile eastward of the town, which I thought from its appearance might have been the site of the Acropolis of Cynætha, but the only remains upon it are those of a modern castle called Trémola, the walls of which follow the crest of a precipice forming a natural defence to the tabular summit. I ride up there

[a] σκληρότατον παρὰ πολὺ τῆς 1. 4. c. 21.
Ἀρκαδίας ἀέρα καὶ τόπον, Polyb.

this morning and from thence to a higher summit half a mile farther, which is covered with a forest of firs: I could not discover the smallest remains of Hellenic antiquity on either hill, but the pure air, the cool temperature, and the extensive prospect, fully compensated for the ride while the greater height gave me some bearings which I could not obtain on the lower hill.

Several points of *Ætolia*, *Locris*, and *Phocis*, known to me, were distinguishable on the opposite side of the *Corinthiac* gulph: the whole of Khelmós, with its glaciers, and forests, and precipices, appeared close at hand: and to the right of them the mountains near Lykúria, Vitína, and Langádha, then the whole range of 'Olono, and in front, on the opposite side of the vale of Kalávryta, the mountain called Tjeftéri [a], upon which Visoká and Kerpení [b] are situated, and behind it Mount Voidhiá. Kerpení contains many large Greek houses with gardens, and is almost as large as Kalávryta.

Beyond Mount Trémola, towards Megaspílio, there is a cultivated hollow from which a rivulet descends to the river of Kalávryta; it contains the village of Vrakhní [c].

May 29.—At 3 this morning I felt two earthquakes, with an interval of two minutes between them; the first was slight, and might not have

---

[a] Τζεφτέρι. [b] Βισοκὰ, Κερπενὴ. [c] Βραχνὴ.

been observable except in the stillness of such an early hour, but the second rattled the wooden framework of the house of Kyr Ianni Papadhópulo, in which I was lodged, in such a manner as would have been alarming at any time. I think it is a remark of Aristotle, that earthquakes in Greece occur frequently at day-break [a].

At 5.30 I quit Kalávryta and begin to pass along the foot of the mountain, leaving the fountain *Alysson* on the left, and at 6 the monastery of St. Laura, situated over against Visoká; from this village there is a regular slope descending into the valley, on the border of which stands a small village, one of the Metókhia of Megaspílio. At 6.8, having crossed a bridge over the river of Kalávryta, which issues from a vale and woody mountain on the left, we proceed to the extremity of the valley in the direction of the north-eastern summit of the range of 'Olono, which here terminates in three separate rocky peaks called Tris Ghynékes[b], or the Three Women. At 6.45, enter at the end of the plain a pass which leads to Kúvelo[c]; this is a small village situated in a narrow valley watered by a stream which rises near Kú-

[a] Vide Meteor. l. 2. c. 8. He observes also, that they often happen in spring and autumn, and when the atmosphere is tranquil. In three respects therefore the earthquakes above mentioned agree with his rules.
[b] Τρεῖς Γυναῖκες.
[c] Κούβελος.

teli[a]; it is a branch of the river which flows into the sea at Tjapes[b] to the east of Vostítza, hence commonly called the river of Vostítza. Our road follows up the vale of Kúvelo, and, at 7.25, enters a picturesque pass, in which, at 7.35, Kúteli remains in a woody situation on the mountain's side to the left.

From thence we pass through a wood of oaks and descend into a hollow, where is some cultivation at the foot of one of the peaks of Tris Ghynékes. This mountain is clothed with firs above and oaks below; beyond it I perceive a bare rocky summit covered with snow. At 8.30, we descend towards a valley in which there is a village called Mánesi, some cultivated ground, and a small tributary of the Aivlasítiko, or river of Ai Vlasi. Besides the high mountain on the south, this valley is surrounded with woody hills, on one of which stands Tríklistra[c], three quarters of an hour from Mánesi. Halt a quarter of an hour at a mandhra; at 8.53, arrive at the extremity of the vale of Mánesi which reaches to the last falls of Mount 'Olono. At 9, cross another stream from that mountain flowing in the same direction as the former,— and then pass along the foot of the mountain. At 9.23, the Kalývia of Ai Vlasi are a quarter

---

[a] Κούτιλη.   [b] Τζάπαις.   [c] Τρίκληστρα.

of an hour on the left,—at 9.53 we cross the Aivlasítiko by a bridge.

This river descends from a deep ravine included between two high summits; in the upper part of the ravine are seen the two large villages, Ai Vlasi, or Aio Vasili [a], and Lower Ai Vlasi, encircled by trees and verdure. A high snowy peak rises immediately above the villages to the south-eastward, called Krýa Vrysi [b]. Not far beyond the sources of the river of Ai Vlasi, are those of the principal branch of the *Peneius*, which follows in the opposite direction a narrow valley, similar to the gorge of Ai Vlasi. Thus the ravines of the two streams form a continued opening, which separates the great summits to the westward, known generally by the name of 'Olono, from those of Krya Vrysi, Trís Ghynékes, and another farther southward, called Astrá, which is near the town of Dhívri. There are some extensive forests of firs upon these mountains. In the valley of the Upper *Peneius* just mentioned, stand a village and monastery called Ghermótzana, or Ghermotzáni [c]. A road from Ai Vlasi to Lalla passes along the left side of the valley near Ghermotzáni, and for the most part through woods of fir. The slope of the mountain below Ai Vlasi to the north-

---

[a] Ἅγιος Βασίλειος, St. Basil.   [b] Κρύα Βρύσις, cold spring.
[c] Γερμότζανα, Γερμοτζάνη.

ward is covered with vineyards and cornfields. The two villages produce good butter and small cheeses, which are considered better than those of *Parnassus*. The mountains at the back of the villages are covered with firs.

At 10.5 we arrive at Kastrítza, as the vestiges of a Hellenic fortress are called. The place is about two miles in a direct line to the northward of Ai Vlási, on a height along the western side of which flows a brook to join the Aivlasítiko. So little of the walls remains that neither the form nor the size of the inclosure can be exactly traced, nor could I find any remains of an Acropolis on the upper part of the hill. But though the remains are not extensive, I think it probable that they mark the position of Tritæa, that having been one of the inland cities of Achaia, and the nearest to Arcadia, to which province it was once considered as belonging[a]. The distance of Kastrítza from the sea seems to accord also with the data of Pausanias, who places Pharæ on the river Peirus, at the distance of seventy stades from the mouth of that river, and Tritæa 120 stades inland from Pharæ[b].

According to Polybius, Tritæa lay in a direction from Rhium towards Arcadia[c]; its territory bordered upon the Patræa and Pharæa[d].

[a] Pausan. Eliac. post. c. 12.
[b] Pausan. Achaic. c. 22.
[c] Polyb. l. 4. c. 6.
[d] Pausan. Achaic. c. 22.

Like Pharæ, it was made a dependency of Patræ, by Augustus. In the time of Pausanias it preserved a temple of the gods called the Greatest, with their statues made of clay; and a temple of Minerva, from which the ancient statue (probably made of brass) had been removed to Rome, and its place supplied by one of marble. Before the entrance into the town from Pharæ, there was a sepulchre of a young man and his wife, constructed of white marble and adorned with a painting by Nicias, which represented the woman seated on an ivory chair, her female servant holding an umbrella[a] over her head; the young man was standing before her clothed in a shirt[b], with a purple cloak[c] over it, and was attended by a servant holding javelins in one hand, and leading dogs by the other.

We quit Kastrítza at 10.30, and enter the pass of Nezerá at 10.50. Here a large and rapid torrent, I presume the ancient *Peirus*, descending from the summit of Mount 'Olono in a northerly direction, suddenly turns westward through a deep rocky ravine, inclosed between 'Olono and a lower mountain, which is separated from Mount Voidhiá only by the pass of Makhelería, on the direct road from Kalávryta to Patra. The highest summit of 'Olono slopes with a rapid descent into the ravine

[a] σκιάδιον. [b] χιτών. [c] χλαμύς.

of Nezerá, and admits only of a scanty cultivation around a few small villages on its sides. The mountain which bounds the pass on the northern side is rather more cultivable. We proceed along the side of the latter, and at 11.17, pass through the village of Vendrá[a], which is opposite to that of Kombigádhi[b] on the slope of 'Olono.

From Kombigádhi, which contains about twenty houses, there is an ascent of three hours to the summit of 'Olono, where, between the two highest tops, there is a small plain not yet free from snow, but which in summer affords both corn and pasture. The season for conducting the flocks thither does not begin until June, or a little sooner or later, according to the weather. A too early pasture there is said to be fatal; this the shepherds attribute to a poisonous plant which dies in June, but it is more probably owing to the damp ground and watery food. About the beginning of that month they sow barley in the same plain, while it is yet moist with the melted snow: the harvest is in August.

As we approach Nezerá, I observe on the opposite side of the river, at the foot of 'Olono, a monastery, with a pretty garden formed in terraces under a projection of rock. It is dedicated to the Panaghía, and inhabited only by three or four monks. Opposite to it, on the

---

[a] Βεντρὰ.   [b] Κομπιγάδι.

right bank, are the remains of a castle of the time of the lower empire, built undoubtedly for the purpose of commanding this strong pass, which, like all passes, is rendered more strong and important by the general want of roads in the country. The peasantry alone might here arrest a large force by merely rolling down stones upon them.

At 11.45 we arrive at Nezerá, sometimes called Great Nezerá[a], as being the principal village of a subordinate division of the Kalávryta Kázasi, but belonging to the ecclesiastical province of Patra. Besides Nezerá, the district contains two considerable villages, Kalánistro and Kálano; six smaller, Lópesi, Plátano, Spodhiána, Lefkómata, Kombigádhi, Vendrá; and three convents, the Panaghía, Kalógrio, and Kakolangádhi[b]. The village of Nezerá is situated about half way up the mountain, above the right bank of the river, in a spot where are some good springs and a few fruit trees: it contains about fifty houses. It suffered much from the Albanians in the Russian war; before that time the accommodations were so good, that the consuls at Patra were often in the habit of retiring here during the hot months, when the elevated situation, and

[a] Μεγάλη Νεζερά.
[b] τὰ χωρία Καλάνιστρον, Κάλανος, Λόπεσι, Πλάτανος, Σποδιάνα, Λευκώματα, Κομπιγάδι, Βεντρά· τὰ Μοναστήρια τῆς Παναγίας, τοῦ Καλογραίου, καὶ τοῦ Κακολαγναδιοῦ.

the free current of the maestrale through the *Aulon*, must make it a very agreeable and healthy residence. The village stands about the middle of the Stená of the river, which below these straits receives several other streams, winds over the plains in a north-westerly direction, and joins the sea at Alikí, a salt work, near two villages called the Akhaíes[a], where, if this be the *Peirus*, as I cannot doubt, I should expect to find *Olenus*. I am told that the villages from whence the ascent to the summit of Mount 'Olono is most easy, are Kompigádhi, in the district of Kalávryta, Alupokhóri, in that of Patra, and Ghermotzáni, in Gastúni.

May 30.—I quit my lodging in a lofty new pyrgo belonging to the hodjá-bashi of Nezerá at 5.10, and, crossing over the heights adjacent to the ravine of the *Peirus*, leave it to the left and descend into a valley, watered by a branch of the same river. At 6.25 arrive at Lópesi, a village of twenty houses, where is a dervéni, or guard-house, and some fine fountains from which a stream descends into the Peirus. We halt fifteen minutes, and at the end of another hour along the foot of the mountain, begin at 7.40 to mount the hills which are connected northward with Voidhiá. I look down to the left upon Khalandrítza[b], a village a mile distant, at the foot of the mountain, divided into two parts.

[a] Ἀχαίαις.   [b] Χαλαντρίτζα.

Though it now only contains thirty or forty families, there are several churches, more or less ruined, which shew that it was once a place of greater importance. A small stream descends through it, and joins the *Peirus* a mile below the village. Lálusi, or Lalúsia is two miles farther in the same direction over the plain; a little behind Lálusi, towards 'Olono, is Zoga[a], and a bridge over the *Peirus* called Polykhroniá[b]. This river, in the upper part of its course, is now commonly called the 'Olono, or the river of Nezerá; in the lower it is usually known by the name of Kamenítza, from a village upon its banks which is situated towards the sea.

At 8, having passed the ridge, we traverse a small elevated plain about a mile in length, which contains some cultivated land but no village, and begin to descend the north-western slope of the ridge, with the Gulf of Patra and Mount Paleovúni in *Ætolia* before us,—leave a ruined castle of the lower empire called Sidherókastro, on a height to the left. The descent into the plain of Patra is stony and rugged: we enter it at 9.20. The land is prepared for kalambókki, and is watered by derivations from a torrent which is first collected from the southern face of Mount Voidhiá, and afterwards turns westward along a narrow ravine which separates Voidhiá from the ridge which we have

[a] Ζώγα. [b] Πολυχρονιᾶς τὸ Γεφύρι.

crossed: the ravine is called the Pass of Makellaría[a], the direct road from Patra to Kalávryta by Guzúmistra leads through it. In the mountain to the southward of the pass is situated the monastery of Babióti[b], half an hour northward of which is another called Omblós[c]; the latter is reckoned three hours from Patra. Our road now crosses the torrent-bed, which is not less than half a mile wide; it is strewed with large stones and shaded in many places by oleanders, myricæ, agnus-castus, and other philocharadrous shrubs. At 9.35, in the midst of this stony little desert, we pass the stream itself, which, though now scanty, is sometimes very formidable: it is certainly the ancient Glaucus[d], being still called by the corrupted form of Lefka, or Lafka. At 9.47 begin the currant plantations of Patra: at 10 we enter the town, and at 10.15 arrive at the house of Mr. Consul Strane.

It would seem, from the present name of this city in use among the Franks, that the Hellenic Πάτραι first passed into the usual Romaic form of the accusative στὰς Πάτρας, and that from the word in that shape was derived the Italian Patrasso, and the English and French Patras: it

[a] This word, derived from the Italian, and analogous to the Greek Sphacteria, is said to have been derived from the frequent murders committed in the pass by the robbers, who often infest the surrounding mountains.
[b] Μπαμπιώτη.
[c] Ὀμπλὺς.
[d] Pausan. Achaic. c. 18.

has now, however, become a neuter instead of a feminine plural, and is called Patra[a]. It still preserves that pre-eminence over all the places of *Achaia* and the *Peloponnesian* coast, which it acquired after the battle of Actium, when the victorious Augustus, having resolved to establish two Roman colonies on the western coast of Greece, made choice of Nicopolis and Patræ for that purpose, granting lands in their vicinity to some of his followers, endowing the cities with the valuable privileges of Roman colonies, and augmenting their importance at the expense of the territory and population of all the declining townships in the neighbourhood[b]. Nicopolis has again become the same desert place which it was before the time of Augustus; the changes which have occurred in navigation and ship-building, since that age, have rendered the situation unadapted to the maritime commerce of the present day: but Patræ still justifies the choice of Augustus.

Its advantages consist in the great fertility of the plain and surrounding hills, but still more in the convenience of the situation for communication by sea with the adjacent islands, with the whole western coast of Greece, with Italy and the Adriatic, as well as with eastern Greece and the Ægæan Sea, by the Gulf of Corinth.

[a] τὰ Πάτρα.
[b] Strabo, pp. 324. 387. 450. 460. Pausan. Achaic. c. 18.

Of late years its prosperity has been, in great measure, the result of the cultivation of a fruit unknown to, or, at least, unnoticed by the ancients, and of its sale to nations who were then in a state of barbarism. The demand in Great Britain and other northern countries for the dwarf grapes, commonly called currants, has brought the greater part of the plain of Patra into a state of cultivation not exceeded in any part of Europe, while Corinth, from whence the fruit originally derived its name, has ceased to possess any of the vineyards which produce it.

When Pausanias visited Patræ it was noted for its manufacture of cotton, which was abundantly grown in the Eleia[a], and was woven at Patræ into cloth and women's caps[b]. The persons employed in the manufactures of Patræ were chiefly women, and so great was the number of them attracted to the place by this employment, that Pausanias states the female population to have been double that of the men, a circumstance which seems not to have been very favourable to the morals of the city[c]. Before the time of Augustus the place had so much declined, having particularly suffered in the first invasion of Greece by the Gauls, when the Patrenses joined their old allies the Æto-

---

[a] Pausan. Eliac. post. c. 26. Achaic. c. 21.
[b] κεκρυφάλοι, Paus. Achaic. c. 21.
[c] 'Αφροδίτης δὲ εἴπερ ἄλλαις γυναιξὶ, μέτεστι καὶ ταύταις.

lians, that the greater part of the residue had quitted Patræ and had resumed their ancient dwellings in Messatis and Antheia, occupying also the neighbouring villages of Boline, Argyra, and Arba[a]. Messatis and Antheia were two very ancient places, the inhabitants of which had been withdrawn from thence into Patræ, when Patreus, soon after the Ionic migration into Asia, increased the circuit of Aroe and gave to the city the new name, which it still bears[b]. We can hardly doubt, as well from this circumstance as from the name of Aroe having been often used by the ancients as synonymous with Patræ[c], that Aroe occupied the site of the Acropolis of the city of Patreus.

The objects described by Pausanias[d] were in four different quarters. 1. The Acropolis.—2. The Agora.—3. A quarter into which there was a gate from the Agora.—4. The quarter near the sea.

[a] Pausan. Achaic. c. 18.—Some of the editors and translators have taken the liberty to change Ἀρβᾶν into Ἀρόαν, the objections to which are— 1. That Pausanias in every instance writes Ἀρόη, Ἀρόην, and not Ἀρόα, Ἀρόαν.—2. That the accents of Arba and Aroa are different.—3. That Aroe was the ancient name of a part of the site of Patræ itself. Arba, therefore, must have been a place *near* Patræ, like Boline and Argyra.

[b] Strabo says that Patræ was formed from seven demi, p. 337.

[c] There is a Roman coin of Patræ, with the legend Col · A · A · Patrens. i. e. Colonia Augusta Aroe Patrensis.

[d] Pausan. Achaic. c. 18, 19, 20, 21.

The chief object of veneration in the Acropolis was the temple of Diana Laphria, containing a statue of the goddess, which had been removed with the spoils of Calydon to Patræ by Augustus, at the same time that he withdrew the population of the declining places of Ætolia and Acarnania to people Nicopolis, and conveyed thither the greater part of the statues from the temples in those provinces. The statue of Diana Laphria was a very ancient work of ivory and gold, by two artists of Naupactus named Menœchmus and Soidas: it represented the goddess as a huntress. At her annual festival there was a magnificent procession, closed by the priestess in a chariot drawn by stags. The following day was devoted to a sacrifice, which was distinguished by a degree of cruelty very rare in the religious practices of the Greeks: wild hogs, stags, roebucks, and the cubs of wolves and bears were collected together, as well as fowls of those kinds which were the food of man, and every sort of cultivated fruit, and they were all burnt with dry wood upon the altar of the goddess, which had been previously surrounded with a strong inclosure of timber. Pausanias tells us that he witnessed some of the animals, when endeavouring to escape, forcibly driven back, and thus roasted alive. Between the altar and the temple of Diana stood the monument of Eurypylus. Within the same peribolus which inclosed the temple of Diana, there was a temple of Minerva Panachais, of which the statue was chryselephantine, like the Laphria. Above the Acropolis, near the gate leading to Messatis, stood a temple of Æsculapius; and on the descent from the citadel into the city, the temple of Dindymene and Attes, containing a statue of the former made of stone. In the Agora there were temples of Jupiter Olympius and of Apollo: the statue of Jupiter Olympius was seated, Minerva standing by him; the Apollo was of brass, naked, with the exception of sandals on the feet[a], one foot rested on the skull of an ox, in allusion to his protection of cattle. Between this temple and that of Jupiter stood a statue of Juno. In the open part of the Agora[b] there was a statue of Minerva, and before it the sepulchre of Patreus.

The Odeium adjoined the Agora: it was the most magnificent of any in Greece, except the Odeium of Herodes at Athens, and it contained a very remarkable statue of Apollo, dedicated from the spoils of the Gauls, when the Patrenses alone of the Achaians aided the Ætolians. On a gate which, near the temple of Apollo, led out of the Agora, stood gilded statues of Patreus, Preugenes, and Atherion, represented as

---

[a] ὑποδήματα ὑπὸ τοῖς ποσίν.   [b] ἐν ὑπαίθρῳ τῆς ἀγορᾶς.

boys. Not far beyond the gate[a] there was a temenus of Diana, containing a temple of Diana Limnatis, and sanctuaries of Æsculapius and of Minerva, to which there were approaches through a stoa. The statue of Æsculapius was made of stone, except the drapery (of wood). The statue of Minerva was of ivory and gold. Before the sanctuary of Minerva was the monument of Preugenes, father of Patreus. In this quarter stood the theatre, and near it temples of Nemesis and Venus, containing statues of those deities in white marble, of colossal magnitude;—also a temple of Bacchus, surnamed Calydonius, because the statue was brought from Calydon; and the temenus of a native woman, containing three statues of Bacchus, with the surnames of Mesateus, Antheus, and Aroeus. These in the Dionysiac festival were carried to the temple of Bacchus Æsymnetes, which was situated on the right-hand side of the road leading from the Agora to the maritime quarter of the city. Below the temple of Æsymnetes there was a temple and statue in stone of Soteria, (Safety,) said to have been dedicated by Eurypylus. At the harbour[b] stood an upright statue of Neptune, in stone, and near it two sanctuaries of Venus, each containing a statue of the goddess. Close to the harbour

[a] Τῆς ἀγορᾶς ἀντικρὺς κατὰ ταύτην τὴν ἔξοδον.   [b] πρὸς τῷ λιμένι.

were brazen statues of Mars and Apollo, and a temenus of Venus, in which there was an acrolithic statue of the goddess[a].

On the sea-side there was a grove, containing places of exercise and shady walks, as well as temples of Apollo and Venus, in which were statues of those deities in stone. Near the grove were two temples of Sarapis, one of which contained the monument of Ægyptus, son of Belus, and contiguous to the grove a temple of Ceres, containing upright statues of Ceres and Proserpine, and a sitting statue of Earth[b]. In front of this temple there was a source of water[c], which was inclosed by a wall on the side towards the building, and had a descent to it on the opposite side[d]. The well was consulted, as an oracle, which foretold the fate of sick persons; a mirror was suspended, so that the circumference touched the water[e]; prayers were

---

[a] The words "acrolithic" and "chryselephantine", which I have often used, are not employed by Pausanias, nor the latter by any of the ancient Greek writers; but they are convenient to describe in a single word two kinds of draped statues which were common among the Greeks: in the former, the naked part of the statue was in marble, the drapery, or other attributes, in painted or gilded wood: in the chryselephantine, the flesh was in ivory, the remaining part in the same material, coloured, and inlaid with gold in various parts of the dress.

[b] ἄγαλμα τῆς Γῆς καθήμενον.
[c] πηγή.
[d] Τὰ πρὸ τοῦ ναοῦ λίθων ἀνέστηκεν αἱμασία, κατὰ δὲ τὸ ἐκτὸς κάθοδος ἐς αὐτὴν πεποίηνται.
[e] ὅσον ἐπιψαῦσαι τοῦ ὕδατος τῷ κύκλῳ τοῦ κατόπτρου. The

then offered to Ceres and incense was burnt, after which there were certain appearances in the mirror indicating whether the sick person would live or die.

The modern Patra occupies the same site as the Roman city. It stands upon a ridge about a mile long, which projects from the falls of Mount Voidhiá[a] in a southerly direction, and to the westward is separated from the sea by a level, increasing in breadth from north to south, from a quarter to more than half a mile. The height at the northern end of the ridge, now occupied by the castle of Patra, was the ancient Acropolis, of which some pieces of the walls are intermixed with the modern masonry on the north-eastern side. In this direction the castle is strengthened by a hollow lying between it and the other heights, which form the connection with Mount Voidhiá. Both these and the castle hill are of the most irregular forms, being cut into deep ravines by torrents, and broken into white precipices, like those which are seen in many parts of the northern coast of the Moréa, as well as about *Olympia*, *Elis*, and in the Island of Zákytho. It is observable that all these

Greek mirrors were circular, with a handle, thus: as we know from many specimens of them found in ancient tombs, as well as from representations of them in sculpture.

[a] Βοϊδιᾶς.

places, like Patra itself, are peculiarly subject to earthquakes. According to all I have experienced or can learn, Laconia is by no means so well shaken a country[a].

The ancient town, like the modern, covered the slopes of the ridge which branches from the citadel to the south. The old Achaian city seems, like the modern town, not to have extended nearer to the sea than the foot of this ridge: for we learn from Plutarch, that Alcibiades recommended to the Patrenses to connect the town with the port by means of long walls:—on the contrary it may be inferred, as well from Pausanias as from many existing vestiges of Roman fabrics, that the Augustan colony spread over the plain towards the sea. It may easily be supposed, indeed, that Patræ has at no period been so large as under the Roman Emperors; and all the existing remains which I have seen bear the character of that time.

Masses of masonry constructed of brick and mortar are found among the houses, gardens, ruined walls, and vacant intervals which occupy the ancient position: but none of them are in sufficient continuity or preservation to be ascribed to any particular building among those which Pausanias has described, although the situation of each of the quarters being evident,

---

[a] εὔσειστος ἡ Λακωνική.—Strabo, p. 367.

and the general distribution of the buildings thus known, the position of each monument can be more nearly presumed than in most of the Greek traveller's descriptions.

The Agora seems to have been about the middle of the present town. Here I observed the remains of a small construction of brick upon a foundation of stone near a fountain; and in the house of the Imperial consul, there is part of a circular building of brick, which may possibly have belonged to the Odeium.

As the maritime quarter of the city was towards the west, and as Pausanias descends from the Acropolis to the Agora, afterwards describing the quarter of the theatre which was entered from the Agora by the Gate of the Heroes, and lastly descending from the Agora to the λίμην, or harbour, it may be inferred that the quarter of the theatre was towards the southern end of the modern town. In order to search for the monuments on the road from the Agora to the ancient harbour, and those around the port, it would be necessary to determine the exact position of the latter. This appears to me to be indicated by the form of the coast, and by some foundations of moles to the southward of the street of magazines, which now borders the sea-beach of the roadsted: indeed it is very possible that all the low marshy plain adjacent to the magazines on the south, and which extends from thence towards the southern extremity of the ridge of the town, was anciently the harbour. I cannot conceive, however, that the modern Patrenses are correct in supposing that the port ever reached as far as a Roman wall which supports a terrace at that extremity, notwithstanding there are some holes in the wall, in which, as Mr. Strane tells me, he remembers to have seen rings and staples, supposed to have been those to which the Roman galleys were once attached. I suspect, however, that his memory deceives him; for upon looking into Wheler and Spon, I find that they describe the wall just as it is now, and that Wheler adds, that the consul, Sir Clement Harby, told him, " that many in the town remembered when there was an iron ring fastened to the wall, which they supposed was to tie vessels to;" whence it would seem that the story of the ring is nothing more than a fable, which has been repeated from one generation to another for several centuries. Wheler thought the wall in question had been part of the inclosure of the ancient city. " Under it," he adds, " is a place that seemeth to have been a circus, or a stadium, or perhaps a naumachia, and not far from thence, near a ruined church of the Holy Apostles, a round temple of brick masoned together with a very hard cement." I cannot find any remains of these monuments.

The only position of the ancient Patræ, besides the Acropolis, which seems to be perfectly identified, is that of the temple of Ceres, described by Pausanias as having adjoined a grove on the sea-side, serving as a public walk to the Patrenses; and as having had below it, in front, a source of water, to which there was a descent on the side opposite to the temple. It is evident from the latter circumstance, as well as from what Pausanias says of the oracle, that the source was a perennial well, the surface of which was below that of the adjacent ground; by which description the spring is easily recognized about three quarters of a mile from the town, near the sea-shore, to the southward of the magazines. And hence also it appears that the space between that spot and the magazines, was the situation of the grove which contained the public walks and the temples of Venus and Apollo. There is still a descent of four steps to the well, which is under a vault belonging to the remains of a church of St. Andrew, the patron saint of Patra, who, according to the Greeks, suffered martyrdom at this place, and to whom Ceres appears to have resigned her dwelling[a] on the abolition of paganism. The

[a] ναὸς.

church was already a ruin in the time of Spon and Wheler, but there are still some remains of it, in which prayers are said and incense burnt, as formerly to Ceres; it is particularly resorted to by all the good Christians of Patra on the festival of St. Andrew, when they drink of the fountain which is an ἁγιασμα, or holy water, of the Saint.

According to Ducange[a], the metropolitan church of Patræ stood formerly in the citadel, and was destroyed by Guillaume de Villehardouin, when he obtained possession of Achaia after the Frank conquest of Constantinople in 1204. About 250 years afterwards the patron saint of Patræ suffered another indignity. Thomas, the Greek despot, finding himself under the necessity of retiring to Italy before the conquering arms of Mahomet the Second, could devise no more effectual mode of recommending himself to the Pope, than to carry off the head of St. Andrew from Patræ as a present to his holiness[b]. The greater part of the existing castle of Patra is probably the work of Villehardouin, and he seems to have made liberal use of the remains of the ancient buildings of the Acropolis in constructing it; for besides the pieces of Hellenic wall which I have men-

---

[a] Hist. de Constantinople sous les Emp. François. [b] Phranza, c. 26.

tioned as remaining in their original position, there are several portions of Doric and Ionic fluted columns forming part of the modern masonry, as well as some pieces of architraves with triglyphs and metopes, one of which is adorned with a patera.

As Pausanias says that the temple of Æsculapius stood *above* the Acropolis near the gates leading to Messatis, it seems evident that Messatis occupied a situation on the ridge northward, or north-eastward of the citadel, and as Pausanias also tells us that Messatis was between Aroe, or the site of the Acropolis, and Antheia, the latter must have been situated still further in the same direction. It is in fact very natural that such strong and lofty positions should have been the places of retirement of the inhabitants in those times of insecurity which preceded the foundation of Patreus, as well as when they again dispersed after the Gallic invasion of Greece.

The ruins of the Roman aqueduct of brick, which supplied the town from the heights to the eastward, are still extant on that side of the castle hill. Wheler met with this aqueduct returning into town from the monastery of Ierokómio[a], which is situated on those heights

[a] Γεροκόμειον, or Ἱεροκόμειον.

at a mile and a half to the eastward of Patra. He describes the aqueduct as a very high and stately structure, having two arches one above another, and pilasters propped on both sides with buttresses. He adds, that higher up the stream were two other (arches) better preserved, and that they all united two hills between which flowed a small stream. From the same source which filled the Roman aqueduct, the modern town is now furnished: but the aqueduct itself has suffered very much since the time of Wheler, only a few of the lower arches now remaining. Wheler supposed the stream in the ravine, which is crossed by the aqueduct, to have been the *Meilichus;* but in this he was mistaken, for it passes along the eastern side of the town, and thence into the sea to the southward, whereas the *Meilichus* joined the sea between *Patræ* and *Rhium.* I observed in the convent of Ierokómio a white marble, eight feet long and two feet and a half broad, upon which there is a Latin inscription in large characters in seven lines, but so much worn in consequence of the stone having served as a step to the church, that I was only able to copy a few of the letters.

Mount Voidhiá, one of the most conspicuous hills in Greece, and inferior in height only to a few of the great summits, has been little noticed by ancient authors. It seems evidently, however, to be that Mount Panachaïcum where, in the winter of the second year of the Social War[a], B.C. 219, 220, Pyrrhias the Ætolian established himself at the head of 3000 Ætolians and Eleians, after having made incursions upon the lands of *Patræ*, *Dyme*, and *Pharæ*, and from whence he continued his devastations throughout the Patræa, as well as towards Ægium and Rhium. This mountain is, in fact, most conveniently placed, as the modern kleftes have discovered, for commanding all the western part of Achaia; being surrounded by the Achaian districts of Patræ, Ægium, and Tritæa, and being the only great mountain which belonged entirely to that province, it was very properly called Παναχαϊκὸν. The maritime cities of Achaia, to the eastward of Ægium, possessed only the northern slopes of mountains, the summits of which were in Arcadia.

The Castle of Patra commands a most beautiful and interesting prospect. Nothing can be more perfect in its kind than the great sweep of the coast, forming that vast bay to the south-westward which is separated by the rich plain of Patra from Mount *Panachaïcum*

[a] Polyb. l. 5. c. 30.

and its branches, and which is backed in the view from the castle by the distant summits of *Zacynthus* and *Cephallenia*. Castle Tornese is seen in this direction, a little to the right of the summit of Mount Skopó in Zákytho. To the northward the great lake, for such is its appearance, which forms the outer division of the Corinthian gulf, is bounded by the mountains of *Acarnania* and *Ætolia*, and immediately in face of Patra by the two rocky hills which rise abruptly from the shore, between the lagunes of Mesolónghi and the straits of *Rhium*. In the latter direction the prospect is terminated by the town of Épakto and the mountains above it, which to the right become blended with the slopes of *Panachaïcum*.

Patra is the most populous town in Greece southward of Ioánnina. It contains about 10,000 inhabitants, of whom a third are Turks, the rest Greeks with a few Jews. There are some good Greek and Turkish houses in the town, but those of the European consuls are the most respectable in appearance. Every considerable house is surrounded with a garden of the orange tribe, mixed with pomegranates, figs, almonds, and pot-herbs, which give the place a very agreeable aspect, when seen at such a distance as does not betray the misery of the greater part of the habitations. The convenience of the situation for European trade, the advantages arising from the residence of the consuls, and the export of currants, which are produced in the plain of Patra in greater quantity than in any part of continental Greece, have attracted to this point almost all the European commerce of the Moréa, and of the western coast of Greece. The rising price of currants during the last three years, has led to an increased cultivation of them in the plain of Patra, which, beyond the gardens and olive plantations surrounding the outer houses, consists, for the distance of two or three miles from the town, of a continued vineyard of those dwarf grapes: they are now in blossom, and when the wind blows across the plain, their perfume is almost too powerful to be agreeable.

The average production of currants at Zante, is stated to me by the consul to be eleven millions of pounds, of Kefalonía seven millions, of Patra five millions, of the southern shore of the Gulf of Corinth, together with Mesolónghi and Vrakhóri, in which last place they have been introduced only of late, four millions. In the time of Wheler, 1675, they were grown at Mesolónghi, and not at Patra. There is a bedaat, or extraordinary duty, of exportation of two paras the oke, which is commuted by Patra for 100 purses. Silk, the production of Patra, next in importance to currants, pays a bedaat of nine piastres the oke, according to the last firmahn. The other articles exported from this district are wool, wax, leather, and κεδροκούκι, or juniper berries, which last are sent to England. The plain produces also cotton and tobacco.

The increased cultivation of the plain of Patra is said to have improved the salubrity of the climate, but the excessive heat and the marshy tract to the southward and westward of the town, still create dangerous fevers and dysenteries in summer and autumn, so that with the exception perhaps of Anápli and Corinth, Patra is still the most unhealthy town in the Moréa. It is the prevailing opinion that the fevers are chiefly owing to the wind from Mount Voidhiá, which, say the people of Patra, is unwholesome, because it is heavy. A Corfiote practitioner of physic expressed to me the same opinion. The mountain may, perhaps, be partly in fault, though not, I suspect, as the Patrini[a] and their doctor[b] suppose. The land wind, which blows regularly all the summer in this climate, during the night and early morning, and which at Patra descends immediately from Mount Voidhiá, forms by its coldness a dangerous contrast to the air of the town, still

[a] Πατρινοί.   [b] ἰατρός.

heated by the effects of the preceding day: and hence it happens that a person exposing himself in summer to the night or morning air, without being well clothed, undergoes the greatest risk of laying the foundation of a fever. The violence and heat of the wind from the gulf, in July and August, is extremely disagreeable also; and it is a common custom to keep the shutters closed all the day to avoid its blast. Patra has proved fatal to a great number of new settlers, particularly to the French, who, about forty years ago, had several mercantile houses here: since the revolution they have not had any.

The English consul's house is a large wooden building without much comfort, but well adapted by its timber framing to the frequent earthquakes which occur here. The extremes of lightness or solidity seem to be the best modes of construction in such a country. The ancients I believe adopted both, the former for their private, the latter for their public edifices. I had not been many hours at Patra before I had the opportunity of hearing and feeling the effects of an earthquake in such a house as the consul's. The noise was tremendous, but there cannot be much danger in a structure of this kind, at least in any such concussions as usually occur in Greece. The house was built by a French merchant named Rosa. By a miracle it escaped the plunder and destruction of the Albanians at the end of the Russian insurrection in 1770. General Rosa, who was made prisoner by Alý Pasha, and sent to Constantinople, where he died, was nephew of the merchant.

The rugged hills behind the castle produce a red wine, which is very good when made with care; Mr. Strane gave me some which was not inferior to port. The Greeks chiefly employ it to give body to that which is made from the watery grapes produced in low and moist situations, after which, by adding a little resin from the pine-tree, the mixture will keep sound about a year.

There are 130 villages in the district of Patra, which extends to the south-westward as far as the ancient boundaries of the *Eleia*. The plain of Patra and of the *Peirus* contains three-fourths of the villages, which, with the exception of about forty kefalo-khória of from twenty to fifty houses, and three or four others of larger size, are all tjiftliks, containing from ten to twenty families, some of them even still smaller. The whole population of the district probably is not equal to that of the town.

The terms of cultivation in corn-lands are the same as those in other parts of the Moréa; the farmer is a metayer, and takes his portion of the crop [a], which is a third or a half, according to the portion of stock or instruments supplied by the proprietor. This mode of farming was very common anciently, both among the Greeks and Romans, as appears from the word μορτίτης, which was in use in the time of Solon [b], and from the Latin *medietarius*, from which metayer is derived. But Patra furnishes an example of the most expensive as well as of the poorest mode of agriculture. The currant vineyards are all cultivated by the owners by means of hired labourers, who receive sixty paras a day, without provisions. There are two principal operations, one in February, when the soil is hoed for the purpose of laying open the roots of the plants to the moisture of the spring, at which time the earth is raised into little conical heaps between the vines; and the second in May, when it is levelled again. In other kinds of field-work, the price of day-labour [c] is forty paras, with wine. The labourers in the plain of Patra come chiefly from the district of Kalávryta, but in harvest there are many islanders employed, as well here as in other parts of Western Greece.

When a part of the English army of Egypt

---

[a] πέρνει τὸ μερτικὸν, or τὸ μερίδι του.
[b] J. Poll. l. 7. c. 32.
[c] ἡμεροκάματον, or more vulgarly μεροκάματον.

was ordered to Corfu and the other islands, in September, 1801, two thousand men were destined for Patra, and barracks were ordered to be built for them. The Consul had constructed one and Mehmét Agá, upon whose ground the temporary building was erected, built a kiosk, which still remains in a field near the Roman walls to the southward. In this field Mehmét's labourers found lately in digging, six ancient bottle-shaped cisterns of excellent workmanship, constructed of tiles; the Agá ordered stones to be placed over the mouths of them, and then covered them with earth.

A large quantity of silver coins have been brought to me for sale, which have recently been found by a Zevgalátes of Gastúni, I believe at Paleópoli (*Elis*). As the person who brought them wished to sell them all, and the greater part were either of the commonest sort, Chalcis, Sicyon, Bœotia, &c. or such as I already possessed in duplicate, I refused them, without reflecting that many persons would have been glad to give triple the price for which they were offered to me.

There are three ancient statues in the walls of the castle. The largest is that of a female, complete from the chin downwards; half as large again as life. Its attitude was such that the left shoulder is much higher than the right.

The waist is bound with a thong tied in a bow: the drapery of the finest execution. This fragment stands in a tower which is already cracked, and will probably fall with the first strong earthquake. The two other statues are very inferior in merit: one is of a female and below the human size; the face is destroyed, but in other respects the statue is perfect. The third is of a man, wanting the head and shoulders and feet; it is naked except a fold of garment just under the neck. Besides these there is a colossal head and shoulders of a female, at a fountain just below the castle on the north-eastern side. It is double the human size; the face quite demolished: locks of hair hang down on either shoulder, and each breast is pierced with a round hole. It forms part of a ruined wall belonging to some building of Roman or Byzantine times.

At a mile or two to the southward of the town stands the great cypress tree mentioned by Wheler, who states its girth to have been twenty-one feet, at the height of a foot from the ground: it is now more than twenty-three in the same place.

I rode one afternoon to the castle of the Moréa[a], as the Turkish fortress on Cape *Rhium*

---

[a] τὸ Κάστρον τῆς Μορέας, in Turkish, Mora Kálesi.

is called. Like the castles of the Dardanelles, it contains an interior work which overlooks the outer. The inner is a circular fort with embrasures in the parapet, and appears much older than the exterior inclosure, which is quadrangular and fortified with ravelins on the two land fronts. If the inner castle originally stood on the shore, the sea has retired about 250 yards since it was built; at present there is a broad level between the shore and the outer wall, where boats might land and escalade the fortress. The reality of a gradual retreat of the sea is affirmed by the natives, and appears very probable, if we admit the testimony of the ancient authors as to that great accumulation of soil at the mouths of the *Evenus* and *Achelous*, which is so strongly confirmed by the appearance of the coast near Mesolónghi and by the shallows opposite to Cape Papa. At the strait of the castles the alluvial increase may have been further assisted by the numerous streams descending from Mount Voidhiá, as well as by the great river Morno to the eastward of 'Epakto. At the opposite point of *Antirrhium* I am told that the retreat of the sea is not so rapid. The breadth of the strait appears to me to be little, if at all, short of a mile and a half, a distance which it becomes still more difficult to reconcile with the seven stades of Thucydides[a], if we admit the reality of the progressive narrowing of the strait. Strabo[b], in stating the width at five stades, is more at variance with the present dimensions than Thucydides. Pliny[c], who says that the opening was nearly a mile, appears to have taken his distance from the Greek historian. One cannot but conclude, that here, as at Navarín, there is some error either in the text or in the information of the accurate Athenian.

The castle of the Moréa is surrounded by marshes intermixed with a few plantations of currants, and the land-front is protected by a wet ditch communicating from sea to sea. The Yenitjéir Agá, who commands the fortress, assures me that the air is not unhealthy, but the complexion of the inhabitants seems to declare the contrary. He chiefly complains of the violent winds which blow through the strait in winter, and which make it necessary to build the houses very low and sheltered under the walls. Very few of the inhabitants have the appearance of soldiers. In short, it is a little Turkish fortified town, with a Greek suburb, situated, as usual, on the outside of the walls; I observed in the fortress several good English

[a] Thucyd. l. 2. c. 86. [c] Plin. Hist. Nat. l. 4. c. 2.
[b] Strabo, p. 335.

brass ordnance of the time of the Stuarts,—others of Venetian origin. Anciently each cape was occupied by a temple of Neptune[a], and within land, at the foot of the nearest heights, there was on either side a small town of which the temple was a dependency. The town on the Ætolian side was named Molycria[b], whence Antirrhium was also called Rhium Molycricum[c]. On the Peloponnesian side stood Argyra, situated on the river Selemnus, which joins the sea a little to the eastward of the castle[d].

[a] Thucyd. l. 2. c. 84.—Strabo, p. 335.—Pausan. Bœot. c. 31.—Phocic. c. 11.
[b] Strabo, p. 427.
[c] Ῥίον Μολυκρικόν.—Thucyd. l. 2. c. 84. 86.
[d] Pausan. Achaic. c. 23.

CHAPTER XV.

SECOND JOURNEY.

ACHAIA. ELEIA.

From Patra to Karavostási.—OLENUS.—DYME.—TEICHUS.—To Lekhená, Kastro Tornese, and Gastúni.—MYRTUNTIUM.—CYLLENE.—HYRMINE.

FEB. 16, 1806. I embark at 'Epakto on the outside of the town; one boat carries myself and horse, another my baggage: the wind being contrary, we consume several hours in working up to the Moréa Castle,—disembark at the village behind the castle, and, having procured some horses there, arrive at Patra about 2 P. M.

Feb. 17. Ahmét Agá, brother of the Validé Kiáyassy, and long time vóivoda of Patra, but absent for the last two years, returns here to-day, having, contrary to the expectation or wish of the Patriní, been reinstated in the government. The Validé died last summer, but Yusuf still continues in the superintendence of her property, which devolves to the Sultan, her son. Patra was one of the best of her appanages, and for this reason Yusuf appointed his brother to the government; for though it does not produce much in direct profit to the administrator on the spot, there is a good deal to be gained in the way of plunder, in which Ahmét has always shewn himself expert, by engrossing all the lucrative part of the several powers of Kadí, Dizdár, Bolúkbashi, and Hodjá-bashi. During his absence the place was governed by a servant of Yusuf. Ahmét is received on the sea-side by all the principal inhabitants, and is saluted with the cannon of the fort, and with discharges of musketry, while the consuls hoist their colours.

A new Musellím of Kárlili comes in company with Ahmét Agá. As soon as the former Musellím had been dismissed, the robbers again made their appearance in *Ætolia*, or were said to have done so, whence Alý Pashá had an excuse for sending his negro minister Yusuf, with a body of Albanians, to overrun the country, and lay the villages under contribution. Repeated oppressions of this kind have very much diminished the population of Krávari and Apókuro, whole families and even the entire population of some of the villages having passed over into the Moréa, particularly to Patra and the vicinity.

Feb. 18. The Pashá of the Moréa has succeeded in taking many of the robbers who have long infested the Peninsula, and who have been increasing in numbers for the last year. He has killed one of the Kolotrónis.

Feb. 22. A strong north-easterly wind set in, four days ago, and still continues blowing out of the gulf with such fury, as to prevent all arrivals from the westward. I set out this forenoon at 10 for Gastúni, and follow the sea-shore of that noble curve, which forms so beautiful an object from Patra, trending seven or eight miles to the south-west, before it turns westward, towards *Dyme* and Cape *Araxus*. The shore consists of a shingle, abounding in round pebbles; it was by practising with these that the slingers of Patræ and Dyme acquired the skill in slinging, for which they were renowned, and by means of which Livy adds, that they performed notable service to the Romans, under the Consul Fulvius, at the siege of Samus, in Cephallenia [a]. The left of our road is bordered by currant plantations. This plant succeeds better in a plain than upon hills, whence it happens that the wine made at Patra is better than in many other places, where the hills are equally well adapted to the growth of the vine, but where its cultivators, more anxious about the quantity than the quality of their produce, have preferred the plains for their vineyards: at Patra, on the contrary, the greater part

[a] Liv. l. 38. c. 29.

of the plain being occupied by currants, the Greeks have been contented to plant their vines on the rugged hills behind the castle. A stremma of currant plantation, (i. e. a square of 114 Greek feet the side,) when the plants are in their prime, or from ten to twenty years old, is worth 800 or 900 piastres. According to this valuation, even supposing half the currant grounds in the plain to be new, and not worth more than 500 piastres the stremma, the value of the plain will not be less than half a million sterling.

At 10.54 I cross the mouth of the Lefka, anciently Glaucus, a torrent which descends directly from the highest parts of Mount Voidhiá, crosses the plain in a broad gravelly bed, and retains little or no water in the summer.

At 11.30 arrive at the end of the plain, where low hills, the continuation of the range of *Panachaicum*, meet the sea. These hills are not rocky, but, like those at the back of Patra, they are rugged and precipitous; and they would probably produce good wine, but cultivation ends with the plain of Patra, and a desert begins, which comprehends all Western *Achaia* and the northern part of the *Eleia;* throughout which tract, with the exception of the banks of the *Peirus,* and the vicinity of a few villages, all is forest or pasture. Our road leads along a narrow level, between the low hills and the sea, until we approach the *Peirus.* This river is now called Kamenítza, in the lower part of its course, from a village of that name on its bank, which Wheler [a] erroneously writes Mammenitza, and which he describes as situated on both banks of the river, at a distance of two or three miles from the sea. After emerging from the ravine of Nezerá, the river bends towards Mount Movri, which is a great root of Mount 'Olono, projecting from the central summit of the mountain into the *Eleian* plain. After having skirted the foot of the mountain, the river turns towards the sea, which it joins at the Akhaíes, two villages belonging to Seid Agá, chief Ayán of Patra, and the greatest territorial proprietor there. The lands of these two villages lying on the banks of the Kamenítza, and which are irrigated by its waters, produce rice, cotton, arabóstari, and small kalambókki; the remainder of the arable bears wheat and barley. The river is wide and deep, although no rain has fallen for some weeks. I cross it at 1.25, and soon afterwards, turning out of the straight road to the left, ascend a small height, on which is the village of Kato, or Paleá, Akhaía, containing twenty or thirty families. The word Kato distinguishes it from

[a] Wheler's Travels, p. 292.

another village, higher up the river; the Paleá it derives from some remains of antiquity, which exist in the surrounding fields.

In the village I find a fragment of inscription, containing the name of Pharæ, a most puzzling document, as it formed part of a monument raised by that city, in commemoration of the merits of some individual, and was not likely therefore to have been erected anywhere but in the city itself. On the other hand, we have the strongest testimony of Strabo and Pausanias[a], that this was the situation, not of Pharæ, but of Olenus; Pausanias adding, that Pharæ was seventy stades distant from the sea. We must suppose, therefore, that the stone, which is not large, and forms part of a modern building, has, upon some occasion, been transported hither from the site of Pharæ. Five or six yards behind the village there is a ridge in the plain, which seems to have been formed by the ruins of Olenus. There are traces also of its walls in the adjacent fields, and two or three pieces of Roman masonry. The vestiges extend over a considerable space of ground, and are the more remarkable, as Pausanias tells us that Olenus was never a large city, and as neither he nor Strabo speak of it but as a ruin.

The temple of Æsculapius, which is men-

[a] Strabo, pp. 386. 388. Pausan. Achaic. c. 18.

tioned by Strabo, seems, by the silence of Pausanias, no longer to have existed in his time. The abandonment of the site may be dated from the time of the Roman wars in Greece; for when the Achaic league was revived after its temporary dissolution by the power of the Macedonian kings, the Olenii refused to join it [a], whence it may be inferred, that Olenus was still at that time a place of some importance. On deserting their city, the Olenii settled in the neighbouring towns of Dyme, Peiræ, and Euryteiæ [b].

Peiræ, it may be presumed from the name, stood upon the river Peirus, in the plain between Olenus and Pharæ; this position below Pharæ is probable, as well from the vicinity to Olenus, implied in the fact of the emigration of the Olenii thither, as from the name having been written Πεῖραι, for Pausanias [c] tells us, that the river which at the sea was named Πεῖρος was at Pharæ called Πίερος. Whence it would seem that Peiræ was nearer to the sea than Pharæ. The main stream is joined in the plain by another from the southward, which answers to the Teutheas of Strabo. Apano Akhaía, which stands on the right bank of this tributary, one hour distant from the lower Akhaía, may be

[a] Strabo, p. 384.   Achaic. c. 18.
[b] Strabo, p. 386.—Pausan.   [c] Pausan. Achaic. c. 22.

the site of the town called Teuthea, near which there was a temple of Diana Nemidia[a]. The river Teutheas is stated by Strabo to have been joined by another called Caucon.

I am informed that some vestiges of an ancient site are found on or near the left bank of the Kamenítza, between Prevesó and 'Ysari: as this position corresponds tolerably well with the distance of Pharæ from Patræ, and from the mouth of the Peirus, namely 150 stades from the former and seventy stades from the latter, one can hardly doubt that the vestiges are those of Pharæ. Pharæ, like Tritæa and Dyme, was made a dependency of Patræ by Augustus. In the time of Pausanias there remained a spacious Agora of the ancient fashion[b], containing a bearded Hermes Agoræus in marble, of no great size, which was oracular, and a fountain called Hama, which, as well as the fish contained in it, was sacred to the same deity. Near the statue there were thirty quadrangular stones, to each of which the name of a deity was attached, according to the most ancient practice of the Greeks. Near the river Pierus there was

---

[a] Strabo, p. 342.—M. Pouqueville seems, without knowing it, to have discovered some remains of this temple one mile to the south-east of Apano Akhaía at the foot of Mount Movri, where is a tjiftlik which receives its name, Kolónnes, from the ruins of a temple.

[b] περίβολος ἀγορᾶς μέγας κατὰ τρόπον τὸν ἀρχαιότερον.

a grove of plane trees, some of which were hollow, and so large that persons dined and slept in them. Fifteen stades from the city there was a grove of bay trees sacred to the Dioscuri, whose statues had been carried to Rome [a].

From the village of Lower Akhaía there is an interval of 8 minutes to the khan of Seid Agá, which stands in the direct road at a small distance from the sea-side. It was lately built by the proprietor of the two Akhaíes to save the inhabitants from the expense of Konáks. Here begins a forest of oaks, which extends to the Mavra Vuná, or Black Hills, and nearly to Cape Papa. I leave the khan at 3, and immediately enter the forest. The oaks are crooked, and none of them are handsome trees, though some are of a considerable size. The sea is at a small distance to the right, to the left is the great level which extends as far as the hills near Cape Katákolo. The soil is excellent but quite uncultivated; there are large flocks of sheep, but, from the khan of Seid Agá to Karavostási, where we arrive at 4.35, I see no signs of inhabitants, except a few huts made of mud and wicker for the shepherds. Karavostási [b] is a metókhi belong-

---

[a] Both in this instance and in that relating to the statue of Minerva at Tritæa, Pausanias says only, that the people asserted, [ἐπιχώριοί φασιν— Τριταῖεις λέγουσιν,] that the statues had been carried to Rome, as if he was half afraid of committing the fact to paper.

[b] Καραβοστάσιον.

ing to one of the convents of Nezerá. It is situated between a woody cape and the Mavra Vuná, which are similarly clothed, but it is nearer to the former. The Mavra Vuná[a] terminate to the northward in Cape Papa, between which and Karavostási there is a large lagoon: a mile beyond the village a narrow opening in the hills leads from the village to the lake. The fishery is worth seven or eight purses a year; boats enter it from the sea through a bogház, or opening. Papa, pronounced by the Turks Baba, is a low round peninsular height crowned with a chapel, separated from the Mavra Vuná by the lake and by the adjacent low ground.

Near Karavostási, on the eastern side, I find several remains of Hellenic masonry, others below the village towards the lagoon; and in all the fields around the village fragments of wrought stones and broken pottery, enough, in short, to shew that some Hellenic town occupied this site. Both Strabo and Pausanias[b] place Dyme at forty stades from Olenus, and Olenus at eighty stades from Patræ. My time distance to the *Peirus* from Pátra was 3 hours 25 minutes, and 1 hour 43 minutes from thence to Karavostási,—the proportion between these

---

[a] Μαῦρα Βουνὰ.   [b] Strabo, p. 386.—Pausan. Achaic. c. 18.

numbers is precisely the same as that between the eighty stades and forty; but the time distance, compared with the stades, would indicate a slower movement than usual, which I was not sensible of. I have little doubt that Strabo and Pausanias have underrated the distances, as my construction will not give less than sixteen geographical miles in direct distance from Patra to Cape Papa.

The distance of Karavostási from Cape Papa agrees with Strabo's sixty stades[a] between Dyme and Cape Araxus; nor is his remark as to Dyme having been harbourless[b] opposed to the inference which might be drawn from the modern name Karavostási, signifying a station for ships, for the latter has a reference only to modern navigation, for the purposes of which Cape Papa furnishes a very convenient shelter, when a southerly wind prevents vessels from proceeding in that direction; to the ancients, on the contrary, the lagoon, the ridge which separates it from the sea, and the long sandy beach were not favourable to the construction of those artificial moles or of the cothons, or basins, which were customary among them. The decline of Dyme is to be dated, like that of so many other Grecian cities, from the first Roman

---

[a] Strabo, p. 337. [b] ἀλίμενος.—Strabo, p. 387.

wars in Greece; in consequence of its having been favoured by Philip, son of Demetrius, it was plundered by the Romans[a]; and was already in a half deserted state when a colony of the Cilician pirates, who had been subdued by Pompey, was sent here[b]. Augustus attached Dyme, together with Pharæ and Tritæa, to the Roman colony of Patræ: in the time of the Antonines it preserved little more than a temple and very ancient statue of Minerva; a sanctuary of Dindymene and Attes, and monuments of its ancient heroes Sostratus and Œbotas; the former of these was a companion of Hercules; the latter was the first of the Achaians who gained a victory at Olympia[c]: the distich upon his statue in the Altis, which Pausanias has preserved, shews that before the Ionic migration the city was called Paleia. The name of Dyme, it is natural to suppose, was derived from its westerly position with respect to the rest of Achaia, though Pausanias, following as usual local tradition, which generally preferred a heroic etymon, ascribed it to a woman Dyme, or to Dymes, son of Ægimius. What connexion the Phrygian Dindymene and her priest Attes had with Dyme, Pausanias could not discover.

Karavostási commands a fine view of the

[a] Pausan. Achaic. c. 17.   Achaic. c. 17.
[b] Strabo, p. 665.—Pausan.   [c] V. et Paus. El. post. c. 3.

coast and mountains of *Ætolia*, as well as of the roadsted of Mesolónghi[a], with the coast as far as Oxiá and Kurtzolári, two conspicuous rocky peaks, anciently called the Oxeiæ[b], a name which is correctly descriptive of them. Strabo, however, was mistaken in supposing them both to be islands, unless we imagine the sea to have retreated from this coast more rapidly than I think possible. Kurtzolári is a mountain of the main land opposite to the island still called Oxía or Oxiá. In the opposite direction, or inland from Karavostási, is seen the whole ridge of 'Olono. In a lofty situation, upon Mount Movri, stands the monastery of Filokáli, and at the foot of the same mountain, towards the south-western end, the village of Oriólos.

Feb. 23.—I leave Karavostási this morning at 8, and in forty minutes arrive at the Castle of Kallogriá, situated on the last height of the Mavra Vuná towards the south, at the northern extremity of a chain of lagoons similar to that of Cape Papa, which extend almost as far as Glaréntza, the ancient *Cyllene*. Kallogriá occupies a rocky hill about 100 yards in length,

---

[a] It has been the practice of late, even among the Greeks, to write this name Missolonghi. We might as well say Missopotamia. Μεσολόγγιον is a word *mediæ Græcitatis*, signifying "a place in the midst of a wilderness."

[b] αἱ Ὀξεῖαι.—Strabo, pp. 458, 459.

the entire summit of which is enclosed by a massy wall faced with large shapeless masses of stone, put together without cement, but filled within with small fragments and mortar. There exist also some remains of walls and towers constructed entirely of small stones, the repairs apparently of a later age. Although the masonry of the more ancient part of these ruins is not in the usual Hellenic style, the thickness of the walls, and the massy facing, are of a kind which has not been employed in this country since the time of the Roman Empire. I cannot hesitate therefore in believing that they are the ruins of Teichus, a castle of the Dymæi, which was taken from them in the Social War, B.C. 220, by Euripidas, the Ætolian, who commanded the Eleians, and which was retaken in the following year by Philip[a], for Teichus is described by Polybius as a fortress only a stade and a half in circuit, with walls thirty cubits high, and as having been situated towards the frontier of the Dymæa[b]. That the frontier on which Teichus stood was towards Elis, may be inferred as well from the general position of the Dymæa, as from the tradition noticed by the same historian, that the castle had been first built by Hercules, when

[a] Polyb. l. 4. c. 59. 83.   [b] πρόκειται τῆς Δυμαίων χώρας.

he made war on the Eleians. It is true that Polybius further remarks, that Teichus was near Araxus[a], whereas, in fact, Kallogriá is nearer to Karavostási, the site of Dyme, than to Cape Papa; but perhaps all the hills which form so conspicuous a geographical feature in the western extremity of Achaia were called Araxus, as well as the cape itself. No other name at least is to be found for them in ancient history.

The lake below Kallogriá has an opening to the sea, and a fishery, which lets for 600 piastres a year. It is separated from the sea by a sandy strip of land which is covered with a thick forest of strofília[b], the species of pine which produces the esculent seed[c] eaten like almonds, and often used as a substitute for them in Greek cookery. The greater part of the pine nuts of this forest is sent to the opposite islands. The wood is much esteemed for ship building, but that of the common πεῦκος, or pinus maritima, is more in use for that purpose, the tree being more common.

We quit the castle at 9.7, and in little more than half an hour have a metókhi of Megaspílio on the right, on the edge of the lake. At 10.6 cross a river flowing from Mount Movri in the neighbourhood of Oriólos. It does not

[a] παρὰ τὸν Ἄραξον.   [b] pinus pinea.   [c] κουκουνάρι.

fail in summer, and after rains in winter often does mischief: it is now of considerable width, but not deep. This being the largest stream in the Eleia, north of the Peneius, must, I think, be the ancient Larissus, which divided Achaia from Eleia, though its distance from Dyme is only fifty stades, instead of the 300 or the 400 which are found in the MSS. of Pausanias, and which, it is almost unnecessary to add, must be erroneous, as the Alpheius itself is not so far from Dyme. In another place Pausanias states the distance from the city Elis to the Larissus at 157 stades, which, as it gives a correct rate to the stade measured on the map, confirms the identity of the *Larissus* with the river of Oriólos. At the river we regain the great road from Patra to Gastúni, which we had left at Akhaía. From Karavostási our road has continued to pass among oak-trees as before we arrived at that place, but beyond the *Larissus* the trees are not so thickly planted except at intervals.

At 10.40 we arrive at Alý Tjelebý, a village so called from a Turk who built a large pyrgo here, and owned the village, but who afterwards disposed of it to the monastery of Megaspílio, of which it is now a metókhi. A considerable quantity of flax is still grown, as in former ages, in the plains of *Achaia* and *Elis*, for which the rivers furnish the means of irrigation. At Alý Tjelebý a small rill runs towards a large lagoon which takes its name from this village: the lagoon is separated from the lake of Kallogriá by a narrow branch of the plain, through which there is a stream of communication, flowing, if I am not misinformed, out of the northern into the southern lake; whence it would seem that the discharge of the *Larissus* into the sea, is not directly through the lake of Kallogriá, but at the place where the lake of Alý Tjelebý opens into the sea. There is some reason to think that all these lagoons are comparatively of recent formation, as I suppose that at Old Navarín to have been; for there is no mention in ancient history of any but that of *Letrini*, near the modern town of Pyrgo.

The plain now becomes more open, but is still uncultivated, except around the villages, which however are more frequent. At 11.30 arrive at Monoládha, a metókhi of the Convent of St. Taxiarches[a] which is situated three hours above Vostítza. Monoládha is a village of twenty or thirty families, with a large pyrgo, entered by a high flight of steps and a drawbridge like that of Alý Tjelebý. Leaving it at 12.50, we cross, at 12.58, a small stream called Verga (rod), running towards the lakes. The neighbouring lands produce rice, flax, and maize. At 1.42 cross another small stream. The plain is in some places marshy and overgrown with mas-

[a] St. Michael.

tic bushes and squills, in others, it is clothed only with grass, furnishing pasture for sheep. At 2.25 we have on the right the beginning of another great lagoon, which extends for several miles along the shore towards Lekhená and Glaréntza; it is called Kotýkhi: its fishery is said to be less valuable than that of Papa, where the largest fish are caught.

Kunupéli is a little rocky height and cape on the coast, nearly in a line with the Spiliótiko metókhi, which we passed at 9.40. There is a ruined tower at Kunupéli, and a magazine, a source of hot salt water, a few vestiges of antiquity, and a port which affords good shelter from easterly winds; a ship is now lying there. The ancient name of the place I cannot discover. At 2.25 we have the small village of Mazi half a mile on the left: at 2.41 Retúni, a large village, is at the same distance on the right; soon afterwards, leaving the straight road to Gastúni to the left, we proceed directly towards Lekhená and Khlemútzi, and halt at the former at 3.42. I observe many broken marbles and other symptoms of ancient buildings in this part of the plain.

Lekhená[a] is the most considerable place in the district of Gastúni. It has a large bazar, a mosque in ruins, and about 200 families. As at Gastúni, the houses are dispersed, and each of

[a] Λεχενά.

them surrounded with a mulberry ground or fruit garden. In a large church I find many ancient squared blocks: others also in the wall surrounding the churchyard. The gallery or portico of the church is supported by four columns of gray granite, which, according to the tradition of the place, were brought many years ago from Kiónia, a place near Mazi. The name of Kiónia[a] seems to shew that it was an ancient site, though I am informed that little, or nothing, is to be seen there at present. Its position corresponds with that of Myrtuntium the Homeric Myrsinus, which Strabo places in the road from Elis to Dyme, at seventy stades from the former. Strabo adds, indeed, that Myrtuntium was upon the sea[b]; but this must either be an error in the text, or in the geographer's information; for it is obvious that no part of the road from Elis to Dyme could have passed near the sea. Entering Lekhená, I found all the shops shut, and the people either ranged on seats before the doors of the houses, or dancing, singing, roaring, and, for the most part, drunk, men, women, and children, this being the last day of Carnival. The road from Lekhená to Gastúni passes by Andravídha[c], where are said to be many fragments of ancient architecture in the churches

---

[a] Columns.   [b] ἐπὶ θάλατταν.   [c] Ἀντραβίδα.

and houses; and by Kavásula[a] on the right bank of the *Peneius*, between which and Gastúni the road crosses the river.

Feb. 24. Move from Lekhená at 8, and ride direct for the castle of Khlemútzi: at 8.18 Andravídha is one mile and a half on the left, next to Lekhená, the most considerable town in the district: traverse a plain tolerably well cultivated, principally with flax: 8.36 pass through Sulimán-agá, a small village. At 9.2 through Neo Khóri, belonging to Shemseddín Bey, of Gastúni, who has a handsome pyrgo here: 9.6 the road to Glaréntza turns to the right. As we are now nearly opposite to Paleópoli, (*Elis*,) and have travelled about five hours from the river of Orióli, that stream is evidently the *Larissus*; for the 157 stades which Pausanias places between Elis and the Larissus will answer exactly to the five hours. We now begin to ascend the long ridge of Khlemútzi, which forms so remarkable a feature of this part of the *Peloponnesus*, both by sea and land. It consists of rough hills, apparently well adapted to vines, but which are uncultivated except in some little intersecting valleys, which are now green in most parts with corn. At 10.10 we arrive at Khlemútzi, a considerable village situated

[a] Καβάσουλα.

under a round height which crowns the ridge, and upon the western side of which height, looking towards Zákytho and Kefalonía, stands the ruined castle called Kastro Tornése. The name of Khlemútzi[a] is evidently derived from the Romaic word $\chi\lambda\epsilon\mu\grave{o}s$, or $\chi\lambda o\mu\grave{o}s$, or $\chi\epsilon\lambda\mu\grave{o}s$, which we often find attached in Greece to hills of a regular form.

The gardens attached to the cottages of the village have fences made of the American aloe, two or three of which are in blossom. They are much smaller than the same plant in Sicily, and not above half the size of the agave Americana in the West Indies. According to the people of Khlemútzi, the plant bears a flower once in two years, and never dies, whence they call it athánatos. This undoubtedly is an erroneous idea, though it is a very natural one, as the reproduction is from a shoot of the old plant, which dies soon after it has flowered.

Kastro Tornése standing on a height surrounded by plains or by the sea, and hence easily recognized at a great distance, is one of the finest geographical stations in Greece. It commands a magnificent view of *Elis*, western *Achaia*, and the coast of *Ætolia*, with the islands *Zacynthus, Cephallenia, Ithaca,* the *Echinades,* and *Oxeiæ*. From its commanding position, with

---

[a] $\mathrm{X}\lambda\epsilon\mu o\acute{v}\tau\zeta\eta$, or $\mathrm{X}\lambda o\mu o\acute{v}\tau\zeta\eta$.

regard to the channels of Zákytho and Kefalonía, as well as towards the plains of the *Eleia*, it would be an important military station in any other hands than those of the Turks. Though in ruins, and neither guarded nor armed with cannon, it is still one of the most respectable fortresses in Greece, and might easily be made defensible, being small with a double inclosure, and in a very repairable state. The keep is a long irregular hexagon without any towers: the long sides of the hexagon are two thick parallel walls, about thirty feet asunder, between which there were two stories of apartments built upon arches. There are large windows looking towards the interior of the castle, and smaller looking outwards. The fortress, which was probably built in the thirteenth century, seems afterwards to have been converted into a monastery; for I perceive the remains of the paintings of a Greek church in one part, and such is the tradition of the inhabitants of the village. We are told by Phranza[a] that Khlomútza was taken by Mahomet the Second, in 1460, after he had reduced Arcadia, Laconia, and Messenia; the Beglerbegs, as he calls those who had possessed the place, having previously retreated to Corfu. It seems clear that by Khlomútza he meant this fortress, and that the Beg-

[a] Phranza, l. 3. c. 25.

lerbegs were Albanian chieftains; for Chalcocondylas relates, that the Turks took Sandamerio and other places in this part of the Moréa, from the Albanians, though he does not name Khlomútza. Coronelli has given a view of the fortress, which I think could never have had any resemblance to the reality. We may infer, however, from the minaret which he represents in one angle, that before the Venetians took the place in the year 1685, the Turks had converted some part of the castle into a mosque. At Gastúni I was told that the name of Tornése was derived from the Lire Tornesi, or livres Tournois, which were coined here by the Frank princes of the country before the Turkish conquest; and that the castle was built by Count $T\zeta\epsilon\nu\tau\epsilon\phi\rho\acute{\epsilon}s$ (so my informant wrote the name), who possessed the country soon after the conquest of Constantinople by the French.

At the foot of the hill of Khlemútzi, two miles in direct distance, and bearing N. 14° E. by compass from Castle Tornése, is the port of Glaréntza, or Glarántza, and the remains of a ruined castle apparently of the same date as Tornése. Glaréntza, softened by the Italians into Chiarenza, once gave name to a Venetian duchy, but it appears from Coronelli to have retained nothing, in the time of the last Venetian conquest of the Moréa, 1685, but ditches and other slight traces of its former importance: it is now only a desert harbour, where some rocks furnish a retreat for boats. There can be no doubt that Glaréntza is the ancient Cyllene, as there is no other harbour on this coast, except that of Kunupéli, which is too far to the north to have been the port of *Elis*[a]; whereas Glaréntza, in its distance from Paleópoli, agrees exactly to the 120 stades which Strabo[b] and Pausanias[c] agree in stating to have been the interval between Elis and Cyllene. In the time of Pausanias, Cyllene still possessed temples of Æsculapius and Venus; but the deity held in the greatest veneration among them was Hermes, who was represented by his symbol, upon a basis[d]. Pausanias is silent as to the ivory statue of Æsculapius, by Colotas, of which Strabo speaks in terms of admiration. We may suppose, therefore, that it had been removed, in the long interval which elapsed between the times of the two authors, having perhaps, by its proximity to the sea, proved too tempting a prize to some Roman collector. The convenient harbour[e] which

[a] τὸ ἐπίνειον τῶν Ἠλείων.—Pausan. Messen. c. 23.
[b] Strabo, p. 337.
[c] Pausan. El. post. c. 26.
[d] τοῦ Ἑρμοῦ δὲ τὸ ἄγαλμα, ὃν οἱ ταύτῃ περισσῶς σέβουσι, ὀρθόν ἐστιν αἰδοῖον ἐπὶ τοῦ βάθρου.
[e] ὅρμον ναυσὶν ἐπιτήδειον.

Pausanias describes, must have been chiefly indebted to art for its advantages.

Below Kastro Tornése, to the left of the village, there are the remains of a wall similar, in its construction, to that of the castle. It is called the Englishman's Wall[a], and is said to be the remains of the palace of an English governor. The most projecting point of the heights of Khlemútzi towards the sea, is to the s.w. of Castle Tornése: this point is opposite to Cape Vasilikó, in Zákytho, and here the channel is narrowest. A little on the right of the projection, a rivulet called Linzi joins the sea: It rises at the foot of the castle-hill, and flows through a little cultivated vale, in which it is joined by two or three other rivulets from similar smaller valleys.

Below Khlemútzi, and not far from the Cape of Glaréntza, there is a small island called Kavkalídha[b], and some rocky shoals, which, together, correspond exactly to the νησίον καὶ βραχέα mentioned by Strabo, as having been near Cape Chelonatas, which promontory he places

---

[a] στὸν Ἰγκλίσον.

[b] Καυκαλίδα. — Καυκαλὶς was the name of a plant which is mentioned by Dioscorides, Theophrastus, and Galen, and which Dr. Sibthorp supposed to be the Hasselquistia Ægyptiaca. Καυκαλίδα is still the name of a plant among the modern Greeks, but probably not the same as the ancient caucalis.

to the southward of Cyllene[a]. According to Pliny, Chelonatas was two miles distant from Cyllene[b], which, as it agrees with the statement of Strabo, identifies the cape as that now called Cape Glaréntza. It appears from Strabo, that the name of Ormina, or Hyrmina, was applied, at the time he wrote, to the whole hill or peninsula of Khlemútzi, for he describes it as a hilly promontory near Cyllene[c]. I conceive the fact to have been, that originally the name Chelonatas was given to the whole peninsula, now called Khlemútzi, from its supposed resemblance to a tortoise, and that the Homeric Hyrmine occupied the central and commanding position of Kastro Tornése; that, in process of time, the name of the town, which had ceased to exist, was applied to the whole promontory, and that of Chelonatas to the particular cape, on the western side of the bay of Cyllene.

At 1.45 I begin to descend through the hills along a narrow cultivated valley, and at 2.45 re-enter the plain at the little hamlet of Makhó[d]. At 3.30 cross the *Peneius*, which is here somewhat larger and deeper than the *Peirus* at its

[a] Strabo, p. 338. Some of the MSS. have νησία βραχία, but the real topography shews the other to be the correct reading.
[b] Plin. Hist. Nat. l. 4. c. 5.
[c] ἀκρωτήριον πλησίον Κυλλήνης ὀρεινὸν.—Strabo, p. 341.
[d] Μαχό.

mouth, and, after crossing a peninsular level, again arrive upon its margin, where it makes a great turn eastward, just below Gastúni: we follow the left bank for a short space, and enter Gastúni at 3.55, where I again lodge in the house of Dr. S. S. complains to me, that in the Moréa it is becoming daily more rare among the rich Greeks to give their children any education, and this want of encouragement to schoolmasters makes it difficult to find any good ones. The proestí[a], he observes, are the ruin of the nation in this, as in every thing else. In the Moréa, where so many Greeks have authority, they naturally become, under the Ottoman system, a sort of Christian Turks, with the usual ill qualities of slaves who have obtained power. The chief proofs among them of a good birth and genteel education, are dissimulation and the art of lying with a good grace; which they seem often to exercise rather with a view of shewing their ability in this way, than with any settled design. When I have taxed a Greek with falsehood on some occasion, the answer has been—" Why you know I must say something." The other day, at St. Luke's, I complained to the Igúmenos of the false account of the distance which his brother abbot at Dobó had given

---

[a] The word προεστοὶ is used exactly with the same signification as the ancient προεστῶτες.

me: "That was nothing;" he replied, "he knew very well your Excellency[a] was determined to go to that village, and therefore told you the distance was shorter than the reality, not to alarm you." In other words, he wished to get rid of me, which was natural enough, as he had found, by experience, that such casual guests were both troublesome and costly, and had never before seen any travellers who are in the habit of defraying their expenses. Though it is impossible not to be disgusted with these things, one can hardly blame the Greeks for them; for what other arms have they against their oppressors? Under such a cruel tyranny, deceitfulness unavoidably becomes a national characteristic: a Greek will often answer the simplest question by a falsehood, for the mere purpose of gaining time to reflect on the most advantageous mode of answering it, or to unriddle the inquirer's motive for asking. They will afterwards, perhaps, speak the truth, if, as it appears to them, there is nothing to be lost in so doing; and thus it is only by cross questioning and by repeating inquiries to different people, that any certain information can be obtained in this country. I believe the want of this caution leads travellers into many errors.

[a] ἡ ἐξοχότησου.

CHAPTER XVI.

ELEIA.

Geography of the ELEIA *Proper, in the time of the Trojan War.*—BUPRASIUM, PETRA OLENIA, Mount SCOLLIS, ALEISIUM. — *Geography of the* PISATIS. — LETRINI, PHEIA, *Promontory* ICHTHYS, HERACLEIA, SALMONE, DYSPONTIUM, CYCESIUM, MARGANEÆ, AMPHIDOLI, *Mount* PHOLOE, EPITALIUM, LASIO, ACROREIA, THALAMÆ.—*Geography of* TRIPHYLIA.—EPEIUM, BOLAX, PHRIXA, PISA, SCILLUS.

THE ancient geography of the Eleia is more obscure and difficult to trace than that of any other part of the Peloponnesus: the following are the causes of this difficulty. The city of Elis, after it had obtained the entire management of the Olympian festival, rapidly absorbed the wealth and population of the ancient cities both of Eleia and Triphylia, so that the chief public monuments of the province were collected at Olympia and Elis, and few of those remains of antiquity which elsewhere constitute the evidence of an ancient site are here to be found.

Secondly, the soil of Eleia being either sandy, or argillaceous, or a rich mould, and stone being found only in the mountains, the public works were seldom of so solid a construction as in other parts of Greece, where the ancient walls are almost as lasting as the rocks on which they are so often found to stand. The scarcity of stone rendering the remains of such of the ancient buildings as were formed of that material so much the more valuable for the use of modern constructions, has caused them to be more frequently removed for that purpose, than in any other part of Greece. They are also more readily hidden under a soil which is extremely subject to alluvial changes.

A third cause of the deficiency of Hellenic remains in the Eleia arises from the ancient sanctity of the Eleian territory, which, with a few remarkable exceptions, was respected throughout the history both of independent and Roman Greece; the people therefore were negligent of military architecture, which furnishes so large a proportion of the proofs of ancient locality in other parts of the country. Instead of inhabiting fortified places, like the Greeks in general, and like the Eleians themselves before the sanctity and security of their territory were established, they were attached to a country life, and had but one city of any great note and importance, which was itself unfortified [a].

[a] Xenoph. Hellen. l. 3. c. 2.—Polybius (l. 4. c. 73.) remarks as a peculiarity of the Eleia, that there were

In consequence of these peculiarities, our faithful guide Pausanias finding little to gratify his favourite pursuit of mythology, except at Elis and Olympia, bestows his attention almost exclusively upon those two places, especially the latter; making mention only of two or three others, and treating even these *haud secus ac notas*, or as if their situation was well known to his reader. Strabo, on the contrary, being throughout Greece a commentator on the Homeric geography, which in this province furnished matter in abundance for research and controversy, has been more ample on the Eleia than any other part of the Peloponnesus; and as under the Roman empire, the Eleia comprehended all the maritime country, lying between the Larissus and Neda, and extended inland as far as the Azanes and Parrhasii of Arcadia[a], the extent of the country to which his enquiries were here directed was very considerable.

In the time of the Trojan war, the territory bordering upon the western shore of the Peloponnesus, from Cape Araxus inclusive to the foot of Mount Taygetum, was divided between the Epeii and the Pylii; their line of separation towards the sea appears to have been the cape

country magistrates for the administration of justice, (τὸ δίκαιον αὐτοῖς ἐπὶ τόπου διεξάγηται,) and that there were many Eleians of good property, who for two or three generations had never visited the capital.

[a] Strabo, p. 336.

opposite to the southern extremity of Zákytho, now called Katákolo, the ancient Icthys; thus including to the north of the Alpheius the Pisatis, and the district of the modern Pyrgo. That such was the extent of Pylus, or the dominion of Nestor northward, is shewn, as I have before had occasion to remark[a], by Homer having described the Alpheius as flowing through the land of the Pylii, and it is confirmed by the definition given by the poet of the country of the Epeii in the catalogue[b], as well as by the proportion between the ships of the Pylii and Epeii in the Trojan expedition. None of the towns of the Epeii were near the Alpheius, and the ninety ships of the Pylii, compared with the forty of the Epeii, shew that the former people possessed by much the larger territory of the two, especially on the seacoast.

The towns of the Epeii, according to Homer, were, Elis their capital, Buprasium their ancient capital, where King Amarynceus was buried[c], Hyrmine, Myrsinus, Petra Olenia, and Aleisium. Among these Homeric towns of the Epeii, occupying the country which was after-

[a] See Chapter X.
[b] Οἱ δ' ἄρα Βουπράσιόν τε καὶ Ἤλιδα δῖαν ἔναιον,
Ὅσσον ἐφ' Ὑρμίνη καὶ Μύρσινος ἐσχατόωσα,
Πέτρη τ' Ὠλενίη, καὶ Ἀλείσιον ἐντὸς ἐέργει.
Τῶν αὖ τέσσαρες ἀρχοὶ ἔσαν· δέκα δ' ἀνδρὶ ἑκάστῳ
Νῆες ἕποντο θοαί· πολέες δ' ἔμβαινον Ἐπειοί.—Il. B. 615.
[c] Il. Ψ. 630.

wards the Eleia, exclusive of the Pisatis, I have already alluded to the position of Hyrmine and Myrsinus. Buprasium no longer existed in the time of Strabo, though its name was still attached to a district on the Larissus[a], which river appears from Stephanus to have been hence known by the name of Buprasius[b]. Pausanias tells us, that the Larissus was 157 stades from the city of Elis[c]. The road from Elis to Dyme, therefore, seems to have led as follows: to Myrtuntium, seventy stades, to Buprasium, on the Larissus, eighty-seven stades, to Dyme, about fifty stades. As to the Petra Olenia, Strabo thought it was the same rocky hill, called Scollis in his time;—" the river Larissus ", he says, "has its sources in Scollis, which is a rocky mountain, common to the Dymæi, Tritæenses, and Eleians; contiguous to the Arcadian mountain Lampeia, distant 130 stades from Elis, and 100 from each of the Achaian cities, Tritæa and Dyme."[d] In another place, he adds, that Pylus of Elis, which we know from Pausanias to have been at no great distance eastward from Elis, was towards Scollis[e].

It happens, unfortunately, that no other au-

[a] Strabo, pp. 340. 387.
[b] Stephan. in Βουπράσιον.
[c] Pausan. Eliac. Post. c. 26.
[d] Strabo, p. 341.
[e] κατὰ τὴν Σκόλλιν.—Strabo, p. 339.

thor mentions Scollis, except Stephanus[a], who calls it a town of Achaia; but this testimony is not at variance with that of Strabo, since it is not improbable that there was a town Scollis, homonymous with the mountain, and as Strabo places the mountain partly within the Achaian districts of Dyme and Tritæa. The circumstance of Mount Scollis having confined on Lampeia, which was a part of Erymanthus[b], added to that of its having been only 100 stades distant from Tritæa, to which it partly belonged, tends to place it considerably to the eastward of the Eleian plain; while its distance of 100 stades from Dyme would oblige us to include the summit now called Movri within the denomination of Scollis. It would seem therefore that Strabo, whose knowledge of the places was evidently but slight, comprehended, in his idea of Mount Scollis, all the northern parts of Mount 'Olonos, including the summit now called Movri, and Sandameriótiko. We cannot doubt that these ridges, though appendages of the great mass of 'Olonos, had specific names, or at least one specific name; and hence it becomes highly probable, that the hill of Sandaméri was the summit particularly called Scollis, being in form and position the most remarkable of the minor summits

[a] Stephan. in Σκόλλις. [b] Pausan. Arcad. c. 24.

on this side of the Peloponnesus. I cannot however conceive that Strabo is right in his opinion, that Scollis was the same as the Πέτρη Ὠλενίη of Homer. Hesiod, who from his antiquity must have understood by the Petra Olenia the same place as Homer, adds that it was on the bank of the Peirus [a], and he seems clearly, like Homer himself, to have had a town in view, not a mere rock, as Strabo describes the Scollis. Petra therefore seems to have been a town on the bank of the Peirus, distinguished by the epithet of Olenia, because it was situated at the foot of the mountain Olenus; for I cannot but regard those two very early authorities, coupled with the modern name Ὤλονος, varying from the ancient only in what is a common dialectic difference both in the ancient and modern language of Greece, as a proof that the name Olenus, or Olonus, has in all ages been attached to this great mountain collectively, and perhaps specifically in ancient times to its north-western part, while other summits were distinguished by the names of Scollis, Pholoe, Erymanthus, Lampeia.

Aleisium, which in the time of the geographer was called Alesiæum, stood upon a height in the road across the hills from Elis to Olympia,

---

[a] Ὤκεε δ' Ὠλενίην Πέτρην ποταμοῖο παρ' ὄχθας Εὑῆνος Πείροιο. Hesiod. ap. Strabon. p. 342.

but in what part of that road does not appear from the geographer.

Artemisium and Dioscurium were two unfortified places in the plains of Cœle Elis[a]. These and other similar names, which often occur in ancient history, such as Heræum, Aphrodisium, Dionysium, &c., were undoubtedly common names of villages in every part of the Peloponnesus, in the time of its greatest populousness, receiving those appellations from their place of worship, like the St. Johns, St. Thomases, and St. Marys, of Christendom.

I shall now proceed to offer a few remarks upon the ancient geography of the two other divisions of the Eleia, as it was defined in the time of the Romans, namely, Pisatis and Triphylia.

Had Strabo been better acquainted with Greece, he would hardly have hesitated in preferring the opinion which fixed the northern boundary of the coast of Pisatis at the Cape Ichthys, now Katákolo, to that which placed it at or near Chelonatas[b]. Southward, the Pisatis was considered to extend to the Macistia, or northern district of Triphylia[c], and eastward, to the Erymanthus[d]. Letrini, the nearest place to the western extremity of Pisatis, seems to

[a] Polyb. l. 4. c. 73.
[b] Strabo, pp. 338. 342.
[c] Strabo, p. 343.
[d] Pausan. Eliac. post. c. 21. Arcad. c. 26.—Strabo, p. 37.

have been almost deserted in the time of the Roman Empire. Strabo does not name it: Pausanias says that only a few habitations remained there. It stood on the road from Olympia to Elis, through the plains, at a distance of 120 stades from Olympia, and 180 from Elis [a]. It is evident that the road by the plains must have descended the vale of the *Alpheius*, into the plain of Pyrgo, and from thence have led along the foot of the hills to *Elis*. The distance is three or four miles greater than across the hills, which agrees tolerably with Strabo, inasmuch as, speaking of the same hill-road from Olympia to Elis, he says that it was *under* 300 stades [b], and 300 stades is exactly the sum of the two distances on the road by the plain, as stated by Pausanias.

It seems manifest, therefore, that the plain of Pyrgo was the *Letrinæa*, and this is confirmed by the mention of Letrini, which occurs in the narrative by Xenophon of the march of Agis and the Lacedæmonians into the Eleia (B. C. 400) [c]; the respective distances of 120 stades from Olympia, and of 180 stades from Elis, shew moreover that Letrini was not far from Pyrgo itself; and we may with some confidence there-

[a] Pausan. Eliac. post. c. 22.
[b] Strabo, p. 353.
[c] Xenoph. Hellen. l. 3. c. 2.

fore place it at the village and monastery of St. John, between Pyrgo and the port of Katákolo, where, among many fragments of antiquity, a part of a large statue was found some years ago. The remark of Pausanias[a], that there was a permanent lake[b] of three stades in diameter, at a distance of six stades from Letrini, does not I think invalidate the conclusion; for, though, instead of a small lake of perennial water, there is now a long salt water lagoon, extending from near Katákolo to the mouth of the river of Tzóïa, this lagoon is very probably of recent formation, like several others on the western coast of the Peloponnesus. The permanent fresh water lake may now be enveloped in the lagoon.

Strabo states the distance between the port of Pheia and Olympia to have been 120 stades, τῷ ἐγγυτάτῳ[c]. If we suppose these words to mean direct distance, it accords very well with the 120 stades of road distance given by Pausanias between Letrini and Olympia, Letrini lying in the road from Pheia to Olympia. In the time of Pausanias there were only a few houses left at Letrini, with a temple of Diana Alpheiæa

---

[a] Pausan. Eliac. post. c. 22.
[b] ἀένναος λίμνη.
[c] Strabo, p. 343.

containing a statue of the goddess [a]. It is not impossible that this may have been the same statue which stood in the temple of Diana Alpheiusa, or Alpheionia, mentioned by Demetrius Scepsius and Strabo [b], and that it may have been removed to Letrini in consequence of the ruin of the temple which stood on the borders of the Letrinæa, near the mouth of the Alpheius, at a distance of eighty stades from Olympia. In the time of Strabo, there was an annual festival of the goddess at Olympia; and the temple was celebrated for its pictures [c] by Cleanthes and Aregon of Corinth, in one of which Neptune was offering a tunny to Jupiter when in the pains of bringing forth Minerva [d]; in two others were represented the taking of Troy, and Diana mounted upon a griffin [e]. It is difficult to believe that Pausanias would have omitted to describe such a temple, had it existed in his time.

Pausanias is equally silent on the subject of Pheia, which was a place of very ancient date, if the received version of Homer [f] is correct, for it is there mentioned as one of the scenes of the

[a] Pausan. Eliac. post. c. 22.
[b] Demetrius Scepsius ap. Athen. l. 8. c. 7.—Strabo, p. 343.
[c] γράφαι σφόδρα εὐδόκιμοι. Strabo.
[d] θύννον τῷ Διὶ προσφέρων ὠδίνοντι. Demetr.—Ἀθηνᾶς γοναί. Strabo.
[e] Ἄρτεμις ἀναφερομένη ἐπὶ γρυπός. Strabo.
[f] Homer. Il. H. 135.

youthful exploits of Nestor. Strabo[a], however, states some reasonable doubts as to the accuracy of the poet's text in this place, and suggests that the words Pheia and Celadon should be Chaa and Acidon, thus placing them with the river Jardanus in Lepreatis. That the Jardanus was in that part of the country, and that it was held to be the same as the Acidas, we learn from Pausanias[b]; thereabouts, consequently, the battle was fought between Nestor and the Arcadians. It is indeed much more probable that the parties should have met on the frontiers of Pylia and Arcadia, than on the sea-shore of Pisatis.

Near Pheia was the cape called Ichthys, the southernmost of the three great promontories on the north-western coast of Peloponnesus. This description of Ichthys, derived from the concurring testimonies of Thucydides, Xenophon, Agathemerus, Mela, and Ptolemy[c], leave no doubt of its identity with the remarkable promontory now called the Cape of Katákolo. Nevertheless Strabo, whose inaccuracy, or that of his text, is in this instance at once shewn by the map, speaks of two capes upon this part of

[a] Strabo, p. 348.
[b] Pausan. Eliac. prior. c. 5.
[c] Thucyd. l. 2. c. 25.—Xenoph. Hellen. l. 6. c. 2.—Agathem. l. 1. c. 5.—Pompon. Mel. l. 2. c. 3.—Ptolem. l. 3. c. 16.

the coast; of which the northern was called Pheia from the name of the neighbouring town [a]; of the southern he has not given the name. The small river near Pheia of which he speaks, and which was supposed to be the Jardanus by those who thought that Homer spoke of Pheia and not of Chaa, may possibly be the river of Tzóïa.

Ichthys is a long rocky promontory, or peninsula, united to the main land by an isthmus from which rises a very conspicuous peaked height, crowned by the ruins of a castle of the middle ages, raised upon some remains of Hellenic walls. These walls are undoubtedly those of Pheia. The ruined castle is called Pondikókastro [b]. Below it, to the south-east, is a harbour well sheltered by Cape Katákolo, and much frequented: this, however, was too open and extensive for ancient navigation. The port of *Pheia* was a small creek at the foot of the hill of Pondikókastro, on the western side; a position clearly indicated by Thucydides [c], who tells us that in the first year of the

[a] Strabo, p. 342.

[b] Rat Castle. — Ποντικὸς, Ποντίκι, the modern Greek word for *mouse, rat,* is one of those conversions of Hellenic particulars into Romaic generals, of which there are many instances. The word Pondikó in its present sense originates in the great use made by the moderns of the skin of the ermine, anciently called Mus Ponticus (Plin. l. 8. c. 37.) Μῦς Πόντιος ὁ λευκὸς. (Aristot. Hist. Anim. l. 8. c. 19.)

[c] Thucyd. l. 2. c. 25.

Peloponnesian war the Athenian fleet sailing from Methone attacked and took Pheia, but that rough weather coming on, they sailed round the promontory Ichthys into the port of Pheia. Opposite to its entrance there is a small island, which is mentioned by Polybius under the name of Pheias [a].

The other towns of Pisatis mentioned by Strabo are Marganeæ, Salmone, Heracleia, Harpinna, Cycesium, Dyspontium, Œnoe, or Bœnoa [b], and Epitalium. Of these Pausanias names only Harpinna and Heracleia, the only two perhaps which existed in his time. Of the position of Harpinna I have already spoken.

Heracleia was situated on the river Cytherus at a distance of fifty stades [c], or forty according to Strabo [d], from Olympia. Salmone stood not far from Heracleia at the sources of another branch of the Alpheius called Enipeus, or Barnichius [e]. Two tributaries of the *Alpheius*, rising in the woody heights to the northward of *Olympia*, join the right bank of the *Alpheius* in the plain where now stand the little villages of Strefi and Floka. The river of Strefi I take to be the ancient *Cytherus*, that nearer to Floka the *Enipeus*. Strefi, which stands on a height on the

[a] τὴν Φειάδα, καλουμένην νῆ-σον. Polyb. l. 4. c. 9.
[b] Βοινώα.
[c] Pausan. Eliac. post. c. 22.
[d] Strabo, p. 356.
[e] Ibid.

edge of the plain, corresponds, by its distance from *Olympia*, with the site of *Heracleia*.

In the time of Strabo, the greater part of the inhabitants of Dyspontium had emigrated to Apollonia and Dyrrhachium. The town appears, from the words of the geographer, to have been, as well as Cycesium, in the northern part of Pisatis, towards Elis. As it lay on the road by the plain from Elis to Olympia[a], its situation seems to have been at the foot of the hills between Paleópoli (*Elis*) and the ridge (ending in Cape *Ichthys*) which separates the plain of Gastúni from that of Pyrgo.

If the text of Strabo is correct where he adverts to the position of Œnoe, that place, as I have already remarked, must have been very near the mouth of the *Peneius*, or river of Gastúni.

Regarding Marganeæ, Xenophon relates[b], that in the second year of the war between the Arcadians and Eleians, (B.C. 364,) the latter having marched out of their city against Pylus, which was then in the hands of the Arcadians, and of a party of fugitives from Elis, met the Pylii returning from an unsuccessful expedition against Thalamæ, a town in a lofty situation in the adjacent mountains, and that the Eleians having completely defeated their opponents,

[a] Strabo, pp. 356, 357.   [b] Xenoph. Hellen. l. 7. c. 4.

followed up their victory by taking both Pylus and Marganeæ. The latter, therefore, seems to have been the nearest city of the Pisatis to Pylus of Elis, which is known to have been near the Peneius about ten miles above Elis[a]. Strabo places Marganeæ in the Amphidolia, and describes it as a place not strong by natural position[b]. From Xenophon and Stephanus[c], Amphidolia appears to have received its name from a town named Amphidoli. This place probably stood about the middle of that broad stripe of land which lies between the Erymanthus and the plain of Elis. I say the middle, because we have seen that near Olympia were Heracleia and Salmone, and towards Elis, Pylus, Cycesium, and Dyspontium. Along the tract of land just mentioned, there is a longitudinal ridge, beginning near the bank of the *Erymanthus* above Lalla, following a course parallel to the *Alpheius* as far as Pyrgo, and then trending northward towards Paleópoli (*Elis*). It separates the course of the tributaries of the *Alpheius* from those of the *Peneius*. We have the positive testimony of Pausanias, that these heights were the ancient Pholoe, so celebrated in Grecian poetry and mythology, for he says that the

[a] Pausan. Eliac. post. c. 22.—Plin. Hist. Nat. l. 4. c. 5.—Diodor. l. 14. c. 17.
[b] Strabo, p. 349.
[c] Xenoph. Hellen. l. 3. c. 2.—Stephan. in 'Αμφίδολοι.

Leucyanias, one of the feeders, just alluded to, of the Alpheius, had its sources in Mount Pholoe[a], thus agreeing with Xenophon, who testifies to the proximity of Pholoe to Scillus, though they were on opposite sides of the Alpheius. Pholoe, however, must sometimes have had a much more extensive signification than this ridge, for Strabo, though he strongly confirms the proximity of a part of Pholoe to Olympia[b], also informs us that the Peneius, and another river which flowed into the Eleia, and which he calls the Scarthon, had their rise in Mount Pholoe[c], shewing, as well in this as in other places[d], that he considered Pholoe to have formed a considerable part of those great summits which are now conjointly known by the name of 'Olono. He even describes Pholoe, in one of the passages just referred to, as an Arcadian mountain, of which the lower parts were in Pisatis.

I conceive, therefore, that all the south-western part of the summits of Mount 'Olono were comprised under the name of *Pholoe*, and that in common estimation it comprehended likewise all the slopes in that direction as far as the plain of *Elis*, including the secondary ridge

[a] Pausan. Eliac. post. c. 21.
[b] ἡ Φολόη δ' ὑπέρκειται τῆς 'Ολυμπίας ἐγγυτάτω, ὄρος 'Αρκα- δικὸν, ὥστε τὰς ὑπωρείας τῆς Πισάτιδος εἶναι. Strabo, p. 357.
[c] Strabo, pp. 338. 587.
[d] Id. pp. 336. 388.

extending from *Elis* to Lalla. The remark of Pausanias[a], that the river Erymanthus rising in Mount Lampeia, which was a part of Mount Erymanthus, passed through Arcadia, leaving Mount Pholoe on the right, and the Thelpusia on the left, will agree with both these suppositions. According to Pliny, there was a town of Pholoe[b], but his testimony is not confirmed by any other author.

Epitalium was situated on the left bank of the Alpheius, as may be deduced from a comparison of the words of Strabo, relative to this place, with those of Xenophon, in describing the events of the war between the Lacedæmonians and Eleians[c]. Agis, king of Sparta, entered the Eleia, at the river Larissus; but an earthquake happening, he regarded it as a divine omen, and retreated. The next year (B. C. 400) he entered from the southward through the Aulon of Messenia and the Lepreatis. "Immediately the Lepreatæ, revolting from the Eleians, joined him, and forthwith the Macistii also, and their neighbours the Epitalii. When he had crossed the Alpheius, the people of Letrini, Amphidoli, and Marganeæ came over to him. Proceeding to Olympia, he there sacrificed to Jupiter Olympius, nobody attempting to hinder him.

[a] Pausan. Arcad. c. 24.
[b] Plin. H. N. l. 4. c. 6.
[c] Xenoph. Hellen. l. 3. c. 2.
—Pausan. Lacon. c. 8.

Thence he marched to the city of Elis, destroying and burning the country and carrying away cattle and prisoners in great numbers. Many of the Arcadians and Achaians came willingly to join his army for the sake of partaking in the plunder, so that the expedition became a foraging party for all Peloponnesus. When he arrived at Elis he destroyed the suburbs and the beautiful Gymnasia; as to the city itself, which was unfortified, it was thought that he was more unwilling than unable to take it." Agis then encamped near Cyllene, when an insurrection of the partizans of Sparta in Elis against the popular party having failed of success, he marched back by the same route, by which he came. When he had repassed the Alpheius, he left a garrison in Epitalium near the river, under Lysippus, the leader of those of the Spartan faction who had fled from Elis, after which, having dismissed his allies, he returned home. During the remainder of the summer and the ensuing winter, the country of the Eleians was exposed to the ravages of Lysippus and his men. In the next summer Thrasidæus, who was leader of the popular party in Elis, sent agents to Sparta, who, for the sake of relieving the Eleia from the annoyance caused by the fugitives at Epitalium, were authorized to agree to the destruction of the fortifications of that place, and to promise liberty as well to that as to some other cities which had been in subjection to Elis, namely, Letrini, Amphidoli, Marganeæ, and Phrixa,—also to Cyllene, to the Acroreii, and to Lasion, which was claimed by the Arcadians. The Eleians endeavoured to retain Epeium, which lay between Heræa and Macistus, affirming they had bought the district from the owners for thirty talents, and had paid the money. "But the Lacedæmonians, who considered a compulsory purchase from a weaker party as equivalent to a deprivation by violence, obliged them also to set Epeium at liberty. They did not, however, expel the Eleians from the guardianship of the temple of Jupiter Olympius, conceiving those who claimed it to be peasants, and unfit for so important a charge. These things having been agreed upon, there ensued peace and alliance between the Eleians and Lacedæmonians."

Epitalium, according to Strabo, stood on the site of the Homeric "Thryon at the ford of the Alpheius[b]:" which the poet in another place calls Thryoessa, and describes as a city upon a lofty hill near the Alpheius[c]. The latter description of the place occurs in the narrative by

[a] Strabo, p. 349.
[b] Θρύον, Ἀλφειοῖο πόρον.—Hom. Il. B. 592.
[c] Ἔστι δέ τις Θρυόεσσα πόλις, αἰπεῖα κολώνη,
Τηλοῦ ἐπ' Ἀλφειῷ νεάτη Πύλου ἠμαθόεντος. Hom. Il. Λ. 710.

Nestor, of the contest between the Pylii and Epeii, when his father Neleus ruled over the former, and Augeias over the latter, and when Nestor performed the earliest of his youthful exploits in arms[a]. The Pylii having been reduced to a state of great weakness by Hercules, the Epeii took a *neighbourly* advantage of it; among other injuries, their king Augeias detained a chariot and four horses belonging to Neleus, which had been sent to contend for the prize of the tripod in the Epeian games, in return for which Neleus made a most successful βοηλασία in the enemy's territory, as I have had occasion more particularly to remark in a former chapter. The Epeii then collected an army, and invested Thryoessa, a frontier town of the Pylii, situated at the passage of the Alpheius. The Pylii moved to its relief, and having assembled their forces at the river Minyeius, halted the cavalry all night, while the infantry marched forward, so that all the army arrived at the Alpheius the following noon. They employed the remainder of the day in repose, or in sacrificing to Neptune, Minerva, and Alpheius. On the ensuing morning they attacked and routed the Epeii, whom they pursued with their cavalry as far as Buprasium, Petra Olenia, and Alesium, the in-

[a] Hom. Il. Λ. 669, et seq.

infantry apparently not having crossed the river.

Thus it appears that Thryoessa, like Epitalium, was on the left bank of the Alpheius, near the usual passage of the river, and therefore in all probability upon the identical site of Epitalium; since the same local conveniences would in all ages cause the river to be crossed nearly in the same place, and the same strong position in the neighbourhood to be occupied by a fortress; the more so, as the road from the southward must always have led along the narrow level included between the shore and the woody hills, which, beginning at Khaiáffa, end at the height of Agulenítza, below which to this day is the usual ferry of the Alpheius, not far from its mouth. We may conclude therefore that Thryum, or Thryoessa, afterwards Epitalium, occupied the hill of Agulenítza. It may be thought perhaps that this hill hardly corresponds by its height to the αἰπεῖα κολώνη of the Iliad, or to Θρύον αἰπὺ of the Hymn to Apollo[a], but being surrounded for a considerable distance by much lower ground, it is very conspicuous, and sufficiently in agreement therefore with the words of the poet.

Lasion was a city of considerable strength and importance in or very near the Pisatis;

[a] Hom. Hymn. in Apoll. v. 423.

Diodorus ascribes it in one place to Eleia[a], and in another to Triphylia[b]: but as it is not included among the Triphylian cities by Herodotus or Polybius, both of whom evidently confined Triphylia to the southern side of the Alpheius, it was probably to the northward of that river. Xenophon distinguishes the people of Lasion from those of Triphylia and Acroreia[c]; and we learn from him that, as well at the time of the invasion of Agis, as at the beginning of the quarrel between the Arcadians and the Eleians, Lasion was an Arcadian city[d], though anciently it had belonged to the Eleia[e]. One hundred and forty-five years after the latter event, Lasion, as we are informed by Polybius, was again a fortress of the Eleians[f]. The natural inference from these several authorities seems to be, that Lasion was situated to the westward of the Erymanthus, the natural boundary of the two provinces, but not very far from that river. Lasion appears also to have been not far from the district of Psophis, for Polybius relates in the place just referred to, that the Eleian garrison deserted Lasion in great haste, upon hearing of the capture of Psophis by Philip. These premises suit no place so well as Lalla, of which the com-

[a] Diodor. l. 14. c. 17.
[b] Ibid. l. 15. c. 77.
[c] Xenoph. Hellen. l. 4. c. 2.
[d] Ibid. l. 3. c. 2. l. 7. c. 4.
[e] Ibid. l. 7. c. 4.
[f] Polyb. l. 4. c. 74.

manding position, at the head of a fine slope falling to the Alpheius and Erymanthus, insured to it such a degree of importance as Lasion appears to have possessed. It will be found also, that the situation accords exactly with the circumstance of Lasion having been taken by the Lacedæmonians marching from Arcadia, previously to their occupying the towns of the Acroreii, in their way to Elis [a].

This expedition occurred in the third year of the ninety-fourth Olympiad. Pausanias, king of Sparta, after having taken Lasion, and the four towns of the Acroreii, named Thraustus, Alium, Eupagium, and Opus, occupied Pylus, and thence marched to Elis. Having been repulsed at Elis, the king left garrisons in different parts of the country, and moved into winter quarters at Dyme. It is remarkable that Xenophon makes no mention of this incursion of the Lacedæmonians, related by Diodorus, though it accords with their invasion in the following year under the command of Agis, who, it seems, had in the interval superseded Pausanias, and though it explains also how it happened that the Spartans then entered the Eleia from the northward. The war, therefore, if Diodorus is correct, lasted four years, and there were three

[a] Diodor. l. 14. c. 17.

invasions, one from the Heræitis, the second from the Dymæa, the third through the Aulon of Messenia, and along the coast of Triphylia.

Mention of Acroreia again occurs in Xenophon's account [a] of the beginning of the war between the Eleians and Arcadians, which in the following year interrupted the celebration of the 104th Olympic festival (B. C. 364). The Arcadians, having beaten the Eleians near Lasion, marched into Acroreia, and after having taken all the towns of that district except Thraustus, moved to Olympia, and occupied Mount Croneium, which they surrounded with a pallisading. These are the only two occasions, upon which Acroreia is noticed in ancient history, but they are sufficient to place the district between the Erymanthus and Pylus on the slopes of Mount Pholoe. The towns of the Acroreii were probably on the banks of the Upper Peneius, and of its great branch, the Ladon, which runs nearly parallel to the former, and joins it near Pylus. That situation agrees perfectly with the name Acroreii, which implies mountaineers, or, rather, the inhabitants of the skirts of mountains. As to the position of the several towns of Acroreia, the order of names in Diodorus is the only datum. Upon this authority, Thraustus was the nearest to the Arcadian frontier; it appears also from Xeno-

[a] Xenoph. Hellen. l. 7. c. 4.

phon, in the last passage cited from him, to have been the most capable of resistance. I am inclined therefore to place it at Dhomokó, upon the right bank of the Erymanthus, where exist some remains of Hellenic antiquity, in a strong situation. Opus, which received its name from the same Epeian hero, whose daughter Protogeneia, married to Locrus, caused the name of Opus to be given to the Locrian capital, might perhaps be discovered by means of its river, of which mention is made by the scholiast of Pindar [a].

Thalamæ was another fortress in the mountainous parts of Eleia. When Philip, son of Demetrius, in the second year of the 140th Olympiad, B. C. 219, invaded and plundered Eleia, great numbers of the people retired with their property and flocks to Thalamæ, which is described by Polybius as a strong fortress in an unfrequented situation, defended by narrow passes [b]. It was, however, under the necessity, at last, of surrendering to Philip. Thalamæ is mentioned also in Xenophon's account of an action in the second year of the war between the Arcadians and Eleians, which has already been alluded to in speaking of Marganeæ [c]. The Eleians, as I have stated, met the Pylii on this occasion returning home from an unsuccessful

[a] In Olymp. 9. v. 64.
[b] Polyb. l. 4. c. 75.
[c] Xenoph. Hellen. l. 7. c. 4.

attempt upon Thalamæ. This place seems therefore to have been in the mountains just above Pylus, either in Scollis or in the adjacent part of Pholoe.

I have had occasion, in a former chapter, to advert to the position of some of the Triphylian towns. Herodotus[a] names six towns in Triphylia:—Lepreum, Macistus, Phrixa, Pyrgus, Epeium, and Nudium. Polybius[b] omits Macistus and Nudium, and adds Samicum, Hypana, Typaneæ, Bolax, and Styllangium. Macistus was once the rival of Lepreum, for to a late period all the northern part of Triphylia was called Macistia, as the southern was called Lepreatis[c], though the town of Macistus, mentioned by Xenophon[d], was deserted before the time of Strabo, which may be the reason why it is not named among the Triphylian towns by Polybius. In the time of Strabo it was partially revived, under the new name of Platanistus[e], which leads, as I have already hinted, to the conjecture, that it was not far from the modern Khaiáffa, for this being the only promontory between Ichthys and Cyparissiæ, appears to have been the cape which Pliny calls Platanodes[f], having probably confounded it by the similarity

---

[a] Herodot. l. 4. c. 148.
[b] Polyb. l. 4. c. 77.
[c] Strabo, pp. 343. 345. 349.
[d] Xenoph. Hellen. l. 3. c. 2.
[e] Strabo, p. 345.
[f] Plin. Hist. Nat. l. 4. c. 5.

of name with the Platamodes which Strabo[a] places between Cyparissiæ and Coryphasium, at a distance of 120 stades from the latter. Another reason, as I have before remarked, for supposing that Macistus was not far from Khaiáffa is the remark of Strabo, that the temple of Neptune Samius, near Samicum, was in the custody of the Macistii. The northern boundary of Macistia, according to Strabo, was a mountain which separated it from the district of Epitalium, (Agulenítza,) which he included in Pisatis. According to these data, the site of Macistus might best be sought for near the banks of a stream, possibly the ancient Chalcis, which descends into the maritime level at about three miles to the north of Khaiáffa.

We are told by Xenophon[b] that Epeium, or Æpeium, another Triphylian town, stood between Macistus and Heræa. We can hardly doubt that it was the same as the Homeric Æpy. If Macistus was in the place just described, Epeium was probably on the high peaked mountain which lies between the villages of Vriná and Smerna, about six miles in direct distance from *Olympia;* from whence it forms a very conspicuous object; for on that hill there are said to be some remains of a Hellenic city,

[a] Strabo, p. 348.   [b] Xenoph. Hellen. l. 3. c. 2. Vide supra.

and the lofty situation agrees with the name of Æpy. Strabo remarks, that a position justifying the appellation by its nature[a], was pointed out in his time as the site of Æpy[b]. He perhaps meant the very place I have just indicated; though it is proper to remark that there was another place in the Macistia the name of which indicates a lofty site: it was called Hypsoeis in the time of Strabo, who supposed it to have been the site of the Homeric Amphigeneia[c].

I have already observed, that some remains of Pyrgi still exist near the right bank of the Neda, not far from its mouth[d], and I have offered some conjectures also upon the positions of Hypana and Typaneæ[e]. If we might be allowed to judge from similarity of name alone, unsupported by any other evidence, *Bolax* might be placed at Volántza[f], a village on the left bank of the *Alpheius*, about four miles above its mouth. As to Styllangium, I am unable to offer any conjecture.

The exact situation of Phrixa is known from the following passage of Pausanias[g]; where, upon finishing the description of Olympia, he

[a] ἔρυμα φυσικὸν.
[b] Strabo, p. 349.
[c] Id. ibid.
[d] Vide Chapter II.
[e] Vide Chapter XIII.
[f] Βολάντζα.
[g] Pausan. Eliac. post. c. 21.

most abruptly resumes the route from Heræa to Olympia, which, in his Arcadics, he had carried forward from Heræa as far as the Erymanthus and the boundary of the two provinces. "The frontiers of the land", he says, "towards the Arcadians, belong at present to the Eleians, but formerly were those of the Pisæi. Having passed the river Erymanthus, as far as the ridge called the hill of Saurus, there is a sepulchre of Saurus and a temple of Hercules, both of which are now in a state of ruin. It is said that Saurus infested both travellers and the natives, before he was punished by Hercules. Near the hill which receives its name from this robber, a river flows from the south into the Alpheius, nearly opposite to the Erymanthus. It separates Pisæa from the Arcadians: its name is Diagon. Forty stades from the hill of Saurus there occurs a ruined temple of Æsculapius, surnamed Damænetus from the name of the founder; it was built upon a height near the Alpheius. Not far from hence is the temple of Bacchus Leucyanitas, and near it the river Leucyanias, which descends from the mountain Pholoe and falls into the Alpheius. When you have crossed the Alpheius from thence, you will be in the Pisæan land, not far from a hill with a peaked summit. Here are ruins of the city Phrixa, and a temple of Minerva Cydonia, which is now only a place of sacrifice[a]. Farther on, at the river Parthenia, is the tomb of the Horses of Marmax. There is also another stream called Harpinnates, and not far from that river some ruins of the city Harpinna, consisting chiefly of altars; it is said that Œnomaus built the city and named it after his mother Harpinna. Proceeding a little further you come to a high mound of earth, the tomb of the Suitors of Hippodameia. They say that Pelops, when he ruled over the Pisæi, performed funeral rites every year at this tomb. One stade further on are vestiges of the temple of Diana, surnamed Cordax. Not far from the temple there is a small building, and in it a brazen chest which preserves the bones of Pelops; nothing remains either of the walls or of any of the other buildings of Pisa, but vineyards are planted over all the place where the city formerly stood."

In the preceding passage we may observe a material omission of a kind not uncommon with Pausanias. The Leucyanias joined the Al-

[a] Vestiges of churches similar to those of the temple which Pausanias here describes, are common in Greece at the present day. Sometimes nothing is left but a line of stones to represent the wall, with a single block of stone, commonly of ancient workmanship, for an altar. Here incense is burnt, and prayers are said on the feast-day of the saint.

pheius on its right bank, and Phrixa stood on the opposite bank. So far he is clear.—But he omits to mention that he re-crosses the Alpheius; for it cannot admit of a question that the Parthenius, and Harpinnates, and Harpinna, and Pisa were all on the right bank of the Alpheius, and that the Scilluntia occupied the country adjacent to the left bank.

The position of Phrixa is determined by a pointed hill, rising from the left bank of the Alpheius, upon the summit of which are the remains of Hellenic walls. It is now called Paleofánaro, and is a conspicuous object, as well from the country around *Olympia*, as from the side of *Heræa*. It will follow, that a small stream, which descends from the woody heights of Lalla, nearly opposite to Paleofánaro, was the *Leucyanias*[a].

I have said that Harpinna and the Scilluntia were on opposite sides of the Alpheius, the former on the right bank, the latter on the left. That Scillus was to the left of the Alpheius, is manifest from Pausanias, who arrives at Scillus from Samicum, and then crosses the Alpheius to

---

[a] Ania, or something resembling that word, appears to have signified *water*, or *river* in the old Æolic, or Pelasgic. There were three rivers of the name of Aroanius in Arcadia. The Anio of Italy had probably the same origin, and perhaps also the name of the Ænianes, who inhabited the banks of the Spercheius.

Olympia [a]. Lucian informs us that Harpinna was twenty stades from the Hippodrome of Olympia, on the road leading eastward to Heræa [b], and from Xenophon we learn that Scillus also was twenty stades from Olympia [c]. It is clear, therefore, that the two places were at equal distances from Olympia, on opposite sides of the Alpheius. As Harpinna was on the road along the Alpheius to Heræa, and Lucian measures a distance of twenty stades from the Hippodrome, which was the part of Olympia nearest to the river, it may be presumed that Harpinna was not far from the bank of the Alpheius, on the ridge which stretches from thence to the modern village Miráka. The rivulet which flows on the eastern side of that ridge appears to be the *Parthenius*, and that to the west the *Harpinnates*. It might indeed be inferred from Strabo, who says that the Parthenius flowed by Harpinna, that the Parthenius and Harpinnates were one and the same; but they are both so near the hill of Miráka, that it may fairly be said that *Harpinna* was situated on either of them.

As Pisa appears from Pausanias to have occupied a position between Harpinna and Olympia, which were only twenty stades asunder, its situation could hardly have been any other than

---

[a] Pausan. Eliac. prior. c. 6.
[b] Lucian. de Morte Pereg.
[c] Xenoph. Anab. l. 5. c. 3.

that of the projecting ridge which terminates the vale of *Olympia* to the eastward, and between which and the continuation of Mount *Cronium* is the pass leading from Andílalo to Miráka. This proximity of Pisa to Olympia is confirmed by Herodotus, who, in an accurate statement of distance, refers to Pisa and the temple of Jupiter as one and the same point[a]. Pindar also and other Greek poets employ the words Pisa and Olympia indifferently and with the same meaning. The ruin of Pisa occurred at so remote a period, that the testimony of such ancient authors as Herodotus and Pindar is the more important in shewing its locality.

In the earlier Olympiads the Pisatæ had sometimes the honour of presiding at the Olympic contest, to the exclusion of the Eleians; but the alliance of Elis and Sparta, the two richest nations of the Peloponnesus, was too powerful for the Pisatæ, with only the Messenians and Triphylii for their natural allies. A tacit agreement of the Lacedæmonians and Eleians to share between them the maritime country which separated their possessions, seems to have cemented the alliance of Sparta with Elis, and to have actuated the policy of the two states. The

---

[a] He says that there were 1485 stades, by the road, from the altar of the Twelve Gods at Athens to the temple of Jupiter Olympius and Pisa. Herodot. l. 2. c. 7.

resistance of the Pisatæ appears to have ceased as far back as the forty-eighth Olympiad, when an unsuccessful revolt brought destruction upon Pisa, Scillus, Macistus, and Dyspontium, and annexed all Triphylia to Elis, as great part of Messenia had already been annexed to Laconia. The Arcadians did indeed endeavour afterwards to make use of the name of the Pisatæ in celebrating the games of the 104th Olympiad, which were interrupted by a battle in the Altis between the contending forces of Elis and Arcadia; but Pisa did not then exist as a town, for we have already seen, that in the ninety-fifth Olympiad, when the Lacedæmonians under Agis invaded the Eleià and occupied Olympia, they would not take away the charge of the games from the Eleians, because the Pisatæ were mere *peasants* unfit for so great a charge [a]. Such being the antiquity of the ruin of Pisa, it is not surprising that Pausanias found the site converted into a vineyard, or that it should now be impossible to find any evidences of its position except in ancient history.

Nearly opposite to the mouth of the *Cladeus* the *Alpheius* is joined by a stream issuing from a woody vale, in which stands a small village called Rasa. It cannot be doubted, upon comparing Xenophon and Pausanias, that this river

[a] Xenoph. Hellen. l. 3. c. 2. Vide sup.

was the Selinus, and that Scillus was situated in its valley. The woody hills, abounding with beasts of chase, still agree with the description of both those authors, though it must be confessed, that without the aid of Xenophon, neither the exact situation of Scillus, nor the road by which Pausanias arrived at it from Samicum and the Anigrus, would have been intelligible.

Scillus seems to have remained desolate from its destruction in the 48th Olympiad, until the 96th, when the Lacedæmonians, who had recently obliged Elis to give liberty to the surrounding cities, colonized Scillus, and bestowed it upon Xenophon, then an exile from Athens. Xenophon describes Scillus[a] as situated at a distance of twenty stades from the Hierum of Olympia, on the road to Sparta, amidst woods and meadows and mountains covered with trees, and he adds that the district, not only afforded an abundant pasture to hogs, goats, sheep, oxen, and horses, but was even capable of supplying sufficient refreshment to the beasts of draught[b] belonging to those who frequented the festival of Diana: for Xenophon had devoted to the goddess a part of his share of the spoil, acquired in the Asiatic

[a] Xenoph. Anab. l. 5. c. 3.   [b] ὑποζεύγια.

expedition of the Ten Thousand, and with it had built at Scillus a small temple of Diana, resembling that of Ephesus, ὡς μικρὸς μεγάλῳ, with an altar and a statue in cypress-wood similar in form to the golden statue at Ephesus. He erected also a pillar[a] near the temple, bearing the following inscription. " This land is sacred to Diana[b]. Whoever possesses it and its fruits, shall consecrate a tenth of them, and from the remainder shall keep the temple in repair. If he neglects to do this, he will be answerable to the Goddess."[c]

" It happens," adds Xenophon, " that the river which flows through Scillus is called Selinus, like that which flows by the temple of Diana at Ephesus, and like that, also, it furnishes fish and shell-fish. The country around abounds in beasts of chase of various kinds. Those who attend the festival are supplied at the expense of the goddess with flour, bread, and sweet-meats[d], with animals for sacrifice from the sacred pastures, and with wild hogs, roebucks and stags, which have been procured in Mount Pholoe, or in the Scilluntia by the sons of Xenophon, and of the other citizens[e],

[a] στήλη.
[b] Ἱερὸς ὁ χῶρος τῆς Ἀρτεμίδος.
[c] τῇ θεῷ μελήσει.
[d] τραγήματα.
[e] τῶν ἄλλων πολίτων.

who are accompanied to the chase by all persons disposed to join them."

Pausanias thus mentions Scillus. "After crossing the river Anigrus, on the direct road to Olympia, there is a high place on the right of the road called Samicum, upon which stood the city Samia. Proceeding still further beyond the Anigrus, through a country covered for the most part with sand and wild pine-trees, the traveller will see the ruins of Scillus, behind on the left hand [a]. Scillus was formerly a city of Triphylia, but the Scilluntii having openly assisted the Pisatæ against the Eleii, the latter destroyed the place. Afterwards the Lacedæmonians having separated Scillus from the Eleia, gave it to Xenophon, son of Gryllus, who was a fugitive at Sparta, because he had taken part with Cyrus against the king of the Persians, who was a friend of the Athenians. Xenophon resided in Scillus, and built a sanctuary and temple to Diana Ephesia. Scillus affords a chase of wild hogs and stags. Not far from the temple of Diana a tomb is shewn with a statue upon it, made of stone from the quarries of Pentele, which the inhabitants say is the statue of Xenophon. On proceeding from

---

[a] ὀπίσω ἐπ' ἀριστερᾷ Σκιλλοῦντος ὄψει ἐρείπια.

Scillus, on the road to Olympia, there occurs, before the crossing of the Alpheius, a mountain precipitous with lofty rocks; it is called Typæum, and there is a law among the Eleians, that any woman who is present at the Olympian contention, or who even crosses the Alpheius on the forbidden days, shall be thrown headlong from that summit.

As the Alpheius was not passable when I visited Olympia, I could not explore the valley of Scillus; it is not very probable, however, that any important remains of antiquity should be found there, unless it be some vestiges of the temple of Diana, as Scillus seems never to have attained any great importance after its restoration by Sparta; nor would it probably have been again mentioned in history, had it not been the residence of the illustrious Athenian, and immortalized by his writings.

The route of Pausanias from Samicum appears to have been along the maritime level, for there alone could he have passed through a country which chiefly consisted of sand and pine-trees. Had he moved in the direct line towards Olympia from Samicum, he must very soon have quitted the sand and pine-trees, and have passed to the right of them. It is probable that the lagoons did not then exist. It seems, that after having traversed about half the distance from Khaiáffa to Agulenítza, he then crossed the hills to the ferry of the Alpheius opposite to Olympia, leaving the site of Scillus on the left, and Mount Typæum on the right. This precipitous hill I have already described as being at a small distance from the left bank of the Alpheius, opposite to the eastern end of the site of Olympia, and consequently higher up the stream than the vale of Scillus and the ancient ferry[a] of the Alpheius.

As Xenophon describes Scillus to have been on the road from Olympia to Sparta, it appears that besides the more level route which led along the right bank of the Alpheius to Héræa, there was another more direct, by passing over the ferry of the Alpheius, ascending the valley of Scillus, and then crossing the hills beyond it; this road probably recrossed the Alpheius at the bridge of Heræa, mentioned by Polybius[b], where it joined the other road, and from thence followed the ordinary route to Sparta by Megalopolis[c].

[a] πόρος. [b] Polyb. l. 4. c. 77. [c] Tab. Penting.

CHAPTER XVII.

ELEIA. ARCADIA.

From Gastúni to Tripótamo.—ELIS.—PYLUS of ELEIA.—River LADON of ELEIA.—Tripótamo.—PSOPHIS.—Siege of PSOPHIS by Philip, in the Social War.—Routes of Pausanias to and from PSOPHIS.—To Sopotó.—River and Mountain ERYMANTHUS.—To Karnési.—CLEITOR, town and river.—To Tara.—Rivers AROANIUS, LADON, TRAGUS.—To Levídhi and Tripolitzá.—ORCHOMENIA, MANTINICE.

FEBRUARY 26.—Set out, at 11.10, from Gastúni for Paleópoli, by a more direct road than that which I passed last year. A large portion of the plain is uncultivated. At 12.25 the village of Toshki is half a mile on the right, just before which we pass by a large tract of currant grounds in excellent order; this is the most perfect kind of agriculture to be found in Greece: 12.36 Bukhióti is on the right. At 1.2 arrive at the village of Paleópoli, which is situated on the slope of the hills. I again visit, in the little plain between the village and the Peneius, the few dispersed and shapeless fragments of brick walls which are now the only visible remains of the great Elis.

If the traveller is disappointed at the little of antiquity that remains either here or at Olympia, or indeed upon any of the Hellenic sites of this province, it may be some consolation to him to consider, that a soil, subject like that of the *Eleia,* to alluvial changes, was the best adapted speedily to conceal, and may still therefore preserve some of the works of art which survived the fury of the persecutors of idolatry, whether Christian or Mahometan, and that if there is less above ground in the Eleia than in any of the provinces of Greece, there may be more below the surface.

Enjoying the same sacred protection as Olympia, Elis retained its respectability as long as the Olympic festival existed, and there was scarcely any city in Greece which Pausanias found in a state of better preservation[a]. It was remarkable for the magnitude of its Gymnasium and Agora; that of the former was caused by its being the place of ordination and preparation for the athletæ of the Olympic Games, that of the latter by its antiquity; such having been the ancient method, as Pausanias remarks, in speaking of the Agora of Pharæ[b]. Strabo tells

[a] Pausan. Eliac. post. c. 23, 24, 25, 26.

[b] Achaic. c. 22. Pausanias contrasts this mode with that of Ionia; (Eliac. post. c. 24.;) on several occasions his reference to that country, shews that it was his ordinary residence, though not I think his birth-place, which seems, from the evidence of Stephanus, to have been in Syria—See Topog. of Athens, Introd. p. 31.

us that the Gymnasium stood on the river-side[a]; there seems no doubt, therefore, as to its exact position, and we may suppose that the Gymnasium and Agora together occupied the greater part of the space included between the river and the hill of Kallaskopí, upon which stood the Acropolis. The Gymnasium was surrounded with a wall within which were walks ($δρόμοι$) shaded by plane trees, and called collectively the Xystus; one of the dromi was destined to the use of the runners and pentathli, another was named the Sacred. The Gymnasium contained likewise three subdivisions, called Plethrium, Tetragonum, and Malco; the first so named from its dimensions, the second from its shape, the last from the softness of its soil[b], which was prepared in that manner for the use of the Ephebi, who were admitted into it during the whole period of the Games[c]. The Plethrium contained altars of Hercules Parastatus, of Eros, of Anteros, of Ceres, of Proserpine, and a cenotaph of Achilles. In the Tetragonum, which was contiguous to the Plethrium, but smaller than that inclosure, there was a brazen statue of Jupiter, which, together with another, (in the Altis of Olympia[d],) had been the produce of a fine

[a] Ῥεῖ διὰ τῆς πόλεως ὁ Πηνειὸς ποταμὸς παρὰ τὸ Γυμνάσιον αὐτῆς.—Strabo, p. 337.
[b] τῆς μαλακότητος τοῦ ἐδάφους.
[c] Πανηγύρεως.
[d] Pausan. Eliac. prior. c. 21.

levied upon two men of Elis and Smyrna, for collusion in the Games. On either side of the entrance of the Malco stood a statue of a young pugilist, said to have been Serapion of Alexandria, who, coming to the Games, brought with him corn from Egypt when there was a scarcity in Elis. In one angle of the Malco there was a head and shoulders of Hercules, with a representation, in low relief, of Eros and Anteros, the former holding a palm-branch in his hand, the latter endeavouring to wrest it from him. The Malco contained the Lalichmium, a building so called from its founder: it was adorned within with a range of shields, and served for the meeting of the councils of the Eleians, as well as for the exhibition of literary compositions[a]. There were two passages leading out of the Gymnasium, one by the street of Silence and the temple of Diana Philomeirax to the Baths; the other above the cenotaph of Achilles to the Hellanodicæon and the Agora. The Agora, which was called the Hippodrome because it served for the exercise of horses, had several stoæ intersected with streets. The southern Stoa consisted of a triple row of Doric columns. Here the Hellanodicæ, or prefects of the Games, passed the day. The Hellanodicæon stood at its extremity, to the left: it was a building di-

[a] δείξεις λόγων αὐτοσχεδίων καὶ συγγραμμάτων παντοίων.

vided from the Agora by a street: here the Hellanodicæ dwelt ten months previous to the festival, employed in learning the laws of the Games from the Nomophylaces, and at different hours they marshalled the several kinds of athletæ, and conducted them to the Gymnasium. The southern stoa was separated only by a street from the Stoa Corcyraica, so called because it had been built from the tenth of spoils taken from the Corcyræi. Its construction was remarkable. One side, consisting of a range of Doric columns, was open to the interior of the Agora: the opposite side, adorned with a parallel range, opened towards a sanctuary of Venus: the stoa was divided longitudinally into two parts, by a wall parallel to the columns, along which on either side were ranged portrait statues[a]. Pausanias does not mention the number of them, and names only one, that of Pyrrho the Sophist, which was on the side towards the Forum.

The hypæthral, or open part of the Agora was so large as to contain, besides the principal temple of Elis, that of Apollo Acesius, those also of the Graces and of Silenus, together with the tomb of Oxylus, which was merely a roof supported by wooden columns: there was also a house in which sixteen women were employed to weave the peplus of Juno[b].

[a] εἴκονες.
[b] There was a similar building at Sparta.—Pausan. Lacon. c. 16.

The works of statuary at Elis were not very numerous, which is not surprising when we consider the immense collection possessed by the Eleians at Olympia: but some of them were by the first masters. The statues of the Graces were acrolithic, with gilded drapery: one bore a rose in her hand, another an astragalus, the third a sprig of myrtle. Beside them stood a Love[a]. Silenus was represented receiving a cup of wine from Intoxication[b]. There were also statues of the Sun and Moon in the open part of the Agora. The sanctuary of Venus on the outside of the Stoa Corcyraica consisted of a *vaὸs*, or temple, and a *τέμενος*, or inclosure; in the former stood a Venus Urania, in ivory and gold by Phidias, who had represented the goddess with one foot on a tortoise[c]; in the latter, there was a brazen figure of Venus Pandemus seated on a goat, the work of Scopas. In a ruined temple of the Roman Emperors, which adjoined the Agora, there remained no statue, nor does Pausanias describe any in the temple of Hades, which stood apart from the Agora, and which was only opened once a year. In the portico of the temple of Fortune[d], there was a colossal wooden statue of the goddess,

---

[a] ῎Ερως.
[b] Μέθη.
[c] Signifying, according to Plutarch (in Præcept. Conjug.), that domesticity and silence were becoming in women, (οἰκουρίας σύμβολοι γυναιξὶ καὶ σιωπῆς.)
[d] Τύχης.

gilded in every part except the extremities, which were of white marble. To the left of this temple, there was a small building sacred to Sosipolis, a provincial deity[a] who was there represented in a painting as a boy wrapped in a cloak[b] spotted with stars, and bearing in his hand the horn of Amaltheia (Cornucopiæ). In a very frequented part of the city there was a statue of heroic size[c], representing a beardless man, with one leg crossing the other, and both hands leaning upon a spear: it was called Satrapes, but was said to have been a statue of Neptune brought from Samicum. The temple of Bacchus, which adjoined the theatre, contained a statue, by Praxiteles, of this deity, who was particularly worshipped by the people of Elis. In the citadel there was a temple of Minerva, containing another of the chryselephantine works of Phidias[d], who had represented a cock on the helmet of the goddess.

After riding in several directions over the site of Elis in the plain, I ascend to the summit of Kaloskopí, which lies between the village of Paleópoli and the river. Here are the remains of a Frank house or castle, the foundations of which are formed of the large squared blocks of

[a] Ἠλείοις ἐπιχώριος δαίμων. Paus. El. post. c. 20.
[b] χλαμύδα. c. 25.
[c] ἀδρὸς οὐ μείζων μεγάλου.
[d] Pausanias, however, adds the word φασὶ, as if he had some doubt of its having really been the work of Phidias.

the ancient city. The place well deserves its name of Kaloskopí, or Belvedere, and is a most useful geographical station, though neither in this respect, nor in the interest or extent of the prospect, is it to be compared with Kastro Tornese. It commands a view of the whole plain of *Elis* from the ridge of Pondikó-kastro southward, to about Alý Tjelebý to the north. Zákytho and the range of 'Olono form the mountainous part of the view.

Having returned to the village, I set out from thence, at 3 p.m., on the road to Tripolitzá, which passes through a narrow vale in the hills behind *Elis*. At 3.38 cross a brook from the right, which joins the *Peneius* a little above the ruins of *Elis*: 4.7 the village of Pozaíti, or Bozaíti, is on the right, pleasantly situated on the slope of a hill amidst pine-trees. At 4.22 pass a small stream, deep and sluggish, running to join the *Peneius* near the village of Lukávitza, which stands on a height upon our left: 4.50 cross another rivulet shaded with planes, flowing from a narrow vale on the right. The scenery of this vale, in the bosom of rugged hills covered with pines, is as beautiful as any in the neighbourhood of *Olympia*. In fact the same description of pine-clad hills, intermixed with tracts of cultivated land round the villages, extends all the way from *Elis* to Pyrgo, Agulenítza, and Lalla. At 5.3 Kúlogli is on our left half a mile.

All these villages are small; they belong to Turks of Gastúni or Lalla, and each has its Pyrgo, the proprietor's dwelling and place of security. At 5.15 we pass at the foot of a height, on the summit of which are remains of massy walls, built of rough fragments of stone mixed with mortar. A small plain cultivated with maize lies between this hill and a river, much more considerable than any of those we have just passed; we cross it at 5.27. There are many planes growing on either bank, as well as in the bed of the river itself. On the edge of the bank I observe a piece of brick ruin, like those of Paleópoli. After ascending the heights on the opposite side, we ride over an uncultivated space, covered, like all the rest of the country hereabouts, with a beautiful verdure, till at 5.53 we arrive at Laganá, consisting only of a few wicker huts and one house. I intended to halt here for the night, but finding the house already occupied by a Turk on his road from Tripolitzá to Gastúni, I am obliged to return half an hour to the river we crossed, on the right bank of which stands a little village called Atzídhes[a]. Here I lodge in a small hut with some oxen, in preference to the pyrgo of

[a] Ἀτζίδες.

the Kihayá, a musulman of Lalla, who has purchased the village. Opposite to Atzídhes, on the left bank of the river, is the small village of Kúlogli, mentioned above.

Although Diodorus, Pausanias, and Pliny[a] all give different distances between Elis and Pylus of Eleia, namely, Diodorus seventy stades, Pausanias eighty, and Pliny twelve Roman miles, yet the medium is sufficiently near to the two hours and a quarter of road-distance from the site of Elis to the ancient remains which I passed at 5.15 and 5.27, to leave little doubt that these are vestiges of Pylus. Probably the ruins first encountered mark the site of the town, and the fragments at the river are the remains of a bridge over the Ladon, which river, Pausanias tells us, was a branch of the Peneius, flowing by Pylus, and which therefore is not to be confounded with the great Arcadian Ladon, a tributary of the Alpheius. It is no objection to this conclusion, as to Pylus, that its position, as here indicated, is not immediately in a direct line from Elis to Olympia, or that it is not exactly at the junction of the Ladon and Peneius. The hill road, though shorter than that by the plain, may not have been quite direct. Pausanias, besides, only says that Pylus was *towards* or *near* the hill

---

[a] Diodor. l. 14. c. 17.— Plin. Hist. Nat. l. 4. c. 5. Pausan. Eliac. post. c. 22.—

road[a], and that the Ladon flowed *by* Pylus to the Peneius[b].

Pylus received its name from the same son of Cleson of Megara, who founded Pylus in Messenia, and who, upon being expelled from thence by the Pelasgi under Neleus, settled in this place. The people of Elis not only pretended that this was the Pylus which Homer had in view, when he stated the Alpheius to flow through the land of the Pylii, but that it was the place which Hercules destroyed, and for which Nestor retaliated upon the Eleians. The absurdity of these suppositions, although both of them were credited by Pausanias, but especially that of the latter, is clearly demonstrated by Strabo[c]. It appears that Pylus of Eleia was deserted before the time of the Roman Empire. Pausanias expressly says that it was uninhabited, and the same inference may be drawn from the word ᾠκεῖτο, in Strabo[d].

The *Eleian Ladon* is formed by many rivulets from the gorges of the woody heights which extend to Lalla and *Olympia;* its most distant sources are at the foot of Mount Astrá, which is the name of the south eastern summit of Mount 'Olono, above the village of Dhivri.

[a] κατὰ τὴν ὀρεινὴν ὁδόν.
[b] παρὰ αὐτὴν ποταμὸς Λάδων κάτεισιν ἐς τὸν Πηνειόν.
[c] Strabo, p. 350. et seq.
[d] Strabo, p. 339.

This Ladon I think is very probably the same river called Scarthon in our copies of Strabo, which he describes as flowing from Mount Pholoe into the Eleia, and as being crossed twenty-five times in one road [a].

The main branch of the Peneius, which is considerably larger than the Ladon, issues from a great ravine in Mount 'Olono, through which passes the road from the country around Lalla and Gastúni to Aio Vlasi, by Ghermotzáni. Its chief sources are at a place in that glen called the Dervéni; on issuing from the ravine it turns westward, leaving Kakotári on the right bank, then passes round the foot of the extreme southern point of the summits of 'Olono, receives the *Ladon* at Agrapídho-khori, and not far below that junction another stream, which flows down a vale, separating the hill of Sandaméri from the western parts of 'Olono; the *Peneius* then skirts the southern end of the Sandamerió-tiko, and at the site of *Elis* enters the plain of Gastúni.

Sandaméri is a village situated in the valley just mentioned, and its rocky hill, as I have before remarked, is probably the ancient Scollis. Sandaméri[b] was one of the strongest and most important of the positions held by the Albanians

[a] Strabo, p. 587. [b] Σανταμέριον.

in the northern part of the Moréa, at the time of the Turkish conquest[a].

Feb. 27.—Leaving Atzídhes at 8.20, and proceeding along the heights to the left of the main road by Laganá, we enter the vale of a stream shaded with planes which joins the *Ladon* a little above Atzídhes, follow up this valley, and at 8.50 pass to the right of the village of Simópulo. Here, on the right of the road in a corn-field, I find a single column of coarse marble standing in its original position, but wanting the capital; around it are some excavations, which have been made for the purpose of carrying away the squared foundation stones of the ancient building, and of which no more than two or three are now left. It was probably one of the temples so numerous in the *Eleia*. " All the country ", says Strabo[b], " is full of Artemisia, and Aphrodisia, and Nymphæa, situated for the most part in groves, which are maintained in a state of verdure by the abundance of water[c]; not less frequent are the Hermeia on the roads, and the Poseidia on the promontories and points of land."

After halting five minutes we proceed up the valley, and soon begin to ascend heights

[a] Chalcocond. l. 9.—Phranza, l. 3. c. 25.
[b] Strabo, p. 343.
[c] διὰ τὴν εὐυδρίαν.

covered with birches, large oaks, wild pear trees, planes, and watered by many springs and rivulets. At 9.40 arrive at the summit of this ascent, which is steep and rocky towards the top, and thence called the Skala. Here ends the forest; at 9.45 halt for a quarter of an hour at a fountain; on proceeding, a fine view opens of the country to the left, including the ranges of 'Olono, Voidhiá, and the mountains of Rúmili opposite to Patra. I particularly remark the sharp peak of Arákhova, which forms the north-eastern end of the range of Mount Viéna in *Ætolia*. Two or three degrees to the right of this is the snow-capt mountain, I believe Mount 'Anino, in Apókuro, which is apparently the highest of all those hills, except the peaks of Vardhúsi and Sykiá in the ancient Doris. Our route continues along the summits which are partly covered with trees, and consist partly of pasture land mixed with a little cultivation. Soon afterwards there is a continued forest extending to the foot of Mount 'Olono on the left, and to the right as far as the eye can reach, being a part of that long even slope reaching from the steeps of *Pholoe* to the *Alpheius*, which is bounded in the other directions by the plains of Gastúni and Pyrgo to the westward, and by the river *Erymanthus* to the eastward.

Similar heights occupy the long narrow space inclosed between the *Erymanthus* and the Arcadian *Ladon*.

These woody heights, backed by the higher summits, are admirably adapted to shelter the wild animals which made Pholoe and its vicinity so favourite a resort of Diana and her nymphs, and Scillus so delightful a residence for a sportsman like Xenophon. Of the wild animals which afforded chase to Xenophon and his friends at Scillus, deer[a] are now rare in the lower parts of the mountain, but they are found in the higher regions, as well of Pholoe as of the other great summits of the peninsula; the roebuck[b] and the wild hog[c] are frequently seen as low as *Scillus* and the banks of the *Alpheius*. The bear would seem, from the silence of Xenophon regarding it, not to have been common in the Peloponnesus in his days, though in more ancient times we may be assured that it existed, from its skin having furnished clothing to the Arcadians[d], and from the story of Arcas and Callisto. It is very possible, that as the wild animals diminish with the increase of the human species, the bear may have been driven out of the peninsula in the most populous and civil-

[a] ἐλάφια.
[b] ζαρκάδι.
[c] ἀγριόχοιρος.
[d] Pausan. Messen. c. 11.

ized ages of Greece, nor have regained its footing in the Peloponnesian mountains, until the Roman wars and their consequences had reduced the country to a state of desertion, which it has never recovered. In the time of Pausanias the bear was common in the woods of Arcadia[a]; it is now seldom seen in any part of the Moréa, though the occasional appearance of ἀρκούδια in the mountains both of Arcadia and Laconia, is generally attested by the inhabitants.

We proceed along a good road through a forest, which consists solely of oaks, many of them very large, but all with very crooked stems. At 10.55 we are opposite to the southern end of the great heights of the mountain, which are a mile distant on the left; on its slope, in a lofty situation, stands the monastery of Notená, above which, on the very summit, there is a chapel in a small grove; the rest of the mountain in sight is naked, but soon after passing the monastery I observe a few firs on a summit seen through the glen of the upper *Peneius*, in the direction of Aio Vlasi. This is the southern extremity of the same forest which clothes all the north-eastern part of 'Olono towards Kalávryta;—a quarter of an hour

[a] Pausan. Arcad. c. 24.

beyond the monastery we have Kakotári, on our left at the foot of the mountain, just at the entrance of the glen. Halfway from Kakotári to Aio Vlasi is Ghermotzáni; the waters in its neighbourhood flow to the *Erymanthus*. The trees now become smaller and more thinly planted. At 11.23 we are at the bottom of a deep hollow, along which flows a rivulet, one of the many which hasten from these hills to add their contributions to the *Ladon*. All the waters, to the eastward of the gorge of the *Peneius*, flow to the *Ladon*, which takes a great sweep before it comes down upon Kúlogli, &c. At 11.40 we halt five minutes at Katjarú[a], a place where are the remains of some ruined houses in a hollow of one of the tributary rivulets of the Ladon. The road now ascends gradually, passing over the roots of Mount Astrá, where are numerous sources of water, particularly a very copious one called Kalimáni[b]; it is the reputed source of the *Ladon*; here formerly stood a khan.

We leave the little villages of Andróni and Kumáni on the left in the wood, distant one mile and a half, and continue to mount very gradually, still passing over the roots of the mountain, which are covered, not thickly, with

---

[a] Κατζαροῦ.   [b] Fine spring.

small oaks: we halt to dine at a rivulet at 1.8, this also runs towards the Ladon. The spot commands a fine view of the whole chain of mountains which extend from Karítena to Khaiáffa, as well as of the opposite range of Dhimitzána and Stemnítza, with their snowy and woody summits. The opening of Karítena is seen between them, and through it the great peaks of *Taygetum.* Fanári and Andrítzena would be clearly seen if the state of the atmosphere were favourable. In the direction of those places, but at the distance only of two miles from us, I perceive a large tract of vineyards with cottages dispersed among them, belonging to Dhivri. Below these, on the right bank of the *Erymanthus*, which river is not above a mile in direct distance from the easternmost of the branches of the *Eleian Ladon*, are some ancient remains at a place where once stood a village, called Dhomokó, perhaps the site of *Thraustus.* At 2.30 we proceed towards Dhivri, continuing to ascend along the side of the mountain, and then turning to the north-east; below us, on the right, is the deep ravine of the Erymanthus, to which there is a long and steep descent. We have now the woody summits of Mount Khelmós before us, and nearer the lofty mountains which border the Erymanthus. At 2.48, pass some houses, serving to store the corn of Dhivri, which is grown on the slope below: soon afterwards, taking a turn to the north and north-west, arrive at Dhivri at 3.20. Dhivri, or Divri [a], is situated in a theatre-shaped slope at the head of a torrent, which flows to the Erymanthus; immediately above it to the northward, is the snow-capt mountain, called Astrá: the word is synonymous with the ancient Lampeia; and, like Kandíli, which is another name, not uncommonly applied by the moderns to a high mountain, is derived from the glittering of the snow in the sunbeams. I do not think, however, that Astrá is exactly the summit which the ancients called Lampeia. On each side of the rivulet, and all round the town, rise steep woody mountains, which shut out all view. On the slopes, where the streams trickle down, and where the sun does not reach, there are now great masses of ice. The town occupies a large space, the houses to the number of 200 being dispersed in clusters over the side of the hills, but a great part of them are uninhabited. This is chiefly owing to the angária of the Lalliotes, who come here and force the poor Greeks to carry straw, wood, &c. on their horses to Lalla without payment. The town, which belongs to the vilayéti of Gastúni, was the pro-

[a] Δήβρη, or Ντήβρη.

perty of Halíl Bey of Gastúni, and on his death fell, with the rest of his property, to the Sultan. Its revenue is now for sale. Two persons have hired it temporarily; it is supposed that it will be bought by a cousin of Shemseddín Bey. At Lekhená each head of a house pays 100 piastres a-year for kharátj and other personal taxes, which is much less than in many parts of the Moréa. At Dhivri the direct taxation is nearly the same, but the Lalliotes come and live upon them. On the opposite side of the *Erymanthus* begins the vilayéti of Karítena, and between Dhivri and Tripótamo is the boundary between Kalávryta and Gastúni.

Feb. 28. — It takes half an hour to descend through the town, the houses being much dispersed, and the rocky paths very difficult. At 8.40 we leave the lowest houses,—from thence follow the side of the mountain along a steep paved road above the right side of the torrent, and reach the extremity of the ravine at $9\frac{1}{4}$. Having crossed the torrent, I perceive on a height by the side of the Erymanthus, just below the vineyards of Dhivri at two or three miles distance, the situation of Dhomokó, near which there is a place called Paleó-kastro, situated in a wood. There remain many heaps of stones and fragments of buildings, among which the Dhivriótes described to me a few large tetragonal stones in the Hellenic style. Though Dhomokó is no longer a village, its former importance is shewn by the Dhivriótes having given its name to the *Erymanthus*, which they call the river of Dhomokó. Below Dhomokó the river takes a turn to the left, running under the long woody heights which reach to Lalla. At 9.35, Peta, a small village, is on the slope of the mountain opposite to us above the left bank of the Erymanthus; a mile lower down nearly opposite to the mouth of the ravine of Dhivri, there is another called Vidhiáki. In descending we gradually approach the river, and at 9.55 fall into the dhimosiá, or public road from Gastúni to Tripótamo, which we had left yesterday a little before arriving at the corn magazines. The path is very bad, ascending and descending over rocks, so that we proceed at a very slow pace, although without the baggage, which I left yesterday morning to follow us. The hills are sparingly covered with ugly oaks, short and crooked, but some of them large. Most of these oaks, as well as the plane-trees, have their dry leaves still hanging on them. 10.5, pass a little rill, the boundary of the districts of Gastúni and Kalávryta: 10.25 cross a bridge over a torrent coming from the mountain on the left near the village of Mostenítza. These mountains are more woody than those on the opposite side of the *Erymanthus*, particularly towards the summits, which are now tipped with snow. At 11.4 arrive at the junction of a rapid stream flowing from the same mountains, with another which has its rise to the north-east near Lekhúri and Sopotó. About 100 yards below the junction, the united stream is joined by a third from the south-eastward flowing from Lópesi, in the direction of Strézova: from these three rivers the place derives the name of Tripótamo. The mountain from whence the western branch descends is seen through the ravine of that river on our left, deeply covered with snow, with a few firs on its slope. Ghermotzáni stands near the division of the waters, which flow on one side into the *Peneius*, and on the other to the western river of Tripótamo.

As soon as I have crossed the latter stream I find myself upon the site of *Psophis*. Four roads meet at this point; 1. The Gastúni road, by which we came; 2. The continuation of it up the valley of the river of Sopotó to Kalávryta; 3. That along the right bank of the third river to Lópesi, Skupí, Strézova, and Tara, being the road from Gastúni to Tripolitzá; and 4. That along the western stream to Nussa[a], Morókhova[b], Poretjó[c], and Ghermotzáni. The road from Gastúni to Tripolitzá crosses the two

[a] Νούσσα.   [b] Μορώχοβα.   [c] Πορετζὸς.

principal streams at Tripótamo by bridges, to avoid the steepness of the banks below their junction, and immediately afterwards, turning the point of mountain which divides the valley of the third river from that of *Psophis*, it arrives at the Khan of Tripótamo, where are some huts and vineyards belonging to the village of Mostenítza. All the three rivers are clear rapid streams, flowing over a gravelly bed, and are bordered by plane trees. At the present season the rivers of Nussa and Sopotó are nearly equal in size: that of Lópesi is considerably smaller; the united stream is not above half the size of the *Arcadian Ladon*, near Strézova.

Polybius and Pausanias have left no doubt as to the names of the two larger rivers, for Polybius expressly states, that the Erymanthus flowed along the eastern side of Psophis, and that the river on its western side was an impetuous torrent from the neighbouring mountains, which is perfectly just, both as to its character and origin[a]. From Pausanias we learn that its name was Aroanius[b].

Among the remarkable positions with which Greece abounds, and which seem to have been intended by Nature for the strong holds of small republics, Psophis is one of the most distinguished for strength and singularity of site.

[a] Polyb. l. 4. c. 70.   [b] Pausan. Arcad. c. 24.

A rocky hill, advanced before the main body of the mountains, is defended on the south-eastern, or longest side, by the Erymanthus, on the south-western by the Aroanius; at the southern extremity of the site the streams are united. The banks are precipitous but not very high :— between them and the steep summit of the hill there is a small space of level, or gently rising ground. The summit is a sharp ridge sending forth two roots, one of which descends nearly to the angle of junction of the two streams, the other almost to the bank of the Erymanthus at the eastern extremity of the ancient city. The town-walls followed the crest of the ridge to the northward and the bank above the two rivers on the opposite side. There was probably a citadel on the summit, but I could not trace the inclosure of it. From the foregoing description, and the accompanying plan, it will clearly appear, that Pausanias is not quite correct in saying that the Erymanthus was more distant from the city than the Aroanius[a], since they both flow under the walls, which are traceable along the crest of the bank of either stream, as well as throughout the entire circuit of the place, or nearly so, though in no part extant to any great height. They are irre-

[a] παρὰ δὲ αὐτὴν ὅ τε Ἀροάνιος ποταμὸς, καὶ ὀλίγον ἀπωτέρω τῆς πόλεως Ἐρύμανθος ῥέουσι.

gular specimens of the third order, and are formed of masses not very large. The summit of the hill is separated, by a narrow neck behind it, from a higher summit, which looks down upon it in a manner not so inconvenient in ancient warfare as it would be at the present day. On the slope of the hill there are several parallel walls built of small stones without mortar: on the summit of all stands a small church.

On the north-eastern side of the town, which is the only part not protected by the two rivers, or by the precipices at the back of the hill, there was a double inclosure: the remains of the interior wall are still seen, extending from the upper ridge to the bank of the *Erymanthus*, and nearly parallel to the outer walls. A part of a theatre, not noticed by Pausanias, is seen on the side of the hill towards the *Aroanius*, situated just under the ridge of rocks on that side. It seems to have been small; there remains above ground a part of the circumference of four or five rows of seats; and there may very possibly be some more concealed under a field of maize, which now occupies the place of the scene, and extends below the theatre as far as the river. Three hundred yards above the junction of the two rivers, near the walls on the bank of the *Erymanthus*, I find some remains of a public building thirty-two yards in length, below which there is a source of water in the bank. In the level part of the site, a little above this ruin, some other foundations are seen, and a great quantity of fragments of wrought stones and ancient pottery dispersed about the level. The only other remains of architecture I could find, were the capital of a Doric column and a fragment of its shaft in a ruined church near the centre of the site, and some other pieces of columns of the same size near the city wall below it. The flutings are two inches and a half: there are also some fragments of plain columns nearly of the same diameter. The town was about two miles in circumference. The situation, though important as commanding the passes of the *Erymanthus*, and the communication from the northern part of *Arcadia* into the valley of the *Alpheius*, and the plains of *Elis*, is any thing but agreeable, being too closely surrounded with mountains, which shut out all view, cause occasionally an extreme of heat and cold, and increase the violence of the winds. The neighbouring hills are sprinkled with oaks like those towards Dhivri.

The buildings of Psophis, remaining in the time of Pausanias, were, a temple of Venus Erycina in ruins, heroa of Promachus and Echephron, sons of Psophis, and the monument of Alcmæon, son of Amphiaraus; the latter was a small building without ornament, standing amidst some very lofty cypresses, which were called by the Psophidii " the Virgins." Near the Erymanthus stood a temple sacred to that stream; it contained statues of Erymanthus, Nile, and other rivers, all formed of white marble, except that of Nile which was of black stone, in allusion to the origin of the river in Æthiopia. It is not improbable that the foundations which I noticed near the walls above the fountain on the bank of the *Erymanthus,* are remains of this temple.

The best ancient account of Psophis is by Polybius[a], in his narrative of its siege by Philip, King of Macedonia, in the Social War (B. C. 219). He describes Psophis as " an ancient city of the Arcadians of Azanis, situated in the central parts of Peloponnesus, towards the western frontier of Arcadia, bordering[b] upon the western Achaians, and overhanging[c] the country of the Eleians, with whom the Psophidii were at that time in alliance. Philip having marched hither in three days from Caphyæ, stationed his army upon the hills opposite to the city, where, secure from the enemy, he commanded a view of the city and surrounding places. He was so much struck with the strength of the

[a] Polyb. l. 4. c. 70. [b] συνάπτουσα. [c] ἐπίκειται.

place that he was doubtful what to do." " On the western side", says the historian, " there is a rapid torrent, impassable during the greater part of the winter, and which, rushing down from the mountains, makes the city strong and difficult of access by the magnitude of the channel, which in process of time it has formed. On the side towards the east flows the Erymanthus, a large and impetuous river, concerning which there are many well known stories. As the western torrent joins the Erymanthus on the southern side, the city is thus fortified on three sides. On the remaining side towards the north impends a strong hill, defended by a wall, and serving the purpose of a secure and well placed citadel[a]. The town itself also is provided with walls, remarkable both for their large dimensions and their construction." "The place contained a garrison sent by the Eleians; Euripidas the Ætolian, who had just escaped from his defeat at Apelaurus, was also in the city. The king, considering the great danger to which Arcadia and Achaia were exposed, as long as Psophis served as a secure place of arms[b] to the Eleians; and, on the other hand, how convenient it would be to the Arcadians and their allies, as a

---

[a] τῇ πρὸς ἄρκτον βουνὸς ἐρυμνὸς ἐπίκειται, τετειχισμένος, ἄκρας εὐφυοῦς καὶ πραγματικῆς λαμβάνων τάξιν.

[b] πολεμητήριον ἀσφαλὲς.

post from whence to undertake expeditions[a] into the Eleia, resolved upon attempting to take it. Having ordered his men, therefore, to breakfast[b] at daylight, he crossed the bridge over the Erymanthus without opposition, and prepared for an escalade in three different parts of the town. Euripidas and the garrison, little imagining that Philip would long remain in his position before the town in a winter season of uncommon severity, and still less that he would assault so strong a place, began to suspect some treachery within; finding, however, no evidence of it, they made a gallant defence for some time upon the walls, where many of the Macedonians were thrown down from the ladders, while the Eleian mercenaries sallied from a gate in the upper part of the town. But the garrison having been unprepared, there was a deficiency of javelins and other necessaries: after a short time, the assailants prevailed on all sides, and the Cretans in the king's service having repulsed the sortie of the Eleian mercenaries, and put them to flight, followed them through the upper gate into the town. Euripidas and the whole garrison, as well as the Psophidii, with their wives and children, then retreated into the citadel: the Macedonians took possession of the town, and

---

[a] ὁρμητήριον εὔκαιρον. [b] ἀριστοποιεῖσθαι.

plundered the private houses; and those in the citadel, finding there was a scarcity of provisions, were soon content to accept of the favourable terms which Philip offered. Euripidas was permitted to retire in safety into Ætolia, the city was given up to Aratus and the Achaians, and the king, after having been detained a few days by the snow, marched to Lasion and Olympia."

The bridge over the Erymanthus was very probably in the same position occupied by the present bridge, as in general the communications through the country would be the same in all ages. After crossing the bridge, the greater part of the Macedonians seem to have moved to the right, and to have thus occupied all the narrow space between the walls and the river, after which they fixed the ladders in three places. The Cretans we may suppose to have been on the right of Philip's position on the mountain, and the Eleians to have issued from the north-eastern extremity of the town, at the double fortification which I have mentioned, where undoubtedly there was a gate; the Cretans, having repulsed the Eleians, entered by the same gate at which the latter issued, and joined the Macedonians in the city. Although Polybius speaks ambiguously of the citadel in the former part of his narrative, favouring the opinion, that there was not any regular Acropolis, the latter part seems to indicate that there must have been some interior inclosure on the summit of the hill, though I was unable to trace the plan of it.

Pausanias arrives at Psophis from Caphyæ, and proceeds from thence to Thelpusa[a]. The former of these two routes I crossed last year, on the 27th of May, near Strézova, in my way from the *Thelpusia* to the *Cleitoria*. The road from *Psophis* to *Caphyæ* may be traced from Tripótamo by the valley of Lópesi to the sources of the south-eastern of the three rivers of Tripótamo, from whence it descends a tributary of the *Arcadian Ladon*, which I crossed at half an hour to the northward of Strézova in the plain called Paleá Katúna and Kúvelo. About midway between Tripótamo and Paleá Katúna there are said to be remains of an ancient fortress near the sources of the two streams just mentioned, which flow exactly in opposite directions. These ruins may be those of Paus, for the route from Caphyæ to Psophis is described by Pausanias as "having led from Caphyæ to the source of the river Tragus at Rheunus, fifty stades beyond which it crossed the Ladon, and then entered a forest of oaks called Soron; from whence, having passed through Argea-

[a] Pausan. Arcad. c. 23.

thæ, Lycuntes, and Scotane, it arrived at Paus, a ruined town situated at the end of the forest [a], not far from Seiræ, which was the boundary of the Cleitorii and Psophidii, and distant thirty stades from Psophis." Now this latter distance will carry us exactly to the division of waters between the two rivers of Lópesi and Paleá Katúna, a very natural position for a territorial separation, and to which the ancient name Seiræ, or the Chains, was allusive. It is to be inferred from the preceding passage, that in the time of Pausanias the valley of Paleá Katúna and adjacent hills were covered with the forest Soron, and that it extended nearly, if not quite, to the right bank of the Ladon. "The forest Soron", adds Pausanias, "contains, like the other woods of Arcadia, bears, wild hogs, and tortoises, which last are so large that lyres may be made from them as large as those made from the Indian tortoise." Some small remains of the forest I remarked on the 27th May last, at Paleá Katúna, near the banks of the stream above mentioned, which flows through that valley to the Ladon, and which has not been named by Pausanias.

The road from Psophis to Thelpusa is thus described by Pausanias [b]: "In the way from

---

[a] Σόρωνος πρὸς τοῖς πέρασιν ἔστι Πάου κώμης ἐρείπια.

[b] Pausan. Arcad. c. 25.

Psophis to Thelpusa there is a place called Tropæa to the left of the Ladon [a]. Adjoining to Tropæa is the grove Artemisium, in which are ancient letters engraved upon a column, marking the boundaries of the Psophidii towards the Thelpusia. Within the latter territory is the river called Arsen, having crossed which, and proceeded twenty-five stades, you will arrive at the ruins of the town [b] Caus, and a temple of Æsculapius Causius, situated on the road-side. About forty stades from this temple is the city, which is said to have received its name from the nymph Thelpusa, daughter of Ladon."

As it is manifest from this description that the latter part of the road from Psophis to Thelpusa led along the left side of the Ladon, it follows that in the former part it traversed the ridges which separate the Erymanthus from the Ladon, and that it then crossed the Ladon, although Pausanias has not mentioned the latter circumstance. Seventy stades seem to be as little as the words of Pausanias will allow for the road distance between Tropæa and Thelpusa, but it could not well have been much more, since in that case the former part of the road would not have crossed from Psophis to the Ladon by the shortest line, as it may be presumed to have done.

[a] ἐν ἀριστερᾷ τοῦ Λάδωνος.   [b] κώμης.

Leaving the eastern end of the ruins of *Psophis* at 1.23, I follow up the valley of the *Erymanthus*; it is chiefly grown with maize: fifteen or twenty minutes beyond *Psophis*, we have the small village of Khósova in a lofty situation on the left; at 2, cross a stream coming from a valley on the left, in which stands the Akhúria[a] of Livárzi on a height above the right bank of a stream which unites with the *Erymanthus* immediately below the place where we cross it. Livárzi[b] itself is situated in a ravine in the higher part of the mountain: all the valley hereabout is grown with vines and maize, principally the former. Advancing, we have at 2¼ the Lekhurítika Kalývia, or Akhúria, at the foot of the hill on the left; the village of Lekhúri[c] is in the upper mountain and not in sight; the Kalývia is surrounded with large vineyards. At 2.44 cross a small stream coming from the village of Vamighiáni, which is situated at the head of a valley on the left, nearly in a line with the part of the mountains in which are the sources of the *Aroanius*.

We now turn to the right in the direction of Anastásova, another village situated like the last mentioned, and from whence also flows a

[a] τὰ Ἀχούρια. — A word nearly synonymous with Kalývia, and signifying a dependent hamlet for the convenience of agriculture; literally, straw built huts,—from Ἄχιρα.
[b] Λιβάρζη. [c] Λεχούρη.

small branch of the *Erymanthus*, which we cross, at 2.47, at some mills, just above its junction with the main stream. The mountains on our left, from above *Psophis*, as far as the summit beyond the sources of the river of Anastásova, I conceive to be the true Mount *Erymanthus*, since the river has all its different feeders in that ridge, with the exception of the stream of Sopotó.

According to Pausanias, the Erymanthus originated in Mount Lampeia, which he describes as a part of Mount Erymanthus[a]. From this circumstance, combined with the name Lampeia, which implies a snowy peak, I should judge that it was properly the highest summit of the range of mountains just alluded to, which I have been following in a parallel direction, though it was undoubtedly often confounded with the whole ridge. Such, upon a comparison of several passages in Strabo, already referred to, appears to have been the idea which the geographer had of Lampeia[b], that is to say, that it was a mountain of Arcadia bordering northward upon Pholoe and eastward upon Scollis, Strabo by the latter name intending all the north-western part of the mountainous region now

[a] ἔχει τὰς πηγὰς ὁ Ἐρύμανθος ἐν ὄρει Λαμπείᾳ· τὸ δὲ ὄρος τοῦτο ἱερὸν εἶναι Πανὸς λέγεται· εἴη δ' ἂν τοῦ ὄρους τοῦ Ἐρυμάνθου μοῖρα ἡ Λάμπεια.—Pausan. Arcad. c. 24.

[b] Strabo, pp. 336. 338. 341. 357.

known collectively by the name 'Olono. In other words, he applied the name Lampeia to all the north-eastern side of these mountains. Upon the whole, therefore, it would appear, from all I have said regarding their several ancient denominations, that the southern part, or that which gave rise to the Peneius and its branch, the Ladon, was Pholoe; that the northeastern, in which the Erymanthus originated, was Erymanthus or Lampeia; and that the north-western, in which were the sources of the Peirus and Selinus, was Olenus. I conceive, however, that there must also have been some specific name for Astrá which has not reached us, as there probably was likewise for some others of the more remarkable peaks.

We now leave the direction of Anastásova, and turning again to the right, follow the right bank of the branch of the *Erymanthus*, rising at Sopotó, until, turning to the left, we soon afterwards ascend to some mills, and leave the small village of Agrídhi on the slope of the right hand mountain at 3.10. There are other huts belonging to the same village on the slope of the opposite mountain. Continue along the valley, which is grown with arabosíti and vines, and arrive at its extremity at 3.30. Here stands Sopotó on the lower slopes of a lofty hill, of which the summit is tipt with snow. A torrent runs through the town, and is joined in the plain, a quarter of an hour below, by a copious source from the foot of the mountain to our left. The place consists of about 160 houses, scattered over the slopes like Dhivri, not occupying so large a space as that town, but having the advantage of standing among gardens, in which cherries abound and very large walnut trees: the dhekatía is purchased by Asimáki of Kalávryta, whose worse than Turkish oppression obliges the people to leave the place, so that many houses are empty. We left a large monastery of the Panaghía, pleasantly situated on the side of the right-hand mountain, half a mile before we arrived at the lower extremity of the town.

March 1.—The high ridge above Sopotó is called Tartári. On its northern peak, which is the highest, there is a castle, but I believe not Hellenic. I set out this morning from my konak at the southern end of Sopotó, and having passed through its whole extent, quit the extremity at $9\frac{1}{4}$, and then ascend the steep ridges at the back of the town, to the left of the great height of Tartári. At 10, arrive at the summit of the ridge in the midst of a violent garbino attended with hail and rain; descend through woods of small oaks and underwood, and arrive, at 10.35, at Mostítza, a small village at the head of a valley watered by a torrent which joins another from a village called Klítora[a], similarly situated to the southward; the junction is at an opening which is common to both valleys. Mostítza, like Sopotó, is dispersed amidst gardens and fruit trees. Leaving this place, at 11, we descend the valley and arrive at Kastéli at 11.25: below this place there is a copious spring which flows to the rivulet of Mostítza. At Kastéli are only two families living amidst many ruined houses. The remains of another village of the same name occupy a high situation on the hills on the northern side of the valley. Forming an equilateral triangle with the two, and overlooking the valley which I crossed last year, May 27, in coming from Strézova to Karnési, there is a lofty peaked hill, on which stand a castle, built of small stones, and some ruined houses. Leaving Kastéli at 12.20, I ride up to this peak, and after remaining there five minutes proceed to Karnési, where I arrive at 2, the road leading over the hills in a north-eastern direction, parallel with the course of the river, which is formed of the branches from Klítora and Mostítza. Karnési stands on the right side of the ravine of a third river, which rising in the plain of Sudhená joins the former in the plain below Karnési, where the most conspicu-

[a] Κλείτορας.

ous object, as I remarked on my former visit to Karnési, is a village upon a small round height, called the Mazeítika Kalývia, or Huts of Mázi,—Mázi itself is a large village on the side of Mount Khelmós.

March 2.—I send my baggage by the Tripolitzá road to the khan of Tara, and visit the ruins of *Cleitor*, called Paleópoli, which bear s. 17° E. by compass from Karnési. Set out from that village at 8.40, and descend the hill, leaving on the right a peaked summit bearing a few holley-oaks, which forms the last fall of the Karnési mountain. Towards the foot of the hill, at 9, I see some squared stones on the left of the road, and, at 9.7, the lower pieces of some plain columns standing in their places. At 9.11, arrive at a low ridge which rises from the left bank of the river of Klítora, about a quarter of a mile above its junction with the torrent from Karnési. Along the summit of the hill are some remains of the walls of Cleitor.

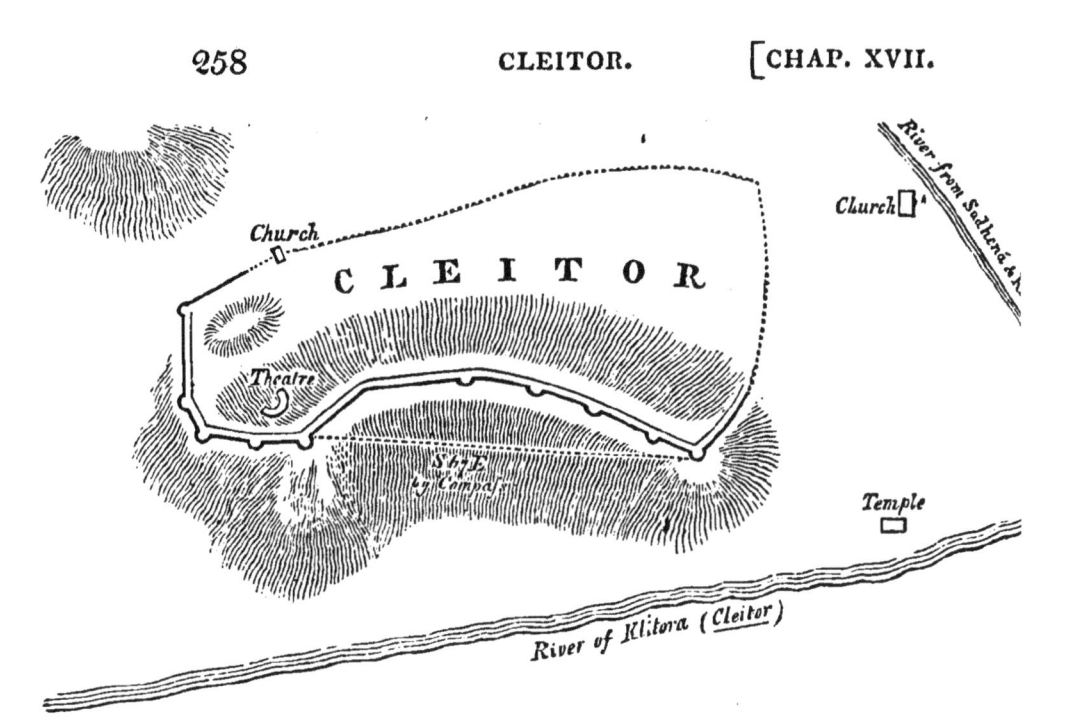

The river was anciently known by the same name as the town, and is properly called by Statius the Rapid Clitor [a]. Vestiges of the fortifications of Cleitor are seen likewise in the plain towards Karnési; where the direction of the walls seems to have been nearly parallel to that of the hill; it may be judged from what remains, that the entire inclosure was less than a mile in circumference, and of a quadrilateral form, but much longer from east to west than from north to south. Beyond the traceable inclosure, however, there appear to have been many buildings, for the whole cultivated plain included between the river of Klítora and the river of Karnési, and between the ancient site and the peak which I mentioned

[a] Stat. Theb. l. 4. v. 289.

as being on my right, descending from Karnési, is covered with stones and pottery, mixed with quadrangular blocks and remains of columns. At a ruined church, under a large oak, towards the river of Karnési, I find some pieces of Doric columns, of which the flutings are two inches and a half; others of the same size are seen also in several parts of the ruins, particularly in the remains of a church at their southern extremity towards the aforesaid hill, on the way to Karnési. I find also a ruined church between the eastern extremity of the hill of *Cleitor* and the junction of the two streams, on the left bank of the river of Klítora, which appeared to have been an ancient temple. There are some remains of a small theatre, about the same size as that of Psophis, towards the western end of the hill, fronting westward: many fragments of the seats are scattered on the slope; they have that small ledge in front usually observable on the seats of ancient theatres. The slope has now almost lost its theatric shape. The town walls are chiefly apparent along the crest of the height; here a few courses remain in several parts both of the walls and of the towers, which are all circular; their gorge is about twenty-six feet, the thickness of the curtains thirteen feet and a half. Towards the western end the wall descends from the ridge, which is there highest, and at the second tower forms a right angle inclosing the theatre, a little beyond which the inclosure is but just traceable through the remainder of its circuit.

All that Pausanias says of Cleitor is as follows[a]: "The city takes its name from a son of Azan. It is situated in a plain surrounded by mountains, not high. The most remarkable temples are those of Ceres, Æsculapius, and Lucina. The Cleitorii have also a temple of the Dioscuri, whom they call the Great Gods: it is four stades distant from the city, and contains brazen statues of the deities. On the summit of a mountain, about thirty stades distant from the city, there is a temple of Minerva Coria containing a statue of the goddess." If the latter distance be correct, the temple of Coria must have been either on Mount Tzipáti[b], as the summit is called which rises from the left bank of the torrent of Karnési, north-eastward of that village, or of the peak above Mamalúka and the monastery of St. Athanasius, a little to the left of which I descended last year, coming from Strézova to Karnési, for neither Mount Karmíri, as the summit is called which rises from the right bank of the river *Cleitor* opposite to the *city*, nor the mountain of Karnési,

[a] Pausan. Arcad. c. 21.   [b] Τζηπάτι.

are more than a third of the distance mentioned by Pausanias, at least in a direct line. As Pausanias has given no other indication of the situation of the temple of the Dioscuri, than its distance from the city, there is no clue to a search for its remains. Karnési sounds like a corruption of Carnasium, as if a temple of Apollo Carneius, a favourite deity in the Peloponnesus, had once given name to a village standing upon this site. I have already shewn that the ancient name Cleitor, although still preserved, is no longer attached to the ruins of the city, which are called Paleópoli, but is now applied in the usual Romaic form, taken from the accusative case[a], to a village situated three miles from the place to which the name formerly belonged. It would seem, that the river having preserved its name after the city had ceased to exist, at length gave that name to a village built at its sources. At 10.35, leaving the ruins, I cross the river of Karnési, and a little beyond it observe, in the road, some ancient sepulchres of the simplest kind, that is to say, four slabs of stone set edgewise in the earth. Pausanias has not noticed the river of Karnési; it may possibly have been called Luseus or Lusiates, as it rises in the district of Lusi, and flows from thence into the Cleitoria.

[a] Κλείτορας, or στὸν Κλείτορα.

On the side of Mount Tzipáti, on our left, I perceive the small village of Stukáni. At 10.55 arrive at the Mazeítika Kalývia standing on an insulated height in the plain of Katzána, or Katzánes, as this angle of the valley is called, and which probably once contained a village of that name. It is traversed by a stream called the river of Katzána, descending from the village of Pladitéri [a], but of which the highest sources are in Mount Khelmós, which overtops all the surrounding summits. The cultivable level on the banks of the Katzánes penetrates for an hour's distance between the mountains, almost as far as Pladitéri. Half an hour higher than the latter is Mázi, another large village situated in a gorge just under the highest part of Khelmós, and now surrounded and deeply covered with snow. Mázi owns the greater part of the plain of Katzánes, which is chiefly grown with kalambókki, the marshy nature of the bottom, and the facility of irrigation being well adapted to the cultivation of that grain. There are also some vineyards; the rest of the plain belongs to Emír Agá, a Turk of Kalávryta, and consists of corn-land and pasture. After a halt of five minutes I quit the Kalývia of Mázi, and

---

[a] Πλαντητέρι, perhaps more properly Πλατυτέρη, and so called because the ground on that part of the mountain is more level than elsewhere.

at 11.9 cross the river Katzánes, which is nearly of the same size as the *Cleitor*, by a curious bridge, not uncommon over the rapid torrents of *Arcadia*: a great branch of a plane tree, which happens to stretch itself obliquely more than half across the river, forms the centre, and all the support, of the bridge. From this branch to either bank are laid large logs, and over them branches and boughs, and on the top of all earth and sometimes stones. I saw a bridge of this kind at *Psophis*, others over the *Neda* in *Messenia*. The river of Katzánes joins the *Cleitor* a little below the Kalývia of Mázi, at a distance from the ruins of *Cleitor*, exactly answering to the seven stades which Pausanias places between that city and the junction of the river *Cleitor* with the *Aroanius*[a]. It appears, therefore, that the river of Katzánes is the ancient Aroanius; but though I think this point is determined, I was not equally successful in verifying the existence of the musical trout, which, according to my excellent but rather credulous Grecian guide, were particularly found in this part of the Aroanius. "Among other fish found in the Aroanius," says Pausanias, "are trout[b], which are said to utter a note not unlike that of the thrush[c]. I have seen",

[a] Pausan. Arcad. c. 21.   [b] ποικιλίαι.   [c] κίχλῃ τῇ ὄρνιθι εἰκός.

he adds, "this kind of fish after it has been caught, but never heard sounds issue from any, even though I remained (for that purpose) on the banks of the Aroanius until the setting of the sun, when the fish is said to be most vocal."[a]

Soon after passing the Katzána, or *Aroanius*, we cross another little stream, and reach the foot of the mountain of Arákhova, so called from a village which no longer exists. Its highest peak is called Turtována, which I take also to have been the name of a village. Here we fall into the road from Tripolitzá to Kalávryta, which, after passing from hence up the vale and gorge of the Katzána, then crosses over a deep neck or hollow between Khelmós and Tzipáti, follows the side of Khelmós to Sudhená, then crosses the mountain at the back of that village, and thus descends upon Kalávryta. A great fall of rain yesterday evening has made

---

[a] The same fable is noticed by Pliny, (H. N. l. 9. c. 19,) who agrees with Pausanias as to the place, (circa Clitorim,) but improperly calls the fish exocœtus or adonis, which was a sea-fish. Athenæus (l. 8. c. 1, 2.) cites three authors in support of the vocal fish of Arcadia, namely, Mnaseas of Patræ, Clearchus the Peripatetic, and Philostephanus of Cyrene. The last only mentions the ποικιλία, or trout, as being the particular fish. In regard to the river, they all differ from Pausanias, but only inasmuch as Philostephanus calls it the Ladon, Mnaseas the Cleitor, and Clearchus the Pheneatic Aroanius, which were all tributaries of the same stream.

the valley of the *Aroanius* a marsh; on the mountains it was snow as low down as Karnési. We continue to follow the valley skirting the foot of the hills on the left. At 11.40 a small stream, which we crossed soon after passing the Katzána, joins that river—a monastery is on the side of the opposite mountain. The valley now becomes narrower, and corresponds exactly with the words of Pausanias, who describes the road which led from the sources of the Ladon to Cleitor as passing along the narrow valley of the Aroanius [a]. Hence we derive an additional evidence that the river of Katzána is the *Aroanius,* as well as a strong presumption that Mount Khelmós, in which this river has its sources, formed, together with the adjacent summits, the mountains called " the Aroanian," [b] though it certainly seems singular that Khelmós, which is very nearly equal in height to Zýria and 'Olono, should not have had some individual and more precise denomination.

Arabosíti grows in the valley, and the banks of the river are shaded with planes. At 11.46 a road on the left ascends to Krenófyta [c], a village on the side of the mountain. At 1, after having lost half an hour in searching for a road

---

[a] ἡ ὁδός ἐστιν αὐλὼν στενὸς παρὰ τὸν Ἀροάνιον ποταμόν.
[b] τὰ ὄρη καλούμενα Ἀροάνια.
[c] Κρενόφυτα.

through the mud of the valley, and the rocks on the left hand side of it, we cross a bridge over the Lykureíko, or river of Lykúria, which descends through a ravine on the left, into a valley forming a *bay* on the northern side of the vale of the *Aroanius*.

The Lykureíko issues in a single body of water at no great distance above the place where we cross it: not far from the summit of the ridge above the sources stands the kefalokhóri called Lykúria. A road across the ridge to Foniá leaves Lykúria on the left. The name of Lykúria, and the issue of the river from an inferior part of the same mountain on which Lykúria stands, prove the river to be the ancient Ladon, the sources of which, according to the information received by Pausanias, were the emissory of the river of Pheneus[a]. Here again, therefore, we have another instance of the exactitude of this diligent traveller, and a confirmation of the several geographical points already alluded to, which, I think, are thus ascertained beyond a doubt.

Pausanias expresses himself as follows: "Proceeding about fifty stades from Lycuria, you will arrive at the sources of the Ladon. I have heard that the water of the lake in the Pheneatice, after passing through caverns in the moun-

[a] Pausan. Arcad. c. 20.

tain[a], here reappears and forms the fountain of the Ladon, but I cannot speak of this positively[b]. The Ladon excels all the rivers of Greece in the beauty of its waters, but it is chiefly celebrated on account of Daphne, and what the poets have sung concerning her. The city of the Cleitorii is sixty stades distant from the sources of the Ladon. The road thither leads along a narrow valley by the river Aroanius, and near the city of the Cleitorii crosses the river Cleitor, which joins the Aroanius seven stades from the city." The only part of this description which appears to me not to be quite correct, is the distance from Lykúria to the sources of the *Ladon*, and from the latter to *Cleitor*, the former of which I think must be less than the fifty stades of Pausanias, and the latter greater. But the other points of conformity are too strong to allow us to attach much importance to a numeral disagreement which may arise either from the miscalculation of an unmeasured distance, or from a textual error.

Beyond the bridge of the Lykureíko, or *Ladon*, the valley of the united stream takes the direction of that river for a mile, and then passes through a ravine between a projecting point of the left hand mountain, and the foot of

---

[a] κατερχόμενον ἐς τὰ βάραθρα τὰ ἐν τοῖς ὄρεσιν.
[b] οὐκ ἔχω σαφῶς εἰπεῖν.

that on the right. We cross the neck of this point at 1.17, and descend into a wide valley, in which the river of Vitína joins the Lykuréiko; five minutes farther we halt to dine on the bank of the former. In the middle of the valley the united stream is crossed by a bridge, near the village of Tzernotá[a]. Our baggage horses, after having crossed over the mountains in front of Strézova, passed over this bridge, and from thence proceeded to Tara. The *Ladon*, not far below the bridge, turns to the right, and after receiving the river of Katúna, flows to the " Bridge of the Lady "[b], and enters the narrow pass, which I traversed last year on the 26th May, coming from Vyzítza to Strézova. The direction of our route to Tara therefore now quits the course of the *Ladon*, and follows the vale of the river of Vitína. On the height which we crossed before entering the plain of Tzernotá, the ground was covered with small stones and vestiges of buildings, but nothing of decidedly Hellenic antiquity. At the foot of the opposite height are similar remains, just above a mill called Kábato-Mylo; on that side of the river also are the Filćika Kalývia, belonging to Filia[c], a village on this side of Strézova. At 1.55, we set out from our halting place, one-third of a mile above the Kábato mill, and immediately enter a

[a] Τζερνοτά.   [b] Τῆς Κυρᾶς τὸ Γεφύρι.   [c] Φίλια.

narrow pass, where the united river from Tara and Vitína, is closely shut in by the mountains on either side: it is called the Dervéni. At 2, arrive at the bridge of the Dervéni, which my baggage crossed, but which we leave on the right. The single guard who is stationed at the Dervéni accompanies us a quarter of an hour to the extremity of the pass, where the valley widens, and from whence it continues to widen to the Khan of Tara, where we arrive at 3. The valley here is upwards of a mile wide; on the foot of the opposite mountain is a pyrgo and tjiftlík of Arnaút-Oglú, a little beyond which the valley branches towards Vitína, and the sources of that branch of the *Ladon* near the ancient Methydrium. One mile and a half above the Khan, to the north by east, at the foot of a long bare mountain, stands the village of Tara, or Apano Tara, so called to distinguish it from Lower Tara, which is situated near the river. To the right of the mountain of Tara appears Mount Saetá, a high peak covered with firs; it is seen from Tripolitzá: to the right of it passes the road from the Khan of Tara to Foniá, over a *col* between two snowy summits. The Khan stands by the right bank of the river of Tara, at a bridge. The road, after crossing the bridge, branches to Vitína on the right, and to Tripolitzá by Levídhi on the left. The Taréiko, or river of Tara, produces trout and other fish, and is a respectable stream, even in summer, though its sources are not more than two or three miles distant, at the foot of a mountain called Kastaniá, where it issues at once in a plentiful stream from the mountain, being apparently, like the sources of the *Ladon*, the emissory of a Katavóthra, probably that of the lake of *Orchomenus*, which cannot be very distant. In this case, it is evident that the Taréiko is the ancient Tragus, which, according to Pausanias, flowed through a mountain of the Caphyatis, and emerged at a place called Nasi, near which was a village named Rheunus[a]. Tara perhaps is a corruption of Tragus. After receiving the river of Vitína a little below the bridge of Tara, the Taréiko flows to the Dervéni, and between that pass and the bridge of Tzernotá is united with the Lykuréiko, or *Ladon*. The Taréiko being, as Pausanias describes the Tragus, a perennial stream, is very useful in irrigating the kalambókki, which grain, in consequence of this convenience, is the principal produce of the plain of Tara. As to the ancient name of the river of Vitína, Pausanias leaves us in doubt. It has been seen that he mentions

[a] κατερχόμενον δὲ ἐς χάσμα γῆς ἄνεισιν αὖθις παρὰ Νάσους καλουμένας· τὸ δὲ χωρίον ἔνθα ἄνεισιν ὀνομάζεται Ῥεῦνος· ἀνατεί- λαντος δὲ ἐνταῦθα, τὸ ὕδωρ παρέχεται ποταμὸν ἀέννaον Τράγον. Pausan. Arcad. c. 23.

two rivers as uniting at Methydrium, named the Mylaon and Molottus (or Malœtas), but which of these names prevailed below the junction, or whether there was any other appellation for the united river, he has not informed us.

Having now seen the greater part of the course of the *Ladon*[a], I shall here compare with the actual topography the description by Pausanias of that portion of its valley to which I have not already adverted, namely, the part above Thelpusa. Pausanias[b] remarks, that "the water of the Ladon had its origin in the Cleitoria, at the place called Pegæ, or the Sources; that it flowed by Leucasium and Mesoboa, and through the Nasi to Oryx, and the place called Alus; and that from thence it descended to Thaliades, and to the temple of Ceres Eleusinia. This temple", he adds, " is within the boundaries of the Thelpusii : it contains statues, not less than seven feet high, of Ceres, Proserpine, and Bacchus, all made of stone. Below the temple of Ceres Eleusinia the Ladon passes the city Thelpusa, which stands on its left bank on (or at) a lofty hill."[c]

The first difficulty in this passage is in the name Nasi, which cannot be the same place as the Nasi where the Tragus issued from the

---

[a] Vide Chapter XIV.   [b] Pausan. Arcad. c. 25.
[c] ἐπὶ λόφου μεγάλου.

mountain of Caphyæ; since there was a distance, as Pausanias remarks, and as my route confirms, of fifty stades between the sources of the Tragus and the Ladon. But in fact the word Nasi[a] was not uncommonly applied by the Greeks to meadows intersected by rivers or channels of water, and the name belonged probably not only to the vicinity of the sources of the *Tragus*, but also to the valley of Tzernotá, as far as the Stená or Straits, through which the *Ladon* passes from thence to the valley of Podhogorá, and "the Lady's Bridge." It is not improbable that *Leucasium* and *Mesoboa* were the two places of which I remarked some vestiges at the upper Stená, or those which are *above* the plain of Tzernotá near Kábato Mylo. As to the three remaining places situated *above* the limits of the *Thelpusia;* those boundaries having been about seventy stades above *Thelpusa*, it will follow, on referring to the distances in my route of the 26th of May last, that the vale of Syriámu on the right of the *Ladon* is the lowest position on the descent of the river, at which we can place *Thaliades*. In this case, the valley northward of Syriamáki, in which a stream joins the *Ladon*, may have been the district of *Alus*, and *Oryx* may have occupied the vale of Podhogorá. And this arrangement of the places is the more

[a] Doric for νῆσοι, islands.

probable, as beyond the Stená of the *Ladon*, which are to the northward of Podhogorá, the river was crossed by the road from *Caphyæ* to *Psophis*, or the modern route from Tara to Tripótamo, upon which was the wood *Soron*, and the places in it named by Pausanias. It happens unfortunately for the geography of this part of Arcadia, that Pausanias has not noticed either the river of Paleá Katúna, or that which joins the *Ladon* near Syriamáki. Nor has he afforded us any assistance in combining his description of the course of the Ladon with his route from Psophis to Thelpusa, not having repeated a single name in the one that he mentions in the other, though the road from Psophis, after crossing the Ladon, could not have been distant from the left bank of the river all the way from that crossing to Thelpusa; whence it follows that the two lines for seven or eight miles must have coincided, or very nearly so. This anxiety to avoid repetition makes it often difficult to follow Pausanias; but though the "brevis esse laboro, obscurus fio" seems often to apply to him, it must be remembered, that his brevity had not the same effect when the names were in use, and the places in existence.

March 3.—A Turk of Arta, who is appointed kadý at Mistrá, lodged in the khan last night. He gives me the news of *Epirus*, of which the most remarkable event is, the secession or flight of the metropolitan bishop of Arta, Ignatius, who having been sent by Alý Pashá to Corfú, had not returned from thence, as he was ordered to do, in consequence of which Alý has closed the mitrópoli at Arta. At 7.55, leave the khan, and crossing the bridge pursue the direct road to Tripolitzá till 8.23, when, turning out of it to the right, I cross the river of Vitína just before arriving at a height, on which are the ruins of a large building of Frank construction, with cisterns and vaulted subterraneous apartments: it is called Anghelό-kastro. A little higher up the river, on the opposite side, there is a high peaked hill, the lower roots of which meet those of the mountain of Agrídhi, the river passing between them through a rocky gorge. The snow-capt summit above Maghulianá appears through the opening; Vitína is about half way thither, three hours distant from the khan of Tara. On a summit on this side of the village of Maghulianá there is said to be a castle similar to Anghelό-kastro, and called Arghyrό-kastro. Return into the direct road at 9.6, a quarter of an hour's distance beyond the spot where I left it. We now ascend the roots of the mountain called Kastaniá, and at 9.40 begin to pass between it and the mountain of Alonístena, which is on our right. The latter is much higher than Kastaniá, and, like the other peaked summits of the *Mænalian* range, is covered with firs, and deeply at present with snow. The snow lies also in our pass. The road is good and level. At 10.5, at a fountain in the road, the small village of Bazeníko[a] is half a mile on the right, standing at the foot of the Mænalian range, and now covered with snow. From hence I look down to the left, through an opening in the hills, upon the plain and lake of Khotúsa; the village of that name is seen three miles distant on the northern side of the lake. At Khotúsa are some remains which mark the site of *Caphyæ*: on the side of the lake just below Bazeníko, are katavóthra, of which the source of the Taréiko is clearly the emissory. At 10.30, arrive at the end of the pass, and enter the plain of Levídhi: the direct road to Tripolitzá crosses the plain diagonally, and then passes over low heights at the foot of Mount Armeniá into the plain of *Mantineia*. We turn from this route to the right, and ride along the side of the great mountain of Alonístena, ascending a little. At

[a] I take this to be the same place called Παζινίκη by Chalcocondylas, who mentions it as having successfully resisted Mahomet the Second in his march through the Moréa in 1458. The Sultan went from Corinth through the Phliasia into the Mantinice, then, after attempting Pazeníki, into the Tegeatis, beyond which he did not penetrate that year.

11.13 arrive at Levídhi[a], a large village which is situated on the slope of the mountain, overlooking the southern end of the plain, and is crowned with a round height, upon which stands a large church. At the opposite corner of the plain is Kalpáki, a small village at the foot of a detached height, on which are Hellenic foundations, undoubtedly the ruins of *Orchomenus*. Beyond Kalpáki the waters of the plain find their way into the lake, through a narrow opening between the hill of Orchomenus and a rocky mountain which there closes the plain. A little to the right of the village there is an artificial canal or trench, probably of very ancient date, for the purpose of conveying all the superfluous waters of the plain to the ravine. A small torrent, which descends on the right of the village of Levídhi, as well as another coming from within the pass of Bazeníko, flow to the canal; but, notwithstanding this drainage, the plain is now little better than a marsh in the middle, where it is chiefly occupied by vineyards, from which a wine is made, resembling small beer in colour, strength, and even taste, as far as the aromatic bitter of the hop flower can be imitated by the resin of the pine tree. There are two valleys branching from the plain of Levídhi, and extending quite to the foot of

[a] Λιβίδι.

Mount Armeniá: in the northernmost of these stands the village of Bútia. Kandíli is situated in a small vale branching eastward from the lower plain, which contains the lake of *Orchomenus* and the *Caphyatice*. On the northern side of the vale of Kandíli rises Mount Kandíli, a lofty summit, between which and Mount Saetá leads the road to Foniá (*Pheneus*). Saetá is the most lofty of the range of mountains, which are in face of Levídhi, to the northward and eastward; they are all a part of the chain which extends from Mount Khelmós, or the *Aroania*, and connects that great summit with *Artemisium, Parthenium,* and *Parnon*. Mount Saetá is covered with firs. The mountain between the plain of Levídhi and Alonístena, or, to speak by the ancient nomenclature, that part of the *Mænalian* range which separates the *Orchomenia* from the valleys of *Helisson* and *Methydrium*, is clothed also with large forests of the same trees; the road across this ridge from Levídhi to Alonístena is now impracticable on account of the snow. The Levidhiótes call the mountain of Alonístena 'Aios Elias, from a ruined church, dedicated to that saint, which stands upon or near the summit.

I am detained all day at Levídhi by a heavy fall of snow, which, before the evening, has covered the ground to half a foot in depth, although the village is not much elevated above the plain, nor in a more lofty situation than Tripolitzá. It contains about 100 families who complain bitterly of their misery, and the extortions to which they are exposed by their position on one of the chief roads of the Moréa, in consequence of which they are obliged to maintain Tartars, soldiers, great Turks with their suites, in short, all persons who travel with the post. Their vicinity to the capital is another misfortune. The annual khartí[a], or acquittance of all direct taxes, to each head of a family is 100 piastres.

In the afternoon I visit an old church twenty minutes below the village on the left bank of the torrent of Levídhi, and find in it two or three pieces of very handsome Doric columns, of which the flutings are three inches and one-sixth in the chord; also some wrought stones, and among them one with two of its sides cut obliquely. In a small ruined chapel close by, there is another fragment of a Doric column, two feet in diameter, with twenty flutings, as usual in that order.

March 4.—At 8½ quit Levídhi, and, instead of descending into the plain, pass between the great *Mænalian* ridge and an insulated round

---

[a] χαρτὶ.

hill which lies on the south-eastern side of the village; the pass is narrow, but soon becomes wider, and then communicates again with the plain by a passage on the southern side of the insulated hill: we leave this opening to the left, and continue to follow the same direction as before, along a narrow elevated valley included between the Mænalian summits and a subordinate parallel range which separates the valley from the northern end of the plain of *Mantineia*. At 9.45, in an opening on the left leading into the plain of Mantineia, stands a small village and another called Simiádhes, a little farther down. Kakúri is opposite to it at the foot of Mount Armeniá, just above a low height which projects into the extremity of the *Mantinic* plain. Having passed this opening, we continue to follow the valley until we come to another similar branch of the *Mantinic* plain, through which we descend into the plain nearly opposite to the ruins of Mantineia at Paleópoli. Kapsá, where we arrive at 10.25, is a village of forty houses standing on the left hand side of the descent. All the adjacent part of the plain is covered with vineyards, interspersed with huts and small platforms constructed of stone, with a coating of stucco. The wine, as at Dhesfína in *Phocis*, is made on the spot by persons who tread the grapes with their feet in the upper part of these platforms; the liquor runs through a hole into a cistern below, from whence it is carried in skins to Tripolitzá. It is a small light-coloured wine, to which resin is added, and often lime. The labourers in the vineyards have fifty paras a day, with wine and bread.

Yesterday afternoon and during the night the snow fell in such quantities as to cover all the plains and adjacent mountains, and the country exhibited this morning as fine a snow scene as Norway could supply. As the day advanced and the sun appeared, the snow melted rapidly, but the sky was soon overcast again, and the snow began to fall.

At 11.18 we cross a bridge over a small stream flowing from left to right, and terminating in a katavóthra at the foot of the hill which borders the vale of Kapsá on the south. This stream I take to be the Ophis, which Agesipolis turned against the walls of Mantineia. It is joined towards Paleópoli by the two united rivulets which now encircle the ancient walls, and which formed a wet ditch to the city. The ruins were on a line with us to the left at the bridge.

It appears, from the description by Pausanias of the road from Mantineia to Methydrium, that the vale of Kapsá is the *plain of Alcimedon*.

His words are these [a]. "The road from Mantineia to Methydrium, once an Arcadian city, but now a town [b] of the Megalopolitæ, leads, at the end of thirty stades, to a plain named Alcimedon. Above this plain rises the mountain Ostracine, which contains a cavern, once the dwelling of the hero Alcimedon, and a fountain called Cissa. Forty stades beyond the fountain is the place named Petrosaca, on the borders of the Megalopolitæ and Mantinenses." It is evident from the map, that the vale of Kapsá being exactly in a line between *Mantineia* and *Methydrium*, the ancient road must have ascended that valley, and then crossed the *Mænalian* ridge; the distance of Kapsá from Paleópoli accords exactly with the thirty stades of Pausanias. The hill which rises at the back of Kapsá seems therefore to be the *Ostracine;* it is separated from the *Mænalian* ridge by the pass which leads to Levídhi, and is therefore an insulated height, which renders it so much the more likely to have had a specific name. Petrosaca we may suppose to have been on the crest of the Mænalium, that being the natural boundary of the two districts.

At 11.40 we reach the end of the vineyards of the plain of Paleópoli, and soon after cross the *Scope*, which, as I have before remarked, is

[a] Pausan. Arcad. c. 12. [b] κώμην.

the projecting point of the *Mænalian* range, separating the plain of Tripolitzá from that of Paleópoli; then, turning a little to the right, along the foot of the mountain, arrive at a hamlet of four houses, called Bedéni. There is another larger village of the same name nearer to Tripolitzá. Having halted half an hour at Bedéni, I set out for Tripolitzá, and arrive there in an hour and ten minutes, without baggage.

The preceding journey from Patra to Tripolitzá has been performed with Agoyatic horses of the former place, but must be reckoned, making the necessary deduction in the mountainous roads, at the rate of the walk of my own horse, which I measured repeatedly in the plain of Athens; the last day has been rather slower, on account of the snow and bad roads.

One hundred and twenty heads of thieves taken by the Pashá have been sent to Constantinople. The thieves were dispersed, and taken in detail. The Pashá hopes, by this achievement, to keep himself in place for another year. A bolúk-bashi, with a large body of Albanians whom he sent against the robbers, deserted, and retired to Bardhúnia, where he was well received by Amús Agá. The Pashá has now sent against him 100 men, who are to be joined by 400 at Mistrá. Only 500 soldiers remain in Tripolitzá. I do not think there are more than 2000 in the whole peninsula, at the disposal of the Pashá, that is to say, exclusive of the people of Lalla, Bardhúnia, and Mani. Not long ago the Pashá summoned all the Turkish vóivodas and Greek hodjá-bashis in the Moréa, for the purpose of consulting them on the best mode of proceeding against the robbers. The vóivoda of Gastúni, an Albanian, and brother of the vóivoda of Mesolónghi, whom I met at Patra, neglected the summons for some time; but at length, after repeated orders, he came, and when the Pashá taxed him with his neglect, answered without shewing any signs of humility. Upon this the Pashá seized a small hatchet, (an instrument often worn by the Turks more for ornament than use,) threw the vóivoda on the carpet, and beat him unmercifully with the hatchet, then turned him out of the room without kaúk or slippers, kept him many days in prison, and finished by obliging him to pay a sum of money. He has driven away Sotiráki and the interpreter, two men who for several years have committed with impunity all kinds of oppression on their countrymen. From Sotiráki, who has retired to Livadhía, the Pashá extorted ten purses before he allowed him to go, and as much more from Asimáki of Kalávryta, by pretending that he had received a firmahn for their heads. Papadhópulo has thus gained a triumph over his enemies; the Tripolitziótes ascribe his influence with the Pashá to his eloquence. He has absolute power in 'Aios Petros and Tzakonía, where the Turkish vóivoda is such an acknowledged cypher that he commonly resides at Tripolitzá.

March 10. The mode in which Sotiráki procured a beautiful antique intaglio which I have purchased here, I learn to-day from a Corfiote practitioner of physic, who was the original purchaser of it from a peasant of Langádha. The peasant was carrying it about the streets for sale, suspended by a string, when the Iatrós accidentally met him, and bought it for two piastres. He shewed it to the brother of Sotiráki, who is an archdeacon, and who perceiving the stone to be valuable, informed his brother of it. The latter, as ignorant as the peasant who found it, but whose avarice was excited by the prospect of selling the gem again for a high price, communicated his wishes to the kadý, a poor Turk, who may at any time be displaced by the influence of the hodjá-bashis and other chief Greeks. They soon agreed that a certain baker should swear it was his property, and stolen from him by his servant, who, if necessary, was to confess the fact before the kadý. The affair did not proceed, however, to such a length. The kadý having sent for the Corfiote Iatrós, attempted at first to alarm him by representing that he had bought stolen goods; and at length obtained it from him as a present, the physician being, as he confessed to me, ignorant of its real value. Suspecting Sotiráki to be at the bottom of the affair, he had at first offered him the stone as a present, in order to ingratiate himself with such a leading character; but Sotiráki preferred obtaining it through the kadý to being under any obligation to the Corfiote. Such are the low intrigues that occupy the time and talents of this naturally gifted people.

Conversing with the same Corfiote on the subject of the wine of this plain, he mentioned that he had boiled a quantity of the unfermented juice of the grape, made from the vines of the plain of *Mantineia*, and that it was reduced to a twentieth of the bulk before it was formed into the syrup called petmés.

CHAPTER XVIII.

ARCADIA.

On the description by Pausanias of the eight roads which centered in MEGALOPOLIS, *namely:*—1. From HERÆA to MEGALOPOLIS.—2. From MEGALOPOLIS to MESSENE.—3. To CARNASIUM.—4. To SPARTA.—5. To METHYDRIUM. 6. To MÆNALUS.—7. To PHIGALEIA.—8. To PALLANTIUM *and* TEGEA.

THE more I see of the Peloponnesus, and the more I read its description by Pausanias, so much the more do I regret the shortness of the time that I have it in my power to bestow upon its geography; for as to the difficulties arising from weather, mountains, torrents, robbers, or, what is worst of all, the want of roads and conveyance, I am persuaded, they may all be surmounted by the man who has time enough at his command, with a sufficiency of perseverance. But these are the more necessary, as the Peloponnesus being a country yet unexplored by the geographer or scholar, every feature, position, and object in it which is described, or more frequently merely alluded to by the ancient authors, is yet to be searched for at an expense of time and labour which will not hereafter be required.

Of perseverance, it must with gratitude be admitted, that we have an excellent example in our guide Pausanias, even without omitting the consideration, that, instead of exploring unknown and deserted sites, he was travelling in an ordinary manner, over the roads of a civilized country, from one celebrated place to another, in each of which he found an exegete[a] to assist him in all his researches. So complete, however, were these researches, and so ardent his curiosity, that it requires the most detailed inspection of the country to be assured that one has not overlooked some still existing proof of his accuracy; and this is the more necessary as it often happens, that by the effect of his *declining Greek* style, and of the abrupt manner in which he mentions things allusively, instead of clearly describing them, not unfrequently also in consequence of the corruptions of his text, his meaning is involved in an obscurity which nothing but an exact knowledge of the locality or the discovery of extant remains of antiquity can clear away. I have every day occasion to remark instances in which it is impossible correctly to understand him, or to translate his words, without actually following him through

---

[a] ἐξηγητής.

the country, and examining the spots described, and it is not always that a single visit to a place is sufficient. In *Arcadia*, I particularly lament that I have been unable to trace the steps of the curious traveller in all the routes which radiated from its capital of *Megalopolis*. I shall however here put together his description of them, including, as I have done upon other occasions, a concise enumeration of the monuments and objects of art, which he met with, and adding to it a geographical sketch for the purpose of elucidating his remarks: this, though very far from completing such an inquiry into the comparative geography as I should have wished, may serve at least to give some assistance to future travellers.

The principal object of Pausanias, in the part of his Arcadics relating to Megalopolis and its vicinity, seems to have been that of describing, in a manner admitting of some method and regularity, the position, mythology, and antiquities of all the old Arcadian cities, the remaining inhabitants of which served to people Megalopolis at the time of its foundation, and which, for the most part, were thenceforward quite deserted, or, at least, preserved little more than their sacred edifices and the remains of some of the other public buildings more or less dilapidated. The method he has adopted is that of describing separately each of the routes which led from the *Great City,* with occasional digressions to places in the vicinity of some of the roads. The routes which he describes conducted to Messene, to Carnasium, to Sparta, to Methydrium, to Mænalus, to Phigaleia, to Tegea;—to these may be added, in order to complete the radiation of roads, that by which the Greek traveller arrived at Megalopolis, being the same also by which I approached the site of the Arcadian capital,—namely, the road from Heræa. I shall begin with the last, which, of course, is described by Pausanias, in an inverse direction to that of the others.

1. " In the road", he says[a], " leading from Heræa to Megalopolis occurs Melæneæ, now deserted and overflowed with water. Forty stades above Melæneæ is Buphagium, at the sources of the river Buphagus, near which are the boundaries of the Megalopolitæ and Heræenses[b]. The Buphagus descends into the Alpheius."

" On proceeding[c] from the sources of the Buphagus, occurs the village Maratha[d], and then Gortys, now a town[e], but formerly a city[f]. Here

[a] Pausan. Arcad. c. 26.
[b] In the Prior Eliacs, c. 7, Pausanias says that the course of the Buphagus was the boundary of the Megalopolitis and Heræitis.
[c] Pausan. Arcad. c. 28.
[d] Μάραθα χωρίον.
[e] κώμη.
[f] πόλις.

is a temple of Æsculapius of Pentelic stone, containing statues, by Scopas, of a beardless Æsculapius and of Hygieia: the natives say that Alexander, son of Philip, dedicated the thorax and spear of Æsculapius; there still remain the thorax and the point of the spear. A river passes through Gortys which, towards its fountains, is called Lusius, because Jupiter was washed there when he was born; but those who dwell at a distance from the fountains name it Gortynius from the town: it is the coldest of all rivers, especially in summer. Its fountains are at Theisoa, on the confines of the Methydrienses; the place where it joins the Alpheius is called Rhæteæ. Teuthis, formerly a city, borders upon Theisoa. It contains temples of Venus and Diana, and a statue of Minerva with a purple bandage bound round the thigh[a]. In the road which leads from Gortys to Megalopolis, there occurs a sepulchre of those who were slain in battle against Cleomenes; the Megalopolitæ call it Paræbasium, because Cleomenes violated his covenant with them. Paræbasium is on the borders of a plain about sixty stades in length; the ruins of the city Berenthe are on the right of the road, and the river Berentheates, which, five stades below the city, falls into the Alpheius.

[a] In allusion to a wound she was said to have received from Teuthis, the hero who gave name to the town.

On the opposite side of the Alpheius[a] is the district called Trapezuntia, in which are the ruins of the city Trapezus; descending again from thence towards the Alpheius, there is a place on the left[b] called Bathos, at no great distance from the river: here the ceremony[c] of the Great Goddesses is celebrated every third year. Here also is a fountain called Olympias, which flows only in the alternate years; near it fire issues from the earth. Ten stades from Bathos is Basilis, a city founded by Cypselus, but of which there are now only ruins, and among them a temple of Ceres Eleusinia. Having proceeded from thence, and again crossed the Alpheius[d], you will arrive at Thocnia, now quite deserted, but once a city standing on a height which rises from the bank of the river Aminius. This stream joins the Helisson, and the latter, not far below the junction, unites with the Alpheius. The Helisson rises in a village of the same name, passes from thence through the district of the Dipæenses and the Lycoatis, and after flowing through Megalopolis, joins the Alpheius thirty stades below the city."

The direct road from Heræa to Megalopolis

---

[a] διαβάντων τὸν Ἀλφειόν.
[b] καὶ αὖθις ἐπὶ τὸν Ἀλφειὸν ἐν ἀριστερᾷ καταβαίνοντι ἐκ Τραπεζοῦντος.
[c] τελετήν.
[d] ἐντεῦθεν προϊὼν τὸν Ἀλφειὸν αὖθις διαβήσῃ.

was the great Roman road through the Peloponnesus. The Peutinger Table agrees with Pausanias in shewing that it passed through Melæneæ, and this is all we learn from the table concerning it; in fact it is almost all we learn from Pausanias as to the direct route, for the rest of the preceding extract relates to the places situated on either side of the road, some of which were at a considerable distance from it.

It may be thought perhaps that the modern name, Karítena, is a corruption of *Gortyna,* and consequently that it indicates the site of that ancient town; but if the river of Atzíkolo is the *Gortynius,* which can hardly be doubted, from the remark of Pausanias as to the sources of the Gortynius being near Methydrium, it is difficult to believe that Gortys could have been situated two miles below the mouth of a river which received its name from that town. It must follow then that Atzíkolo is the site of *Gortys.* The plain of sixty stades can be no other than the great plain of Megalopolis, though the distance from the heights eastward of Karítena, where stood the sepulchral monument called *Parœbasium,* to the foot of the hill of Londári, is I apprehend more, even in a direct line, than the distance mentioned by Pausanias. Karítena will thus answer to *Berenthe;* the ancient position above Mavriá, mentioned in my journal of the 9th May last year[a], to that of Trapezus and Kyparíssia, which also preserves some vestiges of antiquity, to the site of *Basilis;* the latter is somewhat confirmed by the name Vathýrema[b] applied to an adjacent torrent, which we may suppose to be derived from the ancient *Bathos*[c]. After leaving those places, Pausanias seems, by his remark upon the Aminius and Helisson, to have crossed the Alpheius at or very near the modern ford; for those streams occur just in the manner he speaks of them, between the ford and *Megalopolis.* It is evident indeed, from the course of the river through the plain, that this must always have been the most convenient place of passage from Megalopolis to the places in the north-western portion of the plain. *Thocnia* appears to have been nearly in the position of Vromoséla.

2. Road from Megalopolis to Messene[d].—

"In going from Megalopolis towards Messenia, after proceeding about seven stades, there is a temple of the goddesses called Maniæ, by which name the place also is known. It appears to me to be an appellation of the Eumenides, and it is said that Orestes here became insane on account of the murder of his mother. Not

[a] Vide Chapter XII.
[b] Βαθύ-ρευμα.
[c] Βάθος.
[d] Pausan. Arcad. c. 34.

far from the temple there is a small heap of earth, and upon it a finger made of stone, whence the hill is called the Monument of the Finger; it is reported that Orestes here bit off a finger from one of his hands in a fit of madness. Adjacent to this place is another named Ace, where stands a temple of the Eumenides, in which they sacrifice also to the Graces. The place is called Ace because Orestes was here cured of his disorder; near it is another sanctuary named Cureium (?) because Orestes here cut off his hair. From the Maniæ there is a distance of about fifteen stades to the Alpheius, near the place where it is joined by the Gatheatas, this river having previously received the Carnion. The sources of the Carnion are in the district called Ægytis below the temple of Apollo Cereatas, and those of the Gatheatas at Gatheæ of Cromitis, which district is forty stades above the Alpheius, and contains the almost obliterated vestiges of the city Cromi[a]. From Cromi there is a distance of twenty stades to Nymphas, which is a place abounding in water and trees. From thence there are thirty stades to the Hermæum which marks the

[a] Xenophon (Hellen. l. 7. c. 4.) wrote it Cromnus, and describes it as a small town near Megalopolis. Stephanus notices this variety in the mode of writing the name.

boundary of the Megalopolitæ and Messenii, and where is a statue of Hermes upon a pillar."[a]

3. From Megalopolis to Carnasium [b].—

"Such is the road towards Messene, but there is another which leads from Megalopolis towards Carnasium of the Messenii. In this road you meet the Alpheius in the place where the Mallus and Syrus, after having united their waters, fall into the Alpheius. Proceeding from thence with the Mallus on your right hand, after thirty stades you will cross it and ascend an acclivity to the village [c] called Phædria. Fifteen stades from Phædria towards Despœna is the place called Hermæum, which is another boundary of the Megalopolitæ and Messenii; here are small statues of Despœna and Ceres, and others of Hermes and of Hercules: and here I think it was, that a wooden statue of Hercules made by Dædalus, and placed on the confines of Messenia and Arcadia, formerly stood."

As Messene and Carnasium, if the latter be the same place which Pausanias has described near Andania, lay nearly in the same direction from Megalopolis, it is difficult to understand how it happened that there were separate roads

---

[a] πεποίηται ἐπὶ στήλῃ.   [b] Pausan. Arcad. c. 35.   [c] χωρίον.

across the mountain now called Makryplái. The difficulty is not diminished by Pausanias having described the more southern of the two as that which led to Messene, for this seems to place Carnasium, which was a little to the southward of Andania, still more directly in the way to Messene. The question, however, is of little importance; for as Pausanias describes the roads only as far as the frontier of the two provinces, it is sufficient to consider them only as two roads into Messenia. That his road to Carnasium was the more northerly, is clear from this, that he describes the Hermæum near Phædria upon that route as being towards the temple of Despœna, thus clearly shewing, that the road to Phædria and Carnasium was the next southerly to that which led to Phigaleia. The southern route from Megalopolis into Messenia seems to have been exactly that which now leads into that ancient province by the Pashá-Vrysi, or Fountain of the Pashá, and the Kokhla Dervéni[a]: the northern, that which leads by Aiás-bey and Dedér-bey to Krano. The difficulty alluded to above may, perhaps, be thus explained: that as Carneius was a common epithet of Apollo in the peninsula, especially this part of it, and Carneium, or Carnasium, consequently a name common to

[a] See Chapter III.

many places, there may have been two Carnasia between Megalopolis and Messene; in this case the name Krano may be a corruption of the ancient word. Krano may stand upon the site of the northern Carnasium, and the road intended by Pausanias may have been precisely the modern route from Sinánu to Krano. Some remains of Cromi, as I have elsewhere remarked, are still to be seen at Samará, not far from Londári, to the westward, upon a branch of the Alpheius, which seems clearly therefore to be the Gatheatas. The river is said to have its rise in Mount Xero-vúni, at a place called Ianéus[a], which, if this account be correct, is the ancient Gatheæ. A distance of twenty stades from the remains of *Cromi* at Samará, leads us to the "Fountain of the Pashá", which answers therefore to the site of *Nymphas*, as well from the description of that place by Pausanias, as by its lying exactly in the modern southern route into *Messenia*, upon which road, thirty stades beyond Nymphas, stood the Hermæum, or statue of Mercury, which marked the frontier. And hence it appears that Pausanias mentions only on the direct road the Alpheius, Nymphas, and the Hermæum, and that what he says of Cromi and Ga-

[a] Γιανέους.

theæ, and the rivers Carnion and Gatheatas, are digressions.

4. From Megalopolis to Lacedæmon[a].—

" On the road from Megalopolis to Lacedæmon, there is a distance of thirty stades to the Alpheius: you then travel along the river Theius, which is a branch of the Alpheius; leaving the Theius on the left hand, you will arrive, at the end of forty stades from the Alpheius, at Phalæsiæ, which is twenty stades distant from the Hermæum towards Belemina. The Arcadians say that Belemina, which anciently belonged to them, was separated from Arcadia by the Lacedæmonians; but their assertions appear to me improbable, among other reasons, because the Thebans would not have permitted the Arcadians to have been deprived of it, if their right could have been proved."

By this passage, the ancient name of the south-easternmost extreme branch of the *Alpheius*, now called Kutufarína, is shewn to have been *Theius*. It appears that the road, after crossing the Alpheius, followed the left bank of the Theius for forty stades. Phalæsiæ, therefore, was near the modern Gardhíki, a distance of twenty stades beyond which will carry us nearly to the division of the waters flowing

[a] Pausan. Arcad. c. 35.

northward to the *Alpheius* and southward to the *Eurotas*. This was a very natural division of the two territories, of which the Hermæum, mentioned by Pausanias, was evidently intended to mark the common boundary.

5. From Megalopolis to Methydrium [a].—

" But there are other roads leading from Megalopolis to certain places within Arcadia; and first, to Methydrium there is a distance of 170 stades. At thirteen stades from Megalopolis occurs a village [b] called Scias, and ruins of a temple of Minerva Sciatis, which is said to have been built by Aristodemus, tyrant of Arcadia: at ten stades beyond Scias, are some few remains of the city Charisiæ, from whence there are again ten stades to Tricoloni, formerly a city; here still exists a temple of Neptune, which contains a square statue, and stands upon a hill in a grove of trees; it was founded by the sons of Lycaon. Zœtia, which is fifteen stades beyond Tricoloni, is not in the direct road, but to the left of Tricoloni; it is said to have been founded by Zœtius, the son of Tricolonus: Paroreus, the younger of the sons of Tricolonus, built Paroria, which is distant from Zœtia ten stades. Both these places are now deserted; but at Zœtia there remains a temple of Ceres, and another of Diana. There exist also some

[a] Pausan. Arcad. c. 35.   [b] χωρίον.

ruins of the cities Thyræum and Hypsus, the former situated fifteen stades beyond Paroria, the latter in a mountain also called Hypsus, which rises above the plain. All the country between Thyræum and Hypsus is mountainous, and full of wild beasts. Turning to the right from Tricoloni, there is, first of all, an ascent to the fountain Cruni, from whence, after descending thirty stades, occurs the tomb of Callisto, a high artificial hill of earth[a] with many trees upon it, both wild and fruitful; upon the summit is a temple of Diana, surnamed Calliste. Twenty-five stades from thence, and 100 in all from Tricoloni towards the Helisson[b], stands the village Anemosa, in the direct road to Methydrium; [then occurs] the mountain Phalanthum, in which are the ruins of the city Phalanthus. Under Phalanthum is the plain of Palus, (or Polus,) and near it Schœnus, so called from the Bœotian of that name. If this Schœneus ever migrated into Arcadia, it may be that the race-grounds[c] of Atalanta, which are near Schœnus, received their name from his daughter. There remains nothing else worthy of notice, except Methydrium, to which the distance from Tricoloni is 140 stades wanting three. The place was called Methydrium because Orchomenus built it on a lofty

[a] χῶμα γῆς ὑψηλὸν. [b] ἐπί γε τοῦ Ἑλίσσοντος. [c] δρόμοι.

hill between the rivers Malætas, (or Molottus,) and Mylaon."

The preceding route is unusually rich in distances, and there is great reason to trust to their accuracy; the direct line of fifteen geographic miles, compared with the 170 stades of road distance, giving a correct rate to the stade, and the sum of the distances being in perfect agreement with the details as far as they go. Those details however, as often happens with Pausanias, are not complete; the distances from Tricoloni to Cruni, and from Anemosa to Methydrium are wanting, and must be deduced from the others; thus, as there were 100 stades from Tricoloni to Anemosa, and fifty-five from Cruni to Anemosa, it will follow that there were forty-five from Tricoloni to Cruni. In like manner, as there were 137 stades from Tricoloni to Methydrium, and 100 from the former to Anemosa, there will remain thirty-seven over Mount Phalanthum to Methydrium by Schœnus. Pausanias omits likewise to mention the distance between Thyræum and Hypsus; but, as he remarks, that all the country between the two places was a forest full of wild animals, it would seem to have been considerable. His diversion to the left from Tricoloni, appears to have been for the purpose of including the ancient sites along the borders of the plain towards the present Karítena, in the same manner as he digresses for a similar purpose on some of the other routes. In placing the ancient names along this road, I have allowed some increase to the horizontal distance in the plain, and a proportional diminution in the mountains. The latter was principally required from Tricoloni to Cruni, and from Anemosa to Schœnus.

Although Methydrium is the most distant point to which Pausanias has described a route from Megalopolis, there were some other places still more distant, which, according to him, contributed their population on the foundation of Megalopolis, although they were not considered a part of the Megalopolitis in his time, because other districts intervened. The Tripolis, so called as consisting of the three townships of Calliæ, Dipœnæ, and Nonacris, was in this predicament, and, as well as Methydrium and its neighbours, Theisoa and Teuthis, paid its contributions[a] at Orchomenus[b]. The situation of the Tripolis is known only from that of Nonacris, for of the other two places we have no information.

6. Road from Megalopolis to Mænalus[c].—

" Through the pass, called the Gates at Helos, the Megalopolitæ have a road to Mænalus along the river Helisson. On the left of

[a] συντελοῦντες.　　　[b] Pausan. Arcad. c. 27.
[c] Pausan. Arcad. c. 36.

the road stands the temple of the Good God[a]. Not far from thence there is a heap of earth, which is the tomb of Aristodemus, tyrant of Arcadia, surnamed the Good[b]. Here also is a temple of Minerva Machanitis. On the right of the road is the sacred portion[c] of the wind Boreas, to whom the Megalopolitæ sacrifice every year for having assisted them against the Lacedæmonians[d]. Next occurs the monument of Oicles, father of Amphiaraus, and beyond it the temple and sacred grove of Ceres in Helos, into which women only are permitted to enter; it is distant five stades from the city. Thirty stades further is the place called Paliscius; from whence, after leaving on the left hand the Elaphus, which is not a perpetually flowing stream, and advancing about twenty stades, you will arrive at the ruins of the city of the Peræthenses, among which a temple of Pan still remains. But if you cross the torrent [Elaphus] you will arrive at the end of fifteen stades at a plain, and beyond it at a mountain, both of which are called Mænalium. At

[a] Ἀγαθοῦ Θεοῦ.—Pausanias supposed Jupiter to have been meant by this epithet.
[b] Χρηστὸν.
[c] τέμενος.
[d] In a battle gained in this place by Aristodemus, B. C. 265, against Acrotatus, son of Areus. Vide Plutarch in Agid. Pausanias errs in representing Agis as one of the Spartan kings at that time, and Acrotatus as son of Cleomenes. Vide Arcad. c. 27. 30. 36.

the foot of the mountain are vestiges of the city Lycoa[a], and a temple and brazen statue of Diana Lycoatis. In the part of the mountain towards the south is Sumatia, which is no longer inhabited. In the same mountain are the Triodi, (Three Ways,)[b] from whence the bones of Arcas, son of Callisto, were conveyed by the Mantinenses, by order of the Oracle of Delphi. The ruins of Mænalus still remain, and vestiges of a temple of Minerva, together with a stadium for the contest of athletæ, and a place for the running of horses. The mountain Mænalium is considered so especially sacred to Pan, that the inhabitants affirm they have heard him playing on the pipe."

The direction of this road is nearly certain: it followed the Helisson to the foot of Mount Mænalium, and as Pausanias does not mention any crossing of the river, it proceeded probably

---

[a] From Stephanus, as well as Pausanias, it is evident there were two Arcadian cities nearly of the same name; one in Mænalia, the other to the northward of Mount Lycæum. The imperfection of the text of Pausanias leaves their orthography doubtful, but Stephanus, I think, determines it. He informs us that the gentile of Lycoa was Lycoates, (Λυκοάτης,) which being the form of the epithet of Diana in the Mænalia, shews the town in this district to have been Lycoa, whereas Lycæa had the ethnic Λύκαιος, and was sometimes called Lycætha. It is much more probable, moreover, that the town on Mount Lycæum should have been Lycæa, than Lycoa. Cf. Pausan. Arcad. c. 27. 30. 36. Stephan. in Λύκαια, Λύκοα.

[b] Vide et Stephan. in Τρίοδοι.

all the way along the left bank of the river, until it reached the plain at the foot of that mountain. The distances, however, in the text of Pausanias can hardly be correct. It seems evident that the opening through which the *Helisson* enters the plain of *Megalopolis*, and where above the left bank stands the village of Shálesi[a], is the place anciently called the *Gates at Helos*, and consequently that Shálesi is the site of the temple of *Ceres* at *Helos*. Now this point is three miles from the centre of the site of Megalopolis, the number of stades therefore ought perhaps to be twenty-five instead of five. Again, according to the text of Pausanias, Paliscius was only thirty stades beyond Helos, at the confluence of the Elaphus with the left bank of the Helisson; the town of Peræetheæ was at twenty stades to the right of the direct road on the left bank of the Elaphus; and the plain Mænalium, at the foot of the mountain of the same name, commenced at fifteen stades beyond the mouth of the Elaphus. According to these numbers, therefore, the plain Mænalium was only forty-five stades beyond Helos, whereas it appears from the map that the nearest part of the *Mænalian* ridge is seventy or eighty stades distant from thence, so that the plain, if the numbers in Pausanias are correct, was thirty

---

[a] Σιάλεσι.

stades across, which I certainly saw nothing in my two visits to that quarter last year to justify. I must leave the elucidation of this question to future travellers, observing only, that I still think it possible that some vestiges of the walls, or stadium, or hippodrome of Mænalus may exist, though I searched in vain both for this place and for Lycoa. I have already hazarded the opinion, that *Sumatia* stood at or near Sylímna, on the western face of that part of the *Mænalium* which slopes on the other side into the valley of *Pallantium*, and that the *Triodi* was the remarkable pass behind Tripolitzá, which forms a communication from the vale of the Helisson into the great Mantinico-Tegeatic plain.

In speaking of the course of the Helisson in another part of the Arcadics [a], Pausanias says that it "begins from a town of the same name, and passes first through the territory of the Dipæenses, then the Lycoatis, and lastly through the city of Megalopolis;" whence it would seem that neither Mænalus, nor Sumatia, nor Peræetheæ, were very near its banks.

7. Road from Megalopolis to Phigaleia [b].—

"Between the walls of Megalopolis [c] and the temple of Despœna there is a distance of forty stades; the river Alpheius is crossed half-way

[a] Pausan. Arcad. c. 30.   37, 38, 39.
[b] Pausan. Arcad. c. 36,   [c] Μεγαλοπολιτῶν τοῦ ἄστεως.

thither. Two stades from the Alpheius are the ruins of Macareæ, from whence to other ruins which are those of Daseæ, there are seven stades, and as many more to the hill Acacesius, under which stood the city Acacesium. Upon the hill there still remains a statue in stone of Hermes Acacesius. From Acacesium to the temple of Despœna there is a distance of four stades."

The temple of Despœna, (the Mistress,) who was supposed by the Arcadians to be the daughter of Ceres by Neptune [a], was one of the most celebrated places of worship in the Peloponnesus. Before the entrance of the sacred inclosure [b] of the goddess, there was a temple of Diana Hegemone, containing a brazen statue about six feet high, representing Diana with torches in her hands. After entering the inclosure, a stoa on the right contained four sculptures upon white marble in low relief inserted in the wall [c]. On one of these were represented the Fates, with Jupiter as their leader; on the second, Hercules carrying off the tripod of Apollo; between them was a picture relating to the ceremony of Despœna [d]; on the third marble, were nymphs and Pans; the fourth

---

[a] "I dare not", adds Pausanias, "reveal her real name to the uninitiated" (ἀτελέστους).

[b] ἱερὸν περίβολον.

[c] ἐν τῷ τοίχῳ λίθου λευκοῦ τύποι πεποιημένοι.

[d] πινάκιον γεγραμμένα ἔχοντα ἐς τὴν τελετήν.

contained the figure of Polybius, son of Lycortas, with an epigram attesting that Greece would not have erred if she had followed his advice, and that when she suffered for her errors, he, above all others, was useful to her. Before the temple were altars of Ceres, of Despœna, and of the Mother of the Gods. The temple contained a colossal representation, by Damophon of Messene, of Ceres, and Despœna seated on a throne. Each figure was as large as that of the Mother of the Gods at Athens, made by the same artist, and the whole composition was wrought out of a single block of marble. Ceres was holding a torch in her right hand, her left resting upon Despœna. On the knees of the latter deity there was a box[a], upon which her right hand rested; in her left she held a sceptre. Diana was standing by Ceres, clothed in the skin of a deer; a quiver hanging over her shoulders, a torch in one hand, and two serpents in the other; a hunting dog by her side. Anytus, one of the Titanes, in the habit of an armed man, was standing by Despœna. These two were separate statues; below them were represented the Curetes, and on the pedestal of ..... [b] the Corybantes. On the right hand of

[a] κίστη.
[b] ἐπὶ τοῦ βάθρου. Some words seem wanting here to indicate the particular pedestal upon which the Corybantes were represented.

the exit of the temple there was a mirror, which reflected the statues.

"Beyond the temple of Despœna, ascending a little to the right, was the Megarum, in which the Arcadians performed the ceremony [a] in honour of Despœna, and sacrificed numerous victims. Above the Megarum was the sacred grove of Despœna, surrounded with a stone wall [b]. It contained trees of various kinds, among which there was an olive and holly-oak [c] growing from the same root. Above the grove was an altar of Neptune Hippius, and another sacred to all the Gods, inscribed with an epigram. From thence there were steps ascending to a temple of Pan; it had a portico, and a small statue of Pan, before which was burnt a perpetual fire. Here also was an altar of Mars; and a temple of Venus, which contained two statues of Venus, the more ancient of wood, the other of white marble, and wooden statues of Apollo and Minerva;—there was likewise a sanctuary of Minerva. A little above the temple of Pan were the walls of Lycosura, which still contained a few inhabitants." "Of all the cities," continues Pausanias, "on the continent or on the islands, Lycosura is the most ancient. It was the first which the sun beheld, and from it mankind learnt to build

---

[a] τελετή.   [b] θριγκῷ λίθων.   [c] πρῖνος.

cities. On the left hand", he adds, "of the temple of Despœna is the mountain Lycæum, called also Olympus, and by some of the Arcadians 'the Sacred Summit'[a]: it is said, that Jupiter was nursed on this mountain; it contains a place called Cretea, on the left hand of the grove of Apollo Parrhasius, and they relate that the story of the Cretans respecting the education of Jupiter in Crete, applies to this place, and not to the island. They add that the name of the nymphs by whom Jupiter was nursed, were Theisoa, Neda, and Hagno. Theisoa gave name to a city which formerly existed in Parrhasia, and which even now is a town of the Megalopolitis; from Neda the river was denominated. Hagno is the name of a fountain in Mount Lycæum, which, like the Istrus, produces the same quantity of water in winter and summer." Mount Lycæum contained also a temple of Pan, standing in the midst of a grove of trees, together with a hippodrome and a stadium, where the games called Lycæa were formerly celebrated, and where some pedestals remained, from which the statues had been removed. There was a temenus of Jupiter Lycæus, into which men were not permitted to enter. It was said, that he who violated the law was sure to die within the year, and that

[a] ἱερὰν κορυφήν.

neither man nor beast had any shadow within the inclosure. "The same", adds Pausanias, "happens at Syene when the sun enters Cancer, but here at all times. On the highest summit of the mountain there is a heap of earth, which is the altar of Jupiter Lycæus; from thence the greater part of the Peloponnesus is visible. Before the altar eastward are two columns[a], which support gilded eagles of very ancient workmanship. In the eastern part of the mountain there is a temple of Apollo, surnamed Parrhasius and Pythius. To the north of Lycæum is the Theisoæa, where the inhabitants chiefly venerate the nymph Theisoa. Through the Theisoæa flows the river Mylaon into the Alpheius, and into the Mylaon the Nus, and Achelous, and Celadus, and Naphilus."

"To the right of Lycosura are the mountains called Nomia, and in them the temple of Pan Nomius. There is a place[b] called Melpeia, because they say that Pan here first discovered the melody of the pipe. It may easily be conjectured that the mountains were called Nomia, from the pastures[c] of Pan, though the Arcadians themselves say that a nymph gave name to them. To the westward of Lycosura flows the river Plataniston, which river it is necessary to pass in going to Phigalia. Beyond it there is an ascent

[a] κίονες. [b] χωρίον. [c] νομαί.

to that city of thirty stades, or not many more than thirty."

In adverting to the beginning of this route, it seems curious that towns, apparently of some importance, as having taken their names from the royal lineage of ancient Arcadia, should have been situated only half a mile or a mile distant from one another, and not less singular that, as the sum of the several distances from the Alpheius to Macareæ, Daseæ, Acacesium and Despœna, agree exactly with the total from the Alpheius to Despœna, they must have stood exactly in a straight line. It must be admitted, however, that this agreement of numbers is any thing but inculpatory of the text. We ought to find, therefore, some remains of these places, and especially of Despœna, if not of Lycosura, which, if Pausanias is correct, stood in the direction of Phigaleia from Megalopolis, nearly due west from the former, and distant from thence about five miles[a].

[a] After my visit to this part of Arcadia, Mr Dodwell discovered some remains of the walls of Lycosura, nearly in the position which I have stated; but not having proceeded thither from Megalopolis, he was not able either to verify exactly the distances of Pausanias, or to ascertain the three ancient sites between Despœna and the Alpheius. He observed an eminence covered with bushes, a few hundred yards to the south-east of the Acropolis of Lycosura, and another height near it where he saw some fragments of architecture, &c. — Dodwell's Travels in Greece, Vol.

Though Pausanias, in that abrupt manner which is so often unintelligible without a knowledge of the country, says no more of the road from Lycosura to Phigaleia, than that to the westward of Lycosura the Plataniston was crossed at a distance of thirty stades from Phigaleia, it is evident that the whole breadth of the Lycæan ridge, or a distance of eighty or ninety stades, was to be crossed between Lycosura and the Plataniston.

Having already given reasons for believing that Mount Tetrázi was the ancient *Cerausium*, it will follow from that datum alone, that Mount Dhiofórti was the proper *Lycæum*, otherwise called *Olympus*, or the Sacred Summit. This is, in some degree, confirmed by Pausanias having placed it to the left of Despœna; for that temple probably fronted to the plain, especially as that direction was also easterly, which was the most common aspect of Greek temples. Indeed his description of the temple relatively to the places which precede and follow, leads to the same presumption. But there are still stronger proofs of Dhiofórti having been the *Olympus*, or the true *Lycæum*.—First, the extreme difficulty of applying to Tetrázi, which we must otherwise suppose to have been *Olym-*

2. p. 395. These assuredly are the remains of the hierum of Despœna, and would be well worthy of an excavation.

pus, the topography adjacent to that mountain on the east and north, as described by Pausanias; for to the east of Tetrázi lie the places which are mentioned by Pausanias in his routes from Megalopolis to Carnasium and Phigaleia, and to the north there is a continuation of the high ridge of Lycæum itself, and the district of Phigaleia. The abrupt slope, moreover, which falls on every side from the peaked summit of Tetrázi, leaves no situation sufficiently spacious for the celebration of such an important festival as the Lycæa. Dhiofórti, on the other hand, has a round broad summit, and is altogether a much more habitable mountain: in fact, Sir William Gell[a] informs us, that at the foot of the summit of Dhiofórti, in a small elevated hollow on the eastern side, he found some artificial ground and the remains of buildings, which seem clearly to indicate the position of the hippodrome and other appendages of the Lycæan Games; he observed also fragments of columns in several situations in the mountain. To these arguments it may be added, that the first part of the modern name of the mountain Διοφόρτη, strongly indicates a derivation from the word Διὸς, and consequently some local recollection of its having been peculiarly sacred to Jupiter. I do not pretend to adjust the ety-

[a] Gell's Itinerary of the Moréa, p. 108.

mology of the last two syllables of Dhiofórti; but it is not impossible that they refer to the festival[a] celebrated there.

If Dhiofórti, then, was *Lycæum*, the high ridge which connects it with *Cerausium*, and which, like the latter, was considered a part of *Lycæum*, must have been the *Nomia;* its highest summit, and which is little inferior to the other two, is now called Karyátiko, from the neighbouring village of Karyés. Pausanias, in describing the Nomia as being to the right of Lycosura, seems to have meant that they were to the right of the road in proceeding towards Phigaleia. Assuming that Dhiofórti was the Sacred Summit, it becomes probable that the very remarkable source at the foot of the mountain below Tragománo, which forms a large stream flowing immediately to the *Alpheius*, was the fountain *Hagno*, the importance of which is, in some measure, shewn by the superstitious practices connected with it, which are related by Pausanias. These sources are, I believe, the emissory of a river which rises in Dhiofórti and descends into the mountain not far below the village Tragománo. I conceive that the castle of St. Helen, as the ruins of the Greek city above Lavdha are called, was the ancient Theisoa, a place which is clearly distinguished by Pausa-

[a] ἑορτή.

nias from the Theisoa near Methydrium, by his having given to the former the adjunct "near Mount Lycæum,"[a] and to the latter that of "near Orchomenus"[b], not so much from its proximity to that town, as from its having been included in a fiscal arrangement together with Orchomenus, Methydrium, and Teuthis; and Orchomenus having been the place where the contributions were collected[c].

The river *Mylaon* appears to be that which I observed last year, on the 8th of May, flowing through the valley between the hill of St. Helen and Mount Dhiofórti, but of its four tributaries I have no information; indeed, I am rather inclined to suspect here some corruption in the text, and that Pausanias intended to name some of the tributaries of the Alpheius beyond the Theisoæa towards Aliphera.

8. Road from Megalopolis to Pallantium and Tegea[d].—

"Of our discourse upon Arcadia", says Pausanias, "there remains only to speak of the road leading from Megalopolis to Pallantium and Tegea, by the place called Choma [the Dyke]. In this direction the suburb of Megalopolis is named Ladoceia, from Ladocus, son of Echemus. Next to it occurs the place where

[a] πρὸς Λυκαίῳ.
[b] πρὸς τῷ Ὀρχομενῷ.
[c] Pausan. Arcad. c. 27.
[d] Pausan. Arcad. c. 44.

stood the city Hæmoniæ, founded by Hæmon, son of Lycaon: it is still known by the name of Hæmoniæ. Beyond it, to the right of the road, are ruins of the city Oresthasium, and among them some columns of the temple of Diana surnamed Hiereia. In the direct road beyond Hæmoniæ, is the village[a] Aphrodisium, and another called Athenæum, on the left of which there is a temple of Minerva, and in it a statue of stone. Twenty stades beyond Athenæum are the ruins of Asea; the hill upon which formerly stood the Acropolis still retains some vestiges of the wall. The source of the Alpheius is five stades beyond Asea, at a little distance from the road; that of the Eurotas is by the road-side. At the fountain of the Alpheius there is a temple of the Mother of the Gods, without a roof, and two lions of stone. The water of the Eurotas mingles with that of the Alpheius, and they flow together for twenty stades in the same stream, until descending into a chasm, the Eurotas comes forth again in the land of the Lacedæmonians, and the Alpheius at Pegæ of the Megalopolitis. From Asea there is an ascent to the mountain called Boreium, upon the summit of which are vestiges of a temple which is said to have been dedicated by Ulysses, on his return from Troy, to Minerva

[a] χωρίον.

Soteira and Neptune. The place called Choma is the boundary of the Megalopolitæ towards the Tegeatæ and Pallantienses, and from the Choma you turn to the left into the Pallantic plain. To the right is the Manthuric plain, which is within the boundaries of the Tegeatæ, and extends about fifty stades as far as Tegea. To the right of the road there is a mountain, not high, called Cresium, upon which stands a temple of Mars Aphneius; and near the road[a] is the fountain Leuconius, said to have been named from Leucone, daughter of Apheidas; whose monument occurs not far from the walls of Tegea."[b]

Of the latter part of this route of Pausanias, or that between Asea and Tegea, I have already had occasion to speak; of the former there is little to be said, no distance being given but that between Athenæum and Asea. The road must have crossed the ridge which extends from Shiálesi to Mount Tzimbarú, and descended probably into the plain of *Asea* at *Athenæum*. *Hæmoniæ*, one of the old towns of Arcadia, seems to have stood on the edge of the *Megalopolitan* plain near the ascent of the ridge.

Oresthasium, otherwise *Oresteium*[c], I conceive to have occupied the summit of Mount Tzim-

[a] κατὰ τὴν ὁδόν.
[b] τοῦ Τεγεατῶν ἄστεος.
[c] Pausan. Arcad. c. 3.—Euripid. in Orest. v. 1645.

barú, on which conspicuous point there are still some remains of a Hellenic fortress. The situation very much resembles that of many of the ancient Arcadian πόλεις, and indeed that of the fortresses of every part of Greece in the early stages of its society; Tzimbarú lay to the right of the road from *Megalopolis* to *Asea*, in the part where it crossed the ridge between *Hæmoniæ* and *Athenæum*, and this is precisely the point where Pausanias mentions Oresthasium. As to Oresthasium having been ascribed, both by Xenophon and Pausanias, to the Mænalii, which may seem to place it nearer to the proper Mount *Mænalium* and Tripolitzá, it is to be observed that Alea, Asea, Alycæa, and Eutæa, were also in Mænalia[a], and that all these were in or near the basin to the northeastward of Mount Tzimbarú. *Alycæa*, the same place I presume which Plutarch[b] calls Alcæa, and which he states to have belonged to the Achaian league, was probably on the site of the modern 'Alika; *Eutæa* appears to have been on the eastern side of the valley towards Barbítza.

Pausanias, in enumerating the towns which contributed to people Megalopolis, has arranged them under their tribes, which gives us the position of these Ἀρκαδικὰ ἔθνη, or ancient families of Arcadians. "The following", he says,

[a] Pausan. Arcad. c. 27.   [b] Plutarch. vit. Cleomen.

"were the cities, the inhabitants of which, by the effect of the persuasion of the Arcadian community, or by their own patriotism and hatred of the Lacedæmonians, were induced to leave their native places and settle in Megalopolis. Out of Mænalus came Alea, Pallantium, Eutæa, Sumatia, Asea, the Peræthenses, Helisson, Oresthasium, Dipæa, Alycæa. Of the Eutresii were Tricoloni, Zœtia, Charisiæ, Ptolederma, Cnausum, and Paroria. From the Ægytæ[a] were Scirtonium, Malæa, Cromi, Belemina, Leuctrum. From the Parrhasii were Lycosura, Thocnia, Trapezus, the Prosenses, Acacesium, Acontium, Macariæ, Daseæ. From the Cynuræi of Arcadia were Gortys, Theisoa of Lycæum, Lycæa, and Aliphera."

Of these places there are three, Ptolederma, Cnausum, and the Proseis, of which I find no other notice in ancient history[b]. The names Parrhasia and Eutresii are applied by other authors, not to tribes, but to cities. Parrhasia, for instance, by Homer, in the Catalogue, and both of them by Xenophon[c], in his account of

---

[a] For the orthography of this word, see Stephanus in Αἴγυς, Κῶβρυς, Αἶπυ, Κάρυστος. Pausanias, Lacon. c. 2. Strabo, p. 446.

[b] Elea, according to Pausanias, was an Arcadian city founded by Eleatas, son of Lycaon. Stephanus has an Arcadian town, Diope,—the gentile Διοπεὺς, or Διοπίτης. Neither of these names, I believe, occurs elsewhere.

[c] Xenoph. Hellen. l. 7. c. 1.

the movements of the Spartans under Archidamus, when they gained a victory over the Arcadians and Argives, B. C. 367. The action took place in the plain between Parrhasia, Midea, and the Eutresii, that is to say, about three miles to the N.N.W. of Megalopolis.

It is probable that the Parrhasia of Homer was Lycosura, and that after the decline of Lycosura, Basilis was the place which later writers meant by the city Parrhasia, for the etymology of Basilis is not ascribed by Pausanias, like that of most of the other places, to an Arcadian hero, but seems to have been so named by its founder, Cypselus, as being the royal residence and capital of Arcadia[a]. The Parrhasii appear from Pausanias to have possessed the eastern slopes of Mount Lycæum, and all the plain of the Alpheius on its left bank from Karítena to near Londári, together with a part of the right bank at *Thocnia*. Thucydides, however, seems to give them a greater extent towards the south, for he tells us, that in the eleventh year of the Peloponnesian war, the Parrhasii having called in the assistance of the Lacedæmonians, the latter, under their king Pleistoanax, made an incur-

[a] It probably continued to be the capital until the termination of the race of Cypselus in his eleventh successor, Aristocrates, who was stoned to death by his subjects, for having taken bribes from the Spartans to betray the Messenians, B. C. 668. Pausan. Arcad. c. 5. Messen. c. 22.

sion into Parrhasia, and captured the fort of Cypsela in that district, which had been erected by the Mantinenses to annoy the Lacedæmonian district Sciritis[a].

The Ægytæ occupied a territory on the borders of Laconia and Arcadia, extending from Belemina to Cromi, both included, and comprising consequently the termination of the range of *Taygetum* above the modern Londári, together with the two including valleys of the *Theius* and *Gatheatas*. The Ægytæ, it appears from Pausanias, were properly Arcadians, but their city Ægys was conquered by one of the early kings of Sparta[b], and they probably continued under the yoke during the whole period of Lacedæmonian power. Malæa and Leuctrum, two of the towns of Ægytis, are mentioned by Xenophon, who represents Malæa as the chief place of a district, in which Leuctrum was a fortress, well situated for defending one of the passes from Arcadia into the Laconice[c]. Thucydides describes Leuctra as on the frontier of the Laconice, towards Mount Lycæum[d]. From these authorities it should seem, that both Malæa and Leuctrum should be sought for southward of Londári, towards

[a] Thucyd. l. 5. c. 33.
[b] Pausan. Lacon. c. 2. Stephan. in Αἴγυς.
[c] Xenoph. Hellen. l. 6. c. 5.
[d] Thucyd. l. 5. c. 54.

the sources of the Gatheatas, and the passage which leads from the head of its valley, across the Taygetic range, into the vale of the Eurotas. Carystus was a place in the same district, which, like Belemina, was generally ascribed to Laconia. It was celebrated for its wine[a]. As to Londári, the commanding situation of which seems to indicate an ancient site, it is so very near the ruins which I suppose to have been those of Cromi, that one is almost obliged to consider it only as the site of a castle dependent upon that city. It may possibly stand on the site of that Clarium which we find mentioned as a castle of the Megalopolitis by Polybius, who states that it was occupied by the Ætolians, at the beginning of the Social War, as a retreat, and a place of deposit for their plunder, and who adds, that it was soon assaulted and taken by the Achaians[b].

Of the Cynuræi[c] of Arcadia, distinguished, by the termination, from the Cynurenses[d] of Argolis, all the places are determined, except the town of the Lycæi; but the occurrence of its name, with those of Gortys, Theisoa of Lycæum, and Aliphera, concurs with the name itself, in showing, that it was on or near Mount Lycæum,

[a] Strabo, p. 446. Steph. in Κάρυστος.
[b] Polyb. l. 4. c. 6.
[c] Κυνουραῖοι.
[d] Κυνουρεῖς.

and probably on the northern or western side of that mountain. Tragomàno or Andrítzena appear to be the most probable situations. It would seem that Cynuræa was often considered a part of Parrhasia, for Pausanias in one place describes Theisoa of Mount Lycæum, one of the towns of the Cynuræi, as being in Parrhasia[a]. And Strabo[b], who describes the Eleia as extending to the Parrhasii, leads us to the same conclusion.

Of the ancient Arcadian tribes, besides those stated in the passage of Pausanias above quoted, the Azanes are the only people who had a name separate from that of the principal town which they occupied. According to Stephanus, the Azanes had seventeen cities, and were subdivided into Parrhasii, Azanes, and Trapezuntii. It is probable that they possessed originally all the western part of Arcadia, since we find that the Psophidii and Clitorii[c] to the north, and the Phigalenses[d] to the south, were both considered as Azanes. When the chief Arcadian cities, Heræa, Thelpusa, Methydrium, Orchomenus, Pheneus, Mantineia, and Tegea, were strengthened or enlarged by the collection of their small surrounding communities, it was natural that

[a] Pausan. Arcad. c. 38.
[b] Strabo, p. 336.
[c] Clitor was son of Azan, son of Arcas, according to Pausanias, Arcad. c. 4. 21.
[d] See the Delphic Oracle, ap. Pausan. Arcad. c. 42.

the original races of Arcadia should be lost in the names of the cities, and the more so as the territorial boundaries of the cities were so well defined by nature.

Of the several places of the Megalopolitis, which had been ancient Arcadian cities, five only continued to be inhabited in the time of Pausanias, namely, Gortys, Theisoa near Methydrium, Methydrium, Teuthis, and Helisson[a], all places situated in the most central, and mountainous, and poorest parts of the country. This fact, though it may not reflect much credit on the Roman government, as indicating a retreat of the population from the places chiefly occupied by the Romans, is in agreement, at least, with what we learn from Strabo, namely, that the plains of Arcadia, in his days, were no longer noted but for the pasture of cattle[b].

[a] Pausan. Arcad. c. 27. [b] Strabo, p. 388.

CHAPTER XIX.

ARGEIA.

From Tripolitzá to Argos.—Mount PARTHENIUM.—Akhladhókambo.—Ancient Roads from TEGEA to ARGOS and THYREA.—Tribes of TEGEA. — HYSIÆ. — TROCHUS.— Source of the ERASINUS.—Ancient Road from ARGOS to HYSIÆ.—To Anápli.—TIRYNS.—NAUPLIA.

MARCH 12.—I leave Tripolitzá at 1.36 by the Anápli gate, and proceed eastward by a paved road over the plain; the cultivated parts of it are now under the plough. At 2, Aio Sosti is a mile on the right. At 2.30, halt five minutes among the vineyards of Neokhóri, which village is half a mile on the left, at the foot of a range of low hills, advancing into the plain from the foot of Mount *Artemisium*. As we proceed, Zevgaláti, of the same size as Neokhóri, is one mile on the left at the foot of the same hills. On the slope of the *Parnon* range, six or eight miles on the right, is Dhulianá[a]. I have already remarked that the waters which descend into the plain of *Tegea*, from the surrounding mountains, take two opposite directions, both termi-

[a] Δουλιανά.

nating in katavóthra. The Taki, or lake at the foot of Mount *Boreium*, receives the watercourses to the southward of Aio Sosti, while a stream, which has its origin near Dhulianá, collects the waters from the western slope of the range of Parthenium and Parnon, as well as all those which descend into the part of the plain of Tripolitzá which is included between the *Scope* of the *Mantinice*, and the rising grounds near Aio Sosti. The river thus formed enters an opening between Neokhóri and a small rocky height opposite to it, follows the whole length of the branch of the *Tegeatic* plain lying to the eastward of that opening, and terminates in an inundation and katavóthra, above which, to the southward, stands the village of Persová [a]. The waters of the valley of *Pallantium*, and those from Mount *Mænalium*, descend into the plain between Tripolitzá and Mount *Artemisium*, where, joining similar supplies from the latter mountain, they render the plain marshy during a great part of the year. Their natural discharge is into the river of Dhulianá, but, on account of the very level nature of the plain, this discharge requires to be assisted by art: for the same reason the waters might, without much

[a] Περσοβὰ.

difficulty, be diverted into the plain below *Tegea*, and thus carried to the katavóthra of the Taki; for the part of the plain southward of Aio Sosti, towards the Taki, is lower than that in face of Tripolitzá, and there is no ground between Aio Sosti and the entrance into the eastern branch of the Tegeatic plain, sufficiently high to make the operation difficult. These remarks, it will hereafter be seen, are important in reference to a passage in Thucydides.

Having passed Zevgaláti, we enter the κόλπος, or branch of the *Tegeatic* plain just mentioned, which leads towards Persová and the pass of Mount *Parthenium*. The village of Stenó, situated on the point of the left hand hill, just within the opening, takes its name from its situation in the pass. The mountain which rises above the opposite side of the valley, and the summit of which is at a distance of two miles to the right, is called Kuma. Pass to the right of Stenó at 2.46—halt six minutes. At 3.10, Gheorghítika[a] is on the side of the rugged hills to the left: 3.23, a paved road turns up a small valley branching to the left, then mounts the hills and passes over into a glen, by which it de-

[a] Γεωργήτικα.

scends into the plain of Akhladhókambo, where it again joins the beylík [a] or dhimosiá; this by-road is called Ghyro [b], from its being circuitous, but it avoids the rugged rocks of the pass of *Parthenium* on the beylík. I have already mentioned a third road from Tripolitzá to *Argos* by Tzipiuná, which is still more steep and rugged than either of these. At 3.34 we arrive at the end of the valley, and ascend the lower heights of Mount Róani, which close the valley. Two miles on the right, at the foot of the hills in that corner of the plain, stands the large village of Persová.

At 3.50 arrive at the summit of the ridge of Róani; half a mile on the right, at the foot of the mountain, the river terminates in an inundation, through which I perceive the stream winding through the lake and entering the katavóthra, like the Bœotian *Cephissus*, in Lake *Copais*, on a small scale. We now descend the eastern side of Mount Róani, leaving its summits to the right till 4.40, when we enter the plain of Akhladhókambo. This dervéni, or pass, is still known by the ancient name Parthéni. The road is paved all the way, and has been formed with great labour, the mountain

---

[a] Beylik is the Turkish word for a main road, δημοσιά the Greek; but the Greeks often use also the word Μπῄ- λήτικο, adopted from the Turkish.

[b] Γύρος.

consisting entirely of pointed rocks. Half way down there is a kiosk and fountain, and here it is supposed by the Greeks that a church of the Αἴα Parthénos, or Holy Virgin, once stood, from which the mountain derived its present name. This, however, is undoubtedly an error, though a very natural one for Greek Christians ignorant of the ancient geography: ἡ παρθένος is scarcely ever applied by the Greeks as an appellation of the θεοτόκος, or *virgo deipara*, but that of ἡ παναγία. The modern name Parthéni, is evidently the ancient Parthenium, which belonged probably to all the mountain now called Róani. The fountain at the kiosk seems to mark the position of a temple, which anciently stood upon Parthenium, and which was dedicated to a very different sort of personage from the modern saint, namely, the god Pan, upon whom a lying pezodrome[a] of Athens, named Philippides, conferred immortal honour by reporting that he had had an interview with the goat-footed deity, on Parthenium, in returning from Sparta, whither he had gone to demand succours on the arrival of the Persians in Attica, when Pan promised to aid the Athenians in the battle of Marathon[b]. We met in the pass

---

[a] πεζοδρόμος, a foot messenger, by the ancients called ἡμεροδρόμος.

[b] Pausan. Attic. c. 28. Arcad. c. 54.

two bayráks of Albanians, or about 120 men, proceeding from Rúmili to reinforce the Pashá.

Having crossed the Akhladhókambo[a], or plain of Wild Pears, we ascend the side of a mountain on which the village of the same name is situated, immediately opposite to the peaked summit of Mount Róani: arrive there at 5.21.

It must be at the pass of Stenó, that the road from Tripolitzá to Argos joins the ancient route from Tegea to Argos, which Pausanias describes in the following terms[b]:—" The road leading to Argos may be used by wheel carriages, and is much frequented. The first object that occurs upon the road is a temple of Æsculapius with a statue; then, one stade to the left of the route, the ruins of a temple of Apollo Pythius.

" In the direct road there are many oaks[c], among which is situated a temple, called the temple of Ceres in the Corythenses[d]; near it is a temple of Bacchus, surnamed Mysta. Here begins the mountain Parthenium, which contains the sacred portion[e] of Telephus, where Telephus is said to have been nourished by a deer; and a little farther the temple of Pan, where the god is reported, both by the Athenians

---

[a] Ἀχλαδόκαμπος.
[b] Pausan. Arcad. c. 54.
[c] δρῦς.
[d] ἐν Κοριθεῦσι.
[e] τέμενος.

and the Tegeatæ, to have appeared to Philippides. Parthenium produces tortoises excellent for making lyres, but which the natives fear to take, nor will suffer strangers to do so, because they are considered sacred to Pan. After having passed over the mountain and descended again into the cultivated country, there occurs the boundary between the Tegeatæ and Argives, near Hysiæ of Argolis."

Another road, leading eastward from Tegea, conducted to the Thyreatis; it is the fifth of the roads described by Pausanias to or from Tegea; the other four being those of Argos, Sparta, Mantineia, and Megalopolis. He thus briefly speaks of it [a] :—" On the direct way to Thyrea and the towns[b] in the Thyreatis, the first object worthy of mention is the sepulchre of Orestes, son of Agamemnon, from whence, the Tegeatæ say, that a Spartan carried away his bones. This tomb is not now within the gates[c]. The river Gareates flows near the road which leads to Thyrea. After having crossed it, and proceeded ten stades, there occurs a temple of Pan, and an oak sacred to the god." On comparing these two passages, we may safely, I think, con-

---

[a] Pausan. Arcad. c. 54.
[b] κώμας.
[c] This remark refers to the story of Lichas, the Lacedæmonian, who found the bones of Orestes *in* the city of Tegea, and carried them from thence to Sparta. Pausan. Lacon. c. 3.

clude that the *Gareates* is the river of Dhulianá, since it was crossed on the road to Thyrea, and not on that to Argos, which exactly agrees with the course of this stream. The road to Thyrea, beyond the river, must have ascended the ridge to the eastward, which was a continuation of Mount Róani. Though Pausanias proceeds only as far as a temple of Pan, ten stades beyond the Gareates, the boundary of the Tegeatice and Thyreatis was probably much farther, namely, on the summit of the ridge which now separates the district of Tripolitzá from that of Aios Petros; in the same manner, as, farther south, Hermæa, in Mount Parnon, marked the boundaries of Argos, Tegea, and Laconia [a].

The river Gareates appears to have derived its name from one of the nine tribes into which the Tegeatæ were divided, before the foundation of the city by Aleus [b]. *Garea*, I should conceive therefore, was at Dhulianá, or somewhere below it on the banks of the river. The other demi named by Pausanias were the Phylacenses [c], Caryatæ [d], Corythenses [e], Botachidæ [f], Manthurenses [g], Echeuethenses [h], Aphidantes [i]. The ninth were probably the Tegeatæ or those

---

[a] Pausan. 1. 2. c. 38.
[b] Strabo, p. 337. Pausan. Arcad. c. 45.
[c] Φυλακεῖς.
[d] Καρυάται.
[e] Κορυθεῖς.
[f] Βωταχίδαι.
[g] Μανθυρεῖς.
[h] Ἐχευηθεῖς.
[i] Ἀφείδαντες.

who occupied the site of the city of Tegea itself. The positions of Phylace and Manthurium have already been adverted to. That of the Corythenses is indicated by the temple of Ceres in the Corythenses on the road from Tegea to Argos, which having been near the ascent of Mount Parthenium shews that the branch of the Tegeatic plain eastward of Stenó was the *Corythic plain*. In the time of Pausanias it appears to have been chiefly occupied by a forest of oaks. We have already seen that at the southern entrance of the *Mantinic* plain there was a similar forest [a]. The observation of Pausanias upon the various kinds of oak which the latter contained, argues that the forest was large, as well as its name Pelagus, which seems to imply an extensive wilderness, such as the moderns express by the word λόγγος. It is very possible, therefore, that a forest occupied at that time all the central part of the plain of Tripolitzá, together with the branch of it eastward of Stenó.

The village of Akhladhókambo consists of about eighty families and has a pretty appearance, hanging on the side of the hill among olives, prinária, and fruit trees. It belongs to the vilayéti of Aios Petros, and, like all the

---

[a] Pausan. Arcad. c. 11.—See Chapter III.

villages of that district, is a kefalokhóri. As a dervéni village, it has the expense of maintaining some guards for the care of the roads, but enjoys in consequence an exemption from lodging travellers. I see no vestiges of antiquity in the village, though the district was evidently that of the Argolic town *Hysiæ*. The plain is entirely cultivated with corn: it is about two miles and a half long and one wide, running N. 20° W., S. 20° E. by compass; at the upper end of it are several gorges, which bring down torrents from Mount *Artemisium*; these unite in the plain, and, after receiving a small perennial stream, which runs through the village, proceed through mountainous ravines to the sea, a little to the southward of *Lerna*. A snowy summit of the *Artemisian* mountain is seen on this side of the principal peak of Turníki; it is known by the name of Buga. The ridge of Parthéni is a zygós, or lower ridge, which unites Mount Buga with Róani, the peak of which opposite to Akhladhókambo, I take to be the true *Parthenium*. To the north-west of the village rise some snowy summits called ta Kténia, (the Combs). Midway between them and Róani, a rocky summit surrounded with ravines is crowned with the ruins of Mukhla or Mokhlí[a], which in the fifteenth

[a] Τὰ Παλαιὰ Μούχλα, or ἡ Παλαιὰ Μοχλή.

century was one of the chief fortresses in the Moréa. It was taken by Mahomet II. in the summer of the year 1458, when he marched as far as the *Tegeatice,* and from thence, after the capture of Mokhlí, proceeded to take Corinth and Athens. Chalcocondylas, who writes the name Μουχλὴ, describes it as a city of the Tegæa[a], standing upon a very strong hill, but supplied with water from a place without the fortress; this having been taken possession of by the Turks, and their ladders applied to the walls, the garrison capitulated. It is believed among the learned of Tripolitzá that Mokhlí is a colony from Amyclæ in Laconia, and they adduce as a proof of it that the bishop of Amyclæ[b], who is a diocesan of the metropolitan of Lacedæmonia, and who now resides at Tripolitzá, formerly resided at Mokhlí. They assert also that Tripolitzá was so named from the junction of Mokhlí, Tegea, and Mantineia, which in some measure agrees with the fact of Tripolitzá not being mentioned in the Byzantine history, whence it seems probable, that Tripolitzá was not built until after Mokhlí declined. At Akladhókambo the Greeks have some of their usual absurd stories concerning Paleá Mókhlí, such as that there are 366 churches in the ruins. Mokhlí lies be-

[a] Τεγαίης πόλιν.   [b] τῶν Ἀμυκλῶν.

tween the roads Beylik and Ghyros, but nearer to the latter. The ridge which rises immediately above the village of Akhladhó-kambo, branching from Kténia and running north-west and south-east is called Paravunáki. Róani is connected by a long snowy ridge with Mount Málevo, (*Parnon,*) of which the firs, deep snows, and pointed summit are seen to the south.

March 13.—This morning at twelve minutes beyond the village, on the right of the road to Argos, I observe some remains of *Hysiæ*. The town occupied a height, on which now stands a church of the Panaghía. The summit is naturally defended towards the plain by a brow of cliffs; in the opposite direction there is a small hollow between the hill and the slope of Mount Paravunáki; here the fields are covered with broken pottery; I find as I ride over them an ancient weight for spinning and some other trifles of antiquity; some pieces of wall of the second order are traced around the summit. We leave this spot at 8.5 and ascending the mountain obliquely to the southward, arrive, at 8.40, at a khan, where the road to Anápli branches off to the right. Our track continues to cross naked barren mountains till 9.23, when we halt three minutes at a copious fountain and the ruins of a khan called Sta

Nerá (the Waters); a little farther on there are two other sources from the rocks. This perhaps is the site of *Trochus*[a]. The streams, after passing through the gorges of the mountains, unite towards the plain of Argos, and join the sea between the *Erasinus* and *Lerne*, a position which shews the river to be the ancient *Cheimarrhus*[b]; if the conjecture, therefore, as to Trochus is correct, that place stood at the sources of the Cheimarrhus. As we proceed, the shore and plain about Anápli are at intervals in sight. At 9.55 begin to descend towards the plain. The mountains are all of the same barren rugged character as before; the summits of Mount *Artemisium* on our left are of the same description. At 11, having reached the foot of the mountain, we ride down a gradual slope which succeeds it, but do not enter the plain itself until we arrive at the mills of Kefalári. At 11.20, the village of Skafidháki is seen a mile and a half on the right, and, three quarters of a mile beyond it, in the same direction, a peaked hill crowned with a ruined castle, undoubtedly the ancient Mount Pontinus[c]. I here turn out of the road five hundred yards to the left to visit the ruins of an ancient pyramid containing a sepulchral cham-

---

[a] Pausan. l. 2. c. 24.   [b] Ibid. c. 36.   [c] Ibid.

CHAP. XIX.]   ANCIENT PYRAMID.   339

ber; it stands on the right side of the road

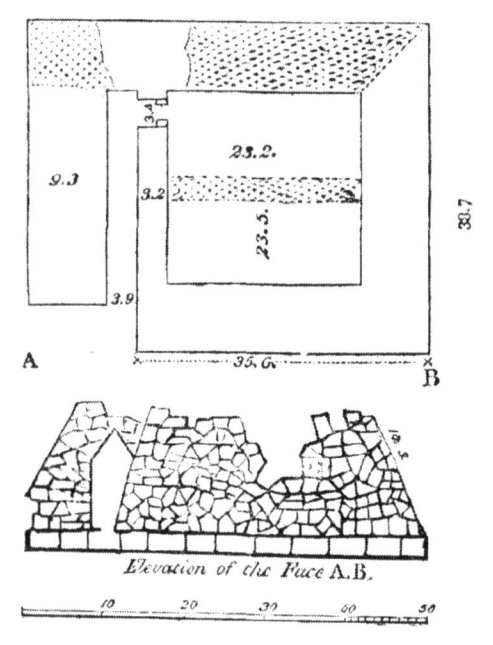

Elevation of the Face A.B.

The parts dotted in the plan are fallen.

which leads from Tripolitzá to Argos by Tzipianá, and which joins that from Akhladhókambo at the mills. The walls are formed of rubble and mortar faced with large polygonal stones, which for the most part are united together with mortar, a rare occurrence in Hellenic masonry, and perhaps the consequence of a repair after some earthquake or other violence. There are some other foundations about the pyramid, and broken pottery in the fields around. I observe also the foundations of a tower thirty-four feet and a half square, built with masonry of the third order; it stood half way between our road from Akhladhó-kambo and the pyramid; there are other foundations on one side of it.

From hence we continue to descend the slope to the " Mills of Argos "[a], and arrive there at 11.35. These mills, so called to distinguish them from the " Mills of Anápli " which are at *Lerne,* are turned by the Kefalári, (anciently the Erasinus,) just below the place where it issues in several large streams from the foot of the rocks of Mount *Chaon.* These at first form a small deep pool, from which several artificial channels are drawn for the mills; the channels reuniting compose a river, which flows directly across the plain to the sea: there are many mulberry trees about the mills. Mount *Chaon* is a mass of rocky precipices overhanging the sources of the Kefalári. Just above the great source there is a fine lofty cavern with a roof like an acute Gothic arch, and extending sixty-five yards into the mountain. Towards the inner extremity it has a branch, which has an opening on the surface of the mountain above it; another branch, at fifteen yards from the entrance, leads to the left so far in, that I could not ascertain the depth on account of the darkness. A third branch to the right communicates with another cavern which has an opening near the great entrance.

---
[a] στοὺς Μύλους τοῦ Ἄργους.

Water drops from the roofs of them all, and the earth in them yields saltpetre in abundance. Pausanias has not noticed these remarkable excavations of nature, but he states that Pan and Bacchus were worshipped at the source of the Erasinus, and we know that caverns were generally sacred to Pan. A wall in the large cavern separates a part of it from the remainder and forms a church.

Leaving the mills at 1.3, we cross the opening of a branch of the plain which is bounded by a peaked mountain on our left—the ancient Lycone. 1.22 cross a small brook flowing from between that mountain and the hills near the castle-hill of Argos; it is probably the ancient Phrixus: beyond it there is a fragment of an ancient building of brick. At 1.30 are some Hellenic foundations in the road; at 1.42 I pass the metropolitan church at the entrance of Argos, and take up my quarters in the house of Kyr V—— in the middle of the town.

Pausanias[a] thus describes the road from Argos to Hysiæ in the contrary direction to that which I followed. " To the right of the road to Tegea is Mount Lycone, on which there are some very fine cypresses. On the summit of the mountain there is a temple of Diana Orthia, in which are statues in white marble of

[a] Pausan. l. 2. c. 24.

Apollo, Latona, and Diana, said to be the works of Polycleitus. After descending from the mountain, there is another temple of Diana, on the left of the highway, and not far beyond it, on the right, the mountain called Chaon, the lower parts of which are clothed with fruit-trees[a]. Here issue forth the copious sources of the Erasinus, which flows from Stymphalus of Arcadia (and has a subterraneous course) like that of the Rheiti from the Euripus to Eleusis, where those salt streams again join the sea. At the place where the waters of the Erasinus emerge, sacrifices are offered to Bacchus and Pan; the festival of the former is called Tyrbe. Proceeding on the road to Tegea, there is a village[b], Cenchreæ, to the right of the place called Trochus; Cenchreæ apparently receives its name from Cenchreus son of Peirene. Here is the Polyandrium[c] of the Argives who were victorious over the Lacedæmonians at Hysiæ. On the descent into the plain, are seen the ruins of Hysiæ: here it was that the Lacedæmonians are said to have been beaten." Although ancient[d] and modern Greeks agree in opinion

[a] δένδρα ἥμερα.
[b] χωρίον.
[c] Conjoint sepulchre.
[d] Herodot. l. 6. c. 76.—Strabo, p. 256.—Senec. l. 3. Quæst. Nat.— Ovid. Metamorph. l. 15. v. 275.—Stat. Theb. l. 1. v. 357.—Diodor. l. 15. c. 49. who says the subterraneous course was 200 stades in length.

that the *Erasinus*, or Kefalári, is the emissory of the lake of Stymphalus, it cannot be said that the opinion receives much confirmation from the preceding passage of Pausanias, in so far as he compares its subterraneous course to that of the Rheiti, which certainly is imaginary, and shews that no constant reliance can be placed upon the ancient traditions on these subjects. But the fable of the Rheiti is of Athenian growth, and as the Athenians had no real katavóthra in their country, they may have been more apt to fall into fiction upon that subject than the Peloponnesians, who, being familiar with these provisions of nature, may have been more disposed to inquire into the real subterraneous courses of the streams with a view to practical utility, and may thus have been truly informed respecting them. There seems little doubt that the Erasinus is really the same river as the Stymphalus. The only other point, on this route of Pausanias, requiring any observation, is Cenchreæ, where stood the Polyandrium of the Argives. The ruined pyramid, a mile to the south-west of the Erasinus, might very well have been a Polyandrium, and I should have been well pleased to have imagined it the tomb of the Argives; but it is impossible to deny, that according to the words of Pausanias, Cenchreæ was situated much nearer to Hysiæ, and that it stood to the right of the road, in some part of the mountain which I crossed in coming from thence. The mountain appears from Strabo to have been called Creopolus [a], and was the same perhaps as the Creium of Callimachus [b]. The pyramid therefore was probably only the sepulchre of some illustrious Argive, or Argive family, and has not been noticed by Pausanias.

The Baratlís and Fermahnlís of the Moréa are much alarmed at the conduct of the Pashá with regard to them; he has taken a list of their effects and property, has summoned them before him, and ordered them, in the name of the Porte, to reside with their consuls. The Porte, it seems, is endeavouring to put an end to the system of European protections, which has become so extensive of late, (particularly that of Russia,) as to give them serious and well-founded alarm. At Argos the measure is supposed to be chiefly aimed at the islands, particularly Ydhra and Petza [c], though it has not yet been executed within the Capitán Pashá's government, of which these islands form a part. Half the opulent men there have now Russian

[a] Εἰσὶ δὲ καὶ Ὑσιαὶ, τόπος γνώριμος τῆς Ἀργολικῆς καὶ Κεγχρεαὶ, αἱ κεῖνται ἐπὶ τῇ ὁδῷ τῇ ἐκ Τεγέας εἰς Ἄργος, διὰ τοῦ Παρθενίου ὄρους καὶ τοῦ Κρεωπώλου. Strabo, p. 376.

[b] Callim. Ad Lavacra Minervæ, v. 40.

[c] Italice, Spezzia.

protections, under which flag they carry corn to the Mediterranean, and wine and colonial produce, &c., in return. About two months ago, a body of the non-protected Greeks of the same islands, envious of the lower duties and other commercial advantages which their protected countrymen partake with Frank traders, and provoked at their insolence, carried a complaint to the Porte: the present order is undoubtedly connected with that complaint.

The late Capitán Pashá, Hussein, desirous of encouraging the Ægæan seamen, but particularly those of Ydhra, Petza, and Psará, because they supply the Turkish fleet with its best seamen, and wishing to place the inhabitants as much as possible on an equal footing, issued forty firmahns for navigating the Black Sea, in favour of some of the islanders who did not enjoy foreign protection, but on his death, the present Capitán Pashá immediately revoked them.

The islanders of Ydhra and Petza are an Albanian colony, who probably occupied the islands about the same time as the peasants of Attica and the Argolis, who have the same origin. The period is no doubt distant in both instances, as I cannot learn, either here or at Athens, of any tradition regarding it. We know from history that the Peninsula was full of Albanians before the Turkish conquest. The higher classes of Moreítes pretend to hold the people of Ydhra in contempt, as a gross, ignorant, Albanian race, good sailors and keen traffickers, but who spend all their money in building and drinking at Ydhra, where they are continually quarrelling among themselves.

I am told that most of the robbers were killed and taken by the Greeks of the villages; while the Turkish troops either remained idle or behaved still worse. V—— and his brothers argue, that if the Greeks of the villages of the Moréa, particularly those about Mistrá, &c., which are most suspected, were attached to the French, and in any intelligence with them, they would not have assisted in destroying those persons who would be the most useful in an insurrection. To get rid of the Turkish troops by removing the cause which brought them, seems to have been the only motivé of the Greek villagers, who certainly would not rashly join a foreign invader, or without the strongest prospect of success. I was informed at Akhladhó-kambó that the Turkish troops destroyed many innocent persons in the thief-chase, and made others prisoners, particularly at Vérvena.

The present Pashá of the Moréa is said to have paid the Porte 400 purses for his appointment for one year, and he will probably squeeze 1000 out of the poor province. Vanlí Pashá, who was removed last year to Candia, paid 600 purses for two years, and greatly enriched himself. The Moréa has the character of being the most profitable pashalik in the empire, of those at least which the Porte has the power of selling annually.

The vilayéti of Argos is an appanage of the Mariem Sultana, and was for a long time exempted in consequence from the burthen of lodging travellers, so that even pashás coming from the northward were obliged to pass outside the town and change their horses without entering it. For the sake of this advantage many persons settled here from other parts of the Moréa, and among others the family of V——, which is of Mistrá. No respect being now paid to these exemptions, the town suffers excessively from the inconvenience of being in the great road from the northward to Tripolitzá, but still more from the insolence of the lawless Turks of Anápli. The Greeks of Argos particularly complain of the havoc which those Nauplians make among their grapes about the time of the vintage. The town of Argos contains 1200 families, and the houses standing far apart, it occupies a large space of ground. There are sixty or eighty Turkish families, all the rest are Greek.

The difference of climate between the plains of Tripolitzá and Argos is very remarkable. There we had frost and snow, and here the heat is that of an English summer; but this is just the time when the spring most rapidly advances on the sea-coasts of Greece.

The dryer parts of the plain of Argos are covered with corn: where the moisture is greater, cotton and vines are grown: and in the marshy parts, towards the sea, rice and kalambókki. The vóivoda, judging that plantations of rice are injurious to health, has lately forbidden the increase of them in the district of Argos. In that of Nauplia many new ones have lately been established. Only one person has ventured to plant currants in this plain, and as yet he is a loser, on account of the time it takes to bring the plant to perfection. The soil is said to be too moist. V——, rather than risk a plantation here, is at the expense of an epítropos at Corinth, who constantly resides there. A milliára the strema is a moderate produce, but it cannot be expected under the first seven years. Seid Agá, at Patra, has had two milliáras the strema; but it is spoken of as the greatest produce in Greece. All the plantations in *Achaia within* the Gulf of Corinth are subject to a rule established by Notará of Tríkkala, the largest proprietor, and agreed to by the rest, that all the produce shall be sold together: the consequence of which is, that V—— has all his last year's crop of currants still lying in his magazines. The regulation is said to have been made for the benefit of the smaller proprietors. Patra seems to be the favourite soil of this plant; there almost all the plantations belong to Turks. The vineyards of the plain of Argos are, as usual, for the most part in low moist situations, and the wine, without an addition of resin, would be sour in the spring; indeed it generally is so, long before that of the new vintage is ready for use. The men now employed in hoeing the vineyards are paid forty paras (about 15*d*. sterling) a day with provisions.

March 15.—From Argos to Anápli. Leave the house of Kyr V—— at 1.51: at 2.3, the last houses of the town;—2.11, cross the river Bánitza;—2.31, pass through Delamanára, where, in a ruined church, are several ancient squared blocks and other remnants of antiquity, and by the side of a well the shaft of a small Doric column, hollowed to serve as a trough for cattle. Hereabouts stood a pyramidal monument, which was the common sepulchre of the Argives who were slain on either side in a drawn battle between Prœtus and Acrisius. It was adorned with representations of Argolic shields, in memory of the tradition that on that occasion the two kings and their followers were for the first time armed with shields[a]. At 3.1 I arrive at Paleó-Anápli, as the ruins of Tiryns are called. They occupy the lowest and flattest of several rocky hills which rise like islands out of the level plain. The length of the summit of that of Tiryns is about 250 yards, the breadth from forty to eighty, the height above the plain from twenty to fifty feet, the direction nearly north and south. There still remains the entire circuit of the walls, more or less preserved. Some of the masses of stone are shaped by art, some of them are even rectangular, but these are probably repairs, and not a part of the original work, which consisted, as Pausanias has described it[b], of rude masses piled upon one another, with small stones fitted in between the larger. The great masses he calls ἀργοὶ λίθοι, and describes them as so large that a yoke of mules could not move the smallest of them: the λιθία, or smaller stones, served to fill up the intervals and complete the work[c]. The finest specimens of this Cyclopian masonry, " for it is the work of the Cyclopes,"[d] are near the remains of the eastern gate, where a ramp, supported by a wall of the same kind, leads up to

[a] Pausan. l. 2. c. 25.
[b] Id. ibid.
[c] λιθία ἐνήρμοσται πάλαι ὡς μάλιστα αὐτῶν ἕκαστον ἁρμονίαν τοῖς μεγάλοις λίθοις εἶναι.
[d] Κυκλώπων μέν ἐστιν ἔργον.

the gate. The ramp is twenty feet wide, the gate fifteen. The ruined wall of the fortress still exists to the height of twenty-five feet above the top of the ramp: this is the only part in which the walls rise to any considerable height above the table summit of the hill within the fortress. On one side of this gateway I measured a stone of 10.6 by 3.9 by 3.6; here the wall is twenty-four and a half feet in thickness, in other parts from twenty to twenty-three. But the principal entrance was not here, I think, but on the southern side, adjacent to the southeastern angle of the fortress, where a sloping approach from the plain is still to be seen, leading to an opening in the walls.

In its general design the fortress appears to have consisted of an upper and lower inclosure, of nearly equal dimensions, with an intermediate platform, which may have served for the defence of the upper castle against an enemy in possession of the lower. The southern entrance led by an ascent to the left into the upper inclosure, and by a direct passage between the upper inclosure and the eastern wall of the fortress into the lower inclosure, having also a branch to the left into the middle platform, the entrance into which last was nearly opposite to the eastern gate already described. Besides the two principal gates, there was a postern in the western side. On either side of the great southern entrance, that is to say, in the eastern as well as in the southern wall, there were galleries in the body of the wall of singular construction. In the eastern wall, where they are better preserved, there are two parallel passages, of which the outer has six recesses or niches in the exterior wall. These niches were probably intended to serve for the protracted defence of the gallery itself, and the galleries for covered communications leading to towers or places of arms at the extremity of them. One of these places of arms still exists at the south-western angle of the fortress, and there may have been others on either side of the great southern entrance.

The passage which led directly from the southern entrance, between the upper inclosure and the eastern wall into the lower division of the fortress, was about twelve feet broad. About midway there still exists an immense door-post with a hole in it for a bolt, shewing that the passage might be closed upon occasion. In these various contrivances for the progressive defence of the interior, we find a great resemblance, not only to Mycenæ, which was built by the same school of engineers, but to several other Grecian fortresses of remote antiquity. A deficiency of flank defence is another point in which we find that Tiryns resembles those fortresses; it is only on the western side, towards the south, that this essential mode of protection seems to have been provided. On that side, besides the place of arms at the south-western angle, there are the foundations of another of a semicircular form, projecting from the same wall fifty yards farther to the north; and at an equal distance still farther in the same direction, there is a retirement in the wall, which serves in aid of the semicircular bastion in covering the approach to the postern of the lower inclosure. This latter division of the fortress was of an oval shape, about 100 yards long, and 40 broad; its walls formed an acute angle to the north, and several obtuse angles on the east and west. Of the upper inclosure of the fortress very little remains: there is some appearance of a wall of separation, dividing the highest part of all from that next to the southern entrance, thus forming four interior divisions besides the passages. The postern gate, the gallery of the eastern wall, and the recesses in the same wall are all angular in the upper part; the angle having been formed by merely sloping the courses of masonry.

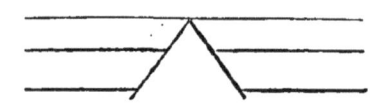

This appears, from many other examples in

Greece, to have been a common mode of construction at a remote period of Greek military architecture [a].

The fortress being only one third of a mile in circumference, could not have been any thing more than the citadel of the Tirynthii, which appears from Strabo to have been named Lycimna [b], probably from Licymnius, son of Electryon, who was slain at Tiryns by Tleptolemus, son of Hercules [c]. There was ample room for the town on the south-western side, where a plain, two or three hundred yards in breadth, separates the ruins from a marsh which extends a mile farther to the sea. Homer, in using the words Τίρυνθά τε τειχιόεσσαν [d], shews that the walls which Pausanias regarded with so much wonder, were equally an object of curiosity in the time of the poet,—no bad proof of their remote and genuine antiquity. It is remarkable, that Euripides, who so often alludes to the works of the Cyclopes at Mycenæ, has not mentioned Tiryns.

According to the ancient history of Argolis,

[a] In an Egyptian building, of a period of time not very distant from that of Tiryns, namely, the Great Pyramid of Memphis, there is an opening formed in a manner more approaching in principle to the arch, by two stones mutually supporting each other in this manner:— Within, however, the gallery is formed by horizontal beams of granite.
[b] Strabo, p. 373.
[c] Pindar, Ol. 7. v. 49.
[d] Hom. Il. B. 559.

Tiryns was founded by Prœtus about 1400 years B. C., and Mycenæ, a generation later, by Perseus. Tiryns is said to have been ceded by Megapenthes, son of Prœtus, to Perseus, and to have become a fortress dependent upon Mycenæ, until the return of the Heracleidæ, when Mycenæ itself, as well as Tiryns, Mideia, Hysiæ, and other places, contributed to increase the population of Argos, and were thenceforth reduced to the condition of dependent towns or castles. The existing ruins of Tiryns, however, indicate by the variety in the style of architecture, or rather of masonry, that it was more than once employed as a fortress in the subsequent ages of Greece. At other times it was probably a deserted place, to which the retiring of the sea from this part of the coast may have contributed. The rudeness of the Cyclopian work, the magnitude of the masses, and the firmness with which their weight keeps them together, have preserved the ruins from the hands of the barbarous masons of modern Greece, who have found more manageable materials in Hellenic constructions of a later date.

As Pausanias gives us no description whatever of the chambers[a] of the daughters of Prœtus, which he places between Tiryns and the sea, we can only conjecture that they were subter-

[a] θάλαμοι.

raneous buildings, like the thalamus of Danae at Argos, or the thesauri of Mycenæ.

From the ruins of Tiryns I ride to another insulated rocky height standing to the north-east of it, passing on the right, at half way, a third, much larger and loftier than either, and the pointed summit of which is crowned with a small church. In a line between this and Anápli, there is a fourth insulated hill, similar to the last. On none of these are there any Hellenic remains. I return to Tiryns; leave it at 4.47, and at 5.27 enter the gate of Anápli. A pleasant kiosk, belonging to an agá of Anápli, is curiously situated on the side of the rock to the left entering the fortress. A little beyond it is a cavern, which was, perhaps, one of those mentioned by Strabo as containing works of the Cyclopes[a].

Nauplia seems never to have attained, in ancient times, an importance equal to that which it acquired during the Byzantine empire, and which was even augmented when it became the chief town of the Moréa under the Venetians and the Turks. As its name is not mentioned by Homer, and very rarely occurs in the history of Greece, it was probably never any thing more than the naval fortress or arsenal of Argos. This was its condition in the time of Strabo; in that of Pausanias the place was deserted. He

[a] Strabo, p. 373.

remarked only the ruins of the walls, a temple of Neptune, the source of water[a] called Canathus, and certain ports[b], by which he meant, probably, such artificial basins as the ancients were in the habit of employing. He observed also the figure of an ass upon a rock, which had been placed there in memory of the origin of the pruning of vines:—a vine which had been cropped by an ass having been found to produce grapes much more plentifully than any others[c]. During the time of the Greek empire, the name ἡ Ναυπλία assumed the form τὸ Ναύπλιον or τὸ Ἀνάπλιον, or the same words in the plural number. The bishop of Argos is still entitled bishop of Anaplia and Argos[d].

The modern town stands upon the northeastern side of a height, with a tabular summit, which projects from a steep ridge at the southeastern angle of the bay of Argos. This height, naturally a peninsula, was made an island by the Venetians when they excavated a wet ditch for the fortifications which they constructed for the defence of the land-front. There are still some remains of the Hellenic fortifications of Nauplia to be seen on the brow of the table-summit, which forms the south-western portion of the peninsula; towards its eastern

[a] πηγή.
[b] λιμένες.
[c] Pausan. l. 2. c. 38.
[d] Ἀναπλιῶν καὶ Ἄργους.

end the modern ramparts are in part composed of the ancient walls, which are constructed very much like those of the citadel of Argos, and appear to be of equal antiquity. There is a large piece of Hellenic wall, also, towards the north-western end of the same height, and another smaller, not far from the middle. But the most curious relic of antiquity at Nauplia, perhaps, is the name Palamídhi[a], attached to the steep and lofty mountain which rises from it to the south-east; for Palamedes having been a native hero, the reputed son of Nauplius, who was son of Neptune and Amymone, the name is so connected with the ancient local history of the place, whether true or fabulous, that we cannot but infer that Palamedium has been applied to this hill from a very early period, although no ancient author has had occasion to notice it.

Before the year 1790, the Pashá of the Moréa resided at Anápli, which brought the agás to Anápli and the Greek primates to Argos, and made the former town the Turkish, and the latter the Greek capital of the Peninsula; many Greeks were attracted also to Argos, as I have already said, by the privileges which the place then enjoyed. Much of the commerce of the Moréa then centered at Anápli, and there were several French mercantile houses. The mov-

[a] Παλαμήδιον.

ing of the seat of government to Tripolitzá in 1790, was followed in 1791 by a plague, which lasted for three years with little intermission; it prevailed in almost every part of the Moréa, but was particularly fatal in Anápli. Since that time the town has not prospered; it is now only inhabited by the agás who possess lands in the *Argolis*, by the soldiers of the garrison amounting to about 200, commanded by a Janissary agá, who resides in the fort of Palamídhi, and by some Greek shopkeepers and artisans. The governor is a mirmirán[a], or pashá of two tails, whose authority does not extend beyond the walls of the fortress; but there is also resident here a vóivoda for the vilayéti, a kadí, or judge, and a gumruktjí, or collector of the Customs, which last office is generally united with that of vóivoda. The houses are, many of them, in ruins, and falling into the streets; the French consulate, a large house like the Okkals at Alexandria, is turned into a khan. The port is filled up with mud and rubbish, and capable only of admitting small polaccas, and to complete this picture of the effects of Turkish domination, the air is rendered unhealthy on one side by the putrid mud caused by the increasing shallowness of the bay, and on the other by the un-

---

[a] Literally, an emír of emírs, a word composed like the similar but superior title of beglerbég (bey of beys).

cultivated marshy lands along the head of the gulf. In the midst of these miseries, however, the fortifications and store-houses of the Venetians still exhibit a substantial grandeur never seen in a town entirely Turkish, and testify the former importance of the place.

March 16.—It is pretended at Anápli that the women are generally handsome, and those of Argos the contrary, and it is ascribed to the water, which, at Argos, is drawn entirely from wells, and at Anápli from a fine source in one of the rocky heights near Tiryns, which is conveyed to the town by an aqueduct. This tale is derived, perhaps, from the μῦθος, relating to the Nauplian spring called Canathus, by washing in which Juno was said to have renewed her virginity every year[a]. I inquired in vain, however, for any natural source of water in Anápli; and could only find an artificial fountain, now dry in consequence of neglect, near the Latin church by the Custom-house: but this source having been supplied from the aqueduct which I have mentioned, could not have been the Canathus which Pausanias describes as a πηγὴ, or natural spring.

Notwithstanding a buyurdí of the Pashá of the Moréa, which I bring with me, as well as a general firmáhn of the Porte, I find some diffi-

[a] Pausan. l. 2. c. 38.

culty in obtaining permission to see the fortress of Palamídhi. Before the Pashá had read the order, and the kadí had summoned the ayáns to take it into consideration, all the forenoon had passed. But at length an order is issued, and in the afternoon I ride up, by a circuitous route, to the southern extremity of the castle, and entering by the gate on that side, find the Janissary agá and his staff waiting for me at the gate; he accompanies me round the fortress. It is of a remarkable construction: the interior part consists of three cavaliers, or high redoubts, entirely detached from one another, and surrounded by an outer and lower inclosure. There are many brass-guns mounted on the ramparts, some of which carry stone-balls of a foot and a half in diameter. The outer wall is low on the side towards the sea, and the rock, though very precipitous on that side, is not inaccessible to a surprise: the profile of these outer works is low also towards the heights on the south, and they have no ditch; but there is an advanced work adjoining the rocks at the southern extremity, the salient angle of which is as high as that of the principal cavalier. Under the sea-face, at the foot of the precipice, there is a road leading along the shore. The rock on the sides towards the town and the plain is nearly as precipitous as towards the sea, and more difficult to ascend: from the town there is a covered passage of steps up to the fort, and on one side of it an open flight, mounting in zigzag, the latter for common use, the former for security in war. From the south-eastward only is the hill easily accessible. There are nine cisterns of water in the fort about thirty feet long, six wide, and six deep. There is a better provision of powder and artillery here than is usual in Turkish fortresses. The body of the ramparts, both of Palamídhi and of Indjé Kalesi, as the Turks call the lower fortress, are built of stone, with merlons of brick. The table-height surrounded with cliffs, forming the summit of the peninsula of Anápli, and around which are the remains of the Hellenic fortress, is unoccupied with houses, and is fortified towards the sea only with a low wall, the steepness of the cliffs furnishing a protection on that side of the peninsula. These cliffs are covered with cactus, from whence, perhaps, has been derived the name of Indjé Kalesi, in allusion to the fig-like fruit of that plant. The small island of St. Nicolas, three or four hundred yards off the north-western point of the peninsula, is occupied by a castle; a little within this the anchorage is deepest.

In returning to Argos, we move from Anápli

at 5.10, and soon afterwards, in order to avoid the rugged pavement of the *kalderím*, or stone causeway of the high road, pass through the shallow water of the bay, and then follow a hard sandy beach till 5.44, when, being at the inner curve of the gulf, we quit the shore and cross the plain directly to Argos. This is precisely the line which the Long Walls of Argos should have followed, but I see no traces of any; nor do I believe, although the distance is not greater than that between Athens and the Peiræeus, that Argos ever had Long Walls, except in the fifteenth year of the Peloponnesian war, when they were erected to ensure a communication with Athens, but were destroyed by the Lacedæmonians in the following winter [a]. I arrive at the house of V—— at 6.45. The rate of travelling from Tripolitzá has been that of the *menzil*, with a deduction for mountains where they occur.

[a] Thucyd. l. 5. c. 82.—Diodor. l. 12. c. 81.—Plutarch. in Alcibiad.

CHAPTER XX.

ARGEIA.

Mycenæ.—Heræum.—Argos.—Ancient routes from Argos.—Œnoe.—Lyrceia.—Orneæ.

March 17.—From Argos to *Mycenæ*. At 11.20 quitting the outside of the town of Argos, and turning the point of the rocky height which projects from the *Larissa*, or rock of Argos, north-eastward, I soon after cross the Rema, or torrent of Argos[a], which joins the Bánitza[b] between the crossing and Delamanára. The Rema, when it contains any water, flows over a wide gravelly bed, which it sometimes, though rarely fills, and thus it corresponds to the ancient Charadrus, as well in the kind of stream indicated by that name, as it does in its position with regard to Argos. The Argives had a custom of holding a military court at the Charadrus on the return of their armies from abroad, before the troops were permitted to enter the city[c]. At 11.45 we pass the Bánitza, which has no water in this place, though it had where I crossed it in the road

---

[a] τὸ Ῥεῦμα τοῦ Ἄργους.
[b] Μπάνιτζα.
[c] ἐν τῷ Χαράδρῳ, οὗπερ τὰς ἀπὸ στρατιᾶς δίκας πρὶν ἐσιέναι κρίνουσιν.—Thucyd. l. 5. c. 60.

to Tiryns; it is evidently the ancient Inachus. At 12.38 arrive at Kharváti [a], a village of fifteen or twenty Greek houses, with a tower for the Spahí.

Pausanias is our only ancient guide at Mycenæ, and his account, though short, is highly curious and satisfactory by its conformity with actual appearances. Quitting, at Cleonæ, the road which led from Corinth to Argos, he turned to the right to Nemea, and from thence rejoined the road to Argos in the pass of the Tretus. "Proceeding", he then says [b], "from the Tretus on the road to Argos, you have the ruins of Mycenæ on the left hand. Among other parts of the inclosure of Mycenæ there remains the gate upon which lions stand. These are said to be the works of the Cyclopes, who built also the fortress of Tiryns for Prœtus [c]. Among the ruins of the city are the fountain called Perseia, and the subterraneous buildings of Atreus and his sons, in which their treasures were deposited [d]. There are likewise the tombs

[a] Χαρϐάτι.
[b] Pausan. l. 2. c. 15, 16.
[c] Here the words of Pausanias do not very clearly indicate that any thing more than the gate of the Lions was the work of the Cyclopes; but in the Achaics, c. 25, he says, that Mycenæ, as well as Tiryns was fortified by the Cyclopes. — Μυκηναίοις τὸ τεῖχος ἐτετείχιστο κατὰ ταῦτα τῷ ἐν Τίρυνθι ὑπὸ τῶν Κυκλώπων καλουμένων. All the allusions to Cyclopean walls by Euripides relate to Mycenæ.
[d] ὑπόγαια οἰκοδομήματα, ἔνθα οἱ θησαυροί σφισι τῶν χρημάτων ἦσαν.

of Atreus, of Agamemnon, of his charioteer Eurymedon, of Electra, who was given in marriage to Pylades by Orestes, and a sepulchre in common of Teledamus and Pelops, who are said to have been twin sons of Cassandra, and to have been slain at the tomb of their parents by Ægisthus. There is a monument of Cassandra, concerning which the Amyclæi dispute[a]. But Clytemnestra and Ægisthus were interred at a little distance from the walls, being thought unworthy of burial where Agamemnon lay, and those who were slain together with him."

Mycenæ was built upon a rugged height situated in a recess between two commanding summits of the range of mountains which border the eastern side of the Argolic plain. This retired position, near the upper extremity of the plain, Homer describes by the words μύχῳ Ἄργεος, using the word Argos as Euripides does in all his dramas relating to the Perseidæ and Atreidæ, that is to say, in the same sense as Ἀργεία and Ἀργολίς were afterwards employed. It would seem from Aristotle, that the situation was chosen because the lower part of the plain of Argos was then so marshy as to be unproductive; whereas in his own time, or about eight

[a] *i. e.* They affirmed that Cassandra was buried at Amyclæ, where she had a sanctuary under the name of Alexandra. Pausan. Lacon. c. 19.

centuries afterwards, the plain of Mycenæ had become dry and barren, and that of Argos well drained and fertile[a]. At present the Argolic plain suffers under both inconveniencies; the upper part is unproductive from a deficiency of moisture, and a great part of the lower from a want of drainage. As to the doubts raised by Strabo upon the meaning of Homer's epithet of πολυδίψιον applied to Argos, they can only be ascribed to his ignorance of the country, of which indeed he gives a sufficient proof, when he says, that there was not a vestige of Mycenæ extant in his time[b]. Pausanias, who evidently assented to the common interpretation of πολυδίψιον, relates a μῦθος, or fable, in allusion to this dryness of Argos[c]. A dispute having arisen between Neptune and Juno on the subject of the Argolis, Phoroneus, son of the river Inachus, was appointed, together with the rivers Cephissus, Asterion, and Inachus, to decide the difference. They adjudged the country to Juno, upon which Neptune caused all the water to disappear. It is for this reason, adds Pausanias, that the Inachus, as well as the other rivers, have no other supply than such as falls

---

[a] ἡ μὲν ἀργὴ γέγονε καὶ ξηρὰ πάμπαν· τῆς δὲ τὰ τότε διὰ τὸ λιμνάζειν ἀργὰ νῦν χρήσιμα γέγονεν.—Aristot. Meteor. l. 1. c. 14.

[b] ὥστε νῦν μηδ' ἴχνος εὑρίσκεσθαι τῆς Μυκηναίων πόλεως. Strabo, p. 372.

[c] Pausan. l. 2. c. 15.

occasionally in showers, and that in summer, all the waters of the Argolis are dried up, except those of Lerne. It was, probably, this part of the Argolic mythology which particularly suggested the epithet πολυδίψιον to Homer, who generally took care to flatter his readers, or rather hearers, by an allusion to their local fables.

The Acropolis of Mycenæ resembled many other fortresses in Greece, in its situation on the summit of a steep hill between two torrents, and below a higher mountain. Its length is not much less than 400 yards, its breadth about half as much. Within the walls the ground rises considerably, and there appear to have been several interior inclosures, indicating a mode of fortifying similar to that of Tiryns. On the summit I found several subterraneous cisterns, or granaries, built of large stones of irregular shapes, lined with plaster.

The entire circuit of the citadel still subsists, and in some places the ruined walls are fifteen or twenty feet high. There are found among them specimens of Hellenic masonry of various ages. The most ancient parts, although not so massive as the wall of Tiryns, are built exactly in the same manner: there are pieces also of the second order of the most accurate kind, and others which appear to be of a still later date. We know from history, that Mycenæ and

Tiryns in conjunction sent 400 men to the battle of Platæa, and that Mycenæ was not deserted until the first year of the seventy-eighth Olympiad, (B. C. 468.,) when the place having been taken and destroyed by the Argives, more than half the inhabitants took refuge in Macedonia, and the remainder in Ceryneia and Cleonæ [a]. The later reparations of the walls may easily be recognized; with this exception, every thing left at Mycenæ dates from the heroic ages; and notwithstanding this remote antiquity, the description of Pausanias shews that Mycenæ has undergone less change since he travelled, than any place in Greece.

The citadel had a great gate at the N. W. angle, and a postern towards the N. E. The great gate stands at right angles to the adjoining wall of the fortress, and is approached by a passage fifty feet long, and thirty wide, formed by that wall and by another exterior wall parallel to it, which, as it seems to have had no other purpose than the defence of the passage, we may suppose to have been a place of arms, and not a mere wall, especially as it commanded the right or unshielded side of those who approached. The opening of the gateway or door-case widens from the top downwards; two-thirds of its

[a] Herodot. l. 9. c. 28. Achaic. c. 25. Diodor. l. 11. c. 65. Pausan.

height, or perhaps more, are now buried in the ruins. The width at the top of the door is nine feet and a half. It was formed of two massy uprights, covered with a third block, fifteen feet long, four feet wide, and six feet seven inches high in the middle, but diminishing at the two ends. Upon this soffit stands a triangular stone, twelve feet long, ten high, and two thick, upon the face of which are represented in low relief two lions, standing on their hind legs, on either side of a round pillar or altar, upon which they rest their fore-paws; the column becomes broader towards the top, and is surmounted with a capital, formed of a row of four circles, inclosed between two parallel fillets.

Thus we have an illustration of the brief and otherwise obscure description of Pausanias [a], as well as an example of the difficulty which often occurs in understanding him, without a view of the objects described. As he remarks only that the sculpture was the work of the Cyclopes, without adding any suggestion as to its meaning, we are left to our own conjectures on this question. The most probable appears to be that it related to the solar worship, which was the most common in Greece at that distant period. Unfortunately, the sculptural repre-

[a] λείπεται δὲ ἔτι καὶ ἄλλα τοῦ περιβόλου καὶ ἡ πύλη λέοντες δὲ ἐφεστήκασιν αὐτῇ.

sentation is not complete; the upper angle of the stone which contained the heads of the lions is deficient, and between the heads there was probably some object on the summit of the pillar [a], or altar [b], which might have explained the whole. The largest stone I could find in the wall adjoining to the Gate of Lions measured seven feet three inches, by four feet seven inches; the thickness I could not ascertain. The gate led into the lower Acropolis, which was separated from the upper by a wall parallel to the outer southern wall, and which appears to have had its communication with the upper Acropolis, at the further extremity from the Gate of Lions, evidently with the view of increasing the length and difficulty of the approach to the summit. The small gate or postern on the northern side of the Acropolis is constructed of three great stones, like the Gate of Lions; and its approach was fortified like that leading to the latter gate. It is five feet four inches wide at the top, and six feet at the bottom; but what is now visible is not more than a third of the original height.

From the Acropolis a ridge stretches to the south, which to the right falls gradually into the great plain, and to the left more steeply into a deep ravine, watered by a stream,

[a] στήλη. [b] βωμός.

the source of which is nearly a quarter of a mile beyond the upper or eastern end of the citadel, in an opening between the southern extremity of Mount Tretus, and the northern end of the peaked rocky mountain, which rises with great steepness from the left bank of the ravine. Along the crest of the aforesaid ridge, below the citadel, an excavation in the rock may be traced, intended apparently for the foundation of a wall, which was connected with the Acropolis at one end, near the Gate of Lions; a part of the wall itself, in a line with the excavated foundation, is to be seen a little below the Gate of Lions: at the opposite or southern extremity this wall appears to have been united with a bridge or wall crossing the torrent: the foundations of which, twenty feet in breadth or thickness, are still in existence. The vein of water flowing from the fountain above the Acropolis, instead of being allowed to take its natural course down the ravine, and under the bridge or wall just mentioned, and from thence into the plain to the south-west of Kharváti, is conveyed by a conduit round the northern side of the Acropolis to that village, and to a garden near it. Between the Acropolis and the village it passes exactly over the upper stone of the Spiliá, as the natives call the ancient building, which is evidently one of those described by Pausanias, as the subterraneous treasuries of the Atreidæ. The rill formerly supplied a Turkish tjismé, or artificial fountain, at a khan, eight minutes below Kharváti, on the post road from Corinth to Argos. But the fountain is now dry, the water being all consumed in or near the village.

The fountain Perseia[a], which Pausanias remarked in the ruins, is no longer to be found; it was probably no more than the discharge of an artificial conduit from the natural source above the citadel; for Pausanias applies to it the word κρήνη, which is constantly employed by him with that meaning, in contradistinction to the πηγὴ, or natural spring. The Spiliá or treasury, is exactly in the same state as when I saw it before. There only wants a little more labour to complete Lord Elgin's excavation, and to shew the depth and nature of the bottom of the monument within. I believe this has been done, but it is now filled up again.

The building was entirely subterraneous, and was constructed under the slope of the hill, towards the Rema, or ravine of the torrent. An approach twenty feet in breadth led through the slope to the door of the building, between two well constructed walls. As these are now ruined, and for the most part buried beneath

[a] κρήνη καλουμένη Περσεία.

the earth which they served to support, the length of the passage can no longer be exactly determined. The doorway in which it terminated was eight feet six inches wide at the top, widening a little from thence to the bottom. On the outside before each door-post stood a semi-column, having a base and capital not unlike the Tuscan order in profile, but enriched with a very elegant sculptured ornament, chiefly in a zigzag form, which was continued in vertical compartments over the whole shaft. These ornaments have not the smallest resemblance to any thing else found in Greece, but they bear some similitude to the Persepolitan style of sculpture. On my former visit to Mycenæ there were several large fragments of these semi-columns lying on the ground: I can now find only one or two very small pieces[a]. They are formed of a kind of green basalt. The same stone was employed for the sculpture over the Gate of the Lions.

The treasury contains two chambers; that into which the great door conducts, and a small interior apartment. The great chamber is of a conical form, but with curved instead of straight sides. The diameter is forty-five feet at the fourth

[a] There are specimens of them in the British Museum, in the Elgin collection.

course from the base, at the base near fifty: the chord of the side is about the same length, its versed sine five feet. The vertical section therefore may be described as an equilateral triangle, with two of its sides curved. Above the door there is a window in the form of an equilateral triangle, of which the side is about ten feet. This window is constructed in the same manner as the gallery and its recesses at Tiryns; that is to say, the courses of masonry are shaped to the form of the window. The doorway is eighteen feet long, and about the same height. The soffit is formed of two enormous slabs, of which the inner is much the larger; it measures seventeen feet and a half on its lower surface, nineteen on its upper, and is three feet nine inches in thickness. In consequence of the form of the building, this stone presents within the building a surface curved both horizontally and vertically. The edge is a curve, of which the chord is twenty-eight feet and a half, or about a fifth of the whole circumference of the building, at the height of the top of the door. The stone has consequently ten feet engaged in the wall on either side of the door-way.

On the right side on entering, at one quarter of the circumference from the great door, is the entrance to the inner chamber. This door is similar in construction to the great entrance, that is to say, there is a large soffit stone, with a triangular window above it; but the slab is little more in length than double the width of the door. The opening is four feet and a half wide, and leads, by a passage eight feet four inches in length, into a square chamber of about twenty-three feet, which, as well as a great part of the passage towards the interior, is not constructed in masonry, but rudely excavated in the natural rock, with an arch-shaped roof. That it was originally constructed in this rough manner may be doubted, for the rock, though apparently of the same kind of breccia which has been employed in all the existing remains of Mycenæ, and which is very hard, as well in the buildings as in the natural external surface, as I remarked near the village of Kharváti, is here soft and crumbling, and was perhaps faced with stones of a harder quality.

There were about forty courses of masonry in the whole building; of these the lower are about one foot ten inches in height, and composed of stones from four to seven feet long: above the great window the courses are narrower than in the lower part of the building. The whole structure being subterraneous, I found it impossible to examine its masonry outwardly[a], though it well deserves a minute inspection, this being the only complete specimen remaining, of a mode of construction peculiar to the early Greeks, and which was not uncommon among them. Its principle is that of a wall resisting a superincumbent weight, and deriving strength and coherence from the weight itself, which in fact seems to be no other than the principle of the arch. The same motive which suggested the circular form to the Cyclopian architect, or

[a] Mr. Cockerell has since made an excavation here, and has discovered that the joints of the stones towards the interior, are nicely fitted together for about three inches, leaving outwards a wedge-shaped opening, into which small stones were tightly driven, a favorite method, it should seem, among the Cyclopian masons. The annexed horizontal section near the apex, may serve to give an idea of the mode of construction.

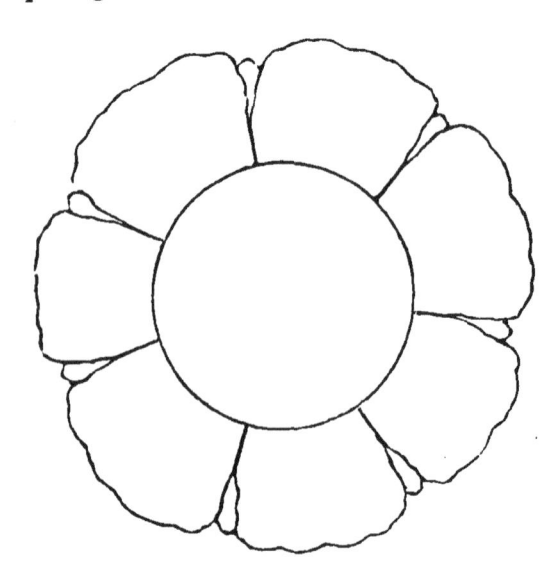

other inventor of this kind of subterraneous building, induced him also to curve the sides vertically, as they derived from that form an additional power of resistance to the lateral pressure. The upper stone of the building has been removed, and lies in fragments on one side of the aperture, made by its removal, which admits a view of the chamber, from the surface of the ground above the treasury. This upper stone, which is hollowed below to form the apex of the parabolic curve of the chamber, was laid upon the upper course, like that course upon the next. In this part of the construction, therefore, the treasury seems to have been built upon a principle different from that of the treasury of Minyas at the Bœotian Orchomenus, of which there are remains sufficient to shew that there was a great resemblance between the two buildings, as might be presumed from their having been nearly of the same age, and intended for the same purpose. Pausanias describes the treasury of Minyas as a circular edifice of stone, having a summit not very pointed; and he adds that the upper stone of all was said to hold together the whole structure; for that such was his meaning in the passage cited below [a],

[a] πεποίηται τρόπον τοιόνδε. λίθου μὲν εἴργασται, σχῆμα δὲ περιφερές ἐστιν αὐτῷ, κορυφὴ δὲ οὐκ ἐς ἄγαν ὀξὺ ἀνηγμένη· τὸν δὲ

may be deduced I think from his employment of the word ἁρμονία on other occasions, to which I have more than once alluded. The first part of his description appears to me to indicate that the Orchomenian building was not subterraneous, the second part that it was terminated above in a key-stone; the latter peculiarity being perhaps a consequence of the former, and the building differing in both from the subterraneous treasury at Mycenæ, where the heavy external pressure was met by a lateral as well as a horizontal arch, and where the upper stone was simply superimposed and kept in its place by the earth which lay upon it. It would seem, from the words of Pausanias, that the treasury at Orchomenus was a more obtuse cone than that of Mycenæ, and his comparison of it to the pyramids of Egypt[a], would lead us to suppose that it was a larger building, though its remains do not give that idea. An excavation will some day determine this question[b].

ἀνωτάτω τῶν λίθων φασὶν ἁρμονίαν παντὶ εἶναι τῷ οἰκοδομήματι. Pausan. Bœot. c. 38.

[a] Pausan. Bœot. c. 36.

[b] The circular buildings called Tholi, which were common in Greece in a later age, appear to have been constructed nearly on the same principle as the treasury of Minyas. Pausanias (Eliac. prior. c. 20.) describes the Philippeium of Olympia as terminating in a brazen poppy, which united together all the beams of the roof (σύνδεσμος τοῖς δοκοῖς). The Odeium of Sparta, called Scias, from the resemblance of its roof to a σκιάδιον, or umbrella, seems to have had a

In the middle of the great doorway I perceive the holes made in the stone for the bolts and hinges of the doors, and in the same line with them a row of smaller holes, which were occupied by small brazen nails; most of these have been taken out, evidently not without difficulty, such was the firmness with which they were originally inserted into the hard breccia of the building. Although the stone has been broken away to obtain the nails, the

similar construction (Etymol. Mag. in Scias.) The Scias was built by Theodorus of Samus, who first cast statues in iron, (Pausan. Lacon. c. 12.,) and who lived about 700 B.C. If the architects of Greece executed buildings on the principle of the arch at such a distant period, and even in the time of Minyas, three or four generations before the Trojan war, it is difficult to conceive that their successors, who brought architecture to perfection, should have been ignorant of the mode of applying the arch to the formation of openings in walls. It seems much more probable, that the arch is not found in temples and other great public edifices, because their characteristics having been solidity and a majestic simplicity, the necessity or expediency for employing it never occurred in such buildings, although it may often have been used in the same ages, in the formation of bridges, subterraneous passages, gates, and other similar constructions. Its more general use among the later Greeks and the Romans may be ascribed to the increase of population, wealth, and luxury, and to that ostentation which attended less to solidity than to a speedy result. The arch economized time, labour, and materials; by its means the scale of buildings was enlarged, works were finished more rapidly, and magnificent edifices, both public and private, were multiplied, although generally with the sacrifice of good taste and durability.

points of many have remained, formed of a metal of a deep yellow colour, and of great hardness. I remark many nails of the same kind in the great soffit stone of the door. Within the building there are remains of some much larger nails of the same material; and which appear to have been at least as numerous in the upper as in the lower part of the walls. These nails also have been broken off, and carried away, so that few of them now remain. Near the apex of the building, however, where they are less accessible, I observe several still projecting from the surface of the stones: they were square, with a broad head, and were driven into the middle of the stones, and not into the joints. It is difficult to conceive for what purpose they could have been intended, except that of attaching some lining to the whole inside of the building, for those near the vertex could not have served for hanging up armour or other moveables; and it is observable, that traces of the nails, both holes for their reception, and points of the nails themselves, are to be found in every part of the interior surface: it is evident, moreover, from the highly ornamented semi-columns at the entrance, and the numerous small nails in the door-way, that the structure was finished originally in a most elaborate manner. I am entirely of opinion, therefore, that there were brazen plates nailed to the stones throughout the interior surface, and it is the more credible, as ancient authorities shew that it was customary among the Greeks in early times to finish their constructions in this manner; there seems no other mode of explaining the brazen chambers of which we find mention in the poetry and early history of Greece, particularly that in which Danae was confined at Argos, by Acrisius, and which, according to the sacred guides [a] of that city, was in a subterraneous building still existing in the time of Pausanias, and described by him almost in the same words [b] which he applies to the treasuries at Mycenæ. The small nails about the door-way served probably to attach some delicate ornaments of metal, with which the entrance was decorated.

While I was examining the inner chamber, my attendants thought proper to light a great fire in the middle of the building. The fine figures, the strong contrasts of light, the singularity of the edifice, and the recollections connected with the place, all conspired to produce a picture of the highest effect and interest.

On the slope of the hill just without the line of the town wall, near the Gate of Lions, I find the remains of a second treasury. The door still exists, though nearly buried in the ruins of

[a] ἐξηγηταὶ. [b] καταγαιον οἰκοδόμημα.

the treasury, or of the soil and rubbish of other ancient buildings, washed down from the hill above. The soffit was made of three stones; the dimensions of the door and of a small part of the circular wall shew that it was not so large as the still entire treasury; the courses of masonry forming the sides were narrower and formed of smaller stones. The length of the three stones forming the soffit was seventeen feet ten inches, the width of the passage, seven feet eight inches. The entrance was on the opposite side to the Acropolis, as might have been expected, the hill rising towards the citadel.

Descending from hence, westward, in the direction of the valley which conducts to the pass of Tretus, I arrive, half way down, at the entrance of a third building of the same kind. It is smaller than the last; the soffit is of three stones, measuring fifteen feet eight inches for the length of the doorway: part of the circumference of this treasury remains above ground, sufficient to shew that its diameter was about twenty-five feet towards the top of the door, and probably about thirty at the bottom. The great treasury, as I have said, was about fifty at the bottom. All this part of the slope of the hill, which is now ploughed land, is strewed with ancient pottery, and seems to indicate that the town of Mycenæ covered the slope towards the plain. But in this case the great treasury being to the eastward of the wall on the ridge, must have been without the town, which is not very probable. On the other hand, if both the great Spiliá and the treasuries on the western slope were within the ancient town, it is difficult to understand the purpose of the wall along the ridge.

Ascending from the third treasury just described, towards the Spiliá, I come to a wall intended apparently for the support of the terrace of a building, and proceeding from thence in the same direction as before, I arrive, a little short of the crest of the ridge, at the ruin of a fourth circular building of the same kind as the others; this last I had observed on my former visit to Mycenæ. The second and third I had not seen. Of this fourth the door-way only remains, and the whole is so much ruined that there is no proof on which side of the door the building stood, though it may be presumed, from the direction in which the hill rises, that the door was on the same side as in the second and third treasuries. The soffit was formed of five stones, forming together a length of entrance of about twenty feet, which is greater than in the second and third treasuries, whereas the breadth of the passage is smaller than in either of them, being only five feet two inches.

The peasants call these buildings the Fúrni (ovens). Their plurality illustrates the plural number in the words ὑπόγαια οἰκοδομήματα in Pausanias. As to their having been the treasuries of the Atreidæ, it was at least a tradition which had descended to Pausanias in an unbroken series; and as there is no reason to doubt that they were built for the purpose which the Greek name implies, it is no more than consistent with the history of Mycenæ, to believe that the largest, or that which is nearly complete, was the treasury of Atreus himself; for Agamemnon having been much engaged in war, and having passed a great part of his reign abroad, was much less likely to have accomplished such a structure. It is by no means improbable that one or two of these edifices may have been more ancient than Atreus and works of the Perseidæ.

Nothing can more strongly shew the extreme antiquity of the remains at Mycenæ, and that they really belong to the remote ages to which they are ascribed by Pausanias, than the singularity of some parts of them, and their general dissimilarity to other Hellenic remains. We find nothing in Greece resembling the lions or the columns before the gate of the great thesaurus or the treasuries themselves, which being nothing more than fabrications in masonry on the barbarous principle of securing treasures by burying them in the ground, seem to argue, from this consideration alone, an early state of society. In the military part of the architecture there is not so remarkable a difference between the Cyclopean ruins and the other most ancient works remaining in Greece, some of which may perhaps be as remote in date as Tiryns and Mycenæ. The greater part of them, even of those which afford the most finished examples of the polygonal kind, appear to me to have been originally built, like Mycenæ, without towers, which, wherever they exist, are probably additions of a later age. To compensate for their neglect or ignorance of this mode of protecting the walls of fortresses, which became universal in the meridian ages of Grecian civilization, the early engineers seem to have bestowed greater labour than their successors on the approach to the gates, and to have devised various modes of protracting the defence of the interior by numerous inclosures and an intricacy of communication.

At a distance of two miles from Mycenæ, in

a small hollow branching from the Dervéni or pass of *Tretus*, there is the lower part of an ancient tower, which I visited on a former occasion, and which I now recognize from the summit of the citadel of Mycenæ, from whence it bears N. 50° W. by compass. I am informed there are no other ruins near it. The peasants call it στὸ ἑλληνικὸν. It appears to have been a guard tower for the pass of Tretus, in several other parts of which I remember to have seen foundations of buildings.

Having returned to Kharváti I descend to the khan, and from thence follow the post road from Corinth to Anápli for about two miles in search of the Heræum, which, according to Pausanias, was situated exactly in the direction of this route at the foot of the hills, at a distance of fifteen stades from Mycenæ. Not finding any traces of the temple, I cross the plain obliquely to Kutzopódhi[a], a cluster of detached hamlets near the foot of a hill which projects into the plain between the *Tretus* and the left bank of the *Inachus*. In the middle of the ploughed land in the plain I arrive at two small ruined churches, in the wall of one of which I observe a part of a Doric column of such a large diameter, that I have little doubt of its having been brought from the ruins of the Heræum;

[a] Κουτζοπόδι, lame foot.

in the other ruined church there are some square blocks of stone of ancient fabric. Soon afterwards I cross the dry bed of the stream which flows from the Dervéni, or ravine of *Tretus*, and a quarter of an hour beyond arrive at the nearest of three or four hamlets, which all bear the name of Kutzopódhi. Here, in a church, I find a piece of a small Ionic cornice and some wrought stones; there are others about the walls of the village. A man of Kutzopódhi found, two or three years ago, in the fields, after a fall of rain, a statue, an arm of another, and many silver medals, seven of which, all Roman, were brought to me at Argos. Returning from Kutzopódhi to Argos, I soon cross the Bánitza and then the Rema of Argos, and enter the town across the ridge which projects north-eastward from the foot of *Larissa*. Here are some sepulchral chambers cut in the rock. The gate of *Deiras* probably stood exactly where the modern path crosses the ridge. The road by which I went to Mycenæ seems to be nearly the same as that by which Pausanias approaches Argos from thence. The road by which I returned was that leading to Argos from Lyrceia.

The Argolic Heræum, or temple of Juno Argeia, was one of the most celebrated of the sacred edifices of Greece; and though Pausanias supposes it to have been possessed by Prœtus before Perseus founded Mycenæ[a], its situation near the latter city seems to shew that it was the chief place of worship of the surrounding country when Mycenæ was the capital, according to a common practice among the Greeks of placing temples of great resort at a short distance without the city walls. The old Heræum was burnt in the ninth year of the Peloponnesian war[b] (B. C. 423) by the negligence of a priestess, after which accident Eupolemus, of Argos, was employed to erect the temple described by Pausanias[c]. " Above the columns[d] were represented the birth of Jupiter, the Gigantomachia, the war of Troy, and the capture of Ilium. Before the entrance were statues of all the priestesses of the temple, and others of heroes, among which was that of Orestes, inscribed with the name of Augustus. In the pronaos, to the left, were ancient statues of the Graces, to the right, the couch of Juno and the shield which Menelaus took from Euphorbus at Troy[e]. The cella contained one of the most celebrated chryselephantine works in

[a] Pausan. 1. 2. c. 16.
[b] Thucyd. 1. 4. c. 133.
[c] Pausan. 1. 2. c. 17.
[d] ὁπόσα δὲ ὑπὲρ τὰς κίονάς ἐστιν εἰργασμένα, which probably meant the metopes as well as the aeti.
[e] Ipse ego, nam memini, Trojani tempore belli,
   Panthoides Euphorbus eram, cui pectore quondam

Greece, the colossal statue of Juno, by Polycleitus. The goddess was seated on a throne with a pomegranate in one hand, and in the other a sceptre bearing a cuckoo; on her crown were sculptured the Hours and Graces. A statue of Hebe, in ivory and gold, by Naucydes, which once stood by that of Juno, had been removed between the time of Strabo and that of Pausanias[a], but there still remained an ancient Juno upon a column, and a still more ancient seated figure of the Goddess, not large, and made of the wood of the wild pear[b], it had been brought from Tiryns when the Argives destroyed that place: the cell of the Heræum contained also a silver altar, adorned with figures representing the marriage of Hercules and Hebe, a peacock of gold and jewels presented by Hadrian, and a golden crown, and purple robe, the gifts of Nero. The foundations of the burnt temple were seen above the other, and before

Sedit in adverso gravis hasta minoris Atridæ.
Cognovi clypeum, lævæ gestamina nostræ;
Nuper Abanteis templo Junonis in Argis.
Ovid. Metam. l. 15. v. 160.

[a] Pausanias says, λέγεται παρεστηκέναι τῇ Ἥρᾳ, &c. and the removal is confirmed by Strabo, (p. 372,) who mentions the statues by Polycleitus in the Heræum in the plural, τὰ Πολυκλείτου ξόανα. This is not the only instance wherein Strabo applies the word ξόανον to a chryselephantine work.

[b] ἀχράδος.

them the statue of the priestess Chrysis, by whose negligence it had been destroyed."

As Strabo and Pausanias differ by five stades in regard to the distance of the Heræum from Mycenæ, it is difficult to ascertain its position, or to know exactly where an excavation might be made, in search of any remains of the building, which may be still concealed beneath the soil. That it stood to the southward of Mycenæ, at the foot of the hills, seems manifest; for Pausanias shews that it was not in the direct road from Mycenæ to Argos, in which he describes some other monuments; on the other hand, it could not have been very far from the road, since Herodotus says, that its distance from Argos was forty-five stades[a]; and Strabo, who tells us that there was an interval of less than fifty stades between Mycenæ and Argos[b], adds in another place, that the Heræum was ten stades from Mycenæ and forty from Argos[c]. Pausanias thus describes the direct road from Mycenæ to Argos[d], and the situation of the Heræum[e]. "In going from Argos to Mycenæ the heroum of Perseus is by the road side, then the tomb of Thyestes called 'the

[a] Herodot. l. 1. c. 31.
[b] Strabo, p. 372.
[c] Ibid. p. 368.
[d] Pausan. l. 2. c. 18.
[e] Ibid. c. 17.

Rams' from the figure of a ram upon it in stone, then on the left of the road the place named Mysia, from a temple of Ceres Mysia, now roofless, but containing within it a temple made of tiles, in which are wooden statues of Proserpine and Pluto. Beyond Mysia is the river Inachus, having passed which there is an altar of the Sun, and then the Gate [of Argos], which, from a neighbouring temple, is called the Gate of Lucina."[a] "The Heræum is on the left hand of Mycenæ[b], at the distance of fifteen stades; along the road leading thither flows the water Eleutherium, which is used by the priestesses for the purgations and secret sacrifices. The temple stands in the lower part of Mount Eubœa[c], for this mountain they call Eubœa, adding, that Eubœa, Prosymna, and Acræa, were daughters of the river Asterion, and that they were the nurses of Juno. From Acræa the mountain opposite to the Heræum[d] receives its name, from Eubœa the part about the temple[e], and the region which is below the Heræum[f] from Prosymna. The Asterion flows under the Heræum and disappears in a chasm[g]. A herb called Asterion which grows on the banks of the stream is pre-

[a] Εἰληθυίας.
[b] Μυκηνῶν ἐν ἀριστερᾷ.
[c] ἐν χθαμαλωτέρῳ τῆς Εὐβοίας.
[d] τὸ ἀπαντικρὺ τοῦ Ἡραίου.
[e] ὅσον περὶ τὸ ἱερόν.
[f] ὑπὸ τὸ Ἡραῖον.
[g] ἐς φάραγγα.

sented to Juno, and chaplets are formed of its leaves twined together."

As Prosymna lay *below* the Heræum, we may infer that the temple did not stand exactly in the plain; the word χθαμαλωτέρῳ, on the other hand, shews that it was not on very high ground. It seems clear, moreover, in coupling the words " to the left of Mycenæ" with the distances given by Herodotus and Strabo, that Pausanias meant the left hand of a person looking westward from the hill of Mycenæ. Upon the whole, therefore, one cannot but conclude that, unless there is some error in the ancient authorities, one of the eminences bordering the plain southward of *Mycenæ*, at about a fourth of the distance from Kharváti to Argos, was the position of the temple. I say a fourth, and not a fifth, as I think the joint testimonies of Herodotus and Pausanias are to be preferred to that of Strabo. It is hereabouts that the torrent of Mycenæ is lost in the plain, though not in a katavóthra, as Pausanias would seem to imply. As to the words " opposite to the Heræum", by which Pausanias describes the situation of Acræa, it is impossible to apply them without knowing exactly the situation of the temple: but the rocky peak which rises from the southeastern side of the site of Mycenæ, being the highest and most remarkable summit of the range, seems the best adapted to the name Acræa. The water Eleutherium may, perhaps, have been the torrent from Tretus, carried artificially in the direction above stated, which is not very different from its natural course; though it is now lost for the most part in the low grounds below Kutzopódhi.

In the extract from Pausanias just cited, it has been seen that he crosses the Inachus before he enters Argos by the Gate of Lucina, but makes no mention of the Charadrus, whereas the modern road, which cannot possibly be very different in direction from the ancient, crosses both streams, and leaves their confluence at a considerable distance to the southward, instead of which, unless there is an omission in Pausanias, the ancient junction was to the northward of the road. There is nothing improbable in this change. The earth brought down in the course of ages by the two rivers would naturally have the effect of altering their course, and might carry their point of union nearer to the sea.

March 18.—The description of Argos by Strabo[a], shews that in his time it occupied the same position as the modern town, though the latter is so much reduced as to be situated not το πλεον, or, for the most part, as he says, but

[a] Strabo, p. 370.

wholly in the plain: it is evident from still existing remains of the ancient walls, that all the south-eastern side of the mountain anciently called Larissa was included within the ancient city. A ruined castle of lower Greek or Frank construction, which occupies the summit of this rocky hill, still preserves, amidst the rude masonry of its crumbling walls, some remains of those of the famed Acropolis of Argos. They are of various dates; some parts approach to the Tirynthian style of building, others are of the most accurate polygonal kind, and there are some remains of towers which appear to have been a late addition to the original Larissa, which was probably constructed without towers. The modern castle consists of an outer inclosure and a keep, and in both of these a part of the walls consists of Hellenic work, thus shewing that the modern construction preserves very nearly the form of the ancient fortress, and that the Larissa had a complete castle within the outer inclosure. The masonry of the interior work is a fine specimen of the second order, being without any horizontal courses; and the stones are accurately joined and smoothed on the outside; in the latter particular it differs from a piece of the exterior Hellenic wall, observable on the north-western side of the outer inclosure of the modern castle, where the stones, though not less irregular in shape, and joined with equal accuracy, are rough on the outside, and are also of larger dimensions. The interior Larissa was equal to a square of about 200 feet. From either end of the outer fortification, the city walls may be traced on the descent of the hill; but their remains are most apparent on the south-western slope, along a projecting crest, which terminates a little beyond the theatre.

The middle part of the theatre was excavated in the rock at the southern foot of the mountain; its two ends were formed of large masses of rude stones and mortar, faced with regular masonry: these are now mere shapeless heaps of rubbish. The excavated part of the theatre preserves the remains of sixty-seven rows of seats, in three divisions, separated by diazomata: in the upper division are nineteen rows, in the middle sixteen, and in the lower thirty-two, and there may, perhaps, be some more at the bottom concealed under the earth. The width of the seats, as usual in Greek theatres, was about two feet and a half. The upper division was not prolonged to the extremities of the cavea, but occupied only the excavated part in the centre. These extra seats, which the form of the hill rendered of easy construction, seem to have been intended for particular occasions, when the throng was excessive, or, perhaps, for some of the less privileged spectators. As well as may be judged in the present ruinous state of the wings, or ends of the cavea, the theatre was about 450 feet in diameter, that of the orchestra 200 feet. The complete rows of seats, reckoning them at 50, would contain near 13,000 spectators, giving a breadth of seat of two feet to each person, or nearly 17,000 if only one foot and a half were allowed: this is on a supposition that the theatre was a semicircle; but we know from Vitruvius, confirmed by existing remains, that the Greek theatre was generally more than half a circle. If 3000 be added for this difference and for the persons seated on the nineteen or twenty incomplete seats above the centre, the audience in the theatre of Argos may have amounted to 20,000, a multitude still very short of the three myriads[a] and more which appear from Plato to have been sometimes assembled in the Dionysiac theatre at Athens. Contiguous to the south-western angle of the theatre, on the extreme foot of the mountain, are twenty-one rows of seats excavated in the rock. These rows are *rectilinear*, forming a line which is nearly that of the orchestra of the theatre produced: the seats, therefore, must have belonged to some separate place

---

[a] πλέον ἢ τρισμυρίους.—Plato in Conviv.

of spectacle, as they could not have commanded a view of any part of the interior of the theatre. Their position clearly proves that the upper division of the excavated seats of the theatre, was not prolonged to the wings. There are foundations of walls inclosing a level space below the rectilinear seats, and steps in the rocks leading up to them in the manner of the scalæ of Greek theatres. I should have supposed they might have belonged to the Stadium, did it not clearly appear from Pausanias that the Stadium was upon the ridge which projects from the opposite end of Mount Larissa.

In front of the western wing of the theatre, there is a ruin of Roman tiles and mortar, with a semi-circular niche at one end, and arched recesses in one of the side walls; the other walls are quite ruined. On the side of the hill to the eastward of the theatre, and nearly on the same level with it, there is a similar but much smaller building before the mouth of a cavern, the lower part excavated in the rock, and the upper built with tiles and mortar. At the extremity there is a semi-circular niche, below it a semi-circular platform cut in the rock, and behind the niche a narrow passage of brick, forming a communication from without at the eastern corner of the building. It was apparently some secret contrivance of the priests. This ruin, though formed of brick, appears to have been the reparation of some ancient temple, as it stands on a terrace supported by a Hellenic polygonal wall, affording a fine specimen of that kind of work.

At the south-western end of the hill of Larissa there are some remains of a conduit of water made of stone, which seems not to have been long out of use, though apparently of ancient construction. I am informed that the aqueduct is traceable to the village of Belish [a], about five miles from Argos to the north-westward. On the south-eastern side of the hill which projects from Mount Larissa in a north-eastern direction, there are some remains of subterraneous passages, constructed with an angular roof, like the galleries at Tiryns.

The only other vestiges of ancient Argos consist of foundations of walls, inscribed stones, and fragments of sculpture and architecture dispersed in the plain or in the churches and houses of the modern town, particularly at and near the episcopal church which stands on the outside of the modern town to the southward.

The north-eastern projection of the mountain of Larissa, which I have already had occasion to notice, forms a conspicuous feature of Argos, though it rises only to one third of the height

---

[a] Μπέλισσι.

of the mountain. It appears to be the hill by Pausanias called Deiras [a], a word which though better suited to the *neck* uniting this hill with the Larissa, we may easily conceive to have had a more comprehensive meaning, and to have been applied to the entire projection. The proofs of the identity of Deiras are: first, that the ascent to the Acropolis was by Deiras, and the ridge in question furnishes the only easy ascent to the summit of the mountain; secondly, that the gate of Deiras led to the river Charadrus, to Œnoe, to the sources of the Inachus, and to Lyrceia, Orneæ, and Phlius, all places to which the road from Argos would naturally lead out of the city across this ridge. The ancient walls of Argos may be traced along the crest of the neck which unites the projection with the mountain, and I observed an opening in the line of the ancient walls, which I conceive to mark precisely the position of the gate of Deiras [b]. It has been conjectured that the eastern extremity of the projecting height in question was the site of the original settlement by Phoroneus, son of Inachus, and hence called the Asty Phoronicum. But assuredly the same motive of security which induced the founder of Argos to make choice of the hill,

---

[a] Pausan. l. 2. c. 24. [b] αἱ πύλαι αἱ πρὸς τῇ Δειράδι. Pausan. l. 2. c. 25.

would lead him to prefer its highest summit. Ἄστυ Φορωνικὸν I conceive to have been nothing more than an expression allusive to the story of Phoroneus having been the first to collect inhabitants in this place: it signified the city of Argos in its infancy, when it occupied the situation which became the Acropolis of subsequent ages like the Cadmeia at Thebes and the Cecropia at Athens. In later times the eastern extremity of Deiras was probably the position of that second citadel which is alluded to by Livy[a]: the height and magnitude as well as the situation of this steep rock would naturally, in the progress of military science, suggest to the Argives the utility of occupying it with an inclosed work.

By the aid of the ascertained positions of Larissa, Deiras, the theatre, and the temple of Lucina, which last stood, as appears from the words of Pausanias already cited, near the gate leading to Mycenæ, we are enabled to throw some light on the topography of the ancient city as described by the Greek traveller[b].

Of the sacred buildings within the city, the first in sanctity and grandeur was the temple of Apollo Lyceius, the most celebrated temple of

[a] utrasque arces, nam duas habent Argi. Liv. Hist. l. 34. c. 25.
[b] Pausan. l. 2. c. 19, 20, 21, 22, 23, 24.

Apollo in Greece next to that of Delphi. It was supposed to have been originally founded by Danaus. The surname of Lyceius was derived from the same fable which gave rise to the type of the wolf's head upon the money of Argos[a]. The image of Apollo Lyceius which Pausanias found in the temple had been made by Attalus of Athens. The temple contained the throne of Danaus and the following statues: Mercury about to make a lyre from a tortoise's shell, Ladas, who was remarkable for his swiftness, Biton carrying a bull for sacrifice on his back, and figures in wood of Mercury and Venus. Before the temple stood a pedestal[b] on which was represented, in low relief[c], a contest between a wolf and a bull, and Diana throwing a stone at the bull. This alluded to the contest of Gelanor and Danaus for the sovereignty,

---

[a] When Danaus and Gelanor were competitors for the sovereignty, it happened that a wolf attacked a bull in the midst of a herd of oxen near the walls of Argos. The omen was thought to proceed from Apollo; Danaus, a stranger, was assimilated to the wolf, the kingdom was assigned to him, and he founded the temple of Apollo Lyceius. This is the version of Pausanias. According to Plutarch, Danaus, who had landed at a place called Pyramia in the Thyreatis, observed, as he proceeded towards Argos, a wolf fighting with a bull, and the former having prevailed, Danaus received it as an omen of his own success over Gelanor. Plutarch. in Pyrrh.

[b] βάθρον.   [c] ἐν τύπῳ.

and was said to have been dedicated by Danaus, as were two neighbouring columns[a] supporting wooden statues of Jupiter and Diana. The exact position of the temple of Apollo Lyceius is not clearly shewn, but as Pausanias speaks of it immediately after mentioning the Gate of Lucina, and as he proceeds from thence to the theatre, thus apparently continuing to skirt the mountain, the temple would seem from this circumstance to have stood in the northern part of the modern town, not far from the foot of the mountain. On the other hand it may be inferred from a comparison of a part of the preceding extract with a passage in the life of Pyrrhus by Plutarch, that the Lyceium stood on one side of the Agora. He says, that when Pyrrhus advanced into the Agora, he observed the figure of a wolf fighting with a bull, which seems clearly to have been the same work mentioned by Pausanias as standing in front of the temple of Apollo. The same inference may be drawn from Sophocles in the Electra, who calls the Agora " the Lyceian Agora of the wolf-slaying god." [b] And the same seems clear also from a

---

[a] κίονας.

[b] Αὕτη, δ' Ὀρέστα, τοῦ λυκοκτόνου θεοῦ Ἀγορὰ Λύκειος. Sophoc. Elect. v. 6.
The epithet λυκοκτόνος probably referred to Apollo having been the protector of flocks, and consequently the

single word of Pausanias, who, after mentioning the theatre, returns *again*[a] to the Agora.

The following objects were near the temple of Apollo,—the tombs of Linus and of Psamathe, —a statue of Apollo Agyeius,—an altar of Jupiter Pluvius,—the monument of Prometheus —a statue of Creugas the pugilist,—a trophy for a victory over the Corinthians,—a statue of Jupiter Meilichius of white marble, by Polycleitus, —and a groupe in stone of Biton and his brother Cleobis drawing their mother in a car to the Heræum; the last of these was in front of a temple of Jupiter Nemeius, which contained an upright statue in brass by Lysippus. Between this temple and the theatre, Pausanias describes the tomb of Phoroneus,—a very ancient temple of Fortune,—the monument of Choreia, one of the Mænades,—a temple of the Hours,—statues of the Seven Leaders against Thebes as named by Æschylus, with those of the Eleven who took Thebes,—the monument of Danaus,—a common cenotaph in honour of the Argives who fell at Troy or in returning from thence,—a temple of Jupiter Soter,—a building in which the Argive women lamented Adonis,—and a

enemy of wolves. A scholiast on this passage not only confirms the position of the Lyceium in the Agora, but adds, that it stood opposite to the temple of Jupiter Nemeius.

[a] αὖθις.

temple of Cephissus, under which it was believed that the water of that Argive river continued to flow after Neptune had deprived it of water above ground. Here was a head of Medusa in marble, said to have been made by the Cyclopes. Behind the temple of Cephissus was a place[a] still called Criterium, because Hypermnestra was here said to have been condemned by Danaus. The temple of Cephissus was near the theatre.

The theatre, among other things worthy of notice, contained a statue of the Argive Perilaus slaying the Spartan Othryades. Above the theatre stood a temple of Venus, before which there was a figure in relief, on a pillar[b], of Telesilla, the composer of hymns[c]. She was represented with books[d] at her feet, and as about to place a helmet on her head. Pausanias now descends again[e] to the Agora. Between the temple of Venus and the Agora he describes the monument of Cerdo, wife of Phoroneus, temples of Æsculapius and of Diana Peitho, a brazen statue of Æneias, a place called Delta, an altar of Jupiter Phyxius, monuments of the two Hypermnestræ, that of the daughter of Danaus being also the tomb of Lynceus,—the sepulchre

---

[a] χωρίον.
[b] ἐπείργασται στήλη.
[c] ἄσματα.   [d] βιβλία.
[e] κατελθοῦσιν ἐντεῦθεν καὶ αὖθις τραπεῖσιν ἐπὶ τὴν ἀγοράν.

of Talaus, son of Bias, and a temple of Minerva Salpinx, before which was the tomb of Epimenides. In the middle of the Agora was the monument of Pyrrhus, a building [a] of white marble, on which were represented various objects relating to his wars, and among them elephants. "This monument", adds Pausanias, "was erected on the spot where his body was burnt, and it is considered a trophy by the Argives, but his bones are in the neighbouring temple of Ceres, where he breathed his last, and where his brazen shield is affixed above the door." [b] The other monuments in the Agora were a tumulus said to contain the head of Medusa,—the tomb of Gorgophone,—a trophy raised for the victory over the Lacedæmonians under the Argive Laphaes,—a temple of Latona, containing a statue by Praxiteles, with that of Chloris, daughter of Niobe, standing by it,—a temple of Juno Antheia, before which was a tomb of the women called Haliæ,—a temple of Ceres Pelasgis,—the tomb of Pelasgus,—a brazen basis [c] of no great size which supported ancient statues of Diana, Jupiter, and Minerva,—a temple of Neptune Pros-

[a] οἰκοδόμημα.

[b] According to Plutarch, Pyrrhus was wounded in the neck by a tile thrown down upon him by a woman, with whose son he was fighting; he was then dragged into a neighbouring portico and slain by Zopyrus, an officer of Antigonus.

[c] χαλκεῖον.

clystius,—the tomb of Argus,—a temple of the Dioscuri, which contained statues by Dipœnus and Scyllis of the Dioscuri, of their sons Anaxis and Mnasinous, and of the mothers of the latter Hilaeira and Phœbe; these works were of ebony, with the exception of a small part of the horses, which was in ivory. There were likewise in the Agora a temple of Lucina dedicated by Helene, —a temple of Hecate, containing an image of the goddess in stone by Scopas, and two others in brass by Polycleitus and Naucydes.

The third part of the description of Argos by Pausanias comprehends his route from the Agora to the Cylarabis. The Cylarabis was a gymnasium named from its founder the son of Sthenelus. It contained a statue of Minerva Pania, and tombs of Sthenelus and Cylarabus. Near it was a polyandrium of the Argives who fell in the Athenian expedition to Sicily. Like most of the gymnasia and places of public exercise, the Cylarabis stood a little without the city-walls. Livy says it was less than 300 paces distant from the city[a]. The gate which led to it appears from Plutarch to have been called Diampares[b]: a little without the gate, according to Pausanias, was the tomb of Sacadas. Pyrrhus, in the attack upon Argos which terminated his restless career, having marched by

[a] Liv. l. 34. c. 26.   [b] Plutarch in Pyrrh. and Cleomen.

night from Nauplia, entered the city by the gate Diampares. His death and the destruction of a great part of his army was occasioned, according to Plutarch, by a mistake in the execution of his orders, by which two divisions of his army moving in opposite directions were brought into contact in a narrow street between the Cylarabis and the Agora. The king fell near the sepulchre of Licymnius, the only monument mentioned by Pausanias between the Agora and the Gymnasium [a].

From the Cylarabis, Pausanias proceeds to Larissa. The monuments which he first describes appear to have been for the most part in or near a street called Cœle. They were as follows:—a temple of Bacchus with a statue, brought from Caphareus by the Argives who had been wrecked there on their return from Troy,—the house of Adrastus,—a temple of Amphiaraus,—the monument of Eriphyle,—a temenus of Æsculapius,—a temple of Baton. Ascending from Cœle [b] was the tomb of Hyrnetho,—a temple of Æsculapius, the principal sanctuary of that deity in Argos,—a sanctuary

---

[a] ἐρχομένῳ ὁδὸν εὐθεῖαν ἐς γυμνάσιον Κυλαράβου. This concurring testimony as to the place where Pyrrhus was killed, proves Strabo to have been mistaken in saying that Pyrrhus did not enter Argos, but fell before the walls: Ἀργεῖοι Πύῤῥον οὐκ ἐδέξαντο, ἀλλὰ πρὸ τοῦ τείχους ἔπεσε. p. 376.

[b] ἐπανιόντι ἐκ τῆς Κοίλης.

of Diana Pheræa[a],—a temple of Bacchus Cresius and a temple of Venus Urania. The statue of Æsculapius in his temple was of white marble; he was represented seated, with Hygieia standing beside him: they were the works of Xenophilus and Straton, of whom there were sitting figures in the same place. Adjacent to the Cresium there was a subterraneous building[b], which, according to the Argive antiquaries, once contained the brazen θάλαμος, or bedchamber, in which Danae was confined by her father, Acrisius. As the words which Pausanias applies to this building are very nearly the same as those employed by him in describing the treasuries of Mycenæ, one cannot but suspect that the building at Argos was of the same kind, and as the side of a hill was necessary to the formation of such a structure, there is reason to presume that it stood at the foot of the Deiras, the more so as Pausanias, after indicating that the monument of Crotopus and the temples of Bacchus Cresius and of Venus Urania were near the subterraneous building, then immediately ascends by the Deiras to Larissa.

On the ascent to Larissa were the temples of

---

[a] Pausanias here adds, that the Argives also shewed the monuments of Dejanira and of Helenus, and the Palladium, or statue of Minerva, which had been brought from Troy, but that he did not believe the objects to have been really what was pretended.

[b] κατάγχιον οἰκοδόμημα.

Juno Acræa, and of Apollo Deiradiotes, the latter so called, because the place in which it stood was called Deiras. It contained a brazen upright statue of the god. To this the temple of Minerva Oxyderces[a] was contiguous[b], and the Stadium to the latter building. In the way from thence to the Acropolis, were monuments of the sons of Ægyptus. On the summit of Larissa there were temples of Jupiter Larissæus and of Minerva. The roof of the former no longer existed, and a wooden statue of Jupiter was removed from its pedestal. But the temple of Minerva was still in good preservation, and worthy of being seen: it contained, besides other offerings, a wooden statue of Jupiter, which had a third eye in the middle of the forehead; it was said to have been brought by Sthenelus from Troy.

Plutarch, on more than one occasion[c], gives the name of Aspis to the citadel of Argos. Cleomenes took it by first entering, in the night, the quarter between the Aspis and the theatre, which the biographer justly describes as rugged and difficult to pass over[d]. Afterwards, when

[a] So called by Diomedes the founder, because the goddess had removed the dimness from his eyes when fighting at Troy.
[b] ἔχιται.
[c] Plutarch in Pyrrh. et in Cleomen.
[d] νυκτὸς ἦγε πρὸς τὰ τείχη τὸ στράτευμα, καὶ τὸν περὶ τὴν Ἀσπίδα τόπον καταλαβὼν ὑπὲρ τοῦ θεάτρου χαλεπὸν ὄντα καὶ δυσπρόσοδον, οὕτως τοὺς ἀνθρώπους ἐξέπληξεν, &c. In Cleomen.

his garrison was defending itself against the Achaians who were in possession of the city, Cleomenes forced his way into the Aspis by breaking down certain vaults which were under it [a].

As no remains of the city-walls are, I believe, traceable in the plain, it is difficult to form an estimate of the dimensions of the ancient Argos; but supposing it to have formed nearly a semicircle, of which the still existing vestiges of the ancient walls across the ridges of Larissa and Deiras were the diameter, the whole periphery could not have been less than five miles. The principal gates appear to have been:—1. That of Deiras, leading to Mantineia, Lyrceia, Orneæ, and Phlius. 2. The gate of Lucina, leading to the Heræum, Mycenæ, and Corinth. 3. The gate Diampares, leading to Nauplia and Epidaurus. 4. The gate of Temenium and Lerna, leading into Laconia by the Thyreatis. 5. The gate leading to the sources of the Erasinus, Hysiæ, and Tegea. It is not improbable that there was a sixth gate, between the gates of Lucina and Diampares, leading to Mideia and the central parts of the plain of Argos.

The second, third, and fifth of these routes I have already travelled, and have added to my itinerary some remarks on their ancient topo-

---

[a] ἐκκόψας δὲ ὑπὸ τὴν Ἀσπίδα ψαλίδας, ἀνέβη καὶ συνέμιξε τοῖς ἔνδον, ἔτι πρὸς τοὺς Ἀχαιοὺς ἀντέχουσι, &c.

graphy. The fourth I propose to follow on leaving Argos. I shall now offer a few remarks on the topography of that which quitted Argos at the gate of Deiras. Two roads issued from this gate, one leading to the left to Mantineia, the other to Lyrceia and Orneæ. Of the first of these, there seems to have been a bifurcation towards the mountains, which contained the common frontier of Argolis and Arcadia; for though in the Argolics Pausanias mentions only one road to Mantineia [a], in the Arcadics he describes two, both leading from Argos to that place, but approaching the city on different sides [b]; and, as in the Argolics, he describes the single road as far only as the boundaries of the Argeia, so, in the Arcadics, he describes the two roads to Mantineia from the borders only of the Mantinice. On the road from Argos to the frontier of the Argeia, "there stood a double temple, of which one of the entrances was to the east, the other to the west; in the eastern was a wooden statue of Venus, in the western a similar statue of Mars; they were said to have been dedicated by Polyneices. After passing the torrent Charadrus, the traveller arrived at the place called Œnoe, above which was the mountain Artemisium, and a temple of Diana on the summit of

[a] Pausan. l. 2. c. 25.   [b] Pausan. Arcad. c. 6.

the mountain."[a] From these words it appears that *Œnoe* stood on or near the left bank of the Rema of Argos, at the foot of Mount Málevo, otherwise called the mountain of Karyá, or of Turníki, which names are those of two villages upon it, and that the ancient road approached the mountain between the two rivers now called the Rema of Argos and the Bánitza. About Bélissi, towards which place, perhaps, some remains of *Œnoe* may be found, the division of the two roads probably took place, the southern anciently called *Prinus*, leading by Turníki, the northern called *Climax*, by Kaparéli and Pikérnes. I shall have occasion to refer to these two ancient routes more particularly hereafter.

The northernmost of the two roads which proceeded from the gate of Deiras, being that which led to Lyrceia and Orneæ is thus described by Pausanias[b]: "The other road from the gates at Deiras leads to Lyrceia. It is said that Lynceus, the only one of the fifty brothers, sons of Danaus, who was saved, escaped to this place, and that he raised a torch from hence as a signal of his safety; it having been agreed upon between him and Hypermnestra, that when he had escaped the snares of Danaus he should shew a torch, and that she should do

[a] ἐπὶ κορυφῇ τοῦ ὄρους.   [b] Pausan. l. 2. c. 25.

the like from Larissa. In memory of the event the Argives celebrate the festival of torches. The city was formerly called Lynceia, but when Lyrcus, the bastard son of Abas, got possession of the place, it received the name of Lyrceia. In the ruins there is nothing remarkable, except the statue of Lyrcus upon a pillar. To this place from Argos there is a distance of about sixty stades, and as many more from Lyrceia to Orneæ. Lyrceia having been already deserted in the time of the expedition to Ilium, Homer has made no mention of it in the Catalogue, but the name of Orneæ occurs as that of an inhabited place of the Argeia, before those of Phlius and Sicyon. The Orneatæ were afterwards expelled from their town by the Argives, and became a part of the Argive community. In Orneæ there is a temple of Diana, containing an upright statue made of wood, and another temple in common to all the gods. Beyond Orneæ are the Sicyonia and the Phliasia."

Strabo describes Orneæ as an uninhabited place situated above the plain of the Sicyonia upon a river, which was also called Orneæ[a]. Thucydides more accurately defines Orneæ as lying between Argolis and Phliasia. And as the road thither was intermediate between the

[a] Strabo, p. 382.

Climax, or northern road into the Mantinice, and the pass of Tretus leading to Nemea, it is obvious that Orneæ must have stood nearly in a line from Argos to Phlius, at a distance of 120 stades from the former; Lyrceia, it appears from Pausanias, was half way thither in a position visible from the Larissa of Argos. The passes over Mount Lyrceium and the adjoining hills, seem to have been the direction followed by Agis in the fourteenth year of the Peloponnesian war[a], when he selected this more rugged road from the Phliasia into the plain of Argos, in order to avoid the Argives, who were waiting for him on the road from Nemea by the Tretus. Saminthus, which Agis destroyed after descending into the plain, may possibly have been at Kutzopódhi, where, as I have already remarked, remains of antiquity are sometimes found.

[a] Thucyd. l. 5. c. 58.

CHAPTER XXI.

Ancient Geography of the Argolic peninsula.—MIDEIA.—LESSA.—Hierum of EPIDAURIA.—EPIDAURUS.—ÆGINA.—Temple of Jupiter Panhellenius.—TRŒZEN.—CALAUREIA.—METHANA.—HERMIONE.—HALICE.—MASES.—ASINE.—Islands of the Argolic and Hermionian Gulfs.

For the purpose of justifying the comparative geography of the Argolic peninsula as indicated on the map, and at the same time of completing that summary view of the state of the Peloponnesus at the end of the second century of the Christian æra, which has been an incidental object throughout this work, I shall here subjoin some observations on that part of the second book of Pausanias which is comprehended between the middle of the twenty-fifth and the middle of the thirty-sixth chapters. These remarks are partly the result of a former tour in Greece, in which I followed the route of Pausanias from Argos to Epidaurus and to Ægina: with regard to Trœzen, Hermione, Mases, and Asine I am indebted either to other travellers, or to oral information which I obtained in the neighbouring districts.

The road to Epidaurus issued from Argos, as

I have already shewn at the gate Diampares. It left the ruins of Tiryns a little on the right, and passed between[a] Nauplia, and Mideia, of which latter "nothing remained but the site[b]. Lessa was a town[c] on the road to Epidaurus; it contained a temple of Minerva and a statue not at all different from that in the Acropolis of Argos [i. e. a wooden statue of Jupiter with three eyes]. Above Lessa rose the mountain Arachnæum, which before the reign of Inachus was called Sapyselaton. It contained altars of Jupiter and Juno, at which there were sacrifices in times of drought. Near Lessa the district of the Epidaurii bordered upon the Argeia, but the road passed by the temple of Æsculapius before it arrived at the city of Epidaurus. The sacred grove was surrounded on every side by mountains. One of them was called Tittheium and the other Cynortium; on the latter stood a temple of Apollo Maleatas. On the ascent to Mount Coryphæum there was an olive tree by the road side called Strepte [twisted]; which was said to have been bent into that form by Hercules. Whether he assigned it for a boundary to the Asinæi," adds Pausanias, " I am not informed, since the country being now desolate, it is not easy to ascertain its bounda-

---

[a] See Pausan. l. 2. c. 25, 26, 27, 28. [b] τὸ ἔδαφος. [c] κώμη.

ries in any part." Upon the summit of the mountain was a temple of Minerva Coryphæa, which was mentioned in a poem of Telesilla. On the descent to the city of the Epidaurii there was a place grown with wild olives called Hyrnethium, and not far from the city a sepulchre of Melissa, wife of Periander, the son of Cypselus.

The exact situation of Mideia I was unable to determine, which is not surprising, as nothing but vestiges of it remained in the time of Pausanias. It is clear, however, as well from this passage as from an expression of Strabo indicating the vicinity of Mideia to Tiryns and to Prosymna[a], which last, as we have seen, was near the Heræum[b], that Mideia stood on the foot of the hills which border the Argolic plain, and about eastward of Tiryns. The road to Epidaurus, after passing these places, leads through a succession of narrow valleys traversed by streams which flow from Mount Arachnæum towards the Argolic Gulf. At three places between Anápli (*Nauplia*) and Lykurió (*Lessa*), I observed vestiges of Hellenic walls, besides the ruins of two castles on the right of the road at the entrance of valleys conducting to the sea. These were all probably works of defence, and as such may

[a] Strabo, p. 373. [b] Pausan. l. 2. c. 17.

have been passed over in silence by Pausanias, because they contained nothing interesting to his favorite objects of inquiry. The further of the two castles, which stands at about two thirds of the distance between *Nauplia* and *Lessa*, is, from its state of preservation, one of the best specimens I know of a Hellenic fortress; and it appears to be of a time when the military architecture of the Greeks was in its perfection.

In approaching the site of *Lessa* the valley becomes wider and more cultivable, and is altogether four or five miles in length, ending eastward at the villages of Lykurió and Koróni: beyond these it is separated from the vale of Ieró by a ridge of heights, in which there is a narrow opening leading into that valley; the opening was anciently fortified by two towers of which the foundations still exist; they mark the common boundary of the Argeia and Epidauria alluded to by Pausanias. The valley of *Lessa* is inclosed between Mount *Arachnæum* and a lower ridge, through a rocky opening in which the waters of the vale of *Lessa*, after uniting into a single stream, find their way to the sea-coast of the *Asinæa*. The foundations of the walls of *Lessa* inclose a hill upon the foot of which stands the village of Lykurió. This hill is a last slope or projection of the range of Arachnæum; I take it to be the ancient Mount

Tittheium. On the outside of the walls of Lessa near the foot of the mountain, I found the remains of an ancient pyramid near a church, which contains some Ionic columns. The lower part only of the pyramid remains, it was faced with masonry of the polygonal kind and had a base of near forty feet square. The name Koróni attached to the village south-eastward of Lykurió is curious, as having evidently been derived from Coronis the reputed mother of Æsculapius, and consequently as having, like the name Palamídhi at Anápli, existed here from the earliest times, although no mention of it occurs in ancient authors.

The temple of Æsculapius and the sacred ἄλσος, or grove of the Epidaurii, one of the most renowned places in Greece for its sanctity, riches, and the splendour of the sacred offerings which adorned it [a], was situated at the upper end of a valley, there terminated by a semicircle of steep hills, from which several torrents descend and unite at the south-western extremity of the valley, from whence the stream passes through an opening in the mountains, and joins, I believe, the river of *Lessa*. The place is now called Sto Ieró [b], that is to say, "the temple or sacred place", probably the name by which it

---

[a] Liv. l. 45. c. 28. [b] στὸ Ἱερὸν.

was always distinguished in common discourse by the Epidaurii, whose city was several miles distant. The buildings described by Pausanias[a] are: first, the temple of Æsculapius, containing a chryselephantine statue of the god, inscribed as the work of Thrasymedes of Parus, and half the size of the Jupiter, by Phidias, at Olympia. Æsculapius was seated on a throne, holding a staff[b] in one hand, resting the other on the head of a serpent, a dog lying at his feet. Upon [the sides of] the throne were represented Chimæra destroyed by Bellerophontes, and Perseus cutting off the head of Medusa. On one side of the temple[c] was a place where the suppliants of the god slept, and sought relief from their complaints by means of the interpretation which was given to their dreams by the priests. Near the temple stood the Tholus, a circular building of white marble, built by Polycleitus of Argos, and containing two pictures by Pausias, one of Love laying aside his bow and assuming the lyre, the other of Methe, or Intoxication, represented by a woman drinking out of a glass[d], through which her face was seen. The sacred peribolus had formerly contained many pillars[e], bearing inscriptions which re-

[a] Pausan. l. 2. c. 27.
[b] βακτηρίαν.
[c] τοῦ ναοῦ πέραν.
[d] ἐκ ὑαλίνης φιάλης.
[e] στῆλαι.

corded the names of persons who had been cured here, together with their diseases and the mode of treatment: but six of them only remained in the time of Pausanias; the inscriptions were in the Doric dialect. Apart from the other columns was one of great antiquity, which commemorated the dedication of twenty horses by Hippolytus. Of the theatre, Pausanias speaks in the following terms: "The Epidaurii have a theatre in their sacred place, which appears to me particularly well worthy of examination: the theatres of the Romans, indeed, excel all others in ornament, and surpass in size even that of Megalopolis in Arcadia, but in harmony and beauty of workmanship what artist can come into competition with Polycleitus, who constructed both the theatre and the tholus of the Epidaurii?"

The other objects in the sacred grove [a], were temples of Venus, of Themis, and of Diana, a statue of Epione, wife of Æsculapius,—a κρήνη, or artificial fountain, covered with a roof and handsomely adorned,—a stadium, which, as usual among the Greeks [b], was constructed of earth, and the following works erected by Antoninus Pius before he was emperor; namely, a bath, called the Bath of Æsculapius, a temple of the Epidotæ, a temple dedicated to Hygieia, and to Æs-

[a] ἐντὸς τοῦ ἄλσους.   [b] οἷον Ἕλλησι τὰ πολλά.

culapius, and Apollo surnamed the Egyptian, and a building erected beyond the sacred precincts for the reception of the dying and of women in labour, because it was unlawful to be born or to die within the inclosure[a]. Antoninus repaired also the stoa of Cotys[b], which was an edifice of unburnt bricks[c], and he added a receptacle for water to the ancient temple of Apollo Maleatas upon Mount Cynortium.

The sacred peribolus is less than a mile in circumference; it was confined on two sides by steep hills, and on the other two by a wall, which appears to have formed a right angle in the lowest and most level part of the valley, and is still traceable in several places. Of some of the buildings described by Pausanias, there are considerable remains, but of the temple which was situated, as might be expected, about the middle of the peribolus, only a part of the foundations are to be seen above ground; by an excavation, not only its dimensions, but many other particulars of its construction would probably be ascertained. There exists also a part of the foundations, and some remains of

[a] There was another regulation of the priesthood, of which one can better understand the motive; namely, that every thing sacrificed in the sacred inclosure should also be consumed within it.

[b] A deity, worshipped also among the Corinthians. Suidas in Κότυι

[c] ὠμῆς πλίνθου.

the circular cell of the Tholus, which shew that it was about twenty feet in diameter. I observed some pieces of it covered with defaced inscriptions, which probably contained records of the same kind as those upon the stelæ mentioned by Pausanias, and which, according to Strabo, were repeated upon numerous tablets suspended in the temple, as occurred also at Cos and Tricca. But the most remarkable ruin at Ieró is the theatre, and, from the renown of its architect, it may be considered as one of the most curious remains of antiquity in Greece. Although no traces of the proscenium remain, and many of the seats made of white marble are displaced by the bushes which have grown among them, it is in better preservation than any other theatre in Greece, except that which exists near Trametzús in Epirus, not far from Ioánnina. Its details, nevertheless, cannot be ascertained with great accuracy on account of the ruined state of the upper part of the edifice, and the accumulation of earth and stones below; enough however remains to shew that the orchestra was about ninety feet in length, and the entire theatre about 370 feet in diameter: thirty-two rows of seats still appear above ground in a lower division, which is separated by a diazoma from an upper, consisting of twenty seats. Twenty-four scalæ, or flights of steps, diverging in equidistant radii from the bottom to the top, formed the communications with the seats. The theatre, when complete, was capable of containing 12,000 spectators.

Of the other remains of antiquity at Ieró, I could recognize only those of the Stadium, and near it the ruins of two cisterns and a bath, which are evidently some of the works of Antoninus. Of the Stadium the circular end and a part of the adjacent sides remain, with parts of fifteen rows of seats.

Coryphæum I take to have been the mountain which rises above the theatre to the south-east, first, because the name seems most applicable to the highest of the summits which surround the valley; secondly, because it appears, from the observation of Pausanias on the olive-tree called Strepte, that the boundaries between the Epidaurii and Asinæi were in Mount Coryphæum, and those boundaries could only have been in a southern direction from Epidaurus. Of the other two mountains named by Pausanias, the one which rises above Lessa I take to have been the Tittheium; for it seems probable that the temple of Apollo Maleatas, which stood upon Mount Cynortium, and which was repaired or added to by Antoninus, was in the more immediate vicinity of the Sacred Grove.

The Hierum of Epidauria enjoyed its fame and riches for a great length of time. Near five centuries before the visit of Pausanias, Æsculapius of Epidaurus was in such repute, that a deputation was decreed at Rome to implore his aid in curing a pestilence which ravaged the city and surrounding country[a]. A ship was soon afterwards sent to Epidaurus, and one of the sacred serpents carried back to Rome. When L. Æmilius Paullus visited the Hierum after the conquest of Macedonia[b], it was rich in gifts presented by those who had here obtained relief from their diseases; in the time of Livy it had been plundered of many of those valuable offerings[c].

Strabo, a contemporary of the Latin historian, describes the Epidaurian sanctuary as "a place renowned for the cure of all sorts of diseases, and always full of invalids;" and he adds, "that the walls of the temple were covered with tablets de-

---

[a] B. C. 293. Liv. Hist. l. 10. c. 47. Valer. Max. l. 1. c. 8. The decree was made in the 19th lustre; the same year in which the custom of rewarding victors in the games with the palm-branch was first introduced from Greece.

[b] B. C. 167.

[c] Epidaurum inclytam Æsculapii nobili templo, quod, quinque millibus passuum ab urbe distans, nunc vestigiis revulsorum donorum, tum donis dives erat, quæ remediorum salutarium ægri mercedem sacraverant Deo.
Liv. l. 45. c. 28.

scriptive of the cures, as in the temples of Cos and Tricca."[a]

It is to the secluded situation of Ieró that we are indebted for what still remains of the monuments of the grove of Æsculapius. When Anápli was the seat of government in the Moréa, they suffered great injury from the Turks of that place, who often made use of the materials in the construction or reparation of their farms, mosks, houses, and fortifications. They are still subject to dilapidation, when the Turkish spahí of a neighbouring village erects a tower or a tjiftlík, or when the Greeks have purchased permission to build or repair one of their churches. It is to be hoped, however, that the retired position, the distance from the sea-coast, and the desolate state of the surrounding country, may long serve to protect these remains, which are equally valuable as works of art, and as furnishing the best preserved specimen of one of those detached hiera, furnished with all the appendages of Hellenic civilization, of which there were not many other examples in Greece. Those which most nearly resembled it were the Altis of Olympia, the Posidonium of the Isthmus, and the Hierum of Jupiter at Nemea; but these were not much frequented, except at the great periodical festivals, whereas the temple of the Epidaurian

[a] Strabo, p. 374.

Æsculapius, besides being a scene of agonistic exhibition in common with every other place in Greece which possessed a stadium and a theatre; and besides being the resort of sick persons, like the other temples of the healing god, far excelled them all in the number of the votaries who frequented it in every season. It was, in short, the most fashionable place of resort of Grecian invalids seeking relief from a change of air or of place, or of medical treatment. Hither they flocked from every part of the country, to commit themselves to the care of the servants of Æsculapius, who, equally dexterous as priests and as physicians, provided themselves with resources in either capacity, which they could turn to the benefit of their patients' infirmities and their own profit. If modern physicians, by means of the pretended virtues of medicinal waters, have often had the art to create a prejudice producing salutary effects on the bodily complaints of their patients, one cannot be surprised that the luxurious valetudinarians of Greece should have here derived ideal benefits of equal efficacy from the *numen loci*, assisted by the interesting diversions which the contests of the Asclepian Games afforded, or the other amusements of the theatre and stadium. On the score of natural advantages, however, the Epidaurian ἄλσος seems to have little to recommend it: it is difficult to believe that a narrow valley, supplied with water only from cisterns, occasional torrents, or distant springs, and closely surrounded with steep woody hills, concentrating an excessive heat in summer, could have been generally beneficial to those diseases which admit of mitigation or cure from a change of place and air. The sea-breezes and delicious climate of Cos, the mountain air, the woods and fountains of Pellene and Titane, or even the wide spreading plains around the Thessalian Tricca, seem to have been preferable to this narrow valley of the Epidauria, of which the long continued reputation, without any mineral waters or other natural peculiarity to mark it for a place of curative influence, furnishes a most remarkable instance of the power of faith among the ancients, and of the permanence of their manners.

It was chiefly by its sacred grove and the reputation of Æsculapius for the cure of human infirmities, that the city of Epidaurus was noted in the later ages of Greece. Its distance from the Hierum was reckoned at five Roman miles[a]. Strabo[b] has accurately described it as situated in a recess of the Saronic gulf, open to the north-east, and as backed by high

[a] Liv. l. 45. c. 28.—Val. Max. l. 1. c. 8.   [b] Strabo, p. 374.

mountains[a]. In the time of the Peloponnesian war, it appears to have been strongly fortified[b]; under Augustus its circuit was no more than fifteen stades[c], whence it appears that Epidaurus was already at that time reduced to the promontory where we now see, in many parts, the foundations of Hellenic walls along the edge of the cliffs. A small neighbouring village is still called Pídhavro[d], which is the ancient name with the same accent, and with the loss only of the initial short vowel, a common Romaic corruption. Around Pídhavro there is a small plain watered by a torrent, and chiefly cultivated with vines as it was in the time of Homer[e]. The slope of the mountain which rises above the valley is covered with wild olives, the descendants of those which formerly surrounded the monument of Hyrnetho, daughter of Temenus and wife of Deiphontes, whose tragic story occupies the greater part of one of the chapters of Pausanias.

The objects noticed at Epidaurus by the Greek traveller, were—in the Acropolis, a remarkable wooden statue of Minerva surnamed Cissæa. In the city, an open temenus of

[a] ἐν μυχῷ τοῦ Σαρωνικοῦ Κόλπου βλέπουσα πρὸς τὰς ἀνατολὰς θερινάς, περικλείεται δ' ὄρεσιν ὑψηλοῖς.
[b] Thucyd. l. 2. c. 56.—l. 5. c. 55.
[c] Strabo, p. 374.
[d] Πίδαυρος.
[e] ἀμπελόεντ' Ἐπίδαυρον. Iliad. B. v. 561.

Æsculapius containing statues, of Parian marble, of the god and his wife Epione; temples of Bacchus, of Diana, and of Venus, and on a cape at the harbour a temple of Juno.

From Epidaurus Pausanias proceeds to Ægina, once a dependence of that city[a]. Strabo describes Ægina with his usual elegance of expression, and with an accuracy for which he is not so often remarkable. "Why need we say", exclaims the Geographer[b], "that Ægina is one of the most celebrated of islands—the native country of Æacus and the Æacidæ, which once enjoyed the dominion of the seas, and contended with Athens itself for the prize of superior glory in the battle with the Persian fleet at Salamis? The circumference of the island is said to be 180 stades. The city, which bears the same name as the island, is on the south-western side. The island is surrounded by Attica, Megaris, and the parts of Peloponnesus towards Epidaurus, and is distant about 100 stades from each. Its eastern and southern sides are washed by the Myrtoan and Cretan seas. Many small islands lie between it and the continent: towards the sea, Belbina only. Its land possesses a deep soil, but is stony on the surface, particularly in the plain; hence it is generally naked,

[a] Herodot. l. 5. c. 83. [b] Strabo, p. 375.

[of trees,] but sufficiently productive of barley. It was anciently called Œnone." Pausanias justly remarks, that "The numerous rocks and shallows which surround Ægina, render it difficult and hazardous of approach." They were fabled to have been provisions of Æacus against the approach of pirates and enemies[a].

The effect of industry excited by necessity, in raising to opulence places the least favoured by nature, has been exemplified in the islands of Greece in every age. The present commercial importance of Ydhra, Psará, and Petza, is not less surprising than that of Ægina in the early periods of Grecian history, though, as the wealth of states so situated, must in great measure be proportionate to that of the surrounding countries, the commercial islands of the modern Greeks are poor compared with the ancient Ægina, which rivalled the most opulent of the Hellenic republics. Before the Athenians had begun to coin a metallic medium of commercial exchange, and when their navy was in its infancy the Æginetæ possessed silver money, had acquired the command of the Grecian seas by their ships, and shaking off their ancient dependence upon Epidaurus, were sufficiently powerful to insult the

[a] Pausan. l. 2. c. 29.

neighbouring coasts, as well those of their late metropolis on the Peloponnesian side, as those of the people on the opposite shore of the Saronic Gulf, who were thereafter to be their masters[a]. According to Thucydides[b], one of the most important events in Grecian history, the Peloponnesian war, originated in great measure in the impatience of the Æginetæ, under the alleged injustice of their neighbours of Athens, combined with the temptation to enter into a war with Athens, which was excited at Corinth and Sparta by the hope of assistance from the Æginetan fleet.

Like the majority of the islands of the Ægæan sea, Ægina preserves its ancient name unaltered. Its western half consists of a stony plain, well cultivated with corn. The remainder is mountainous, and may be divided into two parts; a very remarkable conical hill, now called the Oros[c], which occupies all the southern extremity, and the ridge of Panhellenium, on the north-eastern side. Between the latter and the plain there are some narrow cultivated slopes, lying amidst a cluster of irregular hills. It is among these heights, on a pointed hill towards the northern coast, that the modern town, or rather village, is situated.

[a] Herodot. l. 5. c. 81.— l. 6. c. 89.--Ephorus ap. Strabon. p. 376.
[b] Thucyd. l. 1. c. 67.
[c] τὸ Ὄρος.

The following are the remarks of Pausanias upon the ports and city of Ægina[a]: Near the port principally frequented by shipping, there was a temple of Venus, and in the most conspicuous part of the city the Æaceium, a quadrangular inclosure built of white marble, containing some old olive trees: in the entrance stood statues of the deputies sent by the Greeks to Æacus, to prevail upon him to sacrifice and pray for rain to Jupiter Panhellenius. Near the Æaceium was the tomb of Phocus; it was a barrow surrounded with a circular basis[b], and was crowned with a rude stone; with this stone Phocus was said to have been killed by his half brother Peleus, whose own brother Telamon, afterwards entering the port called Secret by night, raised the tomb to Phocus. Not far from the Secret port there was a handsome theatre, greatly[c] resembling that of the Epidaurii in magnitude and workmanship. Behind it was the Stadium, which, with one of its sides, supported the theatre. There were temples at no great distance from one another, dedicated to Apollo, to Diana, and to Bacchus. That of Apollo had a naked wooden statue, of Æginetan workmanship, the Diana was draped, the Bacchus clothed and bearded. In a different part

[a] Pausan. l. 2. c. 29.
[b] χῆμα περιεχόμενον κύκλῳ κρηπῖδι.
[c] μάλιστα.

of the city was a temple of Æsculapius, with a seated statue of stone. But of all the deities worshipped by the Æginetæ, the greatest veneration was paid to Hecate. Her temple, which stood within a peribolus, contained a wooden statue by Myron, who had represented the goddess with a single head and body; the Athenians, in the opinion of Pausanias, were the first to give her a triple form, as Alcamenes had done in the Hecate Epipyrgidia, which stood near the temple of 'Victory without wings,' in the Acropolis of Athens. On the road towards the mountain of Jupiter Panhellenius there was a temple of Aphæa, to whom Pindar wrote a hymn[a] for the Æginetæ." She was the same as Britomartis, and the Dictynna of the Cretans. Herodotus[b] speaks of a temple of Minerva at Ægina, which has not been noticed by Pausanias.

To the traveller who approaches Ægina from the westward, the position of the ancient city is indicated by a tumulus near the northwestern cape, not far to the southward of which rise two Doric columns, of the most elegant form, one wanting the capital and the upper part of the shaft, the other complete, with a part of the architrave. The column is twenty-five feet in height, including the capital,

[a] ᾆσμα. [b] Herodot. l. 3. c. 59.

and three feet nine inches in diameter at the base. At the foot of the hill, to the southward of where these columns stand, is an oval port, sheltered by two ancient moles, which leave only a narrow passage in the middle, between the remains of towers, which stood on either side of the entrance. Pursuing the same direction, we find another oval port, twice as large as the former. Its entrance is protected in the same manner by ancient walls or moles, fifteen or twenty feet thick, which, though now in many places below the surface of the water, still shelter these two little bays, and furnish a commodious protection to the small vessels which navigate the gulf. Between the two harbours there appear to have been a succession of small basins, separated from the sea by a wall, and communicating with the two harbours. On the northern side of the promontory, upon which stand the two columns, there was an open harbour or roadsted, protected to the north by a breakwater, on which there appears to have stood a wall, which formed a prolongation of the walls of the land-front of the city. There is no more remarkable example in Greece of the labour and expense bestowed by the ancients in forming and protecting their artificial harbours.

The walls of the city are still traced through

their whole extent on the land side. They were about ten feet thick, and constructed with towers at intervals not always equal. There appear to have been three principal entrances, of which that near the middle of the land front, leading to the Panhellenium, was constructed apparently like the chief gate of the city of Platæa, with a retired wall between two round towers. To the southward the town walls abutted upon the mole of the great harbour, which formed a continuation of the city wall, in the same manner as I have just stated that wall to have terminated in the northern roadsted. This appears indeed to have been the usual mode among the Greeks of fortifying their maritime towns, as instanced at Athens, Eleusis, and many other places. The ports were thus κλεῖστοι λιμένες, were placed within the walls of the town, and might be closed by a chain.

At the head of the larger port stand some modern houses and magazines; the rest of the ground inclosed within the ancient walls is uneven, and retains traces of buildings, though none of the remains, except the extant columns, can be referred to any of the buildings described by Pausanias. That no vestiges should be seen of the stadium and theatre, the latter of which was almost equal in size to that of Epidaurus, can only be accounted for by their proximity to the harbour, and the convenience of the wrought masses of the seats for modern constructions. It can hardly be doubted that the larger harbour is that which Pausanias describes as " the port chiefly frequented by ships "[a], and near which stood the temple of Venus. The smaller, consequently, is in all probability the secret port[b], near which was the theatre, the stadium, and temples of Apollo, Diana, and Bacchus. The Æaceium, situated in the most conspicuous part of the city[c], may have been upon the elevated level towards the plain.

The temple to which the existing columns belonged was of such large dimensions, that we may infer from this circumstance alone, that it was the temple of Hecate, the principal deity of the Æginetæ. There are considerable remains of the peribolus, within which it stood; and these walls are prolonged beyond the temple so as to inclose all the cape, and form a kind of citadel.

To judge by the many ruined churches upon the site of the city of Ægina, the place was once occupied by a Christian town of some importance; in later times it became an useful station to the ships of the Venetians, as we find by an inscription which still remained towards the close of the last century on a tower at

---

[a] ἐν ᾧ μάλιστα ὁρμίζονται.   [b] κρυπτὸς λιμήν.
[c] ἐν τῷ ἐπιφανεστάτῳ τῆς πόλεως.

the entrance of the great port which had been erected by Aloys Mocenigo, by order of the Doge, F. Morosini, a short time before his death, in the year 1693. After the Venetians had restored the Moréa to the Turks in 1715, the maritime parts of Greece were again cruelly pillaged by the pirates of various nations, who have in all ages found the rocky coasts and islands of this country propitious to their lawless pursuits. It was probably the fear of these robbers, that drove the people of Ægina from the site of the ancient city into the present town.

It does not appear from Pausanias on what part of the road from the ancient city to the Panhellenium the temple of Aphæa stood, nor do any remains of it exist to supply his deficiency. Its most probable position, I think, is that of the modern town itself.

There was also in Ægina a temple or sanctuary, containing statues of Lamia and Auxesia in a kneeling posture, made of Athenian olive-wood. The place was called Œa; it was twenty stades distant from the city, in the inland part of the island. Herodotus, who has given this description of Œa, confirms its inland position, by relating that the Æginetæ and Argives affirmed, that when the Athenians sent an expedition to Ægina to carry off the statues of Lamia and Auxesia, their retreat from Œa to the coast of the island was cut off by the Argive forces, who destroyed them all[a]. Pausanias, alluding to this passage in the history of Herodotus, adds, that he himself sacrificed to the statues, and that the ceremony was similar to that of Eleusis. He agrees with Herodotus in shewing that the figures were made of olive-wood, but he does not mention their kneeling posture, although there was an absurd fable attached to this peculiarity of statues, precisely of the kind in which Pausanias delighted.

Of the temple of Jupiter Panhellenius, Pausanias, as in the case of some others of the most important buildings in Greece, has told us scarcely any thing, having considered, perhaps, any particular description of such great edifices as not forming a part of the design of his work, and hence, by a natural consequence, being more brief than usual upon such subjects. He remarks only, that Mount Panhellenium contained nothing worthy of notice, except the temple which Æacus was said to have erected to Jupiter[b]. Without our experience of his brevity upon similar occasions, it would be difficult to imagine that by these few words he intended to refer to the great temple, of which the magnificent ruins will continue, as long as they

[a] Herodot. l. 5. c. 83.   [b] ποιῆσαι τῷ Διΐ.

exist, to attract persons of taste to Greece from every civilized nation of the globe.

The temple is situated in the midst of a forest of pines upon the summit of a mountain, separated by a narrow valley from the hill upon which stands the modern town of 'Eghina. At the foot of the mountain there is a small port near the north-eastern cape of the island. The port, the cape, and a small neighbouring island, are all known by the name of Turla. The length of the temple upon the stylobate, or upper step of the κρῆπις, is ninety-four feet, the breadth forty-five. The columns of the peristyle are three feet three inches in diameter at the base, and seventeen feet two inches high, including the capital. Of these columns there were thirty-two when the temple was complete: six at the ends, and twelve in the sides. The cell had a door at either end, opening into the pronaos and posticum, in each of which were two columns of three feet two inches in diameter between antæ. Within the cell were columns, two feet four inches in diameter, standing in a double row. There are now standing twenty-one columns of the peristyle, with their architraves; six of the eastern front, and five of the northern side, are continuous without any interruption. The four columns of the pronaos and posticum are all standing, and the lower parts of five within the cell. The temple was erected upon a large paved platform or peribolus, and must, when complete, have been one of the most remarkable examples in Greece of the majesty and beauty of its sacred edifices, as well as of the admirable taste with which the Greeks enhanced those qualities by an attention to local situation and surrounding scenery. It is not only in itself one of the finest specimens of Grecian architecture, but is the more curious as being in all probability the most ancient example of the Doric order in Greece, with the exception of the columns at Corinth [a].

The Trœzenii bordered upon the Epidaurii to the south-east, and possessed all the eastern promontory of the Peloponnesus [b], together with the peninsula of Methana and the island of Calaureia, each of which incloses, between it and the main coast, a large and well sheltered bay. The most valuable part of the territory of Trœzen was a fine maritime plain bounded to the southward by a chain of mountains, which separated the Trœzenia from the district of Hermione. A city possessing a territory which

[a] On the subject of the date of the Panhellenium, see the additional note to Chapter XXVIII.

[b] ἔσχατον χώρας Πελοπίας προσώπιον. — Eurip. Hippolyt. v. 373.

combined so many advantages, was naturally of considerable importance. Its acropolis was on the summit of a rugged height, overlooking the widest parts of the plain. The city occupied the slope and foot of the same hill, and appears to have been nearly three miles in circumference. It flourished at a very remote age. Like Athens, it was a fabled subject of contest between Neptune and Minerva, of each of whom the emblems, as Pausanias has remarked [a], and as we still see, were represented on its coins; before its original name of Poseidonia had been exchanged for that of Trœzen, it sent forth one of the earliest colonies to Italy, and there founded Poseidonia, or Pæstum, of which the magnificent ruins still subsist.

The Agora of Trœzen [b] contained a temple of Diana Soteira, founded by Theseus, in which were altars of the infernal gods. Behind the temple was the monument of Pittheus, surmounted by three chairs of white marble, in which Pittheus and two assessors were said to have given judgement. Not far from thence stood the Museium, or sanctuary of the Muses, and near it an altar on which the Trœzenii sacrificed to the Muses and to Sleep, whom they considered the most friendly of all deities

---

[a] Pausan. l. 2. c. 30.   [b] Ibid. c. 31, 32.

to the Muses. Near the Theatre was the temple of Diana Lyceia, built by Hippolytus. Before the temple there was a stone, called the Sacred, on which nine Trœzenii were said to have expurgated Orestes for the murder of his mother; near it were altars of Bacchus Saotes, of the Themides, and of the Sun the Liberator. A stoa in the Agora contained statues in stone of some of the Athenian women and children who were committed to the care of the Trœzenii at the time of the Persian invasion. The temple of Apollo Thearius erected by Pittheus, was the most ancient temple which Pausanias knew [a]. It contained a statue [b] of Apollo and wooden statues [c] of the Dioscuri, all the three by Hermon, a native artist. Before this temple stood a building [d], called the Tent of Orestes [e], in which Orestes took refuge before his expiation; before the building grew a bay tree [f]. At the fountain Hippocrene stood a statue of Hermes Polygius, and a wild olive [g], reported to have been a regermination of the club of Hercules, which he cut from a tree at the marsh Saronis, and (after his labours) here dedicated. There

---

[a] It was even much more ancient, remarks Pausanias, than the temple of Minerva at Phocæa, which was burnt by Harpagus the Mede, or than the temple of Apollo Pythius at Samus.
[b] ἄγαλμα.
[c] ξόανα.
[d] οἰκοδόμημα.
[e] Ὀρέστου Σκήνη.
[f] δάφνη.
[g] κότινος.

was a temple of Jupiter Soter, said to have been erected by Aëtius.

But the most noted sanctuary at Trœzen was the inclosure[a] of Hippolytus, who was believed by the Trœzenii not to have been dragged by his horses, and thus killed[b], but to have been deified, and to be the constellation called Auriga. The temenus contained a temple, and ancient statue of Hippolytus, and a temple of Apollo Epibaterius, all dedicated by Diomedes. Lamia and Auxesia were also worshipped here. On one side of the peribolus was the stadium of Hippolytus, above which was the temple of Venus Catascopia, so called, because from thence Phædra beheld Hippolytus, as he exercised in the stadium. Here were a tomb[c] of Phædra, a monument[d] of Hippolytus, a statue of Æsculapius, by Timotheus, and a myrtle, with punctures in the leaves, which were fabled to have been so formed by Phædra, in the agony of her passion, by means of the needle of the clasp of her hair[e]. There was a building, called the house of Hippolytus, before which was a fountain, surnamed the Herculean[f]. In the Acropolis was the temple of Minerva Polias, or Sthenias, with a wooden statue, by Callon of Ægina: on the

[a] τέμενος.
[b] συρέντα ὑπὸ τῶν ἵππων.
[c] τάφος.
[d] μνῆμα.
[e] περόνης, ἣν ἐπὶ ταῖς θριξὶν εἶχεν.—Paus. Attic. c. 22.
[f] κρήνη Ἡράκλειος.

descent from thence a temple of Pan Lyterius. Towards the plain[a] stood a temple of Isis, built by the Halicarnassenses, who were a colony from Trœzen; it contained a statue dedicated by the Trœzenii. Above the temple of Isis was that of Venus Ascræa.

Pausanias, without venturing to express any doubts as to the extraordinary antiquity ascribed to some of their buildings by the Trœzenii, remarks only that they were a people more given to boast of their ancestral dignity, than any whom he knew. In fact, it is more probable that the monuments, of which they attributed the foundation to Pittheus, Theseus, Hippolytus, or Diomedes, were successors on the same site with the same names, than the original buildings themselves. Nothing now subsists of Trœzen but pieces of wall of Hellenic masonry or of Roman brick-work, dispersed over the lower slope of the height, upon which stood the Acropolis, and over the plain at its foot. There are, likewise, many ruined churches and chapels on the site, proving the former importance of Dhamalá, which is still a bishopric of the Corinthian province[b]. Chandler remarked the remains of the temple of Venus Catascopia overlooking the cavity formerly occupied by the Stadium, and he found among the ruins several

[a] διαβὰς ἐς τὴν Τροιζηνίαν. [b] ἐπαρχία.

inscriptions, which he published. Of the Trœzenian rivers, Hylycus and Chrysorrhoas, one flows through the gorges on the eastern side of the height of the Acropolis, the other on the west. As the latter is the larger, and turns some mills, we may infer that it was that Chrysorrhoas which, according to Pausanias, still flowed, when a nine years' scarcity of rain had dried up all the other waters. Another natural feature of the ancient site is the fountain Hippocrene, at the foot of the hill of the Acropolis. By these indications of the topography, some guidance is afforded to the position of the Agora, and of some of the buildings of the city.

Near the Acropolis, on the eastern side, where the road to Hermione left the city, there was a temple of Neptune Phytalmius near the walls, and not far from it that of Ceres Thesmophorus. At a little distance on the road was the rock, more anciently called the altar of Jupiter Sthenius, under which Theseus is fabled to have found the slippers and sword of Ægeus; from hence it was that he set out on his adventurous journey to Athens, and here he afterwards founded a temple to Venus Nymphas, when he espoused Helene[a]. Here also was the source of the river Hylycus, more anciently called

[a] Pausan. l. 2. c. 32.

Taurius; the source was named Hyoessa[a]. It is probably the same fountain alluded to by Euripides in the Hippolytus, as being near the towers of the city[b].

One of the harbours of the Trœzenia was called Celenderis[c]. In descending to it from the city occurred Genethlium, a place[d] so called because Theseus was said to have been born there: before it was a temple of Mars, in the place where Theseus conquered the Amazons.

On the way to the part of the sea called Psiphæa[e] there was a wild olive tree, named the crooked Rhachus[f]; it was said that the branches of this tree having caught the reins of Hippolytus, caused his chariot to be overturned. Not far from the Rhachus was the temple of Diana Saronia. Of this building Pausanias had before said[g] that it was founded by the king Saron, successor of Althepus, near a shallow muddy salt water lake (or part of the sea)[h], called from

---

[a] Sophocles ap. Athen. l. 3. c. 35.

[b] In the scene where the nurse endeavours to console Phædra:

Τί δὲ κρηναίων νασμῶν ἔρασαι;
Πάρα γὰρ δροσερὰ πύργοις συνεχὴς
Κλιτὺς, ὅθεν σοι πῶμα γένοιτ' ἄν.   v. 225.

[c] πρὸς τῇ Κελενδέρει καλούμενον λιμένα.   [d] χωρίον.

[e] ἐπὶ θάλασσαν Ψιφαίαν πορευομένοις.

[f] ῥάχος στρεπτὸς.—Ῥάχος among the Trœzenii, says Pausanias, was a word applied to all fruitless trees of the olive kind. (πᾶν ὅσον ἄκαρπον ἐλαίας, κότινον καὶ φυλίαν καὶ ἔλαιον.)

[g] Pausan. l. 2. c. 30.

[h] ἐπὶ θαλάσσῃ τελματώδει καὶ ἐπιπολῆς μᾶλλον.

the temple the lake Phœbæa, but which name was afterwards changed to that of Saronis, in consequence of Saron having been drowned there in the pursuit of a stag, and having been buried within the sacred peribolus. This description shews the Phœbæa to have been a lagoon, and identifies it, therefore, with that at the head of the bay of Methana, which receives the *Chrysorrhoas*, and several other streams, flowing from the western extremity of the mountain of *Trœzen*. Some words of Euripides also, which allude to the Phœbæa, are exactly applicable to a maritime lagoon[a]. As to Psiphæa, it may be suspected that Ψιφαίαν is a textual error for Φοιβαίαν, the Rhachus Streptus having been near the temple of Diana, which was on the shore of the Phœbæa; on the other hand it must be admitted, that, supposing the word to have been Psephæa, it would be well adapted, in contradistinction to the muddy lagoon, to any part of the shore, which is bold and covered with pebbles [b].

Celenderis I take to have been the Hellenic fortress, which Chandler observed near the northern side of the bay of Trœzen, and that the harbour of Celenderis was the western extremity

---

[a] Δίσποιν' ἁλίας Ἄρτεμι λίμνας.—It is an address of Phædra to Diana, in the same scene of the Hippolytus just referred to. v. 228. [b] ψῆφοι.

of this great bay. The Trœzenii had another port on the shore, immediately below the city, where still exist the remains of a mole, and other foundations.

Strabo says of Trœzen, "that it was formerly called Poseidonia, that it lay fifteen stades above the sea, and that in face of its harbour called Pogon, lay the island Calaureia, which was thirty stades in circuit, and separated from the continent by a strait of four stades." He adds, that "there was a temple of Neptune in Calaureia, enjoying the right of asylum, and formerly the seat of a kind of Amphictyonic council from seven cities, which had charge of the sacrifices in common. These cities were Hermione, Epidaurus, Ægina, Athens, Prasiæ, Nauplia, and Orchomenus of Bœotia. For the Nauplienses the Argives contributed, and for the Prasienses the Lacedæmonians."[a]

In these passages we perceive that Strabo alludes only to one Trœzenian island: from Pausanias, however, we learn[b], that there was a second island named " Hiera, containing a temple of Minerva Apaturia, and a monument of Sphærus, said to have been charioteer of Pelops, from whence the island was called Sphæria, a name afterwards changed to Hiera." He observes likewise, that "the strait between Hiera

[a] Strabo, pp. 369. 373, 374.   [b] Pausan. l. 2. c. 33.

and the main land was narrow, and so shallow that there was a passage over it on foot"; "that Calaureia had been anciently sacred to Apollo, and Delphi to Neptune; but that the two gods having interchanged them, the worship of Neptune was instituted at Calaureia, and a temple built there, and that within the peribolus of the temple there was a monument of Demosthenes, who received honours from the inhabitants of Calaureia as well as in other parts of Greece."

There is now only one island on the Trœzenian coast; but as it consists of two hilly peninsulas united together by a narrow sand-bank, it can hardly be doubted, on a reference to Pausanias, that this bank is of recent formation, and that what is now called the island of Poro comprehends what was formerly the two islands of Hiera and Calaureia, the latter having been the greater, and the former the smaller peninsula. The circumference of the smaller is about equal to what Strabo assigns to Calaureia, namely, thirty stades: it consists of a rocky height, on the southern face of which stands the modern town of Poro. The strait is in general of the breadth which Strabo indicates, and it is fordable, as Pausanias remarks, a circumstance which has given rise to the modern name of the town. The circumference assigned by Strabo to Calaureia can hardly be supposed an error in the text, as he twice mentions the same number, and describes the island as a νησίδιον. It would seem, therefore, that he had never seen the places himself, and had adopted some erroneous information concerning them. In regard to the distance between Trœzen and the sea (fifteen stades), the geographer is more correct; this, in fact, is about the distance of Dhamalá from the nearest part of the shore. We learn from Herodotus as well as from Strabo, that the Trœzenian bay was called Pogon. It was the place of assembly of a part of the Greek fleet before the battle of Salamis[a].

The remains of the town of Calaureia and of the celebrated temple of Neptune, to which Démosthenes fled from the agents of Antipater, and where the orator destroyed himself by poison when he found that the asylum would not be respected by his enemy[b], were discovered by Dr. Chandler in 1765, near the middle of the island. He found here a small Doric temple reduced to a heap of ruins, and copied an inscription from the pedestal of a statue which had been erected by the Calaureitæ to Eumenes, King of Pergamum. The vicinity of the populous modern towns of Ydhra, Petza,

[a] Herodot. l. 8. c. 42.   Pausan. l. 2. c. 30.   Lucian.
[b] Plutarch. in Demosth.   Encom. Demosth.

and Poro, has been detrimental to the preservation of these ruins, as well as those of Trœzen, Hermione, and the other places on the neighbouring coasts. When Chandler visited Calaureia, it was particularly resorted to, notwithstanding its lofty situation and the rugged ascent to it from the sea-coast, by the masons of Ydhra, who employed the ready wrought stones of the ancient building in the construction of a new convent in their native island.

The name Methana appears to have been the Doric form of Methone[a], which latter Thucydides uses, writing in the Attic dialect[b]. The Doric name, however, has prevailed to the present day, exactly the same form in which Strabo and Pausanias employ it, that is to say, as a neuter plural. Pausanias describes Methana[c] as "an isthmus of the Peloponnesus extending far into the sea[d], in which there was a small maritime city called Methana. The Agora contained a temple of Isis, and statues of Mercury and Hercules. Thirty stades from the city were hot baths, said to have first appeared in the reign of

[a] Μεθώνη.
[b] Thucyd. l. 4. c. 45. Strabo, p. 374., in remarking this difference of orthography, says, that it prevailed only ἔν τισιν ἀντιγράφοις; it occurs, I believe, in all the copies now known. Diodorus, l. 12. c. 65., uses also the form Methone.
[c] Pausan. l. 2. c. 34.
[d] ἰσθμὸς ἐπὶ πολὺ διήκων ἐς θάλασσαν.

Antigonus, son of Demetrius. It is reported", he adds, "that the water did not immediately shew itself, but that fire came out of the earth in great quantities, and that when the fire ceased, the water issued, which still continues to flow, and which is hot and extremely salt": he then remarks, that "there is no cold water for the use of the bather, nor can he with safety immerge himself in the sea, as it abounds with sea-dogs and other monsters." Strabo, without quoting any authority, says, that a hill seven stades in height, and a mound of rocks as large as towers were thrown up; that the place was inaccessible from the heat and sulphureous smell; and that the sea, to an extent of eight stades, was heated and rendered turbid[a]. Some lines also in Ovid, beginning "Est prope Pittheam tumulus Trœzena"[b], appear to be an exaggerated and poetical description of the same volcanic eruption. The remark of Pausanias, that the bathers who frequented the hot springs had no cold water for their use, would seem to shew that the Greeks were in the habit of using immersion in cold water after the hot bath, as now practised by some of the northern nations of Europe and Asia.

Methana is lofty and rugged, like the neighbouring islands of Ægina and Calaureia, and is

[a] Strabo, p. 59. [b] Ovid. Metam. l. 15. v. 296.

little cultivated, except around the foot of the mountain, and in a small valley facing the middle of the bay of Methana, where are considerable ruins of the Acropolis, and town walls of the ancient Methana, near a small modern village of the same name. In the seventh year of the Peloponnesian war, the Athenians, by fortifying the isthmus which connects Methana with the mainland, were enabled to make use of the peninsula as a military post, from whence they could carry their incursions at pleasure into the the districts of Trœzen, Haliæ, and Epidaurus[a].

As Pausanias remarks that the islands of Pelops, which were near the coast of Methana, were nine in number[b], those which lie between Epidaurus and Ægina must have been included under this denomination. The principal are named Móni, Metópi, Anghístri, and Kyrá; of which Anghístri is much the largest, and, being chiefly covered with wild pines, answers in this respect, as well as in its distance from the continent, to the Pityonnesus, which Pliny places in face of Epidaurus[c]. Kyrá, being nearer to Epidaurus, corresponds equally well with Cecryphalos. It is probably the same as the Cecry-

[a] Thucyd. l. 4. c. 45.
[b] τὰς νησίδας ἀριθμὸν ἐννέα οὔσας αἳ πρόκεινται τῆς χώρας, Πέλοπος καλοῦσι. Pausan. l. 2. c. 34.
[c] Contra Epidaurum Cecryphalos, Pityonesos vi M. P. a continente. Plin. Nat. Hist. l. 4. c. 12.

phaleia, where the Athenians, in the year B. C. 459, obtained an important victory over the Peloponnesian fleet, which was speedily followed by another over the Æginetans at Ægina [a].

Near the entrance of the Gulf of Methana, on the coast of the main land, are the ruins of a Hellenic fortress, in a small valley to the northward of the village of Fanári; it may possibly be the Ægina which Strabo places in the Epidauria [b].

At the back of the hills which border this entire coast, rising either immediately from the shore, or at no great distance from it, there is a succession of small elevated valleys, through which passes a road from Dhamalá to Piádha, near Pídhavro, and thence by similar valleys almost as far as Corinth. Vestiges of small Hellenic towns or fortresses are seen at several points in these valleys; the most remarkable is at Trakhyá, in a small valley, to the eastward of Fanári. As the name is well adapted to the rugged region in which the place is situated, one cannot but suspect that it indicates the situation of a dependent fortress of Epidaurus, called Trachys, not noticed by any author, and the name of which may have been preserved, either quite

[a] Thucyd. l. 1. c. 105.— Diodor. l. 11. c. 78. Stephan. in Κεκρυφάλεια. [b] Strabo, p. 375.

unaltered, or only with a customary Romaic change of termination. We have already witnessed two other examples, in this part of the country, of the existence of Hellenic names of places, of which there is no mention in ancient history. I mean those of Παλαμήδι and Κορώνι.

The road from Trœzen to Hermione passed, according to Pausanias[a], by the rock of Theseus already noticed, then "through the mountains, in which was a temple of Apollo Platanistius, to the place[b] called Eilei, which possessed temples of Ceres and of Proserpine. On the sea-side, on the frontier of the Hermionis and Trœzenia, stood a temple of Ceres Thermesia, distant about eighty stades from the cape which received the name Scyllæum from the daughter of Nisus. In sailing from Scyllæum towards Hermione there occurred another promontory, called Bucephala, and off it certain islands[c]: the first, named Haliusa, afforded a convenient harbour for ships; the next was Pityusa, the third Aristera. Beyond these there was another promontory, named Colyergeia, then the island Tricrana, and a mountain projecting from Peloponnesus, called Buporthmus, which contained two temples, one sacred to Ceres and her daugh-

[a] Pausan. l. 2. c. 34, 35.   [b] χωρίον.
[c] καὶ μετὰ τὴν ἄκραν νῆσοι.

ter, the other to Minerva, surnamed Promachorma. Before Buporthmus lay the island Aperopia, and not far from it another called Hydrea. Beyond this there was a curved shore on the main land, and near it a peninsula, beginning eastward from the open sea, and extending to the west[a]. This peninsula, which was the site of the ancient Hermione, and contained certain ports[b], was seven stades in length, and three in breadth, in the widest part. On the cape stood a temple of Neptune, from which the place was named Poseidium; higher up from the shore were a temple of Minerva, and the foundations of a stadium; there was also another smaller temple of Minerva wanting the roof, a temple of the Sun, a grove of the Graces, a temple of Sarapis and Isis, and a peribolus of rough stones, within which were performed sacrifices to Ceres. The city of the time of Pausanias[c] stood at a distance of four stades from Poseidium, in a plain rising gradually to the hill called Pron. It was entirely surrounded with walls. The deity held in chief veneration by the Hermionenses was Ceres, to whom there were three temples in the Hermionis. Two of these were dedicated to the goddess with the

---

[a] μετὰ ταύτην αἰγιαλός τε παρήκει τῆς ἠπείρου μηνοειδὴς καὶ ἀκτὴ μετὰ τὸν αἰγιαλὸν ἐπὶ Ποσειδίον, ἐκ τῆς θαλάσσης μὲν ἀρχομένη τῆς πρὸς ἀνατολὰς, προήκουσα δὲ ὡς ἐπὶ τὴν ἑσπέραν.
[b] ἔχει δὲ λιμένας ἐν αὐτῇ.
[c] ἡ ἐφ' ἡμῶν πόλις.

epithet of Thermesia; one on the borders of the Trœzenia already noticed, the other within the city. The third on Mount Pron [a], was sacred to Ceres Chthonia, and was the chief place of worship of the people of Hermione. It was said to have been founded by Chthonia, daughter of Phoroneus, and Clymenus, her brother, to whom there was a temple opposite to that of Chthonia [b]. In front of the latter stood the statues of some of the priestesses; the temple of Clymenus was surrounded with statues of men [c]; near it was a temple of Mars, containing his statue. To the right of the temple of Chthonia was the stoa of Echo, which repeated the voice three times; behind the same temple were three places [d], surrounded with stone fences [e], one named the sanctuary of Clymenus [f], the second that of Pluto [g], the third was called the lake Acherusia. In the sanctuary of Clymenus there was an opening in the earth [h], through which, according to the Hermionenses, Hercules led out the Dog of Hell [i].

[a] ἐπὶ τοῦ Πρῶνος.
[b] There is an inscription extant, brought from Hermione, which makes mention of Ceres Chthonia, Clymenus, and Cora (Proserpine). Boeck. Corp. Inscr. Græc. Vol. 1. p. 593.
[c] εἴκονες.
[d] χωρία.
[e] θριγκοῖς λίθων.
[f] τὸ Κλυμένου.
[g] τὸ Πλούτωνος.
[h] γῆς χάσμα.
[i] τοῦ ᾄδου τὸν κῦνα. Strabo (p. 373.) adds that this was the shortest road to Hades, on

"In the city there were two temples of Venus, of which that of Venus Pontia, or Limenia, contained an admirable colossal statue of the goddess in white marble. Near the temple of Ceres Thermesia stood that of Bacchus Melanægis. The other temples were: that of Diana Iphigeneia, in which was a brazen Neptune with his foot on a dolphin; the sacred place of Vesta[a], containing an altar of Vesta; and three temples of Apollo, each containing a statue, one called Pythaeus, a second Orius, the third had no surname. The temple of Fortune was the most recent of all the public buildings, and contained a colossal statue of Parian marble. There were two public fountains[b], one very ancient, which afforded, though not a copious, a never-failing supply; of the other, which had been constructed in the time of Pausanias, the water was derived from a place called Leimon (the Meadow). At the gate leading to Mases there was a temple of Lucina within the walls, with a statue, which the priestesses only were allowed to behold.

"In the road from Hermione to Mases[c], there was a turning to the left, at the end of seven stades, leading between Mounts Pron and Thornax, otherwise called Coccygium, to Halice.

which account, the dead here paid no freight (ναῦλον).
[a] τὸ τῆς Ἑστίας.
[b] κρῆναι.
[c] Pausan. l. 2. c. 36.

CHAP. XXI.]   HALICE, MASES.   461

On the summit of the latter mountain there was a temple of Jupiter, on that of Pron a temple of Juno. The road to Mases passed by an extremity of Coccygium, upon which stood a temple of Apollo, without doors, or roof, or statue. In the time of Pausanias, Halice was deserted, and Mases, which is enumerated among the Argive cities by Homer, was only a haven [a] of the Hermionenses. From Mases there was a road to the right to the promontory Struthus, from whence there was a distance of 250 stades by the heights [b] to Philanorium and to the Bolei, which were heaps of rude stones [c]. The place called Didymi was twenty stades distant from thence. It contained temples of Apollo, Neptune, and Ceres, with upright statues of white marble. Beyond this [d] were the ruins on the sea-side of Asine, formerly a city of the Argives, among which there still remained a temple of Apollo Pythaeus."

The position of Hermione is now called Kastrí, a modern name often found attached to Hellenic sites. Its situation near the sea, and not far from some islands of recent populousness, has been very unfavourable to the preservation of its remains of antiquity; but there are

[a] ἐπίνειον.
[b] κατὰ τῶν ὀρῶν τὰς κορυφάς.
[c] λίθων σωροὶ λογάδων.
[d] τὸ δὲ ἐντεῦθεν ἐστιν.

still found upon the site many foundations and fragments of Hellenic buildings, and its ancient importance leads to the belief, that many more may be still concealed beneath the surface.

The ancient names have been better preserved at this extremity of the Argolic peninsula than the ruins of the places themselves. Cape *Scyllæum* is now called Skyli, the island of *Hydrea*, Ydhra, *Eilei*, Ilio, and the site of the temple of Ceres *Thermesia*, eighty stades westward of Cape *Scyllæum*, Thérmisi. This temple appears, from the words of Pausanias, to have been just within the boundary line of the Hermionis, which was marked probably by the course of a river falling into the sea a little eastward of Thérmisi. In the other direction the Hermionis comprehended Halice and Mases, and all the south-eastern extremity of the Argolic peninsula as far as the Asinæa. Pausanias says that he could find no proof of the former existence of Halice as a town, except in one of the medical pillars at the Epidaurian Asclepieium [a]: it is evidently, however, the same place as the Haliæ of Thucydides [b] and Diodorus [c], of which the natives, though called Halici [d] by

[a] ἐν στήλαις ταῖς Ἐπιδαυρίων, αἱ τοῦ Ἀσκληπίου τὰ ἰάματα ἐγγεγραμμένα ἔχουσιν.— Pausan. l. 2. c. 36.

[b] Thucyd. l. 1. c. 105.— l. 4. c. 45.

[c] Diodor. l. 11. c. 78.

[d] Ἁλικοί.

Pausanias, are named Halienses[a] by Xenophon[b] and Strabo[c]. Its desertion was not recent in the time of Pausanias, for Strabo describes the Halienses as seafaring men, inhabiting a part of the Hermionis[d]. I think it may be deduced from the account which Pausanias has given of the places beyond Hermione, that Halice was on one of the harbours eastward of Cape Kosmá, which is the southern extremity of the Argolic peninsula opposite to the island of Petza,—that Mases occupied the position of the modern Kiládhia, a village on the side of a harbour one hour below Kranídhi, which is at present the chief place in all this district, and that Struthus was the cape on the northern side of the port of Kiládhia, now I believe called Kóraka. These questions, however, cannot be well determined without the discovery of some remains of the places themselves, because the Greek traveller has not furnished us with the distances between Hermione, Halice, and Mases. If that of 250 stades from Cape Struthus to Philanorium be correct in his text, it will almost of necessity follow that Asine was situated at Port Toló. The position agrees with

[a] Ἁλιεῖς.
[b] Xenoph. Hellen. l. 6. c. 2.
[c] Strabo, p. 373.
[d] Ἑρμιόνη .... ἧς τὴν παραλίαν ἔχουσιν Ἁλιεῖς λεγόμενοι, θαλαττουργοί τινες ἄνδρες.— Id. ibid.

Homer's description of Asine as occupying a deep bay [a], and it agrees also with the expression of Strabo, as to the proximity of Asine to Nauplia [b]. It is impossible, however, for me to advance any confident opinion on this subject without a better and more detailed knowledge than I possess of the real topography of this part of the Argolis.

It might be supposed, that by means of the preservation of the ancient names Scyllæum, Thermesia, and Hydrea, the capes and islands on this coast named by Pausanias would have been easily recognized, but his description is found to be so vague on comparing it with the actual geography, that one cannot but suspect some imperfection in the text. The only writer besides Pausanias, who names these islands, is Pliny. "In the Argolic sea," he says, "are Pityusa, Irine, and Ephyre, and over against the territory of Hermione are Tiparenus, Eperopia, Colonis, Aristera." The three islands which he places in the Argolic Gulf correspond very well with Dhaskalió, Platyá, and Psylí, and the ancient name of the second Irine seems to have some connection with that of Iri, a modern

---

[a] Ἑρμιόνην Ἀσίνην τε, βαθὺν κατὰ κόλπον ἐχούσας.
Hom. Il. B. v. 560.

[b] .... Ἀσίνης καὶ αὕτη δὲ κώμη τῆς Ἀργείας πλησίον Ναυπλίας.—Strabo, p. 373.

place on the coast opposite to Platyá, and which, from this coincidence, we may suspect to be an ancient name preserved. Aperopia, by its connexion in the passage of Pausanias with Hydrea and Posidium, seems to correspond to the island now called Dhokó. In regard to the other capes and islands, I shall offer but one conjecture, namely, that the word Tiparenus, which has no appearance of a Greek name, is an error for Tricarenus, and that the island was the same as the Tricrana of Pausanias, and the modern Tríkhiri. This at least is as probable, as that the modern Petza was called Tiparenus, the only argument for which is the occurrence of the name in Pliny as that of the first of the islands of the Hermionis, following the names of those in the Argolic Gulf. It is to be regretted that we are thus left in ignorance as to the ancient appellation of an island, which is of some importance in the modern history of Greece.

Of all the towns under the government of Agamemnon and Diomedes, Heionæ is the only one of which, in the time of the Roman Empire, the situation was uncertain. Nothing seems to have been known of it to the geographers of those ages, except that, after the expedition to Troy, its inhabitants had been expelled by the Mycenæi, and that it then dwindled into a port dependent upon Mycenæ[a]. Although this fact is quite indecisive of the situation of Heionæ, Mycenæ having been the capital of so large a portion of the north-eastern part of the Peloponnesus, it may safely be inferred from the Catalogue, that it occupied some part of the coast of the Argolic peninsula, but whether between Trœzen and Epidaurus, as Homer places it in his verse[b], or on the northern shore, where a great space of coast between Mases and Asine remains unoccupied on the map by any ancient city, I shall not pretend to decide. As well from the name as from the remark of Strabo, to which I have just referred, it may be presumed that Heionæ was a maritime position.

[a] Strabo, p. 373.
[b] Τροιζῆν' Ἡιόνας τε καὶ ἀμπελόεντ' Ἐπίδαυρον.
Il. B. 561.

ADDITIONAL NOTE.

LATE discoveries have shewn, that the Aeti of the Panhellenium of Ægina were filled with statues, which at both ends represented the same subject, and with some slight variation in exactly the same manner. In the centre stood a colossal Minerva, at whose feet lay a dying hero. On either side of this central groupe stood a warrior, ready to strike his opponent; behind the warrior, to the left of the Minerva, there was an unarmed figure, stooping down, and stretching forward his hands across the warrior, to lay hold of the dying figure. The remainder of the pediment was filled up on either side with a kneeling figure drawing a bow, another protruding a spear, and a third, in the angle of the pediment, dying of his wounds. For further information regarding these fine and indubitable specimens of the Æginetan school of sculpture, I must refer the reader to the remarks of Mr. Cockerell, one of the discoverers of them, in the Journal of Science, No. 12. I shall here subjoin a note of my own, written in reply to his request, that I would give him an opinion on the subject of the composition: it was printed with his paper.

"I am inclined to think that the following noble lines of the Iliad not only explain the subject of the composition, but indicate the exact moment chosen by the sculptor.

"Ἂψ δ' ἐπὶ Πατρόκλῳ τέτατο κρατερὴ ὑσμίνη,
Ἀργαλέη, πολύδακρυς· ἔγειρε δὲ νεῖκος Ἀθήνη,
Οὐρανόθεν καταβᾶσα· προῆκε γὰρ εὐρύοπα Ζεὺς
Ὀρνύμεναι Δαναούς· δὴ γὰρ νόος ἐτράπετ' αὐτοῦ." Il. P. 543.

"The κνημίδες observed on all the figures to the right of Minerva, together with the absence of these Grecian articles of dress in the other division of the work, as well as the Phrygian bonnet upon one of the figures of the latter, seem strongly to mark that the subject is taken from the war of Troy. In the midst of the contest for the body of Patroclus, Jupiter sends Minerva to give new courage to the Greeks. On the western pediment she seems to have just descended from the skies; on the eastern, she has raised her arm against the Trojans, and the contest is decided [a]. It may be objected perhaps, that this is not quite conformable to Homer, who represents Minerva as assuming the shape of Phœnix, and Jupiter as again changing his mind, and once more giving the superiority to the Trojans before the body was finally carried off by the Greeks. But every thing that we know of the productions

[a] This is the only remarkable difference in the two pediments.

of the ancients in the arts of design, shows that they were never servile imitators of the poets; in other words, that a sculptor who had chosen a subject treated of by Homer would represent it in his own manner. Phidias may have been indebted to Homer for a first conception of his Olympian Jupiter, but every thing else about it was his own. It must be remembered also, that in pictures and compositions of statuary, the artist had to pursue a very different route from the poet. The latter had to narrate a succession of events, the sculptor to embody the action of a moment. If it should be thought that the death of Patroclus had little reference to Jupiter, the deity of the Æginetan temple, or to Æacus, its founder, it is to be observed, that it had fully as much reference to local history as the capture of Troy at the Heræum of Argos, or the hunting of the Calydonian boar, and the battle of Telephus and Achilles, in the temple of Minerva Alea, at Tegea, or the contests of the Centaurs and Lapithæ, and of Œnomaus and Pelops, in the temple of Jupiter at Olympia. In all these cases, the artist had to choose from among the mythological actions which were in any manner connected with the worship of the temple, that which in his judgement would produce the finest composition of sculpture, and give the greatest scope to his genius. The defence of the body of Patroclus is represented by Homer as the most conspicuous among the exploits of Ajax, and in the estimation of the Æginetans, Ajax must have been the first of the Æacidæ, superior even to Achilles himself."

CHAPTER XXII.

ARGEIA.   LACONIA.

*From Argos to the Mills of Anápli.—*LERNA.—*Mount* PONTINUS.—*Fountain* AMYMONE.—TEMENIUM.—*To Kivéri.* —GENESIUM.—ABOBATHMI.—*To Astró and Luku.*— ANIGRÆA.—*The* DEINE.—ASTRUM.—THYREA.—ANTHENE.—NERIS.—*To Prastiótika Kalývia.—*PRASIÆ.— CYPHANTA.—*To Kastánitza.—Tzakonía.—Tzakonic dialect.—*EVA.—*To Tzítzina.—River* TANUS.—*Mount* PARNON.—*To the Monastery of the Forty Saints.—Ancient road from* ARGOS *to* SPARTA.—SCOTITA.—SELLASIA.— CARYÆ.—*River* ŒNUS.—*To* SPARTA *and Mistrá.*

MARCH 18.—A pezodhrómo brought me a letter to-day at noon, which had been written at Tripolitzá in the morning, a direct distance of more than twenty-four British miles. Another sent by M. V—— to Mr. Consul Strane, at Patra, was six days absent, and remained an entire day and night at Patra; the road distance from hence to Patra to a pedestrian, is about ninety British miles.

This afternoon I quit Argos for Mistrá, by the way of Tzakonía. The road to the mills of Anápli, by reason of the neglected state of the plain, and its consequent marshiness at this season, instead of coinciding with the ancient route across the plain to *Lerna,* follows that to *Tegea,* as far as the Kefalári, or sources of the *Erasinus.* At 2.35 I quit the theatre of Argos. At 3.16 cross the *Erasinus,* just below the mills of Kefalári, from whence the road, leaving that of Tripolitzá on the right, traverses the plain in a direct line to the other mills, at the north-eastern angle of the gulf, which are called the Afendikí Mýli: 3.41, Skafidháki, a small village, is on the foot of the hills to the right, a little beyond the torrent which I have already mentioned as descending from the opening in Mount *Creopolus,* through which passes the road from Anápli to Akhladhó-kambo, with a branch to Tzipianá. This torrent, as I have already remarked, appears to be the Cheimarrhus of Pausanias, who thus describes the route from Argos to Lerna[a]. "The sea-shore at Lerna is not more than forty stades distant from Argos. In descending to it, the road first arrives at the Erasinus, which falls into the Phrixus, and the Phrixus into the sea, between Temenium and Lerna. On turning from the Erasinus, about eight stades to the left, there is a temple of the Anactes Dioscuri; their statues are of wood, and made after the same fashion as those in the city. Returning into the high road, you will cross the Erasinus, and arrive at

[a] Pausan. l. 2. c. 36, 37.

the Cheimarrhus, near which there is an inclosure of stones, where it is said that Pluto, having seized upon the daughter of Ceres, carried her to the kingdom which is supposed to exist under the earth. Lerna, as I have already said, is on the sea-side. Here the ceremony [a] in honour of Ceres, called the Lernæa, is celebrated. The sacred grove, which consists chiefly of plane trees, begins from the mountain Pontinus, and extends to the sea; it is bounded on one side by the river Pontinus, which flows from the mountain, and on the other by the river Amymone, which received its name from the daughter of Danaus. On the summit of Mount Pontinus are the ruins of a temple of Minerva Saïtis, said to have been founded by Danaus, and the foundations of the house of Hippomedon, who went to Thebes in aid of Polynices, son of Œdipus. The grove of Lerna contains two temples; in one of these there are three statues of stone, of which two are [upright] statues of Ceres Prosymne, and Bacchus; the third, small and seated, represents Ceres. In the other temple is a seated statue in wood of Bacchus Saotes. On the sea-side there is a Venus in stone, which is said to have been dedicated by the daughters of Danaus.

"The Lernæa are reported to have been instituted by Philammon. Between Lerna and Te-

[a] τελετή.

menium the river Phrixus joins the sea. In Temenium there is a temple of Neptune, another of Venus, and a tomb of Temenus, held in veneration by the Dorians of Argos; Nauplia, now deserted, is distant from Temenium, as it appears to me, fifty stades."

As to the Phrixus, the name of which occurs, I believe, no where but in this passage of Pausanias, it can be no other than the brook which issues from the opening between Mounts *Lycone* and *Chaon*, and which is so much smaller than the *Erasinus*, that it would have been more correct to have said that it fell into the Erasinus, than the latter into it.

At 4.7 we arrive at three copious sources which form a stream running to turn the northern Afendikí Mýli, or mills of Anápli[a], to which town they belong. The sources issue from the foot of a rocky hill of a conical form, which terminates the plain of Argos in this corner. The hill and stream are evidently those which were anciently called Pontinus; the river has only a course of a few hundred yards before it joins the sea. The ruins of a castle, made of small stones and mortar, now occupy the summit of the hill, and consequently stand on the site of the house of Hippomedon and of the temple of Minerva, whose epithet Saïtis indicates that her worship

[a] ἀφεντικοὶ, or αὐθεντικοὶ, μύλοι—government mills.

was introduced here from Egypt, and thus agrees with the reputed foundation of the temple by Danaus. At Sais, we know that Neith, the Greek Athene, was held in great honour[a]. Continuing along the foot of Mount *Pontinus*, we arrive, at 4.15, at some copious sources on the road-side much larger than those of the Pontinus; they issue from under the rocks, and immediately enter a deep marsh and a lake, which extends to the sea-beach. They correspond exactly in position to the Amymone of Pausanias. A stream running out of the lake turns the southern mills, which stand close to the sea-side, and to a small wharf where vessels load or disembark their cargoes.

A ship from Smyrna is now in the anchorage, discharging a cargo of iron. There is a range of magazines stretching from the mills along the beach to the northward; the rest of the distance, as far as the northern mills and the river Pontinus, is occupied by a large garden, which extends in breadth from the sea-beach to the road, and occupies a part at least of the site of the ancient Lernæan grove. The lake Alcyonia I conceive to have been the lower part of the marsh above mentioned, towards the southern mills. According to the millers, this part is very deep, abounds in springs, and contains many eels:

[a] Herodot. l. 2. c. 175.

and all around it there are reeds, mixed with a great variety of aquatic plants growing luxuriantly. Pausanias remarks, that grass and rushes[a] grew on the margin of the Alcyonia, that its depth was unfathomable, and that Nero had let down several stades of rope loaded with lead without finding a bottom. Another fable he relates of it was, that although the water appeared tranquil, those who attempted to swim in it were drawn to the bottom, a belief which may have arisen from some persons having been drowned here, in consequence of their having been paralysed by the coldness of the water, an accident not uncommon in similar pools. The station of the celebrated hydra was said to have been under a plane-tree, at the source of the Amymone; " in my opinion", adds Pausanias, " this serpent had only one head, but I believe that it was much larger than any water-snake, and that it was extremely venomous, as appears by the arms of Hercules having been poisoned with the serpent's gall[b]. As to the numerous heads of the serpent, the poet Peisandrus, of Camira, invented[c] them to make the beast more terrible, and his own verses more dignified."

Pausanias, by calling Amymone a river, seems to indicate that it did not mix with the Lake

---

[a] πόα καὶ σχοῖνοι.   [b] χολῆς.   [c] ἐποίησε.

Alcyonia, but flowed to the sea in a separate channel: in fact this would still be the case were there not a stone-dam extending along the sea-beach for 250 yards to the south of the mills, and confining the water of the lake, which is chiefly formed by deep subterraneous sources. This dam, and two shorter walls, built at right angles to the shore on either side of the lake, for the purposes of a mill-head, make the lake much larger and deeper than it would naturally be, or than it was in the time of Pausanias, who describes it as only a third of a stade in circuit[a]. At present the marsh which surrounds the lake almost fills up the space between the shore and the road near Amymone, so that the marsh and lake together are not less than half a mile in circumference. The enlargement of the lake may, perhaps, explain why the fountain of Amphiaraus can no longer be identified, as it may now be enveloped in the lake, or at least in the marsh. The gardens formerly belonged to the Capitán Pashá, but are now the property of a Bey of Anápli. They contain a great quantity of orange and other fruit trees, and would be delightful if kept in order; at present they are in as ruinous a state as the Pyrgo which stands in the midst of them.

[a] εἶδον δὲ καὶ πηγὴν Ἀμφιαράου καλουμένην καὶ τὴν Ἀλκυονίαν λίμνην,—περίοδος δὲ τῆς λίμνης ἐστὶν ὅσον σταδίου τρίτον. Pausan. l. 2. c. 37.

Just below the fountain *Amymone* is a khan; beyond which a road to Akhladhó-kambo branches off to the right: it passes near a ruined khan, in the plain of Akhladhó-kambo.

Pausanias describes two roads from Lerna; one by Temenium to Nauplia, the other to Thyrea. That to Nauplia, concerning which I have cited his words, followed nearly the shore of the bay. As Tiryns was about twenty stades distant from Nauplia, Temenium must have been thirty stades to the westward of Tiryns, between that place and the mouth of the Erasinus, or nearly opposite to Argos, at a distance, according to Strabo[a], of twenty-six stades from thence. The position of Temenium is thus most exactly indicated, but so marshy is that part of the plain of Argos at present, that I have been unable to explore the site.

I now proceed to follow the second route from Lerna described by Pausanias. Leaving the Amymone at 5.12, we cross a small, but fertile plain on the sea-side, where, at 5.25, I pass, on my right, a hamlet of six or eight houses, called Kivéri, situated on the point of a rocky hill, advancing towards the sea. A road here turns away to the right, to Velanidhiá, a village situated higher up the valley, and not in sight. At 5.40, just after having crossed a

[a] Strabo, p. 368.

small, deep, rapid river, I arrive at another, Kivéri, which, though the larger of the two, has only ten families, with a tower belonging to the Spahí, where I am well lodged. The stream at Kivéri is evidently that which is collected from the surrounding mountains in the plain of Akhladhó-kambo. It is joined by some copious sources at Andrítzena. Near the mouth of the river there is a mill, said to have been built in the time of the Venetians. Either here or at the rocky projection below the northern Kivéri, the Genesium of Pausanias seems to have stood; for here begin the difficult mountains which extend to the Bay of Astró, or *Thyreate* gulf[a], and the rugged road which was anciently called Anigræa.

It may be convenient to the reader to cite the words of Pausanias[b], which give these positions; and as I am about to follow his route still farther, I shall continue the extract to the end of the chapter which concludes his Argolics. "There is another road", he says, "from Lerna, which leads, by the sea-side, to a place called Genesium. Here, on the shore, is a small temple of Neptune Genesius, contiguous to which is Apobathmi[c], so called because Danaus and his children are said to have here first landed in Argolis. Beyond

---

[a] Θυρεάτης κόλπος.
[b] Pausan. l. 2. c. 38.
[c] ἔχεται ἄλλο χωρίον Ἀπόβαθμοι.

Apobathmi, after having passed the Anigræa, which is a narrow and difficult road[a], there is a tract of land on the left, which extends to the sea, and is fertile in trees, particularly olives. Ascending inland from thence, occurs the place called Thyrea, where 300 select men of Argos fought for the country against an equal number of chosen Spartans, when all were slain, except one Spartan and two Argives[b]: tombs were erected to the slain[c] on the spot. Afterwards the Lacedæmonians, having beaten the Argives in a general action, obtained possession of the land and cultivated it, and subsequently gave it to the Æginetæ, when the latter were expelled from their island by the Athenians. But now the Argives possess the Thyreatis, and assert that it has been assigned to them by arbitration[d]. Proceeding forward from the Polyandria[e], there is a road to Athene [or Anthene[f]], which was formerly inhabited by the Æginetæ, and another town[g], Neris, and a third, Eva, which is the largest of the three, and contains a temple of Polemocrates, son of Machaon. Above these towns rises the mountain Parnon,

---

[a] ἐντεῦθεν διελθοῦσιν Ἀνιγραῖα καλούμενα, ὁδὸν καὶ στενὴν καὶ ἄλλως δύσβατον.

[b] See also Herodot. l. 1. c. 82.

[c] τάφοι ἐχώσθησαν.

[d] φασὶ δὲ ἀνασώσασθαι δίκῃ νικήσαντες.

[e] i. e. the sepulchres of the Argives and Spartans.

[f] Vide Thucyd. l. 5. c. 41.

[g] κώμη.

which contains the boundaries of the Lacedæmonians towards the Argives and Tegeatæ: the boundary is marked by Hermæ in marble, which give name to the place where they stand. The Tanus is the only river which flows from Parnon through the Argeia; it falls into the Thyreate gulf."

March 19.—I set out at 6.50, and immediately mount the hills which fall steeply to the sea on our left; the road leads along the face of them, and then descends upon a small beach, where a torrent, now dry, discharges itself. Not long afterwards, at 8.45, we arrive again upon the sea-beach at Xeropígadho, where, at the bottom of a retreating curve of the coast, the slope of the hill above it is less steep than in the other parts, and is cultivated with corn and olives. Here I find two boats loading wood for Anápli: the port is a dependency of the town of Ai Ianni, or St. John[a]. On the beach there is a well, not dry as the name indicates, together with a cistern lately built. This may possibly be the position of Pyramia of the Thyreatis, near which Plutarch says that Danaus landed[b].

Our path continues to follow the side of the rugged mountain, and, after having passed another cape, at 9.25 arrives opposite to the Aná-

[a] Ἅγιος Ἰωάννης.   [b] In Pyrrh.

volo[a]. This is a copious source of fresh water rising in the sea, at a quarter of a mile from a narrow beach under the cliffs. The body of fresh water appears to be not less than fifty feet in diameter. The weather being very calm this morning, I perceive that it rises with such force as to form a convex surface, and it disturbs the sea for several hundred feet around. In short, it is evidently the exit of a subterraneous river of some magnitude, and thus corresponds with the Deine of Pausanias, who remarks in the Arcadics, that the waters of the plain in the Mantinice, called Ἀργὸν, or the Inert, flow towards a chasm, and that, after a subterraneous course, they re-appear at the Deine, towards the place in the Argolis called Genethlium; " here sweet water ", he adds, " rises out of the sea in the same manner as near Cheimerium in Thesprotis[b]. Anciently the Argives threw bridled horses into the Deine as a sacrifice to Neptune." It can hardly be doubted, that the Genethlium here mentioned is the same place which Pausanias, in the Argolics, notices by the synonym Genesium[c], or

[a] Ἀνάβολος.
[b] ἀφανισθὲν δὲ ἐνταῦθα ἄνεισι κατὰ τὴν Δείνην. Ἔστι δὲ ἡ Δείνη κατὰ τὸ Γενέθλιον καλούμενον τῆς Ἀργολίδος, ὕδωρ γλυκὺ ἐκ θαλάσσης ἀνερχόμενον..... γλυκὺ δὲ ὕδωρ ἐν θαλάσσῃ δῆλόν ἐστιν ἐν- ταῦθά τε ἀνιὸν τῇ Ἀργολίδι καὶ ἐν τῇ Θεσπρωτίδι κατὰ τὸ Χειμέριον καλούμενον. Pausan. Arcad. c. 7.

[c] Pausanias notices a temple of Neptune Γενέθλιος at

the temple of Neptune Genesius, and which, as I have before observed, was probably situated at the modern Kivéri.

It is obvious that the only chasm or *zerethra*, through which any waters could have passed from any part of the *Mantinic* plain in their way towards the *Argolic* gulf, are the katavóthra near Persová. The word *Dine* or *Deine* seems perfectly descriptive of the Anávolo, and its situation is exactly in the direction in which, from the position of the *Zerethra* just mentioned, and the previous course of the river *Gareates*, from Stenó to the chasm, we might suppose that its emissory would be found. It must certainly be admitted that " towards Genethlium" is an extremely vague and inaccurate description of the position of Deine, if we place the former at Kivéri, and the latter at Anávolo. Nevertheless the phænomenon itself is of too singular a kind, and answers too exactly to the words of Pausanias, to allow of any reasonable doubt of the identity.

At 9.35 we arrive at the brow of the cliffs above the extreme corner of the beach of the bay of Astró, and at 9.40 descend into the plain. All the *Anigræa* is a very rugged bad

Sparta, (Lacon. c. 15.) and Apollodorus (1. 2. c. 3.) uses the epithet in the same form; the Scholiast adds, that Neptune was so called διὰ τῆς γενέσεως αἴτιον εἶναι.

road, and our pace was slow. Except in the few spots which I have mentioned, the sea is bordered throughout by perpendicular cliffs. The side of the mountain is chiefly covered with lentisks and wild olives, in the intervals of which there is at this season a fine pasture for numerous flocks of sheep and goats. Having descended into the plain, which is no longer clothed with olives and other trees, as in the time of Pausanias, we leave on the right the road to the Aianítika Kalývia, and pursue the sea-beach or the fields at a small distance from it, as far as Astró, having crossed at 9.50 a small stream coming from some marshes at the foot of Mount Závitza. This is the mountain which, extending from the plain of Astró along the shore to Kivéri, forms at its maritime foot the pass of *Anigræa*: towards the plain of Astró it is still more abrupt. At 10.23 we arrive at Astró; the name, though applied to all the bay and adjacent plain, belongs specifically to a skala on the southern side of a rocky peninsula, which is conspicuous from Argos and Anápli, and which advances into the sea from the middle of a plain of about four miles in length. At the skala there are a cistern, a khan, a tower inhabited by a sub-collector of customs, and two or three small magazines. The customs are farmed, together with those of the mills of Anápli, by the person who holds those of the town of Anápli, and who has paid this year ninety purses for the whole.

In the plain are kalývia belonging to the towns of Ai Ianni, Meligú, Korakovúni, and Prastó, which are situated on the mountains to the west and south. Three of these kalývia are large villages; here the inhabitants of the towns to which they belong reside in the winter, and here the best part of the territory of those towns is situated, the plain around the kalývia having a fertile soil, and being well cultivated with corn and olives. To the north of the promontory Astró, the beach runs in a line nearly west and east. To the south the direction is about s.s.w. for some distance, after which it turns eastward. Ships seldom anchor in the northern bay; and the southern is too much exposed to south-easterly gales to be much in use, except in summer for embarking the grain, oil, and vallonéa of the neighbouring district. When threatened with a gale, vessels generally run over to Port Toló. The south-westerly direction of the shore of the southern bay causes the inner part of it to approach the mountains, from which it is separated only by a large marshy lake called Mostó, the waters of which are discharged into the sea by a small river. The stream and lake thus form a natural division of the plain into two parts, and in fact they are considered as the separation of Tzakonía from the vilayéti of Aios Petros. All the plain to the northward of the river and lake of Mostó is called Astró, and all to the southward Ai Andhréa. The Aianítika and Melighiótika kalývia are in the former, and the Korakovunítika and Prastiótika in the latter; they lie, in the order just stated, from north-west to south-east, the two first are in the level, the two last on the foot of the mountains. Ai Andhréa takes its name from an old church of St. Andrew, on a height at the south-eastern corner of the southern bay of Astró, near the foot of a rocky mountain which bounds the plain on that side.

At St. Andrew there are some remains of Hellenic antiquity, which indicate the site of Brasiæ, or Prasiæ, the frontier town of Laconia; the boundaries of which province seem to have been the same as those of the modern Tzakonía, namely, the lake and river of Mostó. Towards the western end of the promontory of Astró, I found a piece of Hellenic wall of the second order, without towers, sufficient to shew that the peninsula was once the position of an ancient town or fortress. On the highest point of the promontory, which is towards the south, and immediately over the skala, are the remains of a more modern castle, which commands an admirable view of all the opposite coast of the Argolic peninsula, from the Isle of Petza to Anápli, together with the plain of Argos and its surrounding mountains. Astró[a] is an ancient name, retained without any corruption. Ptolemy is the only author who mentions it, but, by placing the Laco-Argive boundary between Astrum and Prasiæ[b], he confirms the position of Prasiæ at St. Andrew, as well as that the ancient boundaries were those natural ones which I have just mentioned. Astró I conceive to have been the situation of the maritime fortress, in the building of which the Æginetæ were interrupted by the Athenians in the eighth year of the Peloponnesian war[c]. On being attacked here by the Athenians, they retreated into the city of Thyrea, and were followed thither by the Athenians, when, having been abandoned by their Lacedæmonian auxiliaries, who retired into the mountains, the Athenians took Thyrea, and indulged their ancient hatred of Ægina, by murdering the inhabitants and burning the town.

Leaving the Skala of Astró at 1.45, I cross the plain in the direction of the Aianítika Ka-

[a] Ἀστρὸν.
[b] Ptolem. l. 3. c. 16.
[c] Thucyd. l. 4. c. 57.—They had been put in possession of the Thyreatis by the Lacedæmonians, upon being expelled from their own island by the Athenians, in the first year of the war. Thucyd. l. 2. c. 27.

lývia, and at 2.5 pass a small river which rises in the mountains near Aios Petros, and which, leaving the monastery of Luku a mile on the right, crosses the plain in a direction from west to east, and joins the sea in the southern bay of Astró a little to the northward of the mouth of the stream which issues from the Lake of Mostó. This river of Luku is nearly dry in summer, but in winter it is sometimes very large, being formed from many torrents in the mountains. We enter the Kalývia of Ai Ianni at 2.15. The plain around is well clothed with olives, which for the most part are young trees; they are intermixed with cornfields and vineyards. The Kalývia consist of good cottages, many of which have two stories, and they are prettily dispersed among the fields and olive woods. At 2.33 I arrive at the end of the Kalývia, where, at the foot of the mountain which borders the plain on the s. w., stands a Metókhi of the monastery of Luku: there is another at Ai Ianni, and a third on the southern side of Mount Závitza to the left of the river nearly opposite to Luku.

I now proceed to Luku, having obtained some information which gives me the assurance that I shall there meet with some remains of *Thyrea.* Passing along the foot of the mountain in a westerly direction, we leave the river of

Luku at the distance of a mile on the right, flowing in a deep bed between the sloping and woody bases of the two mountains which inclose its valley,—arrive at the monastery at 3.10. It is situated on a tabular hill covered with shrubs and small trees, and having a gentle descent towards the river. On the eastern side, the height is bounded by a deep rocky ravine, at the bottom of which runs a small branch of the river. This rivulet, I am told, does not entirely fail in summer, though the greater part of its waters is turned to supply a small conduit which passes by the Metókhi of Luku to the Aianítika Kalývia. On its left bank, on one side of the garden of the monastery, are seen some remains of ancient walls formed of large squared stones mixed with tiles and mortar. These were evidently the city walls on the eastern side, where the ravine furnished a natural protection. The chief part of the town was below the monastery, from whence, as the monks inform me, many sculptured marbles have been removed, some for embarkation, others for the construction or repair of houses in the neighbouring villages or for the use of the convent itself. By the guidance of the monks, I find among the bushes which cover all the site, and among foundations and other remains of masonry, the following fragments of Hellenic sculpture: A statue in white marble of a woman, the head wanting; some masons at work in the monastery have within these few days beaten off a part of the knee and the feet, which before were perfect. I perceive also the fragments of one arm on the ground near the statue. It was naked; the other arm, which is the left, has a piece of loose drapery wound about it and rests upon the hip, the body being much bent towards the right side. The statue is naked to the hips, the rest of the body is covered with a loose garment in many folds. The garment covers all the back in broad even plaits coarsely executed, as if intended to be set up against a wall, as indeed the form of the pedestal shews. The pedestal and statue are of one stone. The fragment from the sole of the foot to the top of the hip three feet five inches. When the Kaloyéri invited me to go and see this statue, they called it a γυναίκα μαρμαραίνια, a marble woman. The next thing I observe is two fragments of a colossal groupe, which seems to have represented a man carrying the dead corpse of another, with the face upwards, upon his shoulders. The latter figure is much smaller than the other, and is perfect from the neck to the thighs. The body is curved backwards, as a dead body would naturally hang. The hand of the figure which was represented carrying the dead body remains on the side of the body; a part of the other figure, covered with drapery, is also attached to the corpse and forms part of the same stone. Lying close by this fragment is another representing the body from the neck to the waist, of a man having a loose garment thrown over his left shoulder, and bound by a thong passing over the right; there is a girdle of the same kind and size round his waist, but partly hidden under the loose folds of the garment which hang over the left shoulder. All the breast and right side are naked, and are of very good design and execution. The muscles seem exerted; probably this was a part of the figure which was represented as carrying the other on his shoulders. It measures two feet two inches from one shoulder to the other. The hand on the side of the corpse is six inches and one tenth across the knuckles of the four fingers. These two fragments lie close together and are partly covered by the lentisk bushes growing by them, but they are still better secured perhaps from the destructive hands of the masons by the unfit shape of the blocks and by the colour, which, though the stone is white marble, has become brown with the weather and incrusted with a minute moss. Not far from these statues, the Igúmeno[a] conducts me to a spot from which he

---

[a] Ἡγούμενος—head of a convent.

says that ancient materials have at different times been carried away, and where appears to have been a large quadrangular building, which he supposed to have been the principal naós or temple. But that edifice, or at least one of the great temples, seems to have existed to the eastward of this spot, near where lies the female statue; for some very massive foundations are there seen, and some ruins of a semicircular niche are still standing, built, like all the other remaining walls at this place, of large squared stones joined with mortar and mixed with tiles. Close by the niche lie five fragments of shafts of grey granite two feet five and a half inches in diameter, together with two Corinthian capitals of a coarse kind of white marble, of which I find many pieces lying about these ruins; it seems to be of the same kind which was used at Sparta, Gythium, &c. The monks describe to me a mountain of this kind of stone near Vérvena. In the church of the monastery there are four shafts of streaked white marble thirteen feet high and five feet three inches and a half in circumference. I observed among the ruins a single column nearly of the same size, and of a dark brown marble; as well as many fragments and broken slabs of white, of veined, and of green marble, and some of porphyry. The other remains of antiquity consist only of masses of mortar and fragments of stones, dispersed among the bushes which cover the slope towards the river. The Kaloyéri inform me they have found and removed to the convent at various times fragments of small marble statues, two of which I find in the convent; others, they say, have been carried by sea to Anápli, or embarked in vessels casually anchoring at Astró. They have excavated also several sepulchres in the loose soil just behind the monastery, and others at the foot of some cliffs, which seem to have formed the lower termination of the ancient site, but they found only coarse broken vases and bones.

The only inscriptions I could find were three letters ꟽ K A in large handsome characters, on a fragment of marble in the church of the convent, and a sepulchral stone of much later date in the same place in honour of a woman named Marciane, with the word ζήσης misspelt.

ZHCIC
MAPKIANH

In the same church I observed an Ionic cornice; and an Ionic capital on the outside of the gate of the monastery.

An uncultivated level extends from the back of the table height of the convent to the steeps of Mount *Parnon*; in front, in the opposite direction, is the more abruptly rising, though much smaller and lower mountain called Závitza; the latter is separated only from the site of *Thyrea* by the valley of the river, which is covered with bushes and small trees, like the ancient site. The ruins of Thyrea being still so considerable, one is surprised that Pausanias should have been so brief in his description of it. Instead of designating Thyrea as a city, as from history we know it to have been, and a city of some importance too, he applies only the word χωρίον to it, and notices nothing whatever but the Polyandria, or sepulchral monuments (apparently two in number) of the Spartans and Argives. Perhaps it was a complete ruin in his time, and almost in the same state of desolation which it now presents. Thucydides is deficient in his usual accuracy when he states Thyrea to be only ten stades from the sea, for it is at least three times that distance[a]. A road passes from the convent of Luku up the gorge of the small stream which bounds the eastern side of the ancient site and leads to Ai Ianni, three hours distant; and from thence in one hour to Aios Petros. This road leaves on the left a Hellenic fortress which I saw from the plain of Astró, situated two miles above the Aianítika Kalývia; it then enters the cultivated

[a] Thucyd. l. 4, c. 57.

level of Xerokambí near Ai Ianni. On the left of the road from the latter place to St. Peter's, there is another larger Hellenic castle on a hill. As Pausanias, leaving the sepulchres of Thyrea, arrives soon after at Anthene, this seems to have been the first mentioned Kastro; the ruin between St. John's and St. Peter's may have been Neris. Eva, the largest of the towns of Mount Parnon, was probably farther to the southward. These places, together with the Thyreatis, and before the time of the Roman empire, perhaps the Prasiatis also, formed a country called Cynuria; which was of great military importance, as lying between the Argolis and Laconia, and as commanding the passes which separated them [a]. Plutarch tells us, that when Cleomenes was in possession of Corinth he found himself obliged suddenly to evacuate it in consequence of a counter-revolution at Argos, which he feared would place these passes in the hands of his enemies and cut off his retreat to Sparta [b]. The Roman government perfectly understood the importance of the Cynuria when they gave it to Argos, as this alone was sufficient to keep Sparta in order. It is probably to this determination of the Romans that Pausanias alludes when he says, that the

[a] Thucyd. l. 2. c. 56.—l. 5.   [b] Plutarch. in Cleomen. c. 41.

Argives possessed Thyreatis in his time, δίκῃ νικήσαντες, by adjudication.

March 20.—Leaving the convent of Luku at 8 this morning, I return by the same road to the Metókhi near the Aianítika Kalývia; a small aqueduct which conducts water from a mill above the convent, follows the road side as far as the Kalývia; this is the *diverticulum* from the torrent of Luku, which I before noticed. At 8.45, towards the end of the Kalývia, we have the ancient fortress, which I suppose to have been Anthene, two miles on the right on the summit of a high peak. It is called στὸ Ἑλληνικὸ. The summit of the hill is surrounded with a wall of polygonal masonry, flanked with towers. As I stood inquiring the modern name of this ruin, an ill-dressed man issued out of one of the houses and exclaimed: "That is Mount Temenium[a], which contained the tomb of Temenus, and the lake before you is that which produced the seven-headed water snake[b] slain by Hercules."[c] It seems, that he is dháskalo of the village, and has been reading Meletius, who makes these mistakes as to Lerna and Temenium. 8.55, pass the Melighiótika Kalývia, or Huts of Meligú, which village stands on the mountain above them. The Kalývia is a small village situated on the right bank of a torrent. At 9.5, the road

[a] Τημένιον ὄρος. [b] ἑπτακέφαλος ὕδρα. [c] Ἡρακλῆς.

passes at the foot of a rocky height projecting from the mountain. On the summit of this height there is a Metókhi of the convent of Aía Triádha (St. Trinity), which is described to me situated an hour below Meligú and one hour and a half above the Metókhi. 9.17, arrive at the beginning of the marsh of Mostó, which here reaches to the foot of the mountain and extends to our left almost to the sea; two minutes farther I observe a copious spring of water issuing from the foot of the mountain, two minutes beyond it are some other sources still larger flowing from the foot of the rock, above which the road passes. This is the lake which Meletius mistook for the Alcyonia. It occupies the centre of the marsh, and is about a mile and a quarter in circumference. It is deep, abounds in fish, and is now covered with wild ducks. The marsh is about three miles in circumference, and the sea-beach one mile direct from the foot of the mountain. We now enter the plain of Ai Andhréa, halt seven minutes at 9.42, and then leaving the straight road to Prastó, which passes by the Korakovunítika Kalývia, we turn to the left to the Prastiótika Kalývia, more commonly called, by the people of Prastó, Ai Andhréa, or Stó Ialó (at the Sea). These Kalývia form a large village on the foot of the mountain in the southern corner of the plain.

Here I lodge in the house of Kyr Thódhoro Guléli, Proestós of Prastó, with whom I find the Bishop of Prastó. The bishop, whose *undress* official title is ὁ 'Ρέοντος καὶ Πραστοῦ, is making a tour of his diocese for the purpose of collecting ten piastres from every Kalóiero and Papás, in obedience to an order from the Patriarch of Constantinople. This extraordinary levy is for the purpose of supporting a school, at Constantinople, for orphans, who are to be taught Hellenic, φιλοσοφία, whatever that may be, and some of the European languages. A large house has already been bought for the purpose at Tarápia on the *Bosphorus*.

The people of Prastó, whose town stands in a cold and lofty situation, migrate in the winter to Lenídhi, where the bishop has a house, or to the two villages of Melanó and Deró, near it, or to this place. Deró is six hours from hence; thence to Melanó is one hour, and thence to Lenídhi one hour and a half, the villages lying on the cultivated slopes of the mountain in the order mentioned, from west to east. By sea, the direct navigation from St. Andrew to the shore below Lenídhi is about two fifths of the distance to Cape Iéraka, or only twelve geographical miles, so mountainous and circuitous is the road by land. The slopes of the mountain above Lenídhi are, as I have said, cultivated, but there is neither plain nor harbour. Fakhinó is a bad port without any village, two hours under Kunúpia. Kyparíssia is a better harbour, four hours under Kremastí, a large village inhabited by a colony of Albanians, who speak that language. It appears, by the description of my host, that Fakhinó and Kyparíssia form nearly equal intervals between Lenídhi and Iéraka.

In the afternoon I visit the Hellenic ruin at St. Andrew. The height on which it is situated branches from the mountains on the south-eastern side of the plain, and forms a projection of the coast, to the westward of which are a magazine and custom-house; the Skala is known by the name of Ai Andhréa. The walls of the Paleókastro surround the promontory along the edge of cliffs, which encircle its table summit: some of the lower courses of the walls remain, and towers are traced at intervals; there was a small keep or inner inclosure, 110 yards in circumference, at the s.s.w. or highest point, upon which stands a ruined church of St. Andrew. The slope and plain towards the modern buildings were anciently comprehended within a third inclosure, which extended as far as those buildings. The circuit of the walls on the hill, exclusive of the latter inclosure, is a walk of twenty minutes: the masonry is of the second order; there is a fine specimen of it belonging to the outer inclosure a little inland from the magazines. On the hill of the Acropolis there are many foundations of large stones, together with some cisterns roughly cut in the rock and coated with plaster. The masons have opened them for the sake of taking away the stones which covered them; the Venetians also are accused of having plundered these ruins when they built the Palamídhi. Just beyond the magazines the river from Mount Málevo (*Parnon*), which enters the plain near the Kalývia of Prastó, joins the sea. It is called Káni, and is evidently the ancient Tanus; it does not flow in the summer, nor does that from the mountain of St. Peter's, which passes by Luku.

Brasiæ, or Prasiæ, as the town is called by every author who mentions it, except Pausanias, is thus introduced by him[a]. "Brasiæ is the last of the maritime cities of the Eleuthero-Lacones in this direction: the passage by sea from Cyphanta is 200 stades in distance. The Brasiatæ shew the cave where Ino nursed Bacchus, and they call their plain the Garden of Bacchus. They have temples of Æsculapius and Achilles, and they celebrate a yearly festival in honour of Achilles. In Brasiæ there is a small summit

[a] Pausan. Lacon. c. 24.

projecting a little[a] into the sea, upon which stand four brazen statues not more than a foot in height; three of these have hats[b] on their heads; whether they are considered Dioscuri or Corybantes, I know not,—the fourth is a statue of Minerva."

The rocky mountain which rises to the southward of the ruins of Prasiæ, is called Lagovúni: at the foot of the cliffs which border the highest summit, on the side looking towards the sea, there is a fine cavern with a small entrance, the same probably as that shewn by the Prasiatæ to Pausanias as the grotto in which Ino nursed Bacchus. A mile north-westward of the Paleókastro a small rocky height projects into the sea, and divides the southern bay of Astró, which receives the river of Luku, from the small curve of St. Andrew, into which the river Káni discharges itself. This seems to be the promontory upon which stood the four brazen statues. I return in half an hour to the Prastiótika, the distance being about two miles and a half, and pass the evening in obtaining some information from Guléli and the bishop respecting the peculiar dialect of modern Greek which is spoken in this part of the country. They tell me that Prastó has lately engaged in the commerce of Spetzia, has become rich, and now

[a] ἠρέμα. [b] πίλους.

owns many ships. Phranza, in relating an unimportant transaction in which he was engaged in the year 1435, makes mention of the place under the name of Προάστειον. In either form I take the word to be a corruption of Prasiæ, whose inhabitants having retired to the mountains when piracy and bad government had made the maritime position at St. Andrew untenable, probably then carried with them the name, which, in the subsequent ages of barbarism, assumed the form of Proástio, or Prastó.

It has been seen, in the passage above cited from Pausanias, that in the coast southward of Prasiæ there was a place called Cyphanta. It was one of the Eleuthero-Laconic towns, and in the time of Pausanias was in ruins, but there was still a temple of Æsculapius containing a marble statue; and he observed a fountain issuing from a rock, which, it was reported, had been produced by a blow of the lance of Atalanta, when hunting and thirsty. Pausanias adds, that the place was ten stades inland from a part of the coast which was six stades from Zarax[a]. It may be suspected, however, that there is some error in the latter distance, such a proximity of two cities being scarcely conceiv-

[a] Προελθόντι δὲ ἀπὸ Ζάρακος παρὰ τὴν θάλασσαν ἕξ που στάδια, καὶ ἐπιστρέψαντι αὐτόθεν ἐς μεσόγαιαν σταδίους ὡς δέκα, Κυφάντων καλουμένων ἐρείπιά ἐστιν, &c. Pausan. Lacon. c. 24.

able in a country of slender resources, where the other places were widely distant from one another. It is probable that the modern Kyparíssia was the *port* which Ptolemy and Pliny call Cyphanta; that the *town* of Cyphanta stood at a distance of ten stades from it, and that Pausanias wrote ἑξήκοντα instead of ἕξ, as the number of stades between Zarax and the shore below Cyphanta: the total, 260 stades, will then correspond very well with the real distance from Port Iéraka to the ruins of *Brasiæ*, the direct distance from St. Andrew to Port Iéraka being about thirty geographic miles. Taking the distance from St. Andrew to Lenídhi at two-fifths, or twelve geographic miles, and Kyparíssia at two-thirds of the remainder, there will remain six geographic miles direct between that place and the position of Zarax at Iéraka, which is not very different from the sixty stades, which I suppose Pausanias to have written instead of six. Of course this is only a conjecture, the correctness of which remains to be ascertained by a personal examination of the places.

March 21.—At 7.4 I move from the Prastiótika Kalývia, and proceeding up the valley by a road not far from the right bank of the Kani, or river of Ai Andhréa, at 7.35 enter the mountains at the opening through which it issues into the plain. The road ascends the heights, which overhang the right bank of the river, and becomes very rugged and difficult. At 7.56, a piece of Hellenic wall is on the right, upon a level bounded by cliffs, which overhang the river; they are the remains perhaps of a small fortress for the defence of this pass: soon afterwards we lose twenty-four minutes in replacing baggage, one of our horses having fallen in the rugged ascent, with the baggage under him and his legs in the air. A little beyond, a road ascends to the left to the convent of Orthokostá, one hour distant, and the largest of the numerous monasteries of these mountains. 9.49, on the side of the opposite mountain, across the river, stands that of Sároma. The hills which we pass over are covered with corn-fields, and olive-trees cultivated in terraces belonging to Prastó. At 10, an opening in the mountains appears on the right, through which descends a small branch of the Káni between two cultivated declivities. Above its right bank, in the midst of a slope covered with gardens and olive grounds, stands Plátanos, a large village belonging to the vilayéti of St. Peter's. Its principal produce is figs, which are dried and sold all over the Moréa, strung upon rushes. The elevated situation of Plátanos, however, is too cold and moist for this fruit, and the figs of Plátanos are of an inferior kind, having tough thick skins, and not much saccharine matter. The village is distant from our road about three miles in a straight line. Its valley ascends to the north-west at right angles to the ravine of the main river. Our road now turns more westward towards Kastánitza, which is seen in a lofty situation just under the woods of Mount Málevo. The branch of the river which comes from thence joins that of Plátanos at the point which was under us at 10 o'clock.

Ten minutes after changing the direction of our road, we have Sítena[a], a village of 100 houses on the opposite side of the ravine, and a mile and a half from us in direct distance. It is immediately under one of the highest and steepest summits of Mount Málevo. A road leads along the side of that mountain from Sítena to Kastánitza, a distance of one hour. Soon after passing Sítena we begin to descend by a rugged zig-zag path, and at 10.30 arrive at the bottom, at a rill which comes from the open country about Prastó. That town is not in sight, but I perceive the cultivated hills about it. Leaving this opening on our left, we ascend towards Kastánitza, along the side of a deep glen on the right bank of the stream, which flows in a rocky channel below. On the opposite side of the ravine, not far above the river

[a] Σήτενα.

side, is an ἀσκητάριον, or hermitage, but which has not been inhabited for many years. It is a great cavern, in front of which a wall has been built, forming two stories, with a door and windows. We continue to mount, leaving many cultivated terraces on our right, on the opposite side of the ravine, and at 11.40 enter Kastánitza.

This was once a town of some importance, but is now reduced to 100 families; many of the houses are empty, the inhabitants having migrated to Ydhra, Spetzia, or Constantinople; Prastó, which now absorbs all the wealth and population of the neighbourhood, was once so inferior, say the people of Kastánitza, to their own town, as to look like its Kalývia. Their houses are spacious, well built, and well furnished; those of the largest size consist of three stories, of which the lowest is the stable, the middle a kind of magazine for the furniture of show and value, as well as the arms, with which these mountaineers are well provided; the upper story consists of two chambers, the inner having a chimney and hearth, and the outer a divan, as being the room of reception. I am lodged at an old priest's house, one of the best in the place. Ten of the Palikária of the village, after having been out several weeks, have lately returned from the pursuit of the thieves, who would never have been caught, if the Pashá had not adopted the mode of making the villages adjacent to their haunts responsible for their suppression. The Kastanitziótes are a well-made, active, clever race, but jealous, to a degree of malignity, of the prosperity of their neighbours of Prastó. Kastánitza, Sítena, and Prastó, together with the villages on the sea-side dependent on the latter, viz. Lenídhi, Melanó, Deró, and the Kalývia of St. Andrew, form the district of Tzakonía, vulgarly pronounced Tjakoniá. The monasteries of Tzakonía are Kondolína, in the district of Kastánitza, and Orthokostá, Rondinó, Karyá, Klisúra, Sínza, and 'Elona, in the district of Prastó[a]. It is only in these villages and convents that the Tzakonic is spoken, a dialect which is believed by the Greeks to preserve many ancient Doric forms of speech. It appears doubtful, however, whether the pretended Dorisms are not in many instances an effect of the imagination of the $διδάσκαλοι$, or other half-educated persons, in their anxiety to discover some remains of the Doric in a district where they know it to have been anciently spoken,

[a] Phranza, in the same passage in which he notices Proástio, or Prastó; names also all the other principal places of this part of the country. They are thus written by him, $Ἀστρὸν$, $Ἅγιος\ Πέτρος$, $Ἅγιος\ Ἰωάννης$, $Μελιγὸν$, $Ῥέοντας$, $Κυπαρισσία$, $Λεωνίδης$, now $Λενίδι$, $Σίτανας$, now $Σήτενα$.

and where the peasantry still preserve a peculiar *patois*. Thus I was told that ἀμέρα (day) was ancient Tzakonic, not known to the vulgar, which means nothing more, as I remarked to the Bishop of Prastó, than that it is an ancient Doric form. It is certain, however, that there are some Doric words in actual use; Νεμὰ for pasture (in Romaic βοσκὴ), and tamborían, i. e. τὰν πορείαν, for "the road,"[a] are apparently real Dorisms, and they induce me to believe that others might be found, though certainly my informants have not stated any, which, to my conviction, were undoubted instances.

The dialect of Tzakonía appears to be more remarkable for having preserved words of common Hellenic in greater number than are to be found in any of the other unfrequented parts of Greece, in all of which the traveller may observe some Hellenisms which are not generally employed by the modern Greeks. The following Hellenisms are in common use in Tzakonía: ὅρα, see, νομεῖς, shepherds, ἐρίφια, kids, ἠνέγκατε, or ἑωράκατε, τὸν ἔριφον; have you brought, or seen, the goat? παρῆτε, come ye. In some of the following may be discerned traces of Hel-

---

[a] τὰμ πορείαν μ' ἔγγω, "I go my road," is a surly answer, often given by these mountaineers to the question, Where are you going?

lenism, if not of Dorism; others seem mere barbarous corruptions of Hellenic: προύατα, sheep, τζούα, oaks, ἴον, water, βότζια, grapes,—ἄτζαπο, used at Prastó for ἄνθρωπος, I find is not acknowledged at Kastánitza; βρέχου, it rains, πὶ ἔσσα ἐκιού; where art thou? ὀγὶ, here, ἔα ὄρ' ὀγὶ, come hither quickly, ὀγὶ ἐμὲ ἐζού, here I am, νιλείετε, speak ye, δράνιτζε, run ye, τζάχετε, walk on, ἀπὸ κιὰ ἐσπαριού[a]; from whence come ye? ἐγγουντερέμε τὰν τζέαν, let us go home. At Kastánitza, instead of τζέα, for house, they use κέλα, which is a Romaic form, derived from the Latin.

That some of the reputed Dorisms of the Tzakonic are the invention of schoolmasters, I was convinced, on the Bishop of Prastó repeating to me a Tzakonic couplet, upon an eclipse of the sun, composed by a λογιώτατος διδάσκαλος of Prastó, but which was nothing more than an attempt to write two bad lines in Doric:

Ἀμέρᾳ Παρασκευᾷ φθινύσθη ἄλιος ποτὶ τᾶς Σελάνας
Ἐπιλυγαζόμενος ἐν διαστήματι ὥρας μιᾶς.

In short, as the real Tzakonic is seldom or never written, as the common Romaic is used in all transactions which require writing, as it is generally understood by the people, and

---

[a] Apparently from πορεύομαι.

spoken by all lettered and travelled persons, it can hardly be doubted, that the peculiarities of speech of this small district will soon be forgotten, while the words of common Hellenic which it preserves will become universal with the progress of literature in Greece. Nevertheless, a more exact inquiry into this dialect, in the places where it is spoken, than my time will allow, would, undoubtedly, be interesting; and the more so, as the Cynurii were one of the people of Peloponnesus, who, according to Herodotus, were aboriginal inhabitants[a]. Villoison, it appears, made some inquiries concerning the Tzakonic dialect when he was in Greece; but, as he did not visit this district, his information on the subject was very scanty. Some of the examples which he adduces are found in every part of Greece, as $\dot{o}\chi\theta\rho\grave{o}s$ for $\dot{\epsilon}\chi\theta\rho\grave{o}s$, &c.

As it is generally imagined that Tzakonía includes all the range of mountains which rise from the eastern coast of the ancient Laconia, I was particular in my inquiries on this head, and was assured that it contains only the places which I have already mentioned. It may easily be conceived, however, that the name, being a corruption of *Laconia*, may have formerly

[a] Herodot. l. 8. c. 73.

had a more extensive chorographical signification, and that its borders may have been contracted as the dialect which distinguished the original people was gradually displaced by that of settlers from Albania, Bulgaria, the islands, or Greece beyond the Isthmus.

The soil of Kastánitza produces neither oil, nor wheat, nor barley; nothing but apples, chestnuts, vines, and rye. The last is grown in some of the highest parts of the mountain, where they reap the grain in August, and sow immediately. The village now possesses only eight Zevgária; formerly it had between three and four hundred. The inhabitants gain their livelihood (in a manner similar to that of the Vlakhiotes of Mount Pindus, &c.) by keeping shops in Mistrá, Anápli, Tripolitzá, Spétzia, Constantinople; some traffic as far as Russia, while others are engaged in Spetziote ships, as sailors. The fir-woods of Mount *Parnon* they make no use of. The ruined place, from which the bishop takes his title, τοῦ ʽΡέοντος, is near the monastery of Karyá, in the way from Prastó to Korakovúni, on the summit of a high hill above the monastery, two hours from Prastó and one from Korakovúni. The circuit of the walls is described as greater than that of the castle between Ai Ianni and Aios Petros, which is small, like *Anthene,* but preserves both walls and towers; whereas at Réonda, or Paleó Korakovúni, as it is sometimes called, the foundations only remain. The air of these mountains is as pure and healthy in summer, as that of the plain of Astró and St. Andrew is pernicious. The plain, in that season, is quite uninhabited. Prastó is reckoned one hour and a half distant from Kastánitza. A high ridge divides the valleys, and shuts out the view of the one from the other. Thus, at least, the people of Kastánitza have the advantage of being spared the pain of a constant view of their neighbours' prosperity.

I cannot discover any Hellenic remains at Kastánitza; nor do I think that any ancient town stood upon this site, for the route described by Pausanias having undoubtedly led through the pass of Kastánitza, if any town had existed here, it would assuredly have been mentioned by him. The fertile slopes around it formed, perhaps, together with those of Sítena and Plátano, the district of *Eva*, which stood under Mount *Parnon*, and which we may suppose to have comprehended its more southern part; because, as I have already observed, there is reason to believe that *Neris* and *Anthene*, the two other towns of *Parnon*, possessed the cultivable districts now occupied by St. Peter's, St. John's, and Meligú.

March 22.—At 7.55 I set out, and ascend the great steeps of Mount Málevo. The ridge immediately above Kastánitza is covered with a forest of chestnut trees, mixed with a few oaks. Our road is very rugged, and has been furrowed by the melting of the snow, which fell here to a great depth when I was at Tripolitzá, but was all dissolved by the subsequent mild weather, except among the forests of firs[a], on the summit of the mountain, where the thaw has not yet penetrated. In three quarters of an hour we arrive among the firs, and, at 8.55, enter a narrow ravine between two steep heights covered with those trees. This is the principal bed of the waters which form the stream of Kastánitza, and the most distant of the chief tributaries of the Káni. As the high mountain which gives rise as well to this as to the other branches of the river which flow by Sítena, Plátano, &c., is certainly the proper *Parnon*, and as Pausanias seems to connect the Tanus with the boundaries of Laconia, on the road we are following, we have sufficient, I think, to identify the Káni with the *Tanus;* notwithstanding that he describes the Tanus as flowing *through the Argeia* into the Thyreate gulf, which, at first sight, seems to answer better to the river of Luku. But though the *maritime*

[a] ἐλάτια.

country, as far north as the marsh of Mostó, may have been ascribed in his time to the Prasiatis, and consequently to Eleuthero-Laconia, it appears, from the position of the Hermæ, relatively to Sellasia and Sparta, as mentioned by Pausanias, in the tenth chapter of the Laconics, that all the road we have been following was in Cynuria, which, though more often in the power of Sparta than of Argos, was always geographically considered as belonging to the Argeia, and was actually a part of it in the time of the Roman empire. Euripides, I believe, is the only other author who mentions the Tanus. It was the river, according to the dramatist, upon which the father of Electra fed his flocks[a]. According to the scholiast, it divided Argolis from the Spartiatic land; a definition not very objectionable, inasmuch as a part of its course may have been the boundary between Cynuria Proper and the Prasiatis. It is not impossible that Káni may be a dialectic form of the word Tanus, at least as far as the initial letter is concerned. There are several examples of the occasional preference of κ to τ in the Æolic or Doric dialects, as in ὅτε and its derivatives, which were written ὅκα, πόκα, ἄλλοκα[b]. The termination of ι for ος is a common Romaic conversion.

[a] Euripid. Elect. v. 410. —Apollon. Dyscol.
[b] Vide Gregor. de Dialectis.

In ascending, we meet with a great quantity of snow in some parts of the narrow glen of the river, and there is a still greater depth upon the sides of the hills. We arrive at the end of the ravine at 9.22, and then ascend the upper heights through the fir forests. " It is all torch-wood"![a] exclaimed one of our postillions in admiration, and added, " How rich I should soon be by selling it at Mistrá!" At 9.45 we attain the summit of the pass, and immediately begin to descend. Here, and for a quarter of a mile below, the snow is four or five feet deep in the road, and the loaded horses with great difficulty get through it, falling repeatedly. The suridjís grow mutinous, complain that the snow is a boúi[b] in depth, and assert that it is impossible to proceed: we persevere, however, and soon come into a path clear of snow, but which the torrents have made very rugged: our pace is consequently slow; through the whole passage of the mountain not more than that of mules. We left the highest summit of the mountain, now called St. Elias of Málevo, two miles on the left, much higher than the part we crossed, bare of trees, and in many parts without snow: it is in the district of Kastánitza. At the bot-

[a] ὅλο δαδί.
[b] A rough measurement, meaning about the height of a man.

tom of the descent, we enter a broad torrent-bed, like that by which we approached the ascent, on the opposite side of the mountain; it is bordered by heights covered with large firs. After proceeding a quarter of an hour down this ravine, we turn out of it to the left; its waters run to Vérria, and, after uniting with the river of Tzítzina, receive the northern branch from Arákhova below the monastery of the Forty Saints, after which the united river assumes the name of Kelefína, and joins the Iri, or *Eurotas*, a little above *Sparta*. We mount a ridge on the left of the ravine, and, at 10.55, arrive on the summit, where a road from Tzítzina to Babakú turns off to the right. In this spot are the foundations of an ancient Greek edifice; many large wrought stones, entire or broken, and all much corroded by the effect of the exposed and humid situation, are lying on the ground. I search in vain for any remains of architectural ornament or of statuary. On the brow of a peak, to the left of this spot, there is said to be a large cavern or quarry; but the mist and rain conceal every thing above us. Below, in the direction of Mistrá, I perceive two cultivated ravines, meeting at a rocky gorge, through which the united stream from the two ravines finds its way towards the Kelefína. In the valley of the northern branch, to our right, is the village of Vérria[a], an ancient Greek name; towards the sources of that which lies to our left, is Tzítzina[b], a word of Bulgarian origin, and vulgarly pronounced Tjídjina. There is not a single representative hereabouts of the forest of oaks, called Scotita, which existed in the time of Pausanias; but the Hellenic ruins, which now give to the place the name of Mármara[c], correspond to those of the temple of Jupiter Scotitas, which stood in the forest[d]. Leaving the road to Vérria on our right, we continue along the side of the fir-clad mountain to the southward, and, crossing a barren ridge or two, descend into a narrow valley, at the head of which stands Tzítzina, under a rocky summit of Mount Málevo. We arrive at 12.20. The sides of the hills below and around the village are covered with vines in narrow terraces. Along the bottom runs a

[a] Βέῤῥοια.—The Βέῤῥοια of Macedonia appears to have been the same name as Φέραι, which was carried, in the ancient Peloponnesian form, into Macedonia by the Argolic colony. Some of the Peloponnesians were partial to the letter B, in the room of an initial aspirate, as in the instances of Βοίτυλος, Βοιιώα, for Οἴτυλος, Οἰνόη. Vérria, therefore, seems to have preserved its present form from Pelasgic times; and it is remarkable, that Livy mentions a Pheræ in this part of the country.—Liv. l. 35. c. 30.
[b] Τζήτζινα.
[c] στὰ Μάρμαρα.
[d] Pausan. Lacon. c. 10.

small river, descending directly from the mountain behind the village; it is joined by another from a ravine which branches from the valley of Tzítzina to the southward.

Tzítzina contains eighty families, who possess a considerable quantity of land, grown with wheat, barley, rye, and vines; they have also some lands and a kalývia near *Sparta*, and many flocks, which are now feeding on the winter pastures in the low lands, particularly in the plain of Elos; from the milk of these flocks they make cheese, and carry on a considerable traffic in this article. In Bardúnia and the north-eastern part of Mani, they cut plank and timber from the oak and poplar of Mount *Taygetum*, and they procure deal plank in their own mountains. Their contributions of every sort amount to 13,000 piastres a year. Seven armed palikária were lately sent from hence to join those of the other villages against the robbers, and assisted in taking some prisoners at the Mármara.

March 23.—At 7½, having sent the baggage by the direct road to the monastery of the Forty Saints[a], I quit Tzítzina, and following its torrent in the direction of the branch which descends through the ravine on the southern side of the village, mount soon afterwards the hill to the left of it, which is covered with

---

[a] τὸ Μοναστήριον τῶν Ἁγίων Σαράντα.

CHAP. XXII.]   MOUNT MALEVO.   517

firs mixed with a few pines; on the summit there is some cultivated ground, and the trees are burnt to prepare the ground for sowing. These woodlands are said to have been more cultivated in former times, when Tzítzina was a much larger village. According to the information which our guide gives me, as we ride along, there are not many deer[a] in the forests of Mount Málevo; one he saw at the Mármara last year, about as large as a calf of a year old. There are wolves and rabbits in the woods, but no roebucks[b], or bears[c], or wild hogs[d]. The last are plentiful in *Taygetum*, the others are found in many of the forests of Greece, but whether they exist in any part of the Taygetic range, I have not ascertained. At the monastery of Luku I saw a wolf trap, made exactly like that called man trap in England. Wild strawberries are found plentifully in the eastern Laconic mountains. The ὀρνιὰ, or vulture, is often seen soaring about the cliffs; it is common in all very high situations in Greece, much more so than the ἀετὸς, or eagle, which, though smaller, is said to be more bold and powerful. The shepherds are more afraid of the eagle than of the orniá,

---

[a] ἐλάφια.
[b] ζαρκάδια.
[c] ἀρκούδια.
[d] ἀγριοχοίροι, or ἄγρια γρούνια.

by both of which their young lambs are sometimes carried off.

At 8.15 we begin to descend, and soon afterwards leave the forest, and, turning to the left, descend a ravine to the village of Agriána, a Kefalokhóri of thirty houses. At 9.15 quit it and halt fifteen minutes, and soon after enter the dry bed of a torrent leading to the westward, which we follow until 9.49, when we ascend some rocky heights on its left bank, leaving on the right a road conducting to the monastery of St. Prodromus of Sidjáfi[a], and to the left another leading to Perpení[b], the fields of which appear on the slope towards the foot of the mountain. Below Perpení, which is, perhaps, an ancient name, are the remains of a tower, which, by the description, is Hellenic. Our road is very rocky; we are accompanied by a boy on foot: the guide is upon a mule. A little before 11 arrive at the summit of a ridge above Khrysafá[c], from whence I see all the head of the *Laconic* gulf, the plain of Elos, the mountain of Beziané, the peninsula of Cape Xyli, and beyond it the Island of Elafonísi; farther westward appears all the western side of the plain of Mistrá, and behind it Bardúnia,

---

[a] Σιτζιάφι.   [b] Περπενὴ.   [c] Χρυσαφὰ.

the north-eastern part of Mani, the peaks of *Taygetum*, and the majestic rocks of the same mountain, which border the plain of Mistrá. The northern continuation of the *Taygetic* range is visible also as far as its termination towards Londári, to the right of which position is seen Mount Tzimbarú and a long pointed summit, crowned with a single tree near the village of Kólina, which is a conspicuous object from all the surrounding country, and has often served me for a point of measurement. Descend and arrive at Khrysafă at 11.20. The village is situated in an uneven cultivated hollow, among the rocky mountains which form the lower part of the Málevo range towards *Sparta*. It was once a place of importance, as the ruins still attest, but has never recovered the effects of the last Russian insurrection, when it was burnt by the Albanians. A few huts among the ruins are sufficient to contain the present inhabitants. There are two large churches and some smaller still standing. In one of the former I observe an ancient tile one foot ten inches square, and in the other a fluted stele of this form, with fragments of another. These were the only Hellenic remains I could find. Some parts of the walls, which support terraces formerly cultivated on the hills round the village, have almost the solidity of Hellenic works, and the situation of the place, a projecting ridge between two ravines crowned with a peaked height, has very much the air of an ancient site. We leave Khrysafá at 12.43, and, descending through some old olive trees and terraces of corn fields, continue to pass over rugged hills intersected with terrace walls, the vestiges of former cultivation, until, at 1.15, we arrive at a church on the side of a pool formed by a fine source of fresh water; it is situated in a ravine which we follow upwards, until we reach some heights surrounding a little cultivated hollow near the left bank of the river of Tzítzina, in which stands the monastery of Aghíon Saránda, or the Forty Saints: we arrive at 2. From the opposite side of the river rises a steep rocky mountain. The convent was originally founded by the Emperor Andronicus Paleologus, in a lower situation than that of the present house, very near the river, and completely surrounded with precipitous rocks, abounding in caverns which were formed into ascetic cells [a] by the addition of walls in front of them; all these are now deserted. The river of Tzítzina joins that from Arákhova, one mile and a half below the convent, at a mill be-

[a] ἀσκητάρια.

longing to it, hence commonly called Καλογιέρικος Μύλος, the Monkish Mill. On the slope of the mountain which rises from the right bank of the Arákhova river, and from the right bank of the united river or Kelefína, there is much cultivation, and the ruins of two large villages, Potamiá considerably above the junction, and Khitórissa half a mile below it. The hollow around the monastery of Aghíon Saránda is well cultivated with corn and olives, but the steep rocky mountains which surround it prevent a free circulation of air, and make the place, though considerably elevated above the plain of *Sparta*, unhealthy in summer. The situation, nevertheless, is greatly preferable to that which Andronicus chose.

About a mile and a half above the monastery there is a great rocky gorge, through which descends the united river from Vérria and from Tzítzina: it is the same ravine which I observed from Sta Mármara; the common route to the Forty Saints from the northward and eastward passes through it; the hermitages are chiefly in the rocks on the right side of this ravine. The only Hellenic remains I can find at the Forty Saints are two fragments of inscriptions, one in the Doric dialect, in very ancient characters, much defaced, the other of Roman times, in common Greek.

March 24.—We leave the convent of Aghíon Saránda at 8.10, and immediately begin to descend the last falls of Mount Málevo, which are here uneven, and intersected by torrents. The soil is good and well adapted to vines, but entirely uncultivated. It is a part of the country above *Menelaium*, which is described by Polybius as level and covered with soil and well watered[a]. The *level*, however, will apply only to the part immediately above *Menelaium*. At 9.6 we halt for thirty-seven minutes at a ruined church not far short of the river Iri, and immediately opposite to the heights of *Sparta*; then crossing the river at 9.50, a very little below its junction with the Kelefína, I enter the low hills upon which that city stood.

Pausanias describes, in the following terms, the route to Sparta from the Hermæ, which marked the borders of Laconia and Argeia[b]. "In advancing from the Hermæ, the country is full of oaks; the place is called Scotita; at a distance of ten stades to the left of the road stands a temple of Jupiter Scotitas: a little farther along the direct route there is a statue of Hercules to the left of the road, together with a trophy said to have been erected by Hercules, when he slew Hippocoon and his sons. A third

---

[a] ἐπίπεδον καὶ γεῶδες καὶ κάθυδρον.—Polyb. l. 5. c. 24.   [b] Pausan. Lacon. c. 10.

turning from the direct road leads on the right to Caryæ and the temple of Diana. The place is sacred to Diana and the Nymphs: here is a statue of Diana Caryatis in the open air, and here the Lacedæmonian virgins have annual dances, and a dance also peculiar to the place [a]. Having returned into the high road [b], and proceeded onwards, there occur the ruins of Sellasia, which was taken by the Achaians, when they defeated the Lacedæmonians under Cleomenes, son of Leonidas. The next place in advance is Thornax, which contains a statue of Jupiter Pythaeus, made like the statue of Apollo at Amyclæ; beyond Thornax is the city Sparta."

The pass of Kastánitza being the natural passage of the ridge of Parnon, and the direct route between the Thyreatis and Sparta, I think there can be no doubt that the line of my route is the same as that of Pausanias, particularly as he terminates his account of the Thyreatis, or Cynuria, at the end of the second book, by describing the course and sources of the Tanus, which may be said to originate in the pass of Kastánitza. The Hermæ probably stood at the partition of the waters which I passed yesterday at 9.45.

[a] ἐπιχώριος ὄρχησις.   [b] λεωφόρον.

It is no objection to this conclusion, that Pausanias says in the same passage, that the Hermæ, in Mount Parnon, were the Lacedæmonian boundary towards the Tegeatice, as well as the Argeia. A Hermæum in the pass of Kastánitza could not indeed have separated Laconia from the Tegeatice, but there may have been another Hermæum on the Tegeatic frontier, towards Vérvena and the sources of the *Alpheius;* on the ridge between Vérvena and St. Peter's, there may even have been a common boundary of all the three districts.

As the ruin called Sta Mármara appears to have been that of a solitary building, such as a temple, and as I turned out of the direct road to the left towards Tzítzina, after descending for some distance along the torrent bed before I reached the Mármara, its position agrees exactly with that of the temple of Jupiter Scotitas. The forest Scotita, no remains of which are now to be seen in the place, described by Pausanias, seems to have been obliterated by a process of gradual diminution, during the two or three centuries which preceded his visit to the country. It is evident from Polybius, that in his time it covered a much larger portion of the country around Sellasia; for he describes it as lying between Sparta and Tegea. On one occasion Philopœmen concealed himself with a body of Achaians in Scotita, whither he had marched suddenly from Tegea, while he sent another body to plunder the country about Sellasia, with orders to retreat into the Scotita if they should be attacked. Some mercenaries of Nabis moved against them from Pellana, (a town on the Eurotas, about ten miles above Sparta,) and having pursued them into the Scotita, there fell an easy sacrifice to Philopœmen[a]. On another occasion, Philopœmen, marched from Tegea, by Caryæ, to Mount Barbosthenes, which was ten miles distant from Sparta, and defeated Nabis between that place and a strong post nearer to Sparta, called Pyrrhi Castra. Livy[b], who relates this transaction, copying from Polybius, adds, that the troops of the tyrant suffered greatly from the enemy in the defiles of the forest, through which they were under the necessity of retreating to Sparta. The historian shews also that one of the gates of Sparta led to Barbosthenes and a second to Pheræ; and it is clear, from the circumstances, that both the roads conducting from them were different from that of Sellasia. There can be little doubt, therefore, that Pheræ was the same place as the modern Vérria, the difference between the two names being only dialectic[c]. Bar-

[a] Polyb. l. 16. c. 21.
[b] Liv. l. 35. c. 27, et seq
[c] See note, p. 515.

bosthenes was, probably, the mountain which rises above Potamiá.

If the temple of Jupiter Scotitas stood at Mármara, on the descending ridge which separates the two branches of the river flowing by the monastery of the Forty Saints, it may be inferred, that the statue of Hercules, having been, like the temple of Jupiter, to the left of the direct road, stood on the same ridge in a lower situation.

It is unfortunate that neither Pausanias, nor any other author, has furnished us with the distance of Sellasia from Sparta, of which it was evidently the key towards the Thyreatis and Argeia. The inscriptions, however, which I found at the convent of the Forty Saints, though they contain no topographical evidence, are sufficient, I think, when combined with the description of the pass of Sellasia, by Polybius, to leave little doubt that Sellasia stood at the monastery.

It is in relating the celebrated defeat of Cleomenes, by Antigonus, which, in the year B.C. 221, opened the gates of Sparta for the first time to an invader, that Polybius describes the pass of Sellasia[a]. Cleomenes, judging that Antigonus, who was at Argos, was preparing to advance from thence upon Sparta, occupied Sellasia with

[a] Polyb. l. 2. c. 65.

20,000 men, and stationed the remainder of his forces in the other entrances into the Laconice, which he directed to be fortified with trenches and obstructed with trees. At Sellasia, Cleomenes entrenched himself on the hills Eva and Olympus, which were separated from each other by the river Œnus, and by a narrow marshy level on its banks, along which lay the road to Sparta. Antigonus, on arriving in presence of the enemy, placed his army in a position opposite to that of the Spartans, with the river Gorgylus in his front; his forces amounted to 28,000 men, of whom about 13,000 were Macedonians, the remainder mercenaries and contingents of the Achaian league. After a few days' hesitation, caused by the strength of the enemy's position, Antigonus resolved upon an attack. Cleomenes commanded the Spartans and mercenaries upon Mount Olympus, and his brother, Eucleidas, the auxiliaries upon Mount Eva.

The cavalry of both armies were in the valley of the Œnus. In the night previous to the attack, Antigonus placed a part of his army in the river Gorgylus[a], at the foot of Mount Eva, with orders to ascend the hill upon seeing a signal, which he should give in advancing with the rest of his forces against Cleomenes upon

[a] ἐν τῷ Γοργύλῳ ποταμῷ.

Mount Olympus. The movement took place accordingly: the division which ascended Mount Eva was at first placed in a hazardous situation by some light infantry stationed with the Lacedæmonian cavalry, who assailed their rear, but they were soon relieved from danger by the gallantry and conduct of Philopœmen, then a young officer in command of the Megalopolitan horse, who, diverted the attack of the light infantry by charging without orders the Lacedæmonian cavalry, to which they were attached. The action now became general, both between the main bodies on the heights, and the cavalry in the valley. Eucleidas, having allowed the enemy to ascend Mount Eva too far before he met them, lost the advantage of his position, and was routed; when Cleomenes, perceiving his brother's distress, and convinced that it could only be relieved by the defeat of the enemy on his side, drew the Spartan phalanx out of its entrenchments, and came to close engagement with the allies. The Lacedæmonians fought with their accustomed valour, and the battle was for some time favourable to them, but they were unable to resist the weight of the Macedonian phalanx in a last desperate charge, and at length were entirely defeated. Cleomenes fled to Sparta and to Gythium, from whence he sailed to Egypt, and

Antigonus entered Sparta without further resistance [a].

The description given by the historian, of two hills separated by a river, flowing in a narrow valley, along which led the road to Sparta, sufficiently identifies the pass with that to the eastward of the Forty Saints; it is highly probable also that the river of Tzítzina, being the principal branch, and that which now gives name to the united stream, was the *Œnus*: consequently that the river of Vérria, which joins it just above the pass, was the *Gorgylus*. Unfortunately we obtain no certainty on this question from Polybius, who, instead of alluding to the right and left of either force, as might have been expected from a military writer, has fallen into a common defect of the ancient authors, that of presupposing the reader's knowledge of the scene of action. It is probable that Antigonus, having marched from Argos by Cynuria, descended the ridge of Mármara, or *Scotita*, until he arrived at the fork of the two streams above the pass of *Sellasia*, and that, in the position which he then assumed, with the Gorgylus and Mount Eva in his front, the Œnus protected one of his flanks, towards the position of

[a] Polyb. l. 2. c. 64, 65. See also Plutarch, in the lives of Cleomenes and Philopœmen; but, as usual, he adds little or nothing to elucidate the historian.

Cleomenes on Mount Olympus. There is nothing, however, in the narrative of Polybius to shew on which flank the Œnus flowed. We have only, therefore, the probability, derived from the magnitude of the two rivers, to which I have already alluded; and which leads to the consequence, that Mount Olympus was to the left of the united stream in the pass, and Mount Eva on its right bank, and that the position of the two armies previously to the battle was that which is described in the annexed sketch.

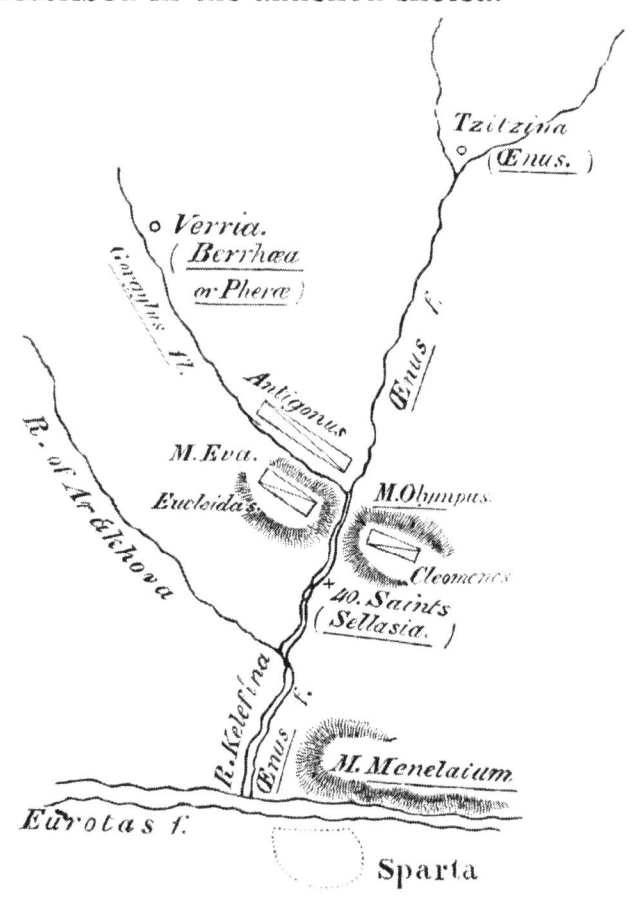

The omission by Pausanias of the distance of Caryæ from the turning which led thither out of the road to Sellasia, leaves us in doubt as to its exact site, though Polybius and Livy both agree with Pausanias, regarding its position between Sellasia and the Tegeatic frontier. When Titus Quinctius, in the third year of his command of the Roman army in Greece (B. C. 195), marched against Nabis, he crossed Mount Parthenium from Argos, and passing Tegea, encamped on the third day at Caryæ, within the enemy's territory. On the next day he moved to Sellasia, on the river Œnus, and thence, by a circuitous route, to the banks of the Eurotas, under the walls of Sparta[a]. When Philopœmen, about three years afterwards, marched against Nabis, he also moved to Caryæ, and thence to Mount Barbosthenes, ten miles from Sparta[b], as I have already had occasion to notice. These authorities have a tendency to place Caryæ not so near the road leading to Sellasia from the Laco-Thyreatic Hermæum of Mount Parnon, as the words of Pausanias would seem to indicate, but nearer to the *Tegeatic* frontier, perhaps not far from the khan of Krevatá.

It would appear from Athenæus[c] and Stephanus[d], that the river Œnus derived its name

[a] Liv. Hist. l. 34. c. 26. &c.
[b] Ibid. l. 35. c. 27.
[c] Athen. l. 1. c. 44.
[d] Stephan. in Οἰνοῦς, ubi citantur Androtion et Didymus.

from a town on its banks, so called, because it was noted for its wine. Denthiades, another place in Laconia, celebrated for its wine, was perhaps in the same part of the country, for the rugged slopes of this range of mountains are well suited to the vine, which is successfully cultivated as high up as Tzítzina. Indeed, it is not improbable, that Tzítzina itself, being in one of the best situations of the upper Œnus, near the sources of that river, and giving the modern name to it, may stand exactly upon the site of the town of Œnus. We have seen that wine is still produced there, though, in common with all the wines of Greece, it has degenerated from its ancient quality, in consequence of a want of care in the manufacture. Vréstena, which is a bishoprick under the metropolitan of Lacedæmonia, written Εὐριστένη in the ecclesiastical books, has so great a resemblance to the Spartan name Eurysthenes, that one cannot but suspect that it stands on the site of an ancient place, called Eurystheneia, which has not been mentioned by any ancient author. It occupies an elevated situation on the south-western face of Mount *Parnon*, from whence descend the tributaries which form the northern branch of the Kelefína or *Œnus*.

The only remains of antiquity which I did not observe on my former visit to Sparta, is a small piece of Hellenic wall on the brow of the principal height on the north-eastern side at the contrary extremity of the theatre. It may have been a part of the ancient walls, which were first built in the time of the Roman wars in Greece. Having seen several theatres since my first journey, I am struck with the comparative smallness of the stones which formed the supporting wall of the cavea of the theatre of Sparta, though they are finely wrought, accurately squared, and are united without any external cement. They favour the supposition, that the part of the theatre now extant is a work of Roman times.

In describing Sparta on the former occasion, I applied the word Circus to the circular building which stands near the road in entering the site of Sparta from the ford of the *Eurotas*, without adverting to the impropriety of the word circus, as belonging to another kind of Roman construction of a very different description. In fact, it is difficult to know what to call this circular building. It seems to resemble a roofed theatre or odeium, in which case it is probably more ancient than the walls surrounding the principal height, for these, as I have before remarked, appear to be the walls of Sparta in its last stage, when an odeium would hardly have been required or suited to the spectacles then in fashion, which were rather those of the amphitheatre. Although placed relatively to the existing walls in the position in which Roman amphitheatres are usually found, it was not an amphitheatre, these buildings having always been oblong, as we see instanced on every scale, —on some of the smallest at Corinth, and at Silchester and Caerleon, in England.

On the left bank of the Eurotas, near the position which I conceive to have been occupied by Therapne, stands a ruined church of St. John. I am informed that there are some ancient columns in this spot, and a stone figure of a man and woman in relief, with an inscription under the figures. It seems to be a common sepulchral design, and is not sufficiently interesting to induce me to recross the river to examine it.

Thornax, a suburban village, like Therapne, was probably situated on the edge of the narrow plain on the left side of the *Eurotas*. After having passed all the morning at *Sparta*, I proceed to Mistrá, to the house of our agent, V. D.

END OF VOL. II.

G. Woodfall, Printer, Angel Court, Skinner Street, London.

ADDITIONS AND CORRECTIONS.

VOL. II.

Page 164. For "B. C. 220" read "B. C. 219."

Page 397, Note a. For "τρισμυρίους" read "τρισμυρίοις." This reference to Plato is repeated from a former work, (Topography of Athens, p. 59,) where I inserted the whole passage and adduced it as a proof that the theatre of Athens was capable of containing 30,000 spectators. Socrates, comparing his own doubtful and shadowy pursuits (σοφία ἡ ἐμὴ ἀμφισ-βητήσιμος ὥσπερ ὄναρ οὖσα) with those of Agathon, whose tragedy had been successful over that of his competitors in the theatre, says, " your wisdom, Agathon, was manifested in the presence of 30,000 Greeks," ἐξέλαμψε καὶ ἐκφανὴς ἐγένετο πρώην ἐν μάρτυσι τῶν Ἑλλήνων πλέον ἢ τρισμυρίοις." There may be some doubt, however, whether this evidence can be considered as conclusive. In the first place, on comparing the space of ground formerly occupied by the theatre of Athens, with the dimensions of other theatres in Greece, of which there are remains sufficient to enable us to form a tolerable judgement of their numerical capacity, it is very difficult to believe that the Athenian theatre could possibly have contained so great a number: 2dly, it appears that "30,000" or "more than 30,000" was an expression not uncommonly used by the Athenians, about the time of Plato, to express the body of Athenian citizens. Thus, Herodotus (l. 5. c. 97,) says that Aristagoras deceived 30,000 Athenians; and Aristophanes, in the Concionantes, v. 1131, employs the words πλεῖον ἢ τρισμυρίων,—

both of them exactly in that sense, and neither author with any reference to the Dionysiac theatre. So that Plato may merely have put a familiar expression into the mouth of Socrates, without any intention of defining the number of spectators in the theatre.

Page 441. For "six of the eastern front, and five of the northern side are continuous without any interruption," read "six of the eastern front, five of the northern side, and three of the southern, are continuous without any interruption."

Page 526. For "B. C. 221" read "B. C. 222."

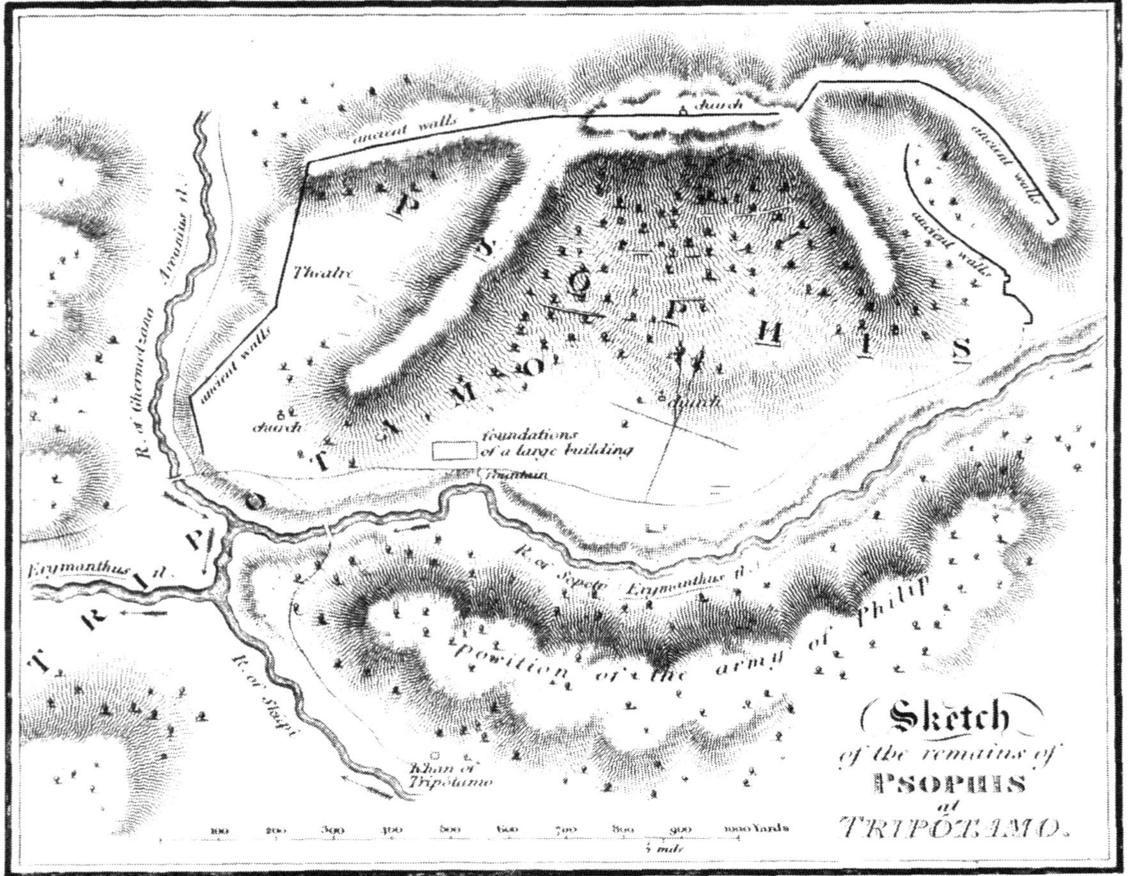

(Sketch)
of the remains of
PSOPHIS
at
TRIPÓTAMO.

J. Walker Sculpt

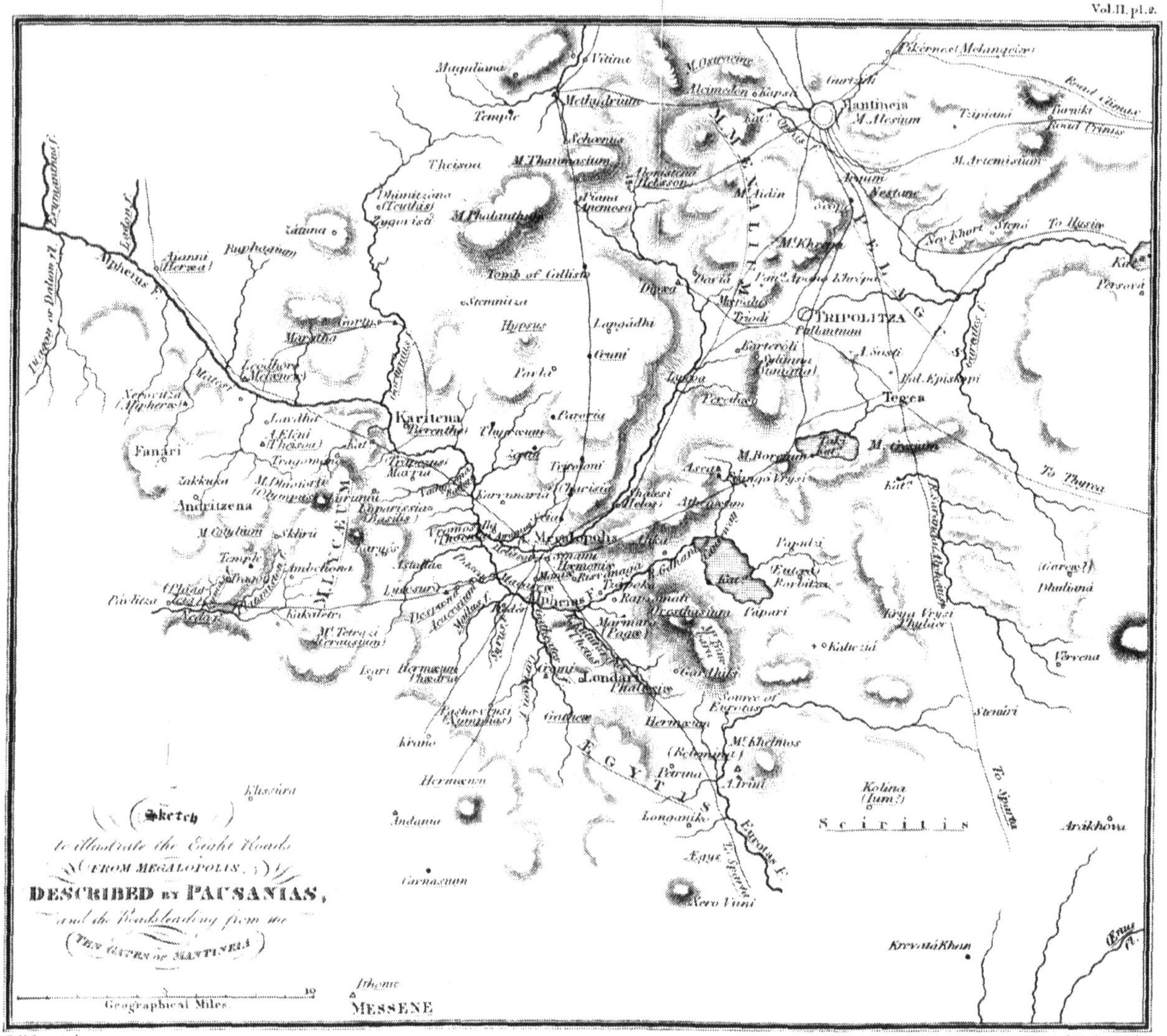

W. M. L. m. & d. J. Walker Sculpt.

FORTRESS of TIRYNS.

Vol. II. pl. 4.

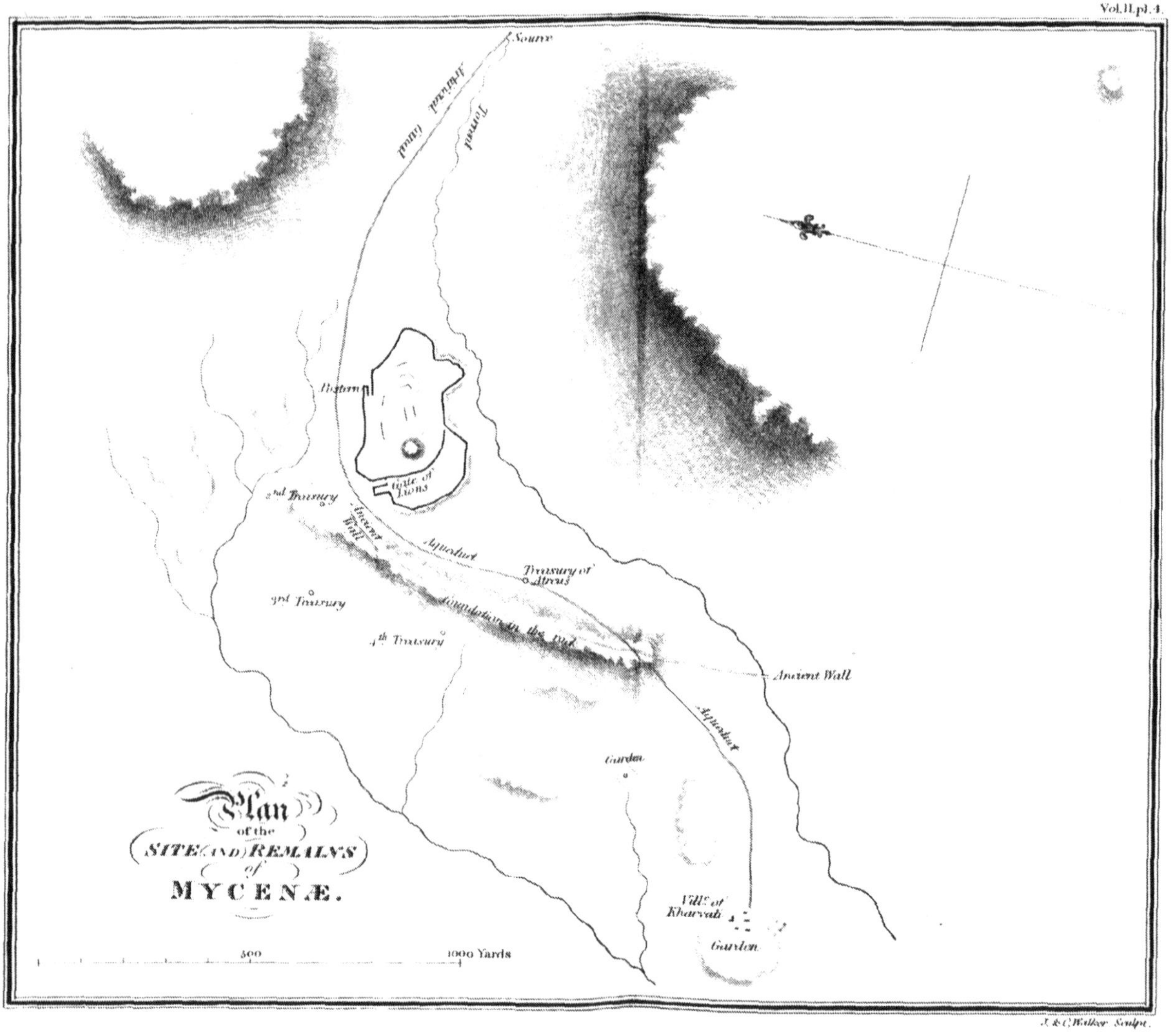

J. & C. Walker Sculpt.

TREASURY OF ATREUS at MYCENÆ

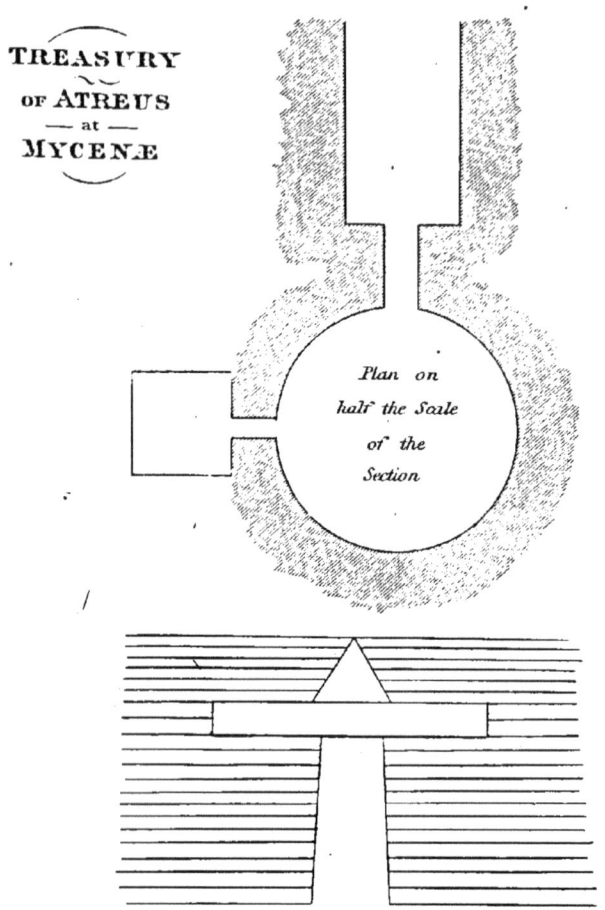

Plan on half the Scale of the Section

Elevation of the Great Door & Window from within

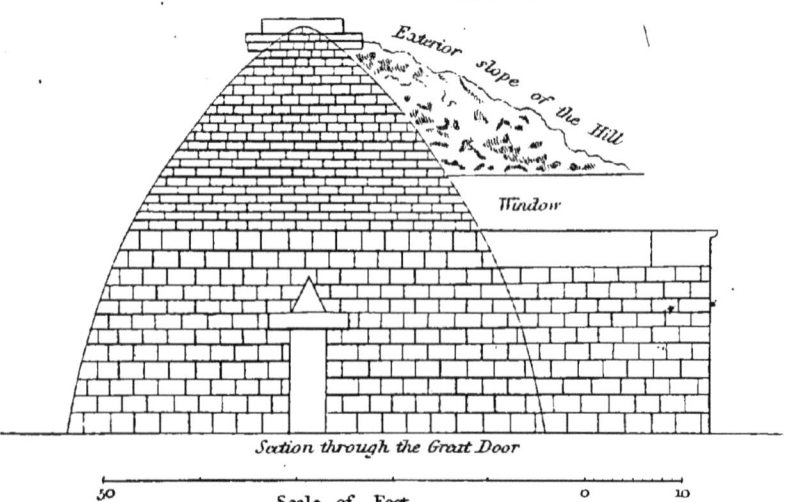

Exterior slope of the Hill

Window

Section through the Great Door

Scale of Feet

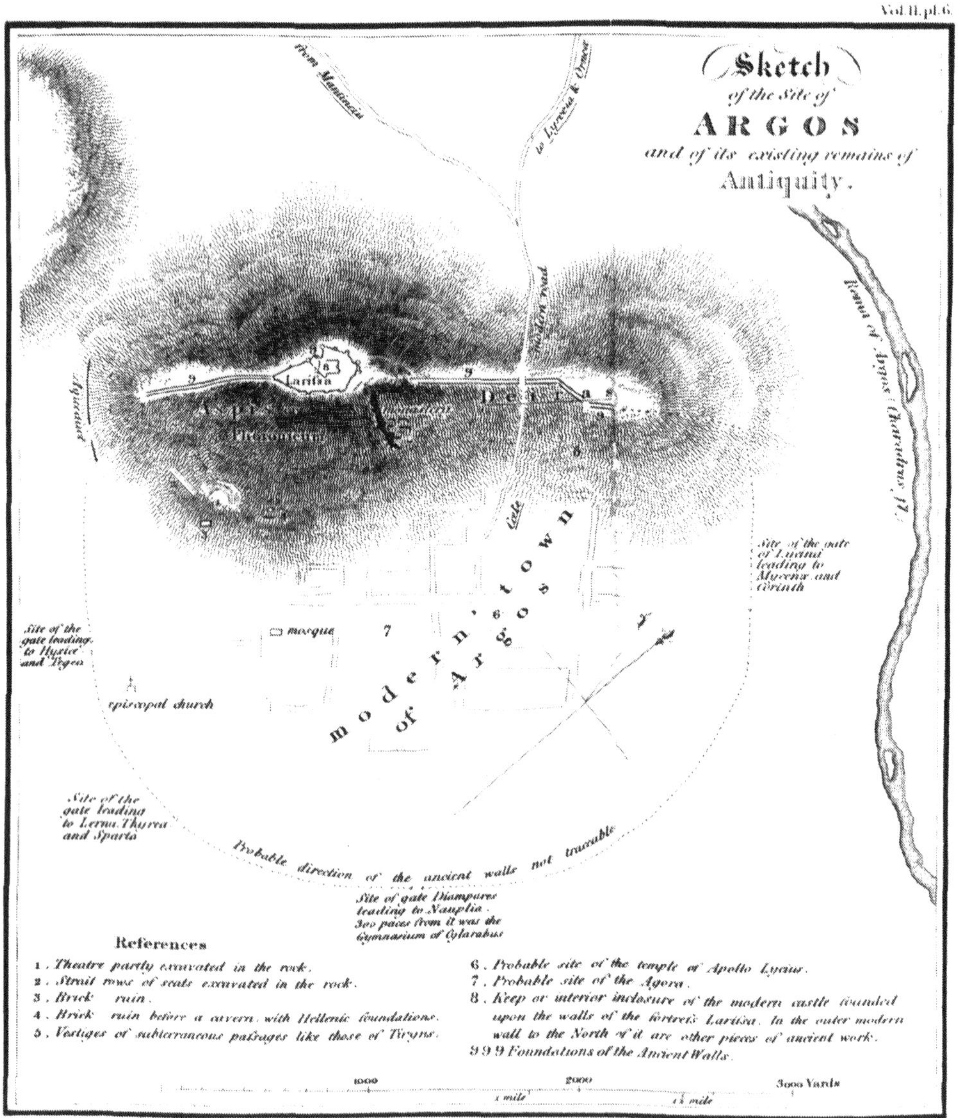

W. M. L. del.

J. Walker Sculpt

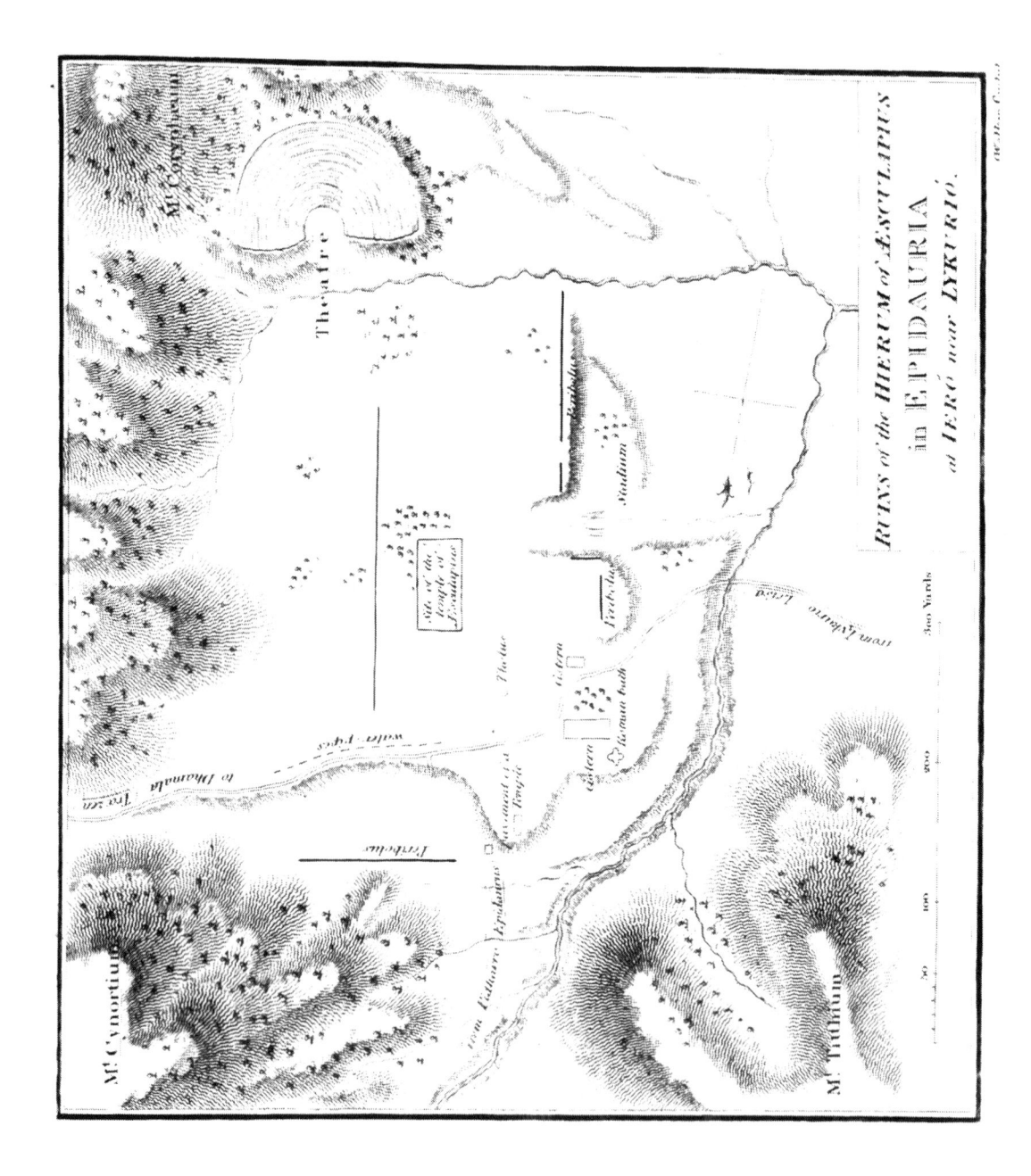

RUINS of the HIERUM of ÆSCULAPIUS in EPIDAURIA at IERÓ near LYKURIO.

PRESERVATION SERVICE

SHELFMARK 10.4.7.D.8
VOL II

THIS BOOK HAS BEEN
MICROFILMED (1996)

MICROFILM NO P.B.M.C.
33807